In the Public Eye

In the Public Eye

A HISTORY OF READING IN MODERN
FRANCE, 1800–1940

James Smith Allen

PRINCETON UNIVERSITY PRESS

PRINCETON, NEW JERSEY

Library of Congress Cataloging-in-Publication Data
Allen, James Smith.
In the public eye : a history of reading in modern France,
1800–1940 / James Smith Allen.
p.   cm.
Includes bibliographical references and index.
1. Books and reading—France—History—19th century.
2. Books and reading—France—History—20th century.
3. France—Intellectual life—20th century. 4. France—
Intellectual life—19th century.
I. Title.
Z1003.5.F7A45   1991
028′.9′0944—dc20   90-28810   CIP

ISBN 0-691-03162-2

Publication of this book was made possible by a grant from the
Publications Program of the National Endowment for the Humanities,
an independent Federal agency

This book has been composed in Linotron Times Roman

Princeton University Press books are printed on acid-free paper,
and meet the guidelines for permanence and durability of the
Committee on Production Guidelines for Book Longevity of the
Council on Library Resources

Printed in the United States of America by Princeton University Press,
Princeton, New Jersey

1   3   5   7   9   10   8   6   4   2

À Anne

Tu n'as pas perdu ces heures
Si légère tu demeures
Après ces beaux abandons;
Pareille à celui qui pense
Et dont l'âme se dépense
À s'accroître de ses dons!

—Paul Valéry, ''*Palme*''

———————————————

CONTENTS

PART I: *The Historical Context*

PART II: *Historical Interpretive Practices:*
The Art of Reading

PART III: *Historical Interpretive Practices:*
The Act of Reading

LIST OF ILLUSTRATIONS

LIST OF TABLES

ACKNOWLEDGMENTS

IN THE PAST eight years I have incurred many debts, too many in fact to acknowledge properly. But I must express my sincere appreciation to the following people and institutions.

For permitting me to reprint articles that appeared first in their journals, I thank Frank Kafker and James Laux of *French Historical Studies* (the Introduction was published originally in Autumn 1987); and T. H. Goetz of *Nineteenth-Century French Studies* (the pages in Chapter 9 on Michelet were in the Fall-Winter 1987–88 issue).

For funding research, time to read and write, or both, I am grateful to the Phillips University Faculty Research and Decision for Excellence Funds (1983, 1984); the National Endowment for the Humanities (1983, 1988–89); the Andrew W. Mellon Foundation and the University of Pennsylvania (1984–85); the American Council of Learned Societies (1985); the Institut français de Washington (1985); and the U.S. Department of Education's Fund for the Improvement of Post-Secondary Education (1987, 1988).

For writing the necessary letters of recommendation, I thank Robert Darnton, Priscilla Parkhurst Ferguson, Pierre-Henri Laurent, Robert Nye, Gerald Prince, Alan Spitzer, and Peter Stearns.

For carefully critiquing an unruly first draft, I am deeply indebted to Frank Bowman, Jean Hébrard, Gerald Prince, Robert Nye, and Alan Spitzer.

For shaping my ideas—and much else—I owe most to Robert Nye.

And finally, for her enduring generosity, devotion, and support, I am fortunate to have married Anne Winston.

May such blessings come to you.

Enid, Oklahoma
September 1990

ABBREVIATIONS

ADSVP   Archives du département de la Seine et de la ville de Paris
AMG   Archives du ministère de la guerre
AN   Archives nationales
APP   Archives de la préfecture de police
BA   Bibliothèque de l'arsenal
BHVP   Bibliothèque historique de la ville de Paris
BIPN   Bibliothèque de l'institut pédagogique national
BN   Bibliothèque nationale
BSL   Bibliothèque Spoelberch de Lovenjoul
BTF   Bibliothèque du théâtre français
Coll.   Collection
Corr.   *Correspondance*
Delteil   Loÿs Delteil, *Le Peintre-graveur illustré (XIXe–XXe siècle)*, 32 vols. (1906–26)
EZRP   Émile Zola Research Program
HEF   *Histoire de l'édition française*, ed. Roger Chartier and Henri-Jean Martin, 4 vols. (1982–86)
MdF   *Mercure de France*
MNE   Musée national de l'éducation
NAFr   Nouvelles acquisitions françaises
RdDM   *Revue des deux mondes*

Unless noted otherwise, all books cited here and in the footnotes were published in Paris. All translations from the French are the author's.

In the Public Eye

INTRODUCTION

"DOCUMENTS" in the history of reading can appear in curious guises, such as the portrait of Henri Fantin-Latour's two sisters completed by 1859 (see Ill. I.1).[1] Seated in the corner of a sewing room, Marie is portrayed with an open book before her, while Nathalie appears in a deeply pensive mood. The two women are apparently reading together, an ordinary middle-class activity in nineteenth-century France. And yet Fantin-Latour's treatment of this familiar domestic scene leaves the attentive viewer uneasy. Is Marie reading aloud here or not? Her lips are neither parted nor pursed, and her sister seems absorbed if not entirely distracted by her own thoughts. Their immediate relationship is made no clearer by the artist's odd choice of title, "The Two Sisters, or The Embroiderers"; reading is not even mentioned. Knowledge about the women complicates still further an adequate understanding of their situation. The pensive Nathalie, for instance, suffered from schizophrenia and was committed to the Maison nationale de Charenton in the same year that the painting was completed. Was Marie then reading aloud to comfort her tragically deranged companion? Or was she reading silently to herself out of despair, or simply out of neglect? Without closer study, answers to these queries may not be ventured, especially in light of the other, equally curious double portraits by Fantin-Latour. All of them show the same detachment between the sitters, as do similar portraits by Berthe Morisot, Édouard Manet, Auguste Renoir, and Edgar Degas, to name some of the many painters of this common cultural practice.[2]

However ambiguous, the artistic image does suggest one major theme in the history of reading that appears repeatedly and more clearly in other, less problematic historical sources: a new context was rapidly undermining the collective nature of reading. Personal letters, diaries, and autobiographies indicate that the circumstances in which people read and interpreted texts were changing in the nineteenth century. For centuries literacy had been the preserve of a small religious, political, and social elite who used their mastery of the printed word, in part at least, to maintain control of the illiterate majority of French men and women. The church protected its privileged reading of the scriptures

[1] See Douglas Druick and Michel Hoog, *Fantin-Latour* (Ottawa, 1983), 94–95; and Edward Lucie-Smith, *Fantin-Latour* (Oxford, 1977), 11–37.

[2] Cf. Druick and Hoog, *Fantin-Latour*, 89–90, 145–46; Lucie-Smith, *Fantin-Latour*, pl. 7; and John Rewald, *The History of Impressionism*, 4th ed. (New York, 1973), 201, 243, 276, and 327.

I.1 Henri Fantin-Latour, "The Two Sisters, or The Embroiderers" (1859). Courtesy of the Saint Louis (Missouri) Art Museum

in monasteries and universities; the king's officials monitored all secular publications and carried word of royal edicts to the populace; and the landed nobility shaped the world of letters by their patronage. Reading had long served a public purpose—in the church, in the courts, in the salons, even in the family. Within this historical setting, relatively few people read alone or silently, much less pondered the meaning of the restricted number of books available without the assistance or intrusion of others. Moreover, the face-to-face relations of a preliterate culture lingered on after literacy had become an ordinary feature of private life in the nineteenth century.[3]

From the early nineteenth century onward, however, the practice of oral reading appears less prominently in the personal accounts of literate individuals. Reading aloud, once a common element of intellectual life in the Old Regime, became a special event at church, in the classroom, on the rostrum, or for children at bedtime. Accordingly, as political, religious, and social controls over printed matter weakened, the rapidly growing number of literate people was surrounded less and less intrusively by authorities, neighbors, and relations. Freed from a traditional milieu, individuals increasingly sought the meaning of more freely available texts in deeply personal, isolated acts. These literate activities, moreover, occurred within a diffuse context of institutions and networks—such as primary schools, literary reviews, reading circles, even bookstores—that suggested rather than determined what and how people read. By the end of the nineteenth century, women like Marie Fantin-Latour could well have neglected their nearby companions or family members for the sake of a book. Nineteenth-century portraits of such readers not only made effective use of a familiar artistic setting, however intriguing on close inspection; they also illustrated a remarkable transition in the historical circumstances of reading in the last two hundred years.[4]

A rich variety of artistic and literary sources also suggests another significant theme in the history of reading: the development of private interpretive practices. In Fantin-Latour's portrait it is clear that even if Marie were reading

---

[3] See HEF 2:402–45, 498–514, 3:24–45, 470–509, and 4:528–41, 564–71; Daniel Roche, *Le Peuple de Paris. Essai sur la culture populaire au XVIIIe siècle* (1981), 204–41; Roger Chartier, ed., *Pratiques de la lecture* (Marseille, 1985), 62–88, 126–55; Martyn Lyons, *Le Triomphe du livre. Une Histoire sociologique de la lecture dans la France du XIXe siècle* (1987), 221–48; Roger Chartier, *Lectures et lecteurs dans la France d'Ancien Régime* (1987), 223–44; and idem, ed., *Les Usages de l'imprimé* (1987), 7–20, 83–127. Cf. Robert Escarpit et al., "La Lecture," in *La Vie populaire en France du Moyen Âge à nos jours* (1965), 2:278–353; John Lough, *Writer and Public in France from the Middle Ages to the Present Day* (London, 1978), 274–399; Claude Labrosse, *Lire au XVIIIe siècle. 'La Nouvelle Héloïse' et ses lecteurs* (Lyon, 1985), 241–73; and Jean Hébrard and Anne-Marie Chartier, *Discours sur la lecture (1880–1980)* (1989).

[4] Cf. Peter Berger et al., *The Homeless Mind: Modernization and Consciousness* (New York, 1974), 63–82; Richard Sennett, *The Fall of Public Man* (New York, 1977), 1–44, 123–255; and Jürgen Habermas, *The Structural Transformation of the Public Sphere*, trans. Thomas Burger (Cambridge, Mass., 1989), 1–56, 141–80.

aloud, she surely paid far closer attention to the text than her sister did. The two women must have experienced the author's world in very different ways, Marie more immediately than Nathalie. Given the apparent psychological distance from her sister, the latter may have pursued another train of thought entirely. Similar interpretive differences appear in the responses of readers to other texts. For example, letters that people wrote about the books they read in the nineteenth and early twentieth century express a surprisingly wide range of interpretation, not all of which was based on careful attention to the texts. Like critics who failed to recognize the merit of their contemporaries, usually for extraneous reasons, the correspondents tended to read personal concerns into their books. Controversial works frequently elicited responses having less to do with the authors' intentions than with the audiences' preoccupations. Consequently, predispositions and prejudices also played a prominent role in the reception of literary texts, past and present.[5] To that extent, Nathalie Fantin-Latour was not exceptional in the way she must have responded to print; her distraction was only more extreme.

But the complexities of interpretation remained no more the same from 1800 to 1940 than did their circumstances. Just as the social and institutional context of reading was moving from public and collective to private and individual, readers' responses to texts developed accordingly. From the evidence in personal correspondence, journals, and autobiographies about the reading experience from the eighteenth century onward, men and women were less and less given to seeking out identifiable individuals, most often the author, in the books they read; meanwhile, they came more and more to look for themselves. Over time, readers' predispositions evolved from the expectation that the novel, most notably, would represent and explain external reality, to the expectation that it would provide new sources of inspiration for self-discovery. The specific emotional and introspective concerns of the romantics, like those of Chateaubriand early in the nineteenth century, took fully one hundred years or more to become those of readers, like Anatole France's audience in the early twentieth century. In the interim, rational and neoclassical preoccupations, prominent features of the Enlightenment, lingered on in the presuppositions of many French readers who considered literary texts in an immediate, often quite utilitarian fashion. Reading as a self-consciously textual and interpretive experience thus developed much later than did self-consciously literary and artistic creation in the history of modern culture.[6]

---

[5] See Levin L. Schücking, *The Sociology of Literary Taste*, trans. Brian Battershaw (Chicago, 1966), 31–108; I. A. Richards, *Practical Criticism: A Study in Literary Judgment* (New York, 1929), 1–18; Walter J. Slatoff, *With Respect to Readers: Dimensions of Literary Response* (Ithaca, 1970), 57–90; and Pierre Bourdieu, *Distinction: A Social Critique of the Judgement of Taste*, trans. Richard Nice (Cambridge, Mass., 1984), 440–51.

[6] See César Graña, *Modernity and Its Discontents: French Society and the French Man of Letters in the Nineteenth Century* (New York, 1967), 1–83; F.W.J. Hemmings, *Culture and So-*

At the same time, the readers who can be documented in available historical sources barely acknowledged the changing creative concerns of the major writers. The new forms that authors explored from the early romantic to the late symbolist movements attracted the attention of relatively few contemporary readers (most of them authors themselves). In the experience of literate French men and women, literary and intellectual trends appeared in a personal guise remarkably different from what scholars have studied so diligently.[7] The reception of literary works, especially, meant an equally complex process of filtering colored by various factors, including the psychological disposition, social context, and cultural background of the reader. In any case, the reader rarely shared the author's concerns in the text. It was not until the twentieth century, in more deliberately ambiguous creations like Marcel Proust's *À la recherche du temps perdu*, that reception reflected creation, perhaps because the author had come to accept reading as a legitimate complement to writing.[8] But the reader's creative participation was still more easily elicited by a text than directed by it. Other external factors were also clearly involved and continued to confound the direct relationship between the reader and the printed page.

Thus many sources, such as Fantin-Latour's portrait of his sisters, suggest the need for a careful historical examination of readers and reading. Writers and texts changed over time, of course, but so did readers, their responses, and their circumstances. Interpretive practices and their temporal milieus require serious consideration—and for good reason. Study of interpretations and contexts elucidates the larger forces affecting the reception of texts central to the transmission and evolution of culture. Publishing, education, censorship, and taste, for example, all affected the way texts were perceived from one generation to another. But a history of reading also reveals the influence of textual reception on the very nature of literate culture, and more, on the historical periods in which it developed. As with all cultural activities, reading was not solely the object of changes occurring around it; it was as well an active agent of those changes. Textual reception became increasingly important in France as literacy came to pervade public and private life (if only because there were more people responding to print). How certain documents

---

ciety in France 1848–1898: Dissidents and Philistines (London, 1971), 1–6; and Michel Raimond, *La Crise du roman. Du lendemain du naturalisme aux années vingt*, rev. ed. (1985), 9–22.

[7] Cf. Robert Escarpit, " 'Creative Treason' as a Key to Literature," *Yearbook of Comparative and General Literature* 10 (1961): 16–21; David Bellos, "Reconnaissances: Balzac et son public féminin," *Oeuvres et critiques* 11 (1986): 253–62; and Anne-Marie Thiesse, *Le Roman quotidien. Lecteurs et lectures populaires à la Belle Epoque* (1984), 37–60.

[8] Cf. Marcel Proust, *À la recherche du temps perdu*, ed. Pierre Clarac and André Ferré (1954), 3:883–86; Douglas Alden, *Marcel Proust and His French Critics* (Los Angeles, 1940), 67–82; and Umberto Eco, *The Role of the Reader: Explorations in the Semiotics of Texts* (Bloomington, Ind., 1984), 47–66.

were interpreted—such as France's many constitutions since 1791—informed subsequent political events, at times even more profoundly than the composition of the texts themselves.[9] Clearly, the interpretive activities of readers mattered to the course of history as well as to the nature of culture. And yet a comprehensive study of this pervasive and profound feature of earlier centuries remains unwritten.

APPROACHES

Reading requires examination over time, first of all in its larger historical context. Most historians, of course, know how important a milieu is to cultural developments.[10] For instance, the industrial economy made possible the proliferation of print to ever larger numbers of people who could easily spare the money to acquire books and the time to read them. In the early modern past, a recently published novel cost more than a worker's weekly earnings. But after 1800, new commercial practices in publishing and new machinery in printing, including the rotary press and the linotype machine, significantly expanded the availability of texts. Publishing shared in both the rapid growth of an industrial economy based on vastly higher productivity and the lower prices this productivity made possible. Higher material standards of living in turn made reading a common leisure and business activity, one represented by the growing delivery of mail: the French sent and received five times more correspondence in 1940 than they did in 1870.[11] Since then, access to the daily newspaper has expanded to the regular clientele of nearly every café in France; its cost is usually a glass of wine, a small fraction of a worker's hourly wage.

Historians also recognize the rapid social dispersion of reading. Once the privilege primarily of religious, political, and social elites in major urban centers of the Old Regime, literacy reached "outward and downward" to the working and rural classes nearly everywhere in France, and by the beginning of the twentieth century was nearly universal.[12] Efforts to establish free, com-

---

[9] E.g., the variations on the "Déclaration des Droits de l'Homme et du Citoyen" of 1789, in Jacques Godechot, ed., *Les Constitutions de la France depuis 1789* (1979), 33–35, 79–83, 101–3, 264–66, 371–76, and 424.

[10] E.g., Pierre Barrière, *La Vie intellectuelle en France du XVIe siècle à l'époque contemporaine* (1961), 551; Germaine Brée, *Twentieth-Century French Literature*, trans. Louise Guiney (Chicago, 1983), 11–80; and Maurice Crubellier, *Histoire culturelle de la France. XIXe–XXe siècle* (1974), 9–17.

[11] Institut National de la Statistique et des Études Économiques, *Annuaire statistique de la France. Résumé retrospectif. 1939* (1940), 56:2*. Cf. HEF 2:544–86, 3:24–121, 4:22–117; Lyons, *Le Triomphe du livre*, 43–104, 193–220; Jean Fourastié, *Machinisme et le bien être* (1951), 93–96; and Crubellier, *Histoire culturelle*, 205–14.

[12] See Michel Fleury and Pierre Valmary, "Les Progrès de l'instruction élémentaire de Louis XIV à Napoléon III d'après l'enquête de Louis Maggiolo (1877–1879)," *Population* 12 (1957): 71–92; and François Furet and Jacques Ozouf, *Lire et écrire. L'Alphabétisation des Français de Calvin à Jules Ferry* (1977), 1:349–69.

pulsory, and secular elementary education, beginning with the Guizot Law of 1833, culminated in Jules Ferry's legislation in the 1880s. More formal instruction affected adults as well as children. By the end of the nineteenth century, more women had acquired this essential skill; three times as many of them could sign their names in 1876 as had been able to do so one hundred years earlier. With the expansion of basic literacy eventually came greater sophistication in the consideration of printed texts, as the time people spent in school lengthened and as the educational requirements of an industrial economy grew. This diffusion of reading skills made possible the remarkable modern demand for textual material—remarkable, that is, before the information explosion in a postindustrial consumer economy after World War II.

Everything French seems to develop a politics, literacy no less than power. The political dangers posed by literate culture in the French economy and the changing social structure were obvious to many fearful observers before and after the 1789 Revolution; legal controls on popular reading seemed necessary.[13] Thus literary and press censorship remained a fact of French intellectual life with few interruptions from the Old Regime to the Third Republic. Though the rapid growth of education and the publishing industry made it anachronistic, censorship of the French theater lasted until 1906. But other political influences on interpretive activity appeared in the various intrusions of new ideologies into literary and nonliterary texts alike. Royalism, bonapartism, republicanism, socialism, and syndicalism, among other important political ideas, colored the way people read as well as wrote during the major revolutionary upheavals in the nineteenth century. As Jean-Paul Sartre noted in his wartime notebooks, even symbolist literature can be subject to politicized readings by opinion leaders in French society.[14] Interpretive communities, like critics and teachers, played important political roles in shaping reception.

Major cultural developments in literature invariably affected the expectations that readers had of French authors.[15] Alfred de Musset's imagined provincials, Dupuis and Cotonet, were bemused by the literary news from Paris

---

[13] See Irene Collins, *The Government and the Newspaper Press, 1814–1881* (London, 1959); Odile Krakovitch, *Hugo censuré. La Liberté au théâtre au XIX siècle* (1985); Fernand Drujon, *Catalogue des ouvrages, écrits et dessins de toute nature poursuivis, supprimés ou condamnés depuis le 21 octobre 1814 jusqu'au 31 juillet 1877* (1879); and Maurice Garçon, "Les Livres contraires aux bonnes moeurs," *MdF* (15 Aug. 1931): 7–39.

[14] See Jean-Paul Sartre, *Les Carnets de la drôle de guerre. Novembre 1939–mars 1940* (1983), 415. Cf. Terry Eagleton, *Criticism and Ideology: A Study in Marxist Literary Theory* (London, 1978), 11–43; Frank Lentricchia, *After the New Criticism* (Chicago, 1980), 102–55; and Fredric Jameson, *The Political Unconscious: Narrative as a Socially Symbolic Act* (Ithaca, 1981), 17–102.

[15] Cf. the introductions to Fernand Brunot et al., *Histoire de la langue française*, 13 vols. (1966–68); Jean-Pol Caput, *La Langue française. Histoire d'une institution* (1975), vol. 3; and Marcel Cohen, *Histoire d'une langue. Le Français (des origines à nos jours)*, 3d ed. (1967).

during the July Monarchy; and they sought out what was romantic in all their reading only to suffer serious disappointment.[16] Their naive literary predispositions were shared by each succeeding generation of informed provincial readers eager to appreciate other "isms" emanating from Paris. But they were no wiser for their eagerness. During the Third Republic, some people in Émile Zola's audience were similarly outraged by the challenge of another literary movement, naturalism. Long after Zola had completed the Rougon-Macquart series, readers were still angry, and they continued to accuse him of obscenity even when his cause had clearly shifted from the naturalist novel to the defense of Captain Alfred Dreyfus.[17] Nevertheless, the contextual interests of intellectual, literary, and political historians neatly intersect in their respective assessments of the climate of opinion and its impact on ordinary readers.

Reading as an historical phenomenon demands more than the elucidation of the historical moment that contributed to the way printed material was perceived. It also requires consideration of interpretation. Whether or not readers are competent, whether or not their texts are part of a scholarly canon, interpretive practices matter. For example, specialists schooled in the Anglo-American New Criticism after the Second World War know full well the importance of the work itself to the reader's response.[18] They consider an exclusive emphasis on contextual concerns to be a serious diversion from the critic's main task. In urging a return to the text, whose meaning is self-contained and apparent to the properly trained reader, the New Critics in fact often attack the "affective fallacy"—the mistaking of readers' responses for the text itself—in the critical reception studies written by continental European scholars.[19] All the same, the history of criticism has been an important feature of literary history, a well-established field that is now complemented by an important new area of literary study, reader-response criticism, also drawing on many of the same textual insights as the New Critics.[20] The text, these reception specialists well know, provides clues to how readers interpret in ways that are of special interest to the historian of reading.

[16] Alfred de Musset, "Lettres de Dupuis et Cotonet," *Oeuvres complètes en prose*, ed. Maurice Allem and Paul Courant (1960), 819–36.

[17] See correspondence in the EZRP, University of Toronto.

[18] See René Wellek, *A History of Modern Criticism 1750–1950* (New Haven, 1955–86), vols. 5 and 6.

[19] Cf. W. K. Wimsatt and Monroe C. Beardsley, *The Verbal Icon: Studies in the Meaning of Poetry* (Lexington, 1954), 21–39; and René Wellek and Austin Warren, *Theory of Literature* (New York, 1956), 73–135.

[20] See Jane P. Tompkins, ed., *Reader-Response Criticism: From Formalism to Post-Structuralism* (Baltimore, 1980); Susan R. Suleiman and Inge Crosman, eds., *The Reader in the Text: Essays on Audience and Interpretation* (Princeton, 1980); Alan C. Purves and Richard Beach, *Literature and the Reader: Research in Response to Literature, Reading Interests, and the Teaching of Literature* (Urbana, Ill., 1972); Charles R. Cooper, ed., *Researching Response to Literature and the Teaching of Literature: Points of Departure* (Norwood, N.J., 1985); Jacques Leenhardt and Pierre Józsa, *Lire la lecture. Essai de sociologie de la lecture* (1982); and Lucien Dällenbach and Jean Ricardou, eds., *Problèmes actuels de la lecture* (1982).

What readers do with texts constitutes a new focus of fruitful inquiry. Depending upon the approaches specialists take, readers can be shown to follow the contradictory clues offered or suggested by the narrative; other readers tend to fill in the gaps left deliberately or unconsciously by the author; still others seek to re-create the work itself according to predispositions defined by schools or styles of interpretation.[21] Here the text can become a pretext for imputing meaning far removed from what the author either intended or achieved. Because a rich variety of perspectives on each literary work sheds light on both the reader and the text, the full range of those perspectives deserves study if the experience of literature is to be assessed more fully. For the historian of reading, this work on reception forms a well-developed body of theory for examining the way actual readers encountered specific works over time. The tools of reader-response critics and theorists, centered on texts and their interpretations, invite the historian to study readers in the past.[22]

The history of reading therefore also demands attention to historical interpretive practices. Whatever the available sources, this subject requires the consideration of responses to many different genres, since historical readers did not read solely what scholars study critically today. Real readers did not limit themselves to drama, fiction, or poetry; they also responded to natural history, political commentary, criticism, letters, journals, newspapers, even advertisements and street signs. Moreover, what they read was of widely varying sophistication—some texts were overdetermined, others were indeterminate, and still more were less interesting. These were interpreted with varying degrees of competence. Informed and uninformed readings of the same texts arose in the same period and in the same culture, as well as over time and across cultures. Children read books that they later considered differently as adults; women often read differently the same texts read by men. Similarly, some people received works in translation from foreign languages they knew poorly. These interpretive differences, among others, the historian must attempt to recapture.[23]

In all these variations of text and response, there remains at least one significant focus that permits a coherent account of them. That focus is the read-

[21] For an example of the first approach, see Louise Rosenblatt, *Literature as Exploration*, rev. ed. (New York, 1968), 25–53; for the second, see Wolfgang Iser, *The Implied Reader: Patterns of Communication in Prose Fiction from Bunyan to Beckett* (Baltimore, 1974), 274–94; and for the third, see Stanley Fish, *Is There a Text in This Class?: The Authority of Interpretive Communities* (Cambridge, Mass., 1980), 1–17.

[22] See James Smith Allen, "History and the Novel: *Mentalité* in Modern Popular Fiction," *History and Theory* 22 (1983): 233–52.

[23] Varieties of text are well illustrated in annual editions of the *Bibliographie de la France*; varieties of response are more difficult to document. Cf. Elizabeth A. Flynn and Patrocinio P. Schweickart, eds., *Gender and Reading: Essays on Readers, Texts, and Contexts* (Baltimore, 1986), 3–30; Laura Bohannan, "Shakespeare in the Bush," *Natural History* 75 (1966): 28–33; and Jean-Paul Sartre, *The Words*, trans. Bernard Frechtman (New York, 1964), 9–135.

er's dialogic relationship to the work.[24] One important source of cultural meaning is found in the interaction between the reader and the text (whose worlds were often quite different from each other). Each contributes something essential to the reading experience. As texts and readers vary, the experience naturally changes, but the relationship between text and reader remains central to an adequate understanding of reading. Any historical study of interpretive practices must therefore attend to this particular interaction. Consequently, "reader/text" studies in adequate numbers over a long enough period elucidate clear, coherent patterns that can be related to the contexts long studied by intellectual, literary, and social historians. However complex, textual reception is not entirely unpredictable. Largely neglected by the New Critics and even some reader-response theorists, the limits to reader subjectivity can be studied most usefully here within the dynamics between text and reader.[25]

Examining reading in this way, within appropriate contexts and within changing modes of interpretation, sheds considerable light on the relationship between large historical developments on the one hand and specific reading practices on the other. The result is a clearer understanding of the different roles played by texts and contexts in the ways people have read over the past two centuries. The full significance of this widespread activity in modern life, however, can be derived most fruitfully from a broad empirical approach to a large range of sources. Given the sizable body of recent work by historical and literary specialists on closely related problems, this synthetic venture in the history of reading becomes imperative. Examination of the responses of readers over an extended period, to elucidate their many different historical roles, thus has implications for at least two fields of study, the historical and the literary, concerned with similar phenomena. But this study also engages issues central to education, psychology, sociology, even anthropology, everywhere culture and its transmission are studied. Research on interpretation, past and present, is particularly interdisciplinary.

Sources

One reason for the neglect of a general history of readers and readings, besides its apparent unimportance to the creative life of great writers, is the problem

---

[24] See Maurice Merleau-Ponty, *The Primacy of Perception and Other Essays on Phenomenological Psychology, the Philosophy of Art, History and Politics*, ed. James M. Edie (Evanston, Ill., 1964), 12–42, 159–92; Jean-Paul Sartre, *What Is Literature?*, trans. Bernard Frechtman (New York, 1965), 61–154; Richard A. Macksey and Eugenio Donato, eds., *The Structuralist Controversy: The Language of Criticism and the Sciences of Man* (Baltimore, 1972), 56–72; and Wolfgang Iser, *The Act of Reading: A Theory of Aesthetic Response* (Baltimore, 1978), 163–231. Cf. Paul Ricoeur, *Temps et récit* (1985), 3:228–63.

[25] Cf. W.J.T. Mitchell, ed., *The Politics of Interpretation* (Chicago, 1983), 271–313; and James Smith Allen, " 'A Distant Echo': Reading Jules Michelet's *L'Amour* and *La Femme* in 1859–1860," *Nineteenth-Century French Studies* 16 (Autumn-Winter 1987–88): 30–46.

of documentation: evidence is often partial, or more precisely, problematic. Whereas intellectual and literary histories have obvious texts to exploit, the history of reading does not, except those texts left by important authors. But authorial accounts pose serious difficulties, most frequently because writers are self-conscious creators, hence self-conscious readers of texts. André Gide's personal journal is a good example of this problem; the more mature this author grew in his craft, the more purposive became his responses to the work of other writers. For him, reading was a logical and necessary extension of writing.[26] Gide's reading experiences served as a principal source of inspiration in the process of creation. Thus, however abundant the personal accounts by such sophisticated readers—that is, by prominent authors—they demand treatment every bit as careful as more complex "documents" such as novels and artwork.

Other problems are posed by similar documents left by less extraordinary individuals. Personal journals and diaries, besides autobiographies and memoirs, are notoriously distorted by motives that compete or conflict with the accurate recording of responses to printed matter. In many cases, reading is not mentioned at all, even though it is almost inconceivable that a writer, however humble, could have been totally unaware of texts by others. Why, for instance, do various military memoirs fail to mention even once the innumerable speeches and bulletins read aloud to the troops during the Napoleonic Wars?[27] One can only speculate. Moreover, much of what is said about reading is extremely anecdotal, entirely unrepresentative of the usual experiences the individual must have had. Reading is usually mentioned by those who have finished school as a mere diversion, even when the diarist's livelihood depends upon this essential literate skill. The historian surely cannot take at face value the evidence of reading, or its absence, in any personal account.

Most critical-reception studies suffer from problematic sources, too. Book reviewers were published authors themselves, often personally acquainted with the writers of the texts under review. A perusal of the work by major critics, like Pontmartin, Nisard, or Sainte-Beuve, reveals the range of personal biases and animosities that clearly intruded into their reviews.[28] Because the world of letters was small, almost intimate, especially in Paris, few critics could completely exclude extraneous considerations from their readings of works by authors known to them. The rapid growth of the publishing industry in the modern period meant that reviewers were often hired to publicize titles they had not even read, or worse, the very titles they had written. Balzac, Dumas *fils*, Sand, Hugo, and Zola, among others, are known to have prepared

[26] E.g., why Gide discontinued reading *Voyage d'un naturaliste*: André Gide, *Journal* (1948), 1:219 [3 May 1906].

[27] E.g., [Jean-Roch] Coignet, *Les Cahiers du capitaine Coignet (1799–1815)* . . . (1885).

[28] E.g., Armand de Pontmartin, *Causeries du samedi* (1875); Désiré Nisard, *Études de critique littéraire* . . . (1858); and C.-A. Sainte-Beuve, *Causeries du lundi*, 15 vols. (1851–62).

review copy of works by close personal friends; in so doing, they contributed another level of complexity to the sources in the history of reading.[29]

A less obvious source appropriate to this study poses similar problems: the fan mail sent to authors about their work. Thousands of letters received by prominent members of the Académie française have been collected and preserved in the Bibliothèque nationale, while the correspondence of still more writers may be found in the Bibliothèque Spoelberch de Lovenjoul in Chantilly. These and other archival collections provide enormous stores of largely unexamined documents in the history of French readers and reading since the eighteenth century.[30] But the insight offered by these responses is limited by another kind of bias. Besides the self-selecting nature of the correspondents, these letters express the selective retention of the recipients, the heirs to the authors' papers, and the libraries that acquired them. Anonymous letters that seemed of no apparent value have been lost out of carelessness or lack of interest. The remainder were written in disproportionate numbers by friends and families of the authors, who were predisposed to their work for obvious reasons. And most of the correspondents unknown to the writers generally had some ulterior motive in writing that very likely interfered with their accounts of reading the authors' works. All too many of the letters were by aspiring authors requesting help in joining the ranks of professional writers.[31]

To be sure, no one is a born reader; this complex skill must be learned. And so records of the way children were taught to read constitute another troublesome though important source. Schools left ample documentation of pedagogical methods at all levels of scholastic achievement—from grade school, when children first learned to decode the written word, to the university, when candidates for higher degrees defended their readings of appropriate texts. Beginning in the Restoration Monarchy at least, circulars, directives, and instructions drawn up by school officials effectively complemented the textbooks, "readers," and exercise books used by instructors and their students.[32] These

[29] E.g., Balzac's revision of Félix Davin's critical introduction to Balzac's own *Études de moeurs* (1834): *Balzac: Corr.*, ed. Roger Pierrot (1960–66), 2:590 n. 1.

[30] On letters addressed to Eugène Sue in the BHVP Fonds Sue: Nora Atkinson, *Eugène Sue et le roman-feuilleton* (1929), 67–77; Rudolf Schenda, "Leserbriefe an Eugène Sue. Ein Beitrag zur Sozialgeschichte literarischer Kommunikation in der Julimonarchie," *Zeitschrift für Literaturwissenschaft und Linguistik* 2 (1974): 73–104; Anne-Marie Thiesse, "Écrivains/Public(s): Les Mystères de la communication littéraire," *Europe* 60 (Nov.–Dec. 1982): 36–46; and Bryna Svane, *Le Monde d'Eugène Sue*, Tome 3: *Les Lecteurs d'Eugène Sue* (Copenhagen, 1986), 7–72.

[31] E.g., Irving Dilliard to Anatole France, 13 Feb. 1922, in BN NAFr 15433 fol. 241.

[32] E.g., see Ministère de l'Instruction Publique, *Circulaires et instructions officielles relatives à l'instruction publique*, 12 vols. (1875–1900); Louis Liard et al., *Instructions concernant les programmes de l'enseignement secondaire (garçons et filles)* (1911); Ferdinand Buisson, ed., *Dictionnaire de pédagogie et d'instruction primaire*, 2 vols. (1882–83); Antoine Prost, *Histoire de l'enseignement en France 1800–1967* (1968), 96–107; Guy Avanzini, ed., *Histoire de la pédagogie du 17e siècle à nos jours* (1981), 281–310; and Pierre Giolitto, *Histoire de l'enseignement primaire au XIXe siècle* (1984), 2:7–67.

materials suggest the nature of the reading experience and its development over time in schools everywhere in France. Yet none of these institutional sources reveals exactly how students actually read texts, not only outside but also inside the classroom. Pedagogical intentions do not always translate into educational achievement. What students learned during their schooling can be more adequately assessed only by a careful examination of student notebooks, a large collection of which is maintained by the Musée national de l'éducation.[33] All the same, the notebooks that have been preserved are not entirely representative of the reading experience in French schools attended by many millions of more ordinary students whose notebooks have been lost.

Given the kinds of sources available, the historian is severely handicapped in a global study of readers over the past two hundred years. None of the available evidence is altogether appropriate to the history of reading. The personal journals and diaries, the novels and artwork, the critical literary reviews and pedagogical materials, as well as the mail received by writers about their work, all pose significant interpretive problems. Individually, they are less than perfect for the purpose of examining the dialogic interaction between reader and text over a long period. Nevertheless, the sheer bulk of the available evidence, the collective insight offered by the thousands of different documents from different kinds of readers about a variety of texts, sheds light on an otherwise obscure but important aspect of intellectual and literary history. When these sources are examined carefully with the tools of critics, theorists, and historians whose concerns are closely related, a genuine history of reading becomes feasible. However tentative the initial results, the study of the reading experience, in modern France at least, seems far more plausible than the inadequacy of any single source would indicate.

ISSUES

This project owes a tremendous debt to previous work done in a variety of disciplines. In historical research, for example, studies have explored many of the issues and sources discussed here, especially for the medieval and early modern periods. Roger Chartier, Daniel Roche, and Robert Darnton identified for Old Regime France the six most logical areas of inquiry in the history of reading: what was read, by whom, when, where, how, and why.[34] But with so recent a definition of this field, social and intellectual historians generally

---

[33] See student notebooks in the MNE near Rouen.

[34] See Robert Darnton, "First Steps toward a History of Reading," *Australian Journal of French Studies* 23 (1986): 5–30; and Henri-Jean Martin, "Pour une histoire de la lecture," *Revue française d'histoire du livre* 46 (1977): 583–609. Cf. Robert Escarpit, *Sociologie de la littérature* (1973), 98–125; Julien Cain et al., *Le Livre français. Hier, aujourd'hui, demain* (1972), 205–46; Jacques Charpentreau et al., eds., *Le Livre et la lecture en France* (1968), 15–50; and Michel de Certeau, *The Practice of Everyday Life*, trans. Steven F. Rendall (Berkeley, 1984), 165–76.

lag behind social scientists, who have already attempted serious answers to the same questions in a contemporary setting. Work by Robert Escarpit and Pierre Bourdieu, especially, can serve as equally appropriate models—subject to the significant constraints imposed by the problematic sources discussed earlier— for historical investigations into readers, readings, texts, and contexts in the modern period. Moreover, this work is a necessary corrective to the less em-pirical interests of reader-response theory and criticism. Despite substantial differences in perspective, methods, and sources, literary specialists are ex-ploring the interpretive implications of essentially the same issues.

Scholars in the social history of ideas have at least made significant progress in determining what materials people read in the past. Using the records of officials responsible for monitoring or censoring the book trade, historians have discovered the material generally available to readers from the sixteenth century to the present. Their research based on the *dépôt légal* and the *Biblio-graphie de la France*, in particular, is complemented by the attention of other scholars to the book catalogs of booksellers, public and private libraries, read-ing clubs, and estate inventories, among other sources of a less global na-ture.[35] Although their well-documented findings are not always consistent, these scholars have assessed with some certainty, albeit indirectly, the mental world of the past, one very different from that inferred from the texts exam-ined by the last generation of intellectual and literary historians.[36] Similarly, sociologists using survey data continue to enrich this study of what printed materials were actually read;[37] they suggest a need for even greater precision in historical research in the modern period, when the publishing industry di-versified its production considerably beyond the fairly simple categories of the early modern book trade. For this reason, notwithstanding their disdain for quantification, intellectual historians have much to learn from the social sci-ences.

Since the number of new titles grew by the thousands after the invention of printing, it is all the more necessary to specify which of these books were read by identifiable social groups. Scholars have addressed this question less well, largely because adequate records are difficult to find. Studies of literacy abound, based as they often are on signatures in ample church and state rec-

[35] E.g., Robert Estivals, *La Statistique bibliographique de la France sous la monarchie au XVIIIe siècle* (The Hague, 1965); idem, "Histoire, sociologie et prévisions économiques quanti-tatives de l'imprimerie," *Bibliographie de la France*, supplement (May–June 1969); and the work surveyed by Chartier, *Lectures et lecteurs*, 87–124, 165–221.

[36] Cf. the Enlightenment in Robert Darnton, *The Literary Underground of the Old Regime* (Cambridge, Mass., 1982), 167–208; and romanticism in James Smith Allen, *Popular French Romanticism: Authors, Readers, and Books in the Nineteenth Century* (Syracuse, 1981), 45–73.

[37] See Janick Jossin, "La Lecture en France," *L'Express* (11 Nov. 1978): 151–62; and André Burguière, "Le Savoir-lire des Français," *Le Nouvel Observateur* (9–15 Jan. 1987): 56–57.

ords.[38] But such work does not define readerships. Though selective and incomplete, some subscription lists compiled by publishers of periodicals and new titles, as well as the registers of books borrowed from libraries, identify past audiences of specific titles. These particular sources tend to support the hypothesis suggested by a German historian, Rolf Engelsing, who claims to have discovered a "reading revolution" at the end of the eighteenth century.[39] From the Middle Ages to shortly after 1750, according to Engelsing, people read repeatedly only a few books, like the Bible, an almanac, or a missal. By the beginning of the nineteenth century, however, their interests ranged more widely to include a variety of titles, which they usually read only once. Engelsing thus saw a progressive movement among the well-heeled burghers of Bremen from "intensive" to "extensive" reading, even though he greatly oversimplified the historical reality of other literate groups in different circumstances elsewhere in Europe. Clearly, some people in the twentieth century, including the devout, the scholarly, the young, and the naive, still read intensively. But the general trend deserves more careful exploration than it has received to date. Like the heuristic but flawed model of historical development offered by modernization theory, Engelsing's reading revolution has served as a useful basis for comparison and revision in a still largely unexplored field.[40]

The other questions—the where, when, how, and most intractably, why—have been subjects of much less successful study for all periods, not just for the Old Regime. Recently, Fritz Nies charted the artistic images of readers in modern Europe to discover the liberation of reading from daytime social settings indoors to include private personal experiences outdoors during the day and indoors at night.[41] The very occasional reading at rural *veillées* during the Old Regime, for example, could only have occurred around a hearth providing light for the rare literate villager with a chapbook. On the other hand, the reading of a modern suburban middle-class youth, alone at home or in the garden, could take place at almost anytime, weather permitting, once wide-

[38] See Harvey J. Graff, *The Legacies of Literacy: Continuities and Contradictions* (Bloomington, Ind., 1987), 192–220, 245–85.

[39] See Rolf Engelsing, "Die Perioden der Lesergeschichte in der Neuzeit. Das statistische Ausmass und die soziokulturelle Bedeutung der Lektüre," *Archiv für Geschichte des Buchwesens* 10 (1969): 944–1002; and idem, *Der Bürger als Leser. Lesergeschichte in Deutschland 1500–1800* (Stuttgart, 1974), 182–215. Cf. Robert Darnton, *The Great Cat Massacre and Other Episodes of French Cultural History* (New York, 1984), 249–51; and Chartier, *Lectures et lecteurs*, 201–3.

[40] Cf. William Nelson, "From 'Listen Lordlings' to 'Dear Reader,' " *University of Toronto Quarterly* 46 (1976–77): 111–24; and Paul Saenger, "Silent Reading: Its Impact on Late Medieval Script and Society," *Viator* 13 (1982): 367–414. On modernization theory, see Eugen Weber, *Peasants into Frenchmen: The Modernization of Rural France 1870–1914* (Stanford, 1976), ix–xiii, 485–96; and John M. Merriman, ed., *Consciousness and Class Experience in Nineteenth-Century Europe* (New York, 1979), 17–44.

[41] See Fritz Nies, "À la recherche de la 'majorité silencieuse'. Iconographie et réception littéraire," *Oeuvres et critiques* 2 (1978): 65–74.

spread literate skills, more portable books, and adequate domestic lighting were developed. But whatever the sources historians use, the problem of specifying the precise circumstances of the reading experience for all literate individuals must remain unresolvable. Those circumstances are much too diverse. As for elucidating actual interpretive practices and the reasons for their change over time in different milieus—an important issue—few scholars in this new field make any attempt. Beyond inferences from texts and their historical context, social historians generally neglect the how and why of reading.[42]

The patient scholarship of literary specialists on the reception of texts has been more significant. With adequate sources, appropriate methods, and well-defined issues, the history of criticism constitutes the first systematic scholarly effort to examine the way in which selected individuals read. There are numerous studies of how major works of important authors were received; and they are complemented effectively by equally numerous intellectual biographies of leading critics whose interpretive practices influenced their contemporaries.[43] Consequently, literary historians, using the ample primary sources available to them, have documented in remarkable detail the principles, habits, prejudices, even the idiosyncrasies guiding the world of letters in modern France.[44] Although their attention may be limited to the canon, their discipline must constitute the core of any proper history of reading. Social historians are obliged to recognize the careful work of literary historians and to adapt it to a much wider range of sources. In this way, the mental lives of more ordinary readers, who are after all only critics of another sort, may be explored within an appropriate field of scholarship.

Despite their exclusive attention to the use of language in texts, reader-response critics and theorists also define a number of central issues in the history of interpretive practice. Among other American practitioners, Stanley Fish, David Bleich, and Norman Holland argue the need to consider the nature and limits of readers' subjectivity in the literary experience, whatever its in-

---

[42] E.g., Jean-Jacques Darmon, *Le Colportage de librairie en France sous le Second Empire. Grands Colporteurs et culture populaire* (1972), 183–212; Françoise Parent-Lardeur, *Lire à Paris au temps de Balzac. Les Cabinets de lecture à Paris 1815–1830* (1981), 130–65; and Michael B. Palmer, *Des petits journaux aux grandes agences. Naissance du journalisme moderne* (1983), 11–21.

[43] E.g., Henri Peyre, *Writers and Their Critics: A Study of Misunderstanding* (Ithaca, 1944), 81–136; David Bellos, *Balzac Criticism in France, 1850–1900: The Making of a Reputation* (Oxford, 1976); W. T. Bandy, *Baudelaire Judged by His Contemporaries (1845–1867)* (New York, 1933); Michael Z. L. Issacharoff, *J.-K. Huysmans devant la critique en France, 1874–1960* (1970); [René] Etiemble, *Le Mythe de Rimbaud*, vol. 1: *La Genèse du mythe, 1869–1949* (1949); and Artina Artinian, *Maupassant Criticism in France, 1880–1940* (New York, 1941).

[44] On French literary history as a field, see Gustave Lanson, *Manuel bibliographique de la littérature française moderne. XVIe, XVIIe, XVIIIe et XIXe siècles*, rev. ed. (1921); René Rancoeur, *Bibliographie de la littérature française du Moyen Âge à nos jours* (1953–); and Hugo Paul Thieme, *Bibliographie de la littérature française de 1800 à 1900*, 3 vols. (1933).

stitutional, educational, or psychological source.[45] French structuralists and deconstructionists emphasize the discursive plasticity of language, in and out of texts, that defines the way readers perceive their world as well as books. Whether or not the historian's documents can define the reading experience, any attempt to characterize it must recognize the indeterminacy of textual meaning. From this perspective, no single reading of a book, even the historian's, is necessarily privileged, an insight calling attention to the trickiness of using texts to study a human activity as linguistically mediated as interpretation.[46] But the answer to that conundrum may lie in the "reception theory" developed by Hans Robert Jauss and Wolfgang Iser, among others in Germany.[47] These theorists have laid the philosophical foundation for relating reading to interpretive understanding. They make clear the necessity of establishing a model of textual reception derived from the reader's actual experience.[48] That their models are invariably centered on their own experiences does not in the least invalidate the models based on the responses of others, especially those of identifiable readers in other periods and cultures. Such self-consciousness is perhaps the ultimate value of recent work in literary theory, particularly the theory immediately relevant to the study of the subjective, linguistic, and theoretical assumptions of historical readers.

LIMITATIONS

In light of these considerations suggested by a host of scholars, it would be presumptuous if not foolish to write a comprehensive history of reading. The initial scope and final conclusions of any study must be carefully defined, at least until more research is focused on a smaller range of issues. For example, it would be wise to choose a restricted period within one culture where a wide variety of historical sources is found. Modern France fits this description best. The French historian is blessed with a reasonably coherent period of national cultural development from the First Empire to World War II, one largely defined by the historical transition from landed wealth to industrial capitalism.[49] Moreover, large stores of documents are located in or near one city: since the Napoleonic Empire, Paris has been the heart of French literate life. Although

[45] E.g., Fish, *Is There a Text in This Class?* 1–17; David Bleich, *Subjective Criticism* (Baltimore, 1978), 213–37; and Norman Holland, *The Dynamics of Literary Response* (New York, 1968), 3–190. See also notes 20, 21, and 25.

[46] See Jonathan Culler, *On Deconstruction: Theory and Criticism after Structuralism* (Ithaca, 1982), 85–225; Harold Bloom et al., *Deconstruction and Criticism* (New York, 1979); and Josué Harari, ed., *Textual Strategies: Perspectives in Post-Structuralist Criticism* (Ithaca, 1979).

[47] See Robert C. Holub, *Reception Theory: A Critical Introduction* (London, 1984), 53–106.

[48] Roman Ingarden, *The Cognition of the Literary Work of Art*, trans. Ruth Ann Crowley and Kenneth R. Olsen (Evanston, Ill., 1973), 3–19.

[49] Cf. J.P.T. Bury, *France 1814–1940* (Philadelphia, 1949), v; and Harry Levin, *The Gates of Horn: A Study of Five French Realists* (New York, 1966), 74–83.

often inimical to free expression, the tight centralization of French culture and politics made possible the remarkable concentration of sources essential to this study. A mandatory depository system for books and newspapers was created during the First Republic for the Bibliothèque nationale, whose well-catalogued archives also contain the personal papers of many major writers since the eighteenth century. In Paris, other collections include invaluable archives on the book industry, literary and press censorship, educational institutions, and public libraries—all important cultural agencies appropriate to a history of reading.

But so many conveniently accessible sources demand other, more conceptual limitations. Given the enormous number of documentable readers and their diverse experiences with printed matter, this study limits itself chiefly to the changing contexts and interpretations of two specific readerships, namely the friends and families of authors and the literary critics of Paris. But government censors of the stage and the teachers and students of elementary and secondary schools also receive attention. These interpretive communities left ample evidence of their literate activities in the correspondence sent to French writers, the reviews written for newspapers and journals, the files maintained in the Interior Ministry, and the books and notebooks required by schools throughout the nineteenth century. Though certainly not representative of all modern French reading publics, the audiences studied here constitute a reasonably diverse sample worth careful analysis. The sharp focus on particular social groups also invites comparison with others suggested by more problematic sources, such as artistic portraits, prose fiction, autobiographies, and memoirs, to validate the conceptions that historians have long had of readers and reading in general.

These communities of interpretation encountered a remarkable range of print, a fact necessitating careful selection of texts as well as readerships. Here again the choices naturally arise from the sources available; they document well the responses to dozens of different works. But because the evidence of audience response is far from complete or comprehensive, the texts selected here were written by the best-documented authors in France from 1800 to 1940 (Stendhal, Balzac, Sue, Flaubert, Baudelaire, Michelet, Augier, the Goncourt brothers, Zola, Anatole France, Proust, and Sartre). Works by these particular authors represent a broad selection of literary genres (mostly prose fiction, but also poetry, drama, essay, correspondence, and political opinion), publication dates (spaced and grouped for appropriate comparison), and response (in newspapers, journals and archival materials, fan mail especially). Moreover, the texts define a coherent pattern from romanticism to existentialism. The cultural unity suggested by these writers owes much to the historical development of modern French literature, of course; but it owes even more to the readers who gave meaning to that development.

Other conceptual limitations define the nature and scope of the present venture, based as it is on the interpretive experiences of more than 1,600 different individuals.[50] Very few of these people read the same work in entirely comparable circumstances. Nearly every respondent to a text, for instance, was subject to the influence of previous readers; the older the text, the more generations there were to interpret it, such that these prior readings themselves altered subsequent experiences with the work, a difficulty that Hans-Georg Gadamer has noted and attempted to incorporate into his hermeneutics.[51] The problem this poses for a history of reading is that the responses of earlier generations often become even more important than the text itself. This is particularly true with works central to the definition of a major literary genre, like the novels of the earliest prose realists. To compensate for this interpretive intrusion—one that can and should be considered by future histories—the present study deliberately examines only the reading experiences contemporary with the publication of each title. Each interpretation was therefore most likely focused on the selected work, permitting more precise study of text, context, and their interaction. These case studies illuminate the readings of various genres (as in Chapters 8 and 9) as well as the responses by successive generations of audiences to a single genre (as in Chapter 10).

Clearly defined by the sources, issues, and methods of the two most relevant scholarly disciplines, history and literature, the present book is divided into sections appropriate to their respective concerns; it considers initially the historical moment, and then the interpretive activity occurring within it. Consequently, the first section, entitled "The Historical Context," develops the historian's interest in the economic, social, political, and cultural forces at work in the period that both shaped and responded to the nature of readers and their experiences. The industrialization, distribution, and consumption of print studied in Chapter 1 provided one major influence that was in turn affected by the growing demand of a more literate and better educated public. A precise analysis of how many and who read this flood of books and newspapers appears in Chapter 2, while the political institutions, ideas, and groups constraining and responding to interpretive practices are the subjects of Chapter 3. Similarly, Chapter 4 considers the roles that cultural, psychological, and pedagogical factors played in the reading experience. In each succeeding chapter of this section, the analytic interest narrows in answer to the basic questions in the field—what was read by whom, when, where, and how—primarily to highlight the historical milieu of the interaction between reader and text from 1800 to 1940.

The second portion of the book, "Historical Interpretive Practices: The Art of Reading" studies textual experiences in art, fiction, and memoir. Using

---

[50] See notes to Table A.8.

[51] See Hans-Georg Gadamer, *Truth and Method*, trans. Garrett Barden and John Cumming (New York, 1975), 245–73. Cf. Dominick LaCapra and Steven L. Kaplan, eds., *Modern European Intellectual History: Reappraisals and New Perspectives* (Ithaca, 1982), 86–110.

artistic evidence, like Fantin-Latour's portrait of his two sisters, Chapter 5 traces the development from collective to individual interactions with print, from the Old Regime to World War II, when images of readers constituted a significant tradition in French portraiture. Similarly, as Chapter 6 discusses, the modern novel provides important insights into the role of reading in people's lives from childhood, through youth, to maturity. The life cycle defined by the *roman de formation* especially has a particular set of powerful reading experiences appropriate to each stage in the development of a work's principal character. No less subject to well-established formalistic constraints like those in art and prose fiction, the journals and memoirs used in Chapter 7 still suggest crucial distinctions among different audiences, defined by region, class, and gender, as they become increasingly self-conscious readers in the period. Urban and rural, middle- and working-class, not to mention male and female readers differed substantially one from another, according to those who left published records of their activities. Part II of this book thus explains how people encountered texts within the specific historical contexts examined in Part I.

An answer to the single most difficult question, why men and women read as they did in modern France, is attempted in Part III, entitled "Historical Interpretive Practices: The Act of Reading." Here the analysis returns to the actual audiences discussed in Part I, this time using sources that permit a closer examination of what meaning these particular communities derived from their contact with the different selected texts. The correspondents' responses to literature are studied in Chapter 8. The last two chapters (9 and 10) consider in detail the actual ways in which readers responded to different literary and nonliterary genres, including correspondence, essays, drama, and prose fiction, whose conventions guided their audiences through the texts. The underlying assumption here is that readers responded as they did as much because of their immediate contact with the work as because of their historical circumstances. Text and context interacted, and they did so in a discernible fashion that ultimately requires close textual analysis.

Although a truly comprehensive history may never be possible, then, interpretive practices and their relevant contexts can be studied more systematically and more empirically than they have been. There can indeed be better informed answers to three fundamental questions: In what circumstances did people read in France from the eighteenth to the twentieth centuries? How did they read? What did their reading mean to them and why? Even partial answers to these questions promise some measure of progress in the study of literate culture and its development over the past two hundred years.[52]

---

[52] See Susan de Castell et al., eds., *Literacy, Society, and Schooling: A Reader* (Cambridge, 1986), 61–86; Eric A. Havelock, *The Muse Learns to Write: Reflections on Orality and Literacy from Antiquity to the Present* (New Haven, 1986); and the bibliography in David R. Olson et al., eds., *Literacy, Language, and Learning: The Nature and Consequences of Reading and Writing*

This book also shares in the scholarly definition of an entirely new field in intellectual history, a field focused on readers and their interpretive practices rather than on authors and their texts. Reading, not writing, is its subject. This new perspective promises further clarification of issues within but also outside the domain of intellectual and literary history. These other concerns include how ordinary men and women perceived important events in the past, from the acceptance of Napoleon's coup d'état in 1799 to the French appeasement of Hitler in 1938. A better understanding of reading over time certainly underlies a better understanding of collective perception, its form and its content—historical problems of interest to historians and literary specialists, whatever their fields.[53] But the history of reading must come first; discussion of its central issues constitutes the more modest intention of the following pages.

(Cambridge, 1985), 412–26. Cf. Eric Auerbach, *Literary Language and Its Public in Late Antiquity and in the Middle Ages* (New York, 1965); and Jacques Derrida, *Disseminations*, trans. Barbara Johnson (Chicago, 1981), 142–71.

[53] Cf. Charles Samaran, ed., *L'Histoire et ses méthodes* (1961), 937–66; Jacques LeGoff and Pierre Nora, eds., *Faire de l'histoire* (1974), 3:76–94; Jacques LeGoff et al., eds., *La Nouvelle Histoire* (1978), 402–23; and Michel Vovelle, *Idéologies et mentalités* (1982), 19–79, 325–29.

PART I

The Historical Context

Chapter 1

THE PRINTED WORD

ON MARCH 19, 1863, a clerk in the Ministry of the Interior recorded a remarkable number in French history. Charged with keeping a register of all publications printed in Paris, he dutifully copied the legal declaration provided by a shop contracted to print military passes: "in-8 [format], 1 [volume], 1 [sheet], 10,000,000 [copies]."[1] Rarely in the nineteenth century did this bureau ever record more than 100,000 copies for any printing job; the annual average ranged from a low of 880 in 1814 to a high of 6,800 in 1878 (see Table A.1). Could this recording have been a mistake? In a hurry or bored by the tedium of his job, the clerk may have misread or miscopied the actual figure. But sixteen days later, on April 4, a different hand registered a similar declaration. Another clerk also noted 10,000,000 copies of a receipt form printed for Parisian coachdrivers.[2] The likelihood of two such large recording mistakes within a three-week period, by two different hands in the same office, seems remote. It could well be that both of them are correct. If so, two Parisian printers in 1863 stated their intentions to produce what amounts to more than twelve copies of printed text for every man, woman, and child in France's largest city.

Although the figure of 10,000,000 falls far short of cumulative production levels in France today, it does represent an important historical trend. This declaration shared in the irregular but rapid growth in print from the First to the Second Empire that then leveled off until the outbreak of World War II. The number of books registered in annual editions of the *Bibliographie de la France*, the most important public catalog of new books, rose from less than 3,000 in 1814 to more than 13,800 in 1866; the latter figure, however, was exceeded only five times in the next 73 years (see Table 1.1). Similarly, the cost of printed material dropped to a new low. The price of daily newspapers, for instance, declined from a standard annual subscription of eighty francs during the Restoration to only five centimes per issue during the Second Empire; by the start of the Third Republic the price of print stopped falling.[3] Thereafter the industrial infrastructure remained largely unchanged for sev-

---

[1] AN F18,II*98, item 3032. Cf. the annual production of French almanacs (4.5–5.0 million) discussed in AN F18,294 d. 1863.

[2] AN F18,II*98, item 3715.

[3] Cf. Michael B. Palmer, *Des petits journaux aux grandes agences. Naissance du journalisme moderne* (1983), 331.

enty years. Renewed growth would have to wait until the *"livre de poche* revolution"* in a more consumer-oriented industry after 1950. In the interim, the uneven market for printed matter would diversify to accommodate the new reading habits of an increasingly literate urban population in France. This, then, was the complex historical development suggested by the printers' declarations recorded by the Interior Ministry's clerks in 1863.

Though apparently unrelated to interpretive practices during the Second Empire, these figures do pertain to the history of reading. French publishing clearly responded to the demands generated by the market for print. How much and what people read eventually had an impact on what printers and publishers together produced for the market. This fact assumes, of course, that the relationship between publishing and reading reflects the close relationship between supply and demand. On the other hand, producers are not necessarily slaves to consumers. The printing and publishing industries themselves had an impact on how much and what people read. The availability of printed matter itself contributes to the nature and extent of the reading experience. New means of production, new modes of distribution, and new patterns of consumption coincided with, responded to, but also influenced the changing readership of France from 1800 to 1940. In this fashion, economic infrastructure was indeed tied to interpretive practice in modern France. For this reason it makes sense to examine the appropriate historical context of the printed word.[4]

PUBLICATION

By the beginning of the Third Republic, the publication of books and newspapers in France no longer resembled what it had been in the Old Regime.[5] Printed matter had been for centuries a luxury good produced for a limited market. Printers and booksellers acted as their own publishers and sold expensive items primarily to a well-defined clientele living in France's few large cities. The major exception to this rule was an extensive colporter network for chapbooks, almanacs, and devotionals sold in a distinctly rural and plebeian market. Otherwise, the prerevolutionary book trade appealed to a small, lit-

[4] See Jean-Alexis Neret, *Histoire illustrée de la librairie et du livre français* (1953), 110–293; Julien Cain et al., *Le Livre français. Hier, aujourd'hui, demain* (1972), 45–93; Theodore Zeldin, *France 1848–1945* (Oxford, 1973–77), 2:349–93; HEF 2:544–86, 3:24–121, 4:22–117; Martyn Lyons, *Le Triomphe du livre. Une Histoire sociologique de la lecture dans la France du XIXe siècle* (1987), 43–104; and Jean-Yves Mollier, *L'Argent et les lettres. L'Histoire du capitalisme d'édition, 1880–1920* (1988). Cf. Frédéric Barbier, "Livre, économie et société industrielles en Allemagne et en France au 19e siècle (1840–1914)," doctoral thesis, Université de Paris IV (1987).

[5] See Robert Estivals, *La Statistique bibliographique de la France sous la monarchie au XVIIIe siècle* (The Hague, 1965); François Furet et al., eds., *Livre et société dans la France du XVIIIe siècle* (The Hague, 1965–70), 1:3–32; Robert Darnton, *The Literary Underground of the Old Regime* (Cambridge, Mass., 1982), 167–208; and HEF 2:20–302.

erate elite, certainly no more than 5 percent of the approximately 26 million inhabitants of France. And this limited demand was easily met by equipment little changed since the invention of printing in the fifteenth century. Wooden hand presses, simple lead typefaces, rag-based paper, and urine-soaked leather ink balls served the needs of an artisanal craft still largely subject to the restrictions of printers' guilds and the inconsistent censorship of a declining monarchy. The largest publishing venture in the eighteenth century, the *Encyclopédie*, could reach only a very small audience, the traditional mixed elite of the Old Regime, so long as the editors depended on the narrow vision and limited possibilities of a traditional craft.[6]

The Revolution of 1789 marked, among many other things, the origins of modern publishing.[7] The awakened political consciousness of the population encouraged interest in literate skills and created a larger market for printed material. In time a new industry arose. Following the Le Chapelier Law of 1791 breaking up the guilds, the Napoleonic Code of 1804 defined the legal conditions for manufacturing and commerce more conducive to expansion and innovation. Despite the tight administrative restrictions on printing and bookselling in 1810, which lasted until the Third Republic,[8] the production of print underwent substantial changes in the course of the nineteenth century. Above all, printers and booksellers made room for a new figure in the trade, the publisher. Printers concentrated their efforts increasingly on producing, while booksellers focused more on retailing for others. They left for the publisher the responsibility of acquiring marketable manuscripts, collecting the necessary capital, overseeing new books into print, and distributing them to appropriate outlets for sale. This specialization took decades to develop; many publishing firms, like Hachette and Nathan, still retain interests in retail outlets, however secondary they are to their main business of publishing new titles for the market. But earlier in the nineteenth century there appeared a more fully differentiated trade than had ever existed before the Revolution.

In time publishers specialized as well.[9] Early in the nineteenth century, booksellers had already staked claims to certain kinds of books. Barba and Tresse, for instance, were known for their holdings in drama, Ladvocat and

---

[6] See Robert Darnton, *The Business of Enlightenment: A Publishing History of the Encyclopédie 1775–1800* (Cambridge, Mass., 1979), 286.

[7] See Neret, *Histoire illustrée*, 110–98; and HEF 2:516–40, 552–86.

[8] See Bernard Veuillot, *Imprimeurs et libraires parisiens du Premier Empire* (1979); and Henri Welschinger, "La Direction générale de l'imprimerie et de la librairie (1810–1815)," *Le Livre . . . Bibliographie retrospective* 8 (1887): 161–82.

[9] Cf. J.-N. Barba, *Souvenirs de Jean-Nicolas Barba, ancien libraire au Palais-Royal* (1846), 175–76; Louis-Désiré Véron, *Mémoires d'un bourgeois de Paris* (1856), 3:51–55; Edmond Werdet, *De la librairie française. Son passé, son présent, son avenir* (1860), 92–119; Maurice Humblot, "L'Édition littéraire au XIXe siècle," *Bibliographie de la France*, suppl. (17 Mar. 1911): 1–18; Maurice Dreyfous, *Ce que je tiens à dire* (1912); and Bernard Grasset, *La Chose littéraire* (1929), 147–66.

Renduel in the romantics, and Levrault and Dupont in textbooks. New publishers soon focused their activities in response to well-defined interests of the booksellers. A hawker of theater programs, Michel Lévy, founded his house on the publication of plays to coincide with their production on the stage. Similarly, the Didot brothers, booksellers and printers since the eighteenth century, concentrated on scholarly and classical texts. Some of the larger provincial publishers, Ardant, Mame, and Pellerin especially, catered to peasant readers who were reached by thousands of itinerant colporters.[10] Others devoted themselves to periodicals; for example, François Buloz began *La Revue des deux mondes* in 1831, and Henri Rochefort started *La Lanterne* in 1868.[11] Even greater diversity in publishing would come with further integration in the financial structure of the French economy after the Second Empire. Family firms then began to incorporate, and these new limited-liability companies created their own *messageries*, or distribution networks.

Besides specializing in the first half of the nineteenth century, the publishing industry developed products appropriate to new market conditions. Instead of expensive multivolume titles in octavo, publishers produced single-volume works in cheaper formats. In 1838, Gervais Charpentier created a minor revolution with a standard eighteenmo edition of new titles costing only 3 francs 50, less than half the price per volume of books published for the lending libraries. His intention was to profit by large runs with lower per unit costs. The price would eventually drop even lower, to one franc, for titles still sold by other publishers for 15 francs or more. A comparable development occurred in the press. In 1836, Émile de Girardin halved the subscription price of *La Presse*, as Armand Dutacq did for *Le Siècle*, in order to enlarge circulation and thereby increase the cost-effectiveness of more expensive advertising copy. Promoted still further by the publication of sensational serial novels, this marketing strategy substantially increased the newspaper's revenues from advertisements.[12] Accordingly, Polydore Millaud sold single issues of *Le Petit journal* for a very small fraction of their actual cost. By the first decade of the Third Republic, publishers issued novels, sold by successive installments of only eight pages, that resembled the daily newspaper in content as well as in format and cost. Some Calmann-Lévy publications even included advertising

---

[10] Cf. BN Q° 10 Catalogues; BN, *Recueil des catalogues et des prospectus des libraires de Paris, 1806–1831* (n.d.); and the indexes to Otto Henri Lorenz et al., *Catalogue général de la librairie française* (1867–1945), vols. 8, 11, 13, 17, 20, 23, 25, 27, and 28.

[11] E.g., see Claude Bellanger et al., eds., *Histoire générale de la presse française* (1969), 2:114–23.

[12] See Pierre Orecchioni, "Presse, livre et littérature au XIXe siècle," *Revue française d'histoire du livre* 43 (1974): 33–44. Cf. Maurice Reclus, *Émile Girardin. Le Créateur de la presse moderne* (1934), 79–97; and James Smith Allen, "Le Commerce du livre romantique à Paris (1820–1843)," *Revue française d'histoire du livre* 49 (1980): 69–93.

copy for pharmaceuticals available to the readers taking cures at various health spas.[13]

To meet the larger audience sought by publishers, printers adopted new equipment.[14] Versions of William Nicolson's rotary press, as modified by Frederick Koenig in 1811, rivaled the hand press nearly everywhere in France by mid-century. At first driven by hand and later by steam and electricity, the new presses were successively refined by the addition of multiple drums to expand their capacity dramatically, especially for newspapers in daily editions of 100,000 or more. Although an experienced team of artisans during the Old Regime could print as many as 250 sheets per hour on the old wooden hand presses, the largely unskilled labor of workers before World War I could easily produce more than ten times that rate on the new presses.[15] In turn, smaller printing jobs, like the small first editions of unknown authors, were facilitated considerably by the adaptation of the hand press to new sources of power. The result was the familiar platen press with its large flywheel and rhythmic clanking. In many print shops it is still used for wedding invitations and calling cards.

Mechanized printing affected other important elements in the production process. During the Restoration, printers began using Louis-Étienne Herhan's stereotypes made from lead poured into molds of previously composed type. Once the plates had been cast, they could be used for printing larger runs, usually on the new rotary presses, without damaging the original type that was now freed for other jobs.[16] This modification to composing became standard practice until the introduction of linotype in the 1880s and monotype in the 1890s. By 1900, whole pages of type could be composed in a fraction of the time it took a skilled compositor to do by hand. Like the platen press, this equipment remains in use today, despite the development of photomechanical processes and equipment. Due to the increased capacity of printers, however, traditional papermaking posed a serious bottleneck to increased production.[17] Consequently, the manufacture of paper was also mechanized and simplified by the replacement of rags by vegetable and wood pulp after 1850. Paper was manufactured in large drums of continuous rolls for newspaper printing; hence the name "newsprint." Even the industrial production of ink

[13] See Jean-Yves Mollier, *Michel & Calmann Lévy, ou La Naissance de l'édition moderne 1836–1891* (1984), 440.

[14] See Maurice Audin, *Histoire de l'imprimerie. Radioscope d'une ère: De Gutenberg à l'informatique* (1972), 247–81, 315–32, 389–404; James Moran, *Printing Presses: History and Development* (Berkeley, 1973), 101–12, 123–42, 157–220; [Frédéric Barbier], *Histoire d'un imprimeur: Berger-Levrault, 1676–1976* (1976), 63–102; and HEF 2:544–50, 3:56–88, 4:36–56, 75–89.

[15] See Moran, *Printing Presses*, 218–19.

[16] On Herhan, see Audin, *Histoire de l'imprimerie*, 215–17.

[17] On paper production, see ibid., 195–99, 280–81, 331–32, 398–400; and HEF 3:58–61.

saw changes with the development of chemical "vehicles," such as mineral oils, that reduced drying time and made possible more rapid printing.

Expanding operations complemented the new equipment.[18] Even though the number of printers was limited by law and their activities were tightly controlled until 1881—one regime after another permitted only 80 printers in Paris—some operations developed the labor structure and the economies of scale typical of modern industry. Print shops were among the largest operations in Paris; 84 percent of them employed more than 10 workers, a percentage matched or exceeded by only 11 percent of all industries surveyed in 1848.[19] Seven years later, the median Parisian printer employed between 30 and 40 workers.[20] By 1865, one outfit run by Napoléon Chaix actually maintained a payroll for 400 workers.[21] But labor was cheaper and more docile in the provinces, where publishers increasingly sent their work. Besides using the printers in nearby Saint-Denis, Sceaux, and Sèvres, Parisian houses sometimes turned to others much farther away, such as Berger-Levrault in Nancy and Mame in Tours, once the railroad network lowered significantly the costs of shipping.[22] By the second decade of the Third Republic, even before legal restrictions on printing were lifted, the structure of the printing industry had altered radically to the advantage of non-Parisian printers. From 1869 to 1889, publishing in Paris experienced a serious slowdown, while provincial publication actually increased elevenfold. By 1900, Paris was no longer the center of French printing that it had been for centuries.[23]

Books and newspapers are more easily printed than sold; much of modern publishing's success resulted from special talents and insights in marketing. Michel Lévy, for example, affected the development of the book trade perhaps more than any other individual in French history.[24] Building on his experience

---

[18] On printing equipment and operations, see BN NAFr 21129 fols. 204 and 239; and C.L.F. Panckoucke, *Budget statistique d'un éditeur* (1837), 3–6. Cf. Frédéric Barbier, "Chiffres de tirage et devis d'édition: La Politique d'une imprimerie-librairie au début du XIXe siècle, 1789–1835," *Comité des travaux historiques et scientifiques. Bulletin de la section d'histoire moderne et contemporaine* 11 (1978): 141–56.

[19] Paris, Chambre de Commerce et d'Industrie, *Statistique de l'industrie à Paris . . . pour les années 1847–1848* (1849), 889. Cf. Paul Chavet, *Les Ouvriers du livre en France de 1789 à la constitution de la Fédération du livre* (1956), 90–113; and Lyons, *Le Triomphe du livre*, 46.

[20] See Kenneth E. Carpenter, ed., *Books and Society in History* (New York, 1983), fig. 5, p. 214. Cf. Frédéric Barbier, "Les Ouvriers du livre et la révolution industrielle en France au XIXe siècle," *Revue du Nord* 73 (1981): 189–206; and HEF 3:91–101.

[21] See Jean Mistler, *La Librairie Hachette de 1826 à nos jours* (1964), 127–30; and HEF 3:73–74, 4:38, 76.

[22] Shops in towns near Paris produced much for the Parisian market; see AN F18,168 and ADSVP DM4,16. Transportation costs are described in BN NAFr 21129 fols. 73–74.

[23] See table in Carpenter, ed., *Books and Society in History*, 213.

[24] See Mollier, *Michel & Calmann Lévy*, 48–431; Gabriel Boillat, *La Librairie Grasset et les lettres françaises* (1974); and Pierre Assouline, *Gaston Gallimard, un demi-siècle d'édition française* (1984).

of publishing dramas only after they had been successfully staged, Lévy relied heavily on both newspapers and literary reviews to identify authors likely to sell well in book form to different audiences. In this way he managed to expand the number of truly marketable titles; these bestsellers included works by Scribe, Hugo, Sand, Daudet, Sainte-Beuve, and Renan. But his most enduring contribution to French publishing, one comparable to the *Bibliothèque Charpentier*, was his practice of variable pricing. Lévy offered titles to several different publics: expensive, well-crafted books for the lending libraries and the wealthy upper classes; high-quality literature in less expensive formats for a more modest middle-class audience; plays, drama news, and programs for Parisian theatergoers; and popular novels in brochure-sized installments for the growing mass market for sensational fiction. Even though Lévy still focused his efforts on literature, he developed a diverse publishing strategy that made his house among the largest in France. In 1872, Calmann Lévy, Michel's heir, published more than 185 new titles and 845 reissues, totalling 1,724,000 volumes, some of them distributed as premiums by chocolate and drug manufacturers.[25]

The founder of Calmann-Lévy was rivaled by another important publisher, Louis Hachette, whose success was derived from yet another growing market.[26] Hachette was concerned less with literature for different audiences than he was with textbooks and dictionaries for the new educational institutions developing in the nineteenth century. Realizing the significance of the Guizot Law of 1833, this entrepreneur bought Paul Dupont's *Bibliothèque de l'enseignement primaire* and published the *Manuel général, ou Journal de l'instruction primaire*. Hachette's specialty in elementary-school books blossomed when his titles were either endorsed or bought in large lots by the Ministry of Public Instruction. This market continued to grow with each attempt to expand formal instruction from the Falloux Law of 1850 to the ministry of Jean Zay in 1936. Joined in this specialty by Delalain, Delagrave, and Larousse, Hachette developed another major interest in dictionaries, encyclopedias, and travel guides; this new investment resulted in the famous compilations by Littré, Vapereau, and Joanne that were consistent with the industry's increasing diversity and scale of operations. In 1854, Hachette received from the Interior Ministry an exclusive authorization to sell his inexpensive, colorfully covered books in designated train stations all over France.[27] Only twenty years after Calmann-Lévy had become a limited-liability corporation in 1898, Hachette made the same transition, but developed additional interests

[25] See Mollier, *Michel & Calmann Lévy*, 450, 441.

[26] See Mistler, *La Librairie Hachette*, 9–210; A. Rétif, *Pierre Larousse et son oeuvre (1817–1875)* (1975); anon., *Les Éditions Fernand Nathan ont cent ans 1881–1981* (1981); and HEF 3:416–42. On the educational market, see Otto Henri Lorenz, "Littérature enfantine," in Lorenz et al., *Catalogue général*, vol. 8.

[27] See authorization in AN AQ48,3549, cited in Mistler, *La Librairie Hachette*, 125.

in printing, binding, and distributing. This expansion led eventually to the establishment of the Messageries Hachette, the largest distribution agency in France. By 1932, the markets for both books and newspapers were coordinated under the management of the most important publisher in twentieth-century Europe.

Lévy and Hachette were not alone; they were joined in the literary marketplace by a host of other prominent French publishers. Besides the founding of Hachette and Dalloz in 1826, Garnier *frères* began in 1833, Belin in 1834, Calmann-Lévy in 1836, Masson in 1837, Privat in 1839, Klincksieck in 1842, Delmas in 1848, Beauchesne in 1851, Larousse in 1852, Fayard in 1855, Dunod in 1858, Delagrave, Gauthier-Villiers, and Lethielleux in 1864, Colin, Picard, and Tallandier in 1870, Flammarion and Champion in 1874, Nathan in 1884, Grasset in 1907, and Gallimard in 1911, to name only the most successful.[28] Their contributions (and failures) coincided with those of still other actors in the industry. As a collective effort, publishing required more than entrepreneurs in production and distribution; it also required authors. Notwithstanding their resistance to the marketplace and their frequent efforts to circumvent it, novelists, historians, educators, and journalists especially created the products that actually made possible modern publishing. Besides printers, booksellers, and publishers, authors learned to adapt their craft to new economic conditions.

Of major concern to most writers in the nineteenth century was the source and magnitude of their compensation.[29] Since the Old Regime, public and private patronage had waned in the face of the developing market for print, whatever the provisions made for some fortunate authors by wealthy individuals and the state. Sinecures for impecunious authors in libraries existed well into the Third Republic (and may be one reason why service in many French public collections was so poor). Nodier, Sandeau, Sainte-Beauve, and Heredia were only the more notable beneficiaries of this practice. Mérimée, Huysmans, Maupassant, and Claudel, among others, found similarly undemanding positions in various ministries that provided them time to create. Annuities and pensions were established and sometimes continued from regime to regime. But the Second Empire actually marked the last period of substantial political patronage. Most subsidies to writers during the Third Republic, with the major exception of Paul Valéry, were purely symbolic. Few of these alternatives to the marketplace provided the kind of independence that the successful sale of manuscripts to newspapers, journals, and publishers did. In fact,

---

[28] See accounts in Gustave Vapereau, *Dictionnaire universel des contemporains*, 5th ed. (1893).

[29] See John Lough, *Writer and Public in France from the Middle Ages to the Present Day* (Oxford, 1978), 275–399; Christophe Charle, *La Crise littéraire à l'époque du naturalisme. Roman, théâtre, et politique. Essai d'histoire sociale des groupes et des genres littéraires* (1979), 27–54; M. Vessilier-Ressi, *Le Métier d'auteur* (1982); and HEF 3:126–56, 4:480–527.

patronage amounted to little more than token support in comparison to the rich returns some writers enjoyed in journalism and publishing.[30]

The growth of the market is well represented by the changing attitudes and productivity of authors from 1800 onward. However unhappy about the sale of his novels, Stendhal never regarded his writing as a serious source of income. He once referred jokingly to his books as lottery tickets.[31] Instead, he relied on money inherited from his family and income from various positions in the military and the foreign service. Despite his publisher's pleas, Stendhal's small output did not particularly trouble him. It took a more marketable talent and an enormous debt to make one of Stendhal's contemporaries more consistently productive. This was Balzac, who often complained of becoming a slave to his work.[32] This became a common complaint during the nineteenth century. The more productive demons at mid-century included George Sand and Eugène Scribe, as well as the more furious serial novelists like Eugène Sue and Alexandre Dumas *père* (whose productivity was reputedly increased by the collaboration of 73 other authors).[33] Often paid by the line, these entrepreneurial authors had much in common with journalists, and even published their work first in newspapers. For the less successful writer, young authors especially, journalistic hackwork was a necessary occupation. From 1862 to 1866, Émile Zola wrote advertising copy as the head of publicity at Hachette before he established a name for himself as a novelist.[34]

While not all writers welcomed the opportunities created by modern publishing—many, like the symbolist poets, refused to sacrifice their art to the marketplace—most experienced its influence on their work for better or for worse.[35] Much of this influence was reflected in the changing contractual agreements between publisher and author from 1800 to 1940.[36] In the first half of the nineteenth century, writers generally sold the rights to publish their manuscripts for a specified number of copies—the more marketable the genre and the more renowned the author, the higher the sum per manuscript paid by

---

[30] See Priscilla Parkhurst Clark, *Literary France: The Making of a Culture* (Berkeley, 1987), 37–60, 78–96.

[31] Stendhal, *Oeuvres intimes*, ed. Henri Martineau (1955), 1456.

[32] E.g., Balzac to Zulma Carraud, 21 Nov. 1831, in *Balzac: Corr.*, ed. Roger Pierrot (1960–66), 1:617. Cf. F. G. Saillard-Huot to Théodore Leclerc, 13 Mar. 1863, in BN NAFr 21129 fol. 108.

[33] See Yves Olivier-Martin, *Histoire du roman populaire en France* (1980), 43–146. Cf. Eugène de Mirecourt, *Fabrique de romans. Maison Alexandre Dumas et compagnie* (1845).

[34] E.g., Émile Zola to Antony Valabrègue in *Émile Zola: Corr.*, ed. B. H. Bakker et al. (Montreal, 1978), 1:435. Cf. Henri Mitterand, *Zola journaliste* (1962).

[35] Cf. F.W.J. Hemmings, *Culture and Society in France 1848–1898: Dissidents and Philistines* (London, 1971), 234–42; César Graña, *Modernity and Its Discontents: French Society and the French Man of Letters in the Nineteenth Century* (New York, 1967), 157–212; and John K. Simon, ed., *Modern French Criticism: From Proust and Valéry to Structuralism* (Chicago, 1972), 41–60.

[36] See Lough, *Writer and Public in France*, 318–24, 374.

the publisher. Some of George Sand's correspondence concerns such contracts.[37] During the Second Empire, authors more frequently sold the rights to their work for a specified period of time; the publisher in turn sold as many copies in as many different formats as the market would bear. Accordingly, the lump-sum payments for manuscripts became much larger, like the 250,000 or more francs paid for Hugo's *Les Misérables* in 1862.[38] In time this system gave way to the payment of a fixed sum per copy printed, terms modified after 1900 to establish the contractual royalties enjoyed by French authors today. Under the modified terms, instead of a fixed fee per volume printed, compensation became a fixed percentage of the profit for each volume sold. Because some writers preferred the payment of a large amount in anticipation of sales, the more successful authors negotiated advances on their royalties, but these expedients constituted only a brief deferment from their growing dependence on the market for an income from their writing.[39] In spite of themselves, authors became the business partners of publishers.[40]

PRODUCTION/DISTRIBUTION

A paucity of reliable sources has frustrated an adequate assessment of French publishing's productive capacity since 1800. Besides compilations by Joseph Marie Quérard and Otto Henri Lorenz, the most frequently used source is the *Bibliographie de la France*. This catalog provides a very crude indication of the actual number of titles published each year.[41] The administrative definition of what constituted a book changed; the ministerial surveillance of the publishing industry varied from regime to regime; and publishers were unwilling to announce every title, particularly those printed in minuscule editions. These considerations limited the completeness of the *Bibliographie*. Cross-references with printers' declarations to the Interior Ministry and with the registrations for new copyrights indicate that about one-third of new works were never

[37] E.g., George Sand, *Corr.*, ed. Georges Lubin (1964–82), 2:219–21, 4:495–97.

[38] See Victor Hugo to Albert Lacroix, 12 Oct. 1862, in Hugo, *Oeuvres complètes*, ed. Paul Meurice et al. (1904–52), 4:391–93; and *Victor Hugo publie 'Les Misérables' (Corr. avec Albert Lacroix, août 1861–juillet 1862)*, ed. B. Leuilliot (1970), 31–32.

[39] Cf. Priscilla Parkhurst Clark, "Stratégies d'auteur au 19e siècle," *Romantisme* 18 (1977): 92–102.

[40] See Maurice Dreyfous, *Ce qu'il me reste à dire* (1913), 282–304.

[41] Cf. Joseph Marie Quérard et al., *La France littéraire, ou Dictionnaire bibliographique des savants, historiens et gens de lettres de la France*, 10 vols. (1827–39); and idem, *La Littérature française contemporaine, 1827–1849*, 6 vols. (1840–57); Lorenz et al., *Catalogue général*, 28 vols.; and A.J.Q. Beuchet et al., eds., *Bibliographie de la France, ou Journal de l'imprimerie et la librairie* (1811–); David Bellos, "The *Bibliographie de la France* and Its Sources," *The Library: Transactions of the Bibliographical Society* 28 (1973), 64–67; idem, "Le Marché du livre à l'époque romantique: Recherches et problèmes," *Revue française d'histoire du livre* 47(1978): 648–51.

even entered before 1881.[42] On the other hand, there are factors that inflate the data from this source. Before the development of cheaper titles during the July Monarchy, for example, multivolume works intended for lending libraries were often listed volume by volume. Publishers also frequently inserted books that had already appeared under different titles or in different editions.[43] This practice was an attractive alternative to remaindering the unsold portion of each edition. Similar comprehensive sources after 1881 do not exist for systematic comparison.

All things considered, the *Bibliographie de la France* probably underestimates the actual number of titles available in France, while it certainly exaggerates the short-term fluctuations of the industry.[44] Pornographic and subversive, hence illicit, titles were not listed, nor were the numerous pirated editions of successful literary works. Foreign publishers such as the Belgians contributed to this large underground market before the bilateral agreements leading to the Berne Convention of 1886 that finally protected the international copyrights of French authors.[45] Moreover, the rapid variation in the figures from year to year is not necessarily significant (see Table 1.1). Like the sudden rise from 8,253 titles in 1855 to 12,027 in 1856, the jump from 8,864 titles in 1924 to 15,054 in 1925 is hard to explain. Administration of the catalog probably changed in these years. Much less puzzling are the precipitous declines. Abrupt reversals occurred during the defeat of Napoleon in 1814–15, the Revolution of 1830, the Franco-Prussian War of 1870–71, and World War I from 1914 to 1918. These dramatic changes reflect the predictable responses of a trade to political as well as economic conditions. Long-term economic trends, from 1860 to 1940 in particular, are more difficult to discern from tabular data, but they tend to follow the irregular pattern of France's industrial growth in the same period.

A clearer picture emerges if one imagines a graph of the data from 1800 to 1940. Here may be seen the stepwise development of book production in France. Rapid growth during the Restoration (1815–30) suggests the remarkable recovery of a basically preindustrial economy after the ravages of the Napoleonic Wars. This phase coincided with certain new commercial practices and the early vogue of the romantic movement. But production soon leveled off. Thanks to a serious economic dislocation after the 1830 Revolu-

---

[42] This discrepancy between the *Bibliographie* and AN F18, II*1–183 appeared during research for James Smith Allen, *Popular French Romanticism: Authors, Readers, and Books in the Nineteenth Century* (Syracuse, 1981), 133–35, 189–91.

[43] E.g., Jules Michelet, *L'Amour*, 1st ed. (1858) and 2d ed. (1859); idem, *La Femme*, 1st ed. (1859) and 3d ed. (1860).

[44] Cf. HEF 4:78–82.

[45] See Hermann Dopp, *La Contrefaçon des livres français en Belgique, 1812–1851* (Louvain, 1932), 106–14; Lyons, *Le Triomphe du livre*, 66–75; Frédéric Barbier, "Le Commerce international de la librairie française au XIXe siècle (1815–1913)," *Revue d'histoire moderne et contemporaine* 27 (1981): 96–117; and HEF 3:267–81, 4:91–103.

TABLE 1.1
Titles Announced in the *Bibliographie de la France*,
1812–1940

Year	Books (N)	5-yr. mean	Year	Books (N)	5-yr. mean	Year	Books (N)	5-yr. mean
1812	5,442		1813	3,749		1814	2,547	
1815	3,357	3,774	1816	3,763		1817	4,287	
1818	4,827		1819	4,568		1820	4,881	4,465
1821	5,499		1822	5,824		1823	5,893	
1824	6,974		1825	7,805	6,399	1826	8,273	
1827	8,198		1828	7,616		1829	7,823	
1830	6,739	7,730	1831	6,180		1832	6,478	
1833	7,011		1834	7,125		1835	6,700	6,699
1836	6,632		1837	6,543		1838	6,603	
1839	6,186		1840	6,369	6,467	1841	6,300	
1842	6,445		1843	6,176		1844	6,577	
1845	6,521	6,404	1846	5,916		1847	5,530	
1848	7,234		1849	7,378		1850	7,608	6,733
1851	7,350		1852	7,787		1853	8,060	
1854	8,011		1855	8,253	7,892	1856	12,027	
1857	12,019		1858	13,331		1859	11,905	
1860	11,882	12,233	1861	12,236		1862	11,753	
1863	12,108		1864	12,065		1865	11,723	11,977
1866	13,883		1867	11,355		1868	11,267	
1869	12,269		1870	8,831	11,521	1871	7,245	
1872	10,559		1873	11,530		1874	11,917	
1875	14,195	11,089	1876	13,642		1877	12,764	
1878	12,823		1879	14,122		1880	12,414	13,153
1881	12,766		1882	13,184		1883	13,701	
1884	13,938		1885	12,342	13,186	1886	12,831	
1887	12,901		1888	12,973		1889	14,849	
1890	13,643	13,439	1891	14,192		1892	13,123	
1893	13,595		1894	13,550		1895	12,927	13,447
1896	12,738		1897	13,799		1898	14,781	
1899	14,595		1900	13,362	13,855	1901	13,053	
1902	12,199		1903	12,264		1904	12,139	
1905	12,416	12,414	1906	10,986		1907	10,785	
1908	11,073		1909	13,185		1910	12,615	11,729
1911	11,652		1912	11,560		1913	14,460	
1914	8,698		1915	4,274	10,129	1916	5,062	
1917	5,054		1918	4,484		1919	5,361	
1920	6,315	5,255	1921	7,726		1922	8,515	
1923	8,748		1924	8,864		1925	15,054	9,781
1926	11,095		1927	11,922		1928	11,548	
1929	10,941		1930	9,176	10,936	1931	9,822	
1932	10,603		1933	8,204		1934	8,389	
1935	7,964	8,996	1936	9,319		1937	8,080	
1938	8,124		1939	7,505		1940	5,549	7,715

Source: *Bibliographie de la France, ou Journal de l'imprimerie et de la librairie*, 2d ser. (1911), 100:230–31 (and subsequent volumes).

tion and the rise of cheaper newspapers after 1836, the July Monarchy (1830–48) marked a period of decline in the book trade. This setback coincided with a pause in the French economic cycles analyzed by François Simiand, even though the long-term development of the century was not undermined by it.[46] A new phase of growth came before the 1848 Revolution, but continued into the early years of the Second Empire (1852–70) to reach levels comparable to those in the twentieth century. Accordingly, it is during this second leap in nineteenth-century productivity that the transition was made in French publishing from a traditional trade to a modern industry.

After a brief decline and recovery around 1870, another, more prolonged pause seems to have set in for the rest of the century, with a serious decline in book production beginning in 1895. Ironically, contemporary with the creative vigor of the Belle Époque's avant-garde, a crisis struck the publishing industry, now characterized by a surfeit of expensive titles for the market.[47] This structural problem was compounded still further by World War I. Recovery from that decline in a period of inflation and depression was not entirely sustained before France's defeat in 1940. Consequently, by the outbreak of World War II, the publishing industry in France was producing no more titles annually than it had during the Second Empire nearly 90 years earlier. It would seem, therefore, that by the 1860s, the production of print had reached a ceiling, despite the continued growth in literacy, cities, and population. There was indeed rapid growth from 1800 to 1870, but productivity was severely limited during the Third Republic (1870–1940). Due to either demand or supply factors—perhaps both—a weak economic infrastructure underlay the modern reading experience in France.[48]

Little more on how much people read can be safely inferred from these crude global figures. Other, more refined sources are necessary for additional information about the development of French publishing. For example, a valuable but less well exploited series of data is found in the printers' declarations to the Ministry of the Interior during the period of administrative control over French printing.[49] From 1814 to 1881 printers in Paris were required to report each publication they printed. These legal declarations were then entered into large registers that listed for each day the appropriate printers' names, the titles

[46] Cf. François Simiand, *Le Salaire, l'évolution sociale et la monnaie. Essai de théorie expérimentale du salaire. Introduction et étude globale* (1932); Tihomir Markovitch, *Industrie française de 1789 à 1964* (1964), 4:71–72; and HEF 3:105–8.

[47] See Henri Baillière, *La Crise du livre* (1904), 9–63; and Paul Giselle, "La Crise du livre en France," *Revue des revues* (1903): 145–66, 341–55.

[48] On the Third Republic's "blocked society," see Stanley Hoffmann et al., *In Search of France: The Economy, Society, and Political System in the Twentieth Century* (New York, 1965), 1–117; Michel Crozier, *The Stalled Society* (New York, 1973), 76–107; and Charles Maier, *Recasting Bourgeois Society: Stabilization in France, Germany, and Italy in the Decade after World War I* (Princeton, 1975), 3–15, 579–94.

[49] AN F18,II*1–183.

of their publications, the formats, the number of volumes, and the number of copies reported. It was in one of these volumes that the Interior Ministry's clerks made their remarkable entries in 1863.

Like the *Bibliographie de la France*, this source poses some serious problems. Although it provides accurate data on formats, volumes, and edition sizes for all printers in Paris over a substantial period, it is not complete. The registers for 1835, 1836, and 1837 are missing. Moreover, the declarations of provincial printers appear in departmental registers for the Restoration and July Monarchies only; national and regional comparisons are extremely difficult and time-consuming.[50] Comparable sources after 1881 do not exist. Only a handful of large publishing houses have kept their printing records for more than a few years, so the series cannot be reconstructed or carried forward to 1940, much less to the present. And finally, printers usually declared only their immediate intentions, not the eventual print run of each book listed. Common practice among publishers was to order a succession of small printings, especially if they thought a title likely to arouse the suspicion of authorities. The more controversial the work, the more circumspect were the printers in their declarations. The total number of copies printed of any work must therefore be compiled by adding up various printings declared over a several-month period.

Despite these limitations, the Interior Ministry's archives provide insight into the development of publishing in nineteenth-century Paris (see Table A.1).[51] The average annual declaration of Parisian printers listing publications of two or more printed sheets in all formats increased nearly fourfold from 1815 to 1881. The statistical means of randomly sampled declarations (5 percent or more in each year) rose significantly from 882 to 3,153. To be sure, not all this growth was regular; its course closely followed the data from the *Bibliographie de la France* in the same period. The Restoration appears to have experienced a more limited growth in print production that leveled off during the July Monarchy. Then a renewed growth occurred on the eve of the 1848 Revolution and continued into the first years of the Second Empire. The 1860s saw a slow decline accentuated by the dislocations of the Franco-Prussian War. But levels roughly comparable to those during the early Second Empire occurred in the last decade of the series. With the single exception of the sudden spurt in 1878, the movement of averages in edition sizes closely resembles the movement in the averages of new titles.

These data also reveal trends in the number of volumes per title and the shifts in their format over the same period. Multivolume titles appeared most often during the Restoration and the July Monarchy. In 1829, no fewer than

---

[50] Only minor discrepancies exist between AN F18,II*1–183, AN F18,43–119, and AN F18,157–67, while serious lacunae occur in AN F18,120–56. See Bellos, ''Le Marché du livre,'' and Lyons, *Le Triomphe du livre*, 77–82.

[51] Cf. Table 7 in HEF 3:116.

45 of the 402 sampled entries listed two or more volumes; one sampled declaration in 1829 actually called for 200 volumes.[52] By 1841, the percentage of records listing more than one volume dropped off precipitously. The practice of publishing books solely for lending libraries or a wealthy clientele must have faded very rapidly in Parisian publishing, more than likely with the competition of far less expensive newspapers. The formats of the books declared show a sharp decline in the octavo and duodecimo editions, the book sizes aimed at a socioeconomic elite. In-8 titles dropped from roughly 70 percent of the trade in 1815 to less than 45 percent in 1880 (see Table A.2). But this decline in expensive formats was not matched by a significant increase in any of the cheaper published formats. The much vaunted eighteenmo, the basis of the Charpentier revolution of 1838, retained a relatively constant share of the production, though its share did rise slightly in the early 1860s to nearly a quarter of the market. Rather, Parisian book production seems to have diversified. As suggested by their mean edition sizes, the in-4 and in-16 formats aimed at different paying publics and gained as much or more than the in-18 titles. These cheap and expensive editions represented roughly equal proportions of book production in 1881.

These figures must indicate a marked shift towards a more diverse market for books. In spite of troublesome administrative surveillance of printing, publishers were willing to take bigger risks in the number of copies and different formats they ordered from printers, presumably to reach both old and new audiences. The statistical trends are supported by less comprehensive figures available in studies of publishing firms and their most important authors. For example, Hachette's publication of the comtesse de Ségur's stories for children, a new and well-defined market, accumulated over time in increments that approximated the number of copies and range of formats described by the printer declaration data. Even though by 1960 the cumulative sales of her four best-known works exceeded 1.5 million copies each, the books were rarely printed by stereotype in lots of more than 10,000. The 1,714,711 copies sold of *Les Malheurs de Sophie*, an unparalleled success in French publishing history, in fact averaged less than 12,000 per printing.[53] Similarly, reprintings of Zola's *Germinal* averaged 10,000 each between 1885 and 1972, although a large portion of its 1.13 million copies actually appeared in *livre de poche* editions after 1956.[54] Despite the crisis in literary publication after 1890, the declaration figures during the first decade of the Third Republic seem to have anticipated later production levels.

The actual number of copies of popular literature printed must have increased, however, by the first decade of the next century. A new practice con-

---

[52] AN F18,II*17.

[53] See HEF 3:440.

[54] See Carpenter, ed., *Books and Society in History*, 229 n. 37; and Colette Becker, "L'Audience d'Émile Zola," *Cahiers naturalistes* 47 (1974): 40–69.

cerning edition sizes arose when Arthème Fayard launched the *Bibliothèque moderne* series in 1904.[55] His illustrated editions of texts by Maurice Barrès, Marcel Prévost, and others cost only 95 centimes, a slim margin of profit offset by printings in the tens of thousands. Within ten years Fayard began at least three more collections of even less expensive titles: *Le Livre populaire*, *Les Meilleurs Livres*, and *Les Maîtres du roman populaire*. Fayard's books were soon joined by the series published by Gallimard and Flammarion after World War I.[56] These progenitors of the cheap paperback hoped that editions printed in the hundreds of thousands would counter the serious competition posed by the cheap popular press and its serial novels. For example, Flammarion published a first edition of 600,000 copies for Victor Marguerite's *La Garçonne* (1922); but in postwar economic conditions this did not mark an enduring trend, as newspapers continued their widespread circulation at the expense of the book trade. Similar-sized editions appeared regularly only with the new market during the "economic miracle" after World War II. Consequently, the so-called "Fayard Revolution"—higher production in order to lower per-unit costs—was in effect the logical outcome of the step first taken by Charpentier sixty-six years earlier within a different context of industrial production.[57]

Perhaps a more valuable indicator of print production during the Third Republic is the daily newspaper. The revolution in book publishing coincided with another in the press; Girardin and Dutacq were contemporaries of Charpentier, just as Millaud was of Lévy. The actual number of periodicals in Paris increased more than sixty times from 1820 to 1936, while the numbers of booksellers and printers rose much more slowly, and even declined after 1900.[58] It should come as no surprise, then, that by 1880 the cumulative circulation of 67 daily newspapers in Paris had reached 2,094,170; *Le Petit Journal* alone accounted for 583,820, more than half of the total circulation of Parisian dailies in 1870 and four times higher than its nearest rival, *La Petite République française*, in 1880. Nevertheless, when book-production levels began dropping in the last decades before World War I, newspaper circulation continued to grow despite the increased competition among the growing number of dailies in Paris and the departments. In 1910, the editions of 80 Parisian newspapers had expanded to 5,336,941, more than double what they had been

[55] Anon., *Histoire de la librairie Arthème Fayard* (1953).

[56] See Assouline, *Gaston Gallimard*; and HEF 4:173–75.

[57] Lyons, *Le Triomphe du livre*, 74.

[58] See Bellanger et al., *Histoire générale de la presse française*, vols. 2–3; Palmer, *Des petits journaux aux grandes agences*; Zeldin, *France 1848–1945*, 2:492–573; Eugène-Louis Hatin, *Histoire politique et littéraire de la presse en France* (1859–61), vol. 8; René Livois, *Histoire de la presse française* (Lausanne, 1965), vol. 3; Francine Amaury, *Histoire du plus grand quotidien de la IIIe République: 'Le Petit Parisien,' 1876–1944* (1972); and Pierre Albert et al., *Documents pour l'histoire de la presse nationale aux XIXe et XXe siècles* (1977). See lists of Parisian printers, booksellers, and periodicals in *Almanach du commerce de Paris* (1819–38); *Annuaire-almanach du commerce* (1857–1903); and *Annuaire de l'imprimerie* (1895–1935).

only 30 years earlier. *Le Petit Journal* had now been eclipsed by *Le Petit Parisien* with a daily readership of 1,375,000. Moreover, a larger portion of the Parisian market was dominated by the four most important papers. Whereas in 1880 they had constituted 49 percent of the circulation, in 1910 they made up nearly 72 percent.

The press was also increasingly dominated by less polemical newspapers, as the circulation of more strident political dailies like *Le Figaro* and *La Lanterne* rapidly declined. In fact, of 40 newspapers continuously in print from 1880 to 1910, only 12 experienced an increase in readership; the remaining 28 suffered losses that made many of them little more than privately printed sheets. At the same time, the number of specialty publications, like the new literary journals that appeared at the turn of the century, increased dramatically. It would seem that during the structural shift in production and distribution, the press was following the same path taken by book publishing toward a greater, more diverse market, only on a much larger, more sustained scale. This trend was especially evident after World War I, when the circulation of the four largest dailies and their share of the market again started to diminish (see Table A.3). As provincial press circulation came to equal that of the Parisian press by 1935, local papers and other regional periodicals played a prominent role in the consumption patterns of French readers.[59]

New products eventually brought new commercial practices. With more print to sell, publishers sought to reach more consumers with uneven success. Older operations had attempted to stimulate demand by subscription schemes, selective rebates, and precipitous remaindering, tried-and-true methods of a conservative trade.[60] Specialization in publishing, however, meant a better targeting of products for different audiences whose interests could now be developed by more effective advertising. Beginning in 1811, for example, book catalogs and prospectuses were supplemented by an annual trade catalog, the *Bibliographie de la France*. Notices of new titles attracted still more attention in the *Bibliographie*'s advertising supplement, which after 1823 permitted different typefaces and illustrations. More flamboyant publishers resorted to the loud-colored street posters first used by Ladvocat during the Restoration.[61] Coinciding with the rapid growth of the press, publishers also advertised discreetly in the daily newspapers, generally by paying for the insertion of flattering copy written by the publisher or by the author. The provision of complimentary review copies to friendly critics, and money to less

[59] Cf. Jean-Pierre Aguet, "Le Tirage des quotidiens de Paris sous la Monarchie de Juillet," *Revue suisse d'histoire* 10 (1960): 216–86; Gilles Feyel, "La Diffusion nationale des quotidiens parisiens en 1832," *Revue d'histoire moderne et contemporaine* 34 (1987): 31–65; and HEF 4:23–27.

[60] See Victor Fouque, *De quelques abus en librairie et des moyens de les combattre* (Chalon-sur-Saône, 1841); and Baillière, *La Crise du livre*, 22–31.

[61] On Dauriat in *Illusions perdues*, see Balzac, *La Comédie humaine*, ed. Pierre-Georges Castex (1976–79), 5:449.

predictable ones, became a still subtler way to advertise new books. The same is true of distinctive covers and bookstore displays. By 1900, publishers had become more adept at maximizing the success of their titles by a clever combination of these commercial ploys.

Besides publicizing new titles, publishers of both books and newspapers were also concerned with developing new channels of distribution. While some producers sought to expand the market by lowering costs, others innovated in other ways. For instance, the number of bookstore outlets in and out of Paris easily outpaced France's population growth from 1841 to 1901, before the demographic fluctuations of the subsequent forty years.[62] In the tradition first established by Edmond Werdet during the Restoration, traveling salesmen sold titles wholesale in the provinces; in time, these *commis-voyageurs* came to resemble their counterparts in Balzac's *La Comédie humaine*.[63] Well into the Second Empire, colporters continued to follow routes in the countryside more than 200 years old, although their numbers dwindled rapidly during the Third Republic. New sources of distribution such as train stations, kiosks, and cafés were running the colporters and hawkers out of business.[64] Some publishers even provided books for distribution by the manufacturers of cheap consumer products. News agencies, like the enormous operations of Havas, took control of information and thus one major sector in the dissemination of print.[65] These innovations in marketing eventually overcame the difficulty readers had in buying what they wanted to read. By the twentieth century, the distribution of print had so improved that André Gide's journal never mentions trouble in acquiring new titles, unlike Balzac's correspondence 100 years earlier.[66] In this context, however uncertain the process may have been, the exclusive market for expensive in-8 editions and yearly newspaper subscriptions had finally made way for the cheaper, more widely available in-18 book and the one-sou daily press.

A major outlet for books and newspapers not actually developed by publishers was the library.[67] Public collections remained bastions of a social and in-

[62] Claude Savart, "La 'Liberté' de la librairie (10 septembre [1870]) et l'évolution du réseau des libraires," *Revue française d'histoire du livre* 48 (1979): 102–3. Cf. HEF 3:237.

[63] Cf. the *commis-voyageurs* in Werdet, *De la librairie française*, 92; and in Balzac's *Illustre Gaudissart* (1833).

[64] Jean-Jacques Darmon, *Le Colportage de librairie en France sous le Second Empire. Grands Colporteurs et culture populaire* (1972), 159–62.

[65] Cf. Pierre Frédérix, *Un Siècle de chasse aux nouvelles. De l'Agence Havas à l'Agence France-Presse, 1835–1957* (1959); and Palmer, *Des petits journaux aux grandes agences*, 103–38.

[66] Cf. *Balzac: Corr.*, 1:537, 553, and 557; and Gide, *Journal* (1948–54), 1:47.

[67] See Cain et al., *Le Livre français*, 191–204; Jean Hassenforder, *Développement comparé des bibliothèques publiques en France, en Grande Bretagne et aux États-Unis dans la seconde moitié du XIXe siècle (1850–1914)* (1967), 33–37, 50–56, 69–73; Noë Richter, *Histoire de la lecture publique en France* (1977); Graham Keith Barnett, *Histoire des bibliothèques publiques en France de la Révolution à 1789* (1987); and HEF 3:261–67, 4:543–52.

tellectual elite well into the Third Republic, but private lending libraries were accessible to a much wider range of readers.[68] During the Restoration and July Monarchies, ten centimes—a sum well within the means of domestics, shop-keepers, and artisans—purchased the right to borrow a book or newspaper in some sections of Paris. Dozens of modest *cabinets* existed in the capital, par-ticularly along the major north-south thoroughfares on both sides of the Seine River. One historian has estimated that there were more than 460 of them in Paris before 1830, even though business directories in any one year list less than one-third that number.[69] Before the Charpentier edition, most publishers produced large, multivolume novels specifically for the lending libraries that rented them at so much per volume, the more volumes the better. Rarely ex-ceeding a few thousand titles and a handful of subscriptions, the Parisian lend-ing library was hardly an imposing social institution. Contemporaries satirized its intellectually naive clientele who often requested books by the color of their bindings, or who mistook newspapers for serial novels.[70] By the end of the century, however, lending libraries had largely disappeared from the cities of France, the victims of less expensive books and newspapers.

By then public libraries had become a more important source of reading material. To expand the few public libraries of the Old Regime, the Directory (1795–99) had ordered that collections confiscated from monasteries and *émi-gré* nobles be deposited in the new central schools mandated for each depart-ment. These were later moved to the town halls. According to reports written during the Empire and the Restoration, more than half of the works consisted of classical and theological texts of limited interest to a large readership, es-pecially in poorly lit, drafty reading rooms open for only a few hours a week.[71] Then the July Monarchy forced public libraries to allocate the money neces-sary to acquire new titles appropriate to a wider readership. In 1867, the li-brary in the 11th arrondissement of Paris began lending books for home use, the first public collection to do so, even though on the first day it had stationed two gendarmes by the front door to maintain order (this was common practice at most early experiments of this sort).[72] By the first decade of the Third Re-public, lending practices had spread to many other libraries elsewhere in France. Later, the Ministry of Public Instruction directed recently created el-

---

[68] See Donald G. Davis, Jr., ed., *Libraries and Culture* (Austin, 1981), 199–209; and Fran-çoise Parent-Lardeur, *Lire à temps de Balzac. Les Cabinets de lecture à Paris, 1815–1830* (1981), 17–43, 87–104, 107–29.

[69] Cf. Parent-Lardeur, *Lire à temps de Balzac*, 25; and *Almanach du commerce de Paris*, ed. J. De La Tynna and Sébastien Bottin (1815–30).

[70] Cf. Robert [L.-P.Solvet], *Cabinet de lecture*, pièce satirique (1808), 25–27, and Harry Whit-more, "Readers, Writers, and Literary Taste in the Early 1830s: The *Cabinet de Lecture* as Focal Point," *Journal of Library History* 13 (1978): 119–30.

[71] One-fourth of all public collections, 1812–34, were in theology alone. E.g., BN NAFr 21045 fol. 143 (Tours), fol. 213 (Grenoble), fol. 332 (Dole); and NAFr 21047 fol. 70 (Orléans).

[72] E.g., the Bibliothèque Forney in 1886, discussed in Richter, *Histoire de la lecture publique en France*, 11.

ementary schools to establish collections for students and their families where a public library did not already exist. This measure established at last an institutional network intended to meet the needs and interests of a growing literate population everywhere in France. In 1890, 38,240 collections totalling 5,111,204 volumes lent nearly 6.1 million books, nearly 55 times more than they had 25 years earlier. This level of activity resembled that of libraries in the Fourth Republic (see Table A.4).

From 1890 to 1946, French libraries experienced a general decline in their collections and service comparable to the troubles experienced by the book trade in the same period. Even though uniform national figures after 1890 are unavailable, the evidence from selected urban centers, like Coulommiers east of Paris, indicates how poorly public collections managed (see Table A.4). Typical of trends elsewhere in France, the number of volumes in Coulommiers grew very slowly after 1890; it increased less than threefold in 45 years (after a long period in which all school libraries had experienced dramatic growth).[73] Moreover, the number of volumes lent peaked during the decade of World War I, perhaps due to a search for diversion from news of international conflict; but it then declined as the depression and alternative forms of leisure detracted from literate activity. Despite reform efforts studied and proposed by private organizations such as the Association des bibliothécaires français, libraries in France failed to keep pace with the overall growth in the literate population. The complex reasons for this stagnation in public collections include the relatively slow rate of industrialization and urbanization; weak private associational life promoting public services; limited holdings appropriate to borrowers' needs and interests; and restrictive library practices limiting borrowing privileges and hours. Not until the decree of 18 August 1945 establishing a national Direction des bibliothèques did public libraries begin to grow once again along with the production of print.[74]

CONSUMPTION

What did people read in modern France? Discussions of national production and distribution practices do not adequately characterize what was actually produced and distributed. Here economic history must give way to intellectual history, for the troubled development of modern publishing coincided with a large-scale transformation in literate culture. On one level of achievement,

[73] Cf. Lyons, *Le Triomphe du livre*, 169–92; AN F17,17314/1–2 d. Anthony, open only Wednesdays from 10 A.M. to noon and Sundays from 9:00 A.M. to 10:30 A.M., with fewer than 3,700 volumes in the collection, lent to merely 300 different borrowers in 1921, the same as in 1909; and AN F17,17402 d. Saint Mandé, Seine, where in 1939, 15,299 borrowers checked out 43,628 titles.

[74] Cf. Hassenforder, *Développement comparé des bibliothèques publiques*, 193–200; and Barnett, *Histoire des bibliothèques publiques en France*, 405–13.

this change in ideas appears in the transition from the Enlightenment in the eighteenth century to the various moral and political engagements of intellectuals in the twentieth.[75] The history of modern French thought in nearly every realm is itself worthy of the volumes written on the subject; by now the contributions of such figures as Voltaire, Rousseau, Chateaubriand, Hugo, Taine, Bergson, Proust, and Sartre are well known and reasonably well enough understood not to merit further discussion here. Consequently, one portion of reading in the past is already well treated in the standard literary and intellectual history texts on the authors, works, and ideas of the nineteenth and twentieth centuries. A glance at the printed catalog of the Bibliothèque nationale indicates how well circulated the leading minds of the past actually were; the titles of Voltaire's works published since his lifetime command two entire volumes and constitute approximately one percent of all books in France's most complete library catalog.[76]

On the other hand, this period was witness to another transformation hardly so well studied or understood. Modern France saw as well a revolution in the material read by the vast majority of ordinary French men and women, people for whom the leading figures of intellectual life were merely names. For centuries, the largest portion of the book market maintained a tradition of its own in addition to that of the great works still read and studied today. What was published in the greatest numbers was a popular literature that did not endure: the chapbooks and broadsides of the eighteenth century, the serial novels of the nineteenth, and the formulaic romances and adventure stories of the twentieth. Like the growing array of print in political posters, shop windows, and advertising flyers, this ephemeral literature occupied the hearts and minds of most people in France; popular readers experienced a change in what they read every bit as significant as that experienced by better-educated audiences in the same period.[77] There were, in fact, as many different markets as there were publics. But the nature and extent of the historical changes in modern reading can at least be suggested in four major areas affecting nearly all French audiences, high and low, namely, religion, education, literature, and news.

[75] See Albert Thibaudet, *Histoire de la littérature de la Révolution à nos jours* (1936); Michel Raimond, *Le Roman depuis la Révolution* (1972); Pierre Barrière, *La Vie intellectuelle du XVIe siècle à l'époque contemporaine* (1974), 433–550; and Maurice Crubellier, *Histoire culturelle de la France. XIXe–XXe siècle* (1974), 52–306.

[76] BN, *Catalogue général des livres imprimés de la Bibliothèque nationale: Auteurs* (1897–), vol. 214, I–II.

[77] Allen, *Popular French Romanticism*, 21–73; Lyons, *Le Triomphe du livre*, 77–144; Crubellier, *Histoire culturelle de la France*, 9–23; Marc Angenot, *Le Roman populaire. Recherches en paralittérature* (Quebec, 1975); Jacques Beauroy et al., eds., *The Wolf and the Lamb: Popular Culture in France from the Old Regime to the Twentieth Century* (Saratoga, 1977), 9–52; Steven L. Kaplan, ed., *Understanding Popular Culture: Europe from the Middle Ages to the Nineteenth Century* (The Hague, 1984), 229–74; and Anne-Marie Thiesse, *Le Roman du quotidien. Lecteurs et lectures populaires à la Belle Époque* (1984), 79–168.

Early in the nineteenth century, the largest body of printed material, by far, consisted of religious works.[78] Prayer books, missals, Bibles, and hymnals dominated the output of most provincial printers and some Parisian ones as well. Few obstacles existed to the publication of these titles, for which a predictable market was more or less guaranteed from the earliest days of printing onward. But an even more important market included the production of religious chapbooks, moralizing tales, saints' lives, and devotionals, together with almanacs and other secular titles in the traditional *bibliothèque bleue*. The latter works were sold by itinerant colporters throughout the countryside until well into the Third Republic. Often in the same published format characteristic of nonreligious offerings, popular religious titles were published in the thousands annually by printers who specialized in the trade: Martial Ardant in Limoges, Mame in Tours, Popelin in Dijon, Vanackère in Lille, Berger-Levrault in Nancy and Strasbourg. Their content, often derived from elite texts first produced in the seventeenth century, changed little over time; the same accounts of Saint Louis, for example, appeared for more than a century.[79] In the course of the 1800s, however, these works were modified to reflect the changing conditions of the rural market with the growth of the elementary-school system and the expansion of literacy among children. According to a bibliography of Canon Johann Schmid, no fewer than 2,666 pious titles for popular consumption had been published by 1890.[80]

In time, a perceptible modernization occurred in this market. More publishers became interested in religious titles and arranged their catalog offerings into series. Ardant established the *Bibliothèque religieuse, morale, littéraire*, while Mégard called his the *Bibliothèque morale de la jeunesse*. A more substantial contribution was the publication of best-sellers in the new formats adopted by the industry. Renduel marked the origin of this trend with Félicité de Lamennais's *Les Paroles d'un croyant*; in 1834, this publisher had 30,000 copies printed in six separate editions, two in octavo and four in eighteenmo. Daubrée and Cailleux issued three more editions of their own in 1835, as did many others less scrupulous about the author's property rights; pirated editions soon accounted for another 70,000 copies.[81] However modest, *Les Paroles* constituted the widest-selling new book of the July Monarchy. A still larger event was Ernest Renan's *La Vie de Jésus*, published by Michel Lévy in 1863. This was probably the single greatest publishing success of the nineteenth century.[82] More than ten different European editions totalling 1.4 million copies

---

[78] See Claude Savart, ''Le Livre catholique, témoin de la conscience religieuse (en France au XIXe siècle),'' doctoral thesis, University of Paris IV (1981); and HEF 3:403–7, 4:271–79.

[79] Cf. Roger Chartier, *Lectures et lecteurs dans la France d'Ancien Régime (1987)*, 247–351; and Robert Mandrou, *De la culture populaire aux 17e et 18e siècles* (1975), 9–33, 182–95.

[80] See BN, *Catalogue général des livres imprimés*, 166:39–270.

[81] See Neret, *Histoire illustrée*, 151.

[82] See Mollier, *Michel & Calmann Lévy*, 319–25.

were sold in the first year alone; successive editions in various formats were issued on a regular basis until 1898. Perhaps because of the Third Republic's anticlericalism, despite the growing secularization of modern French life generally, religious works (broadly defined) retained their importance to French readers into the twentieth century.

Another significant portion of printed material available in modern France was given to children's books.[83] Colporter literature, in either the pious or the secular *bibliothèque bleue* tradition, had targeted readers of all ages, even though in time it formed the core of a folk literature largely reserved for youngsters. Children still memorize the timeless accounts of *la mère Oye* and learn to retell the stories of the brothers Aymon. But this market was soon joined by schoolbooks, one of the largest sources of reading in France after the establishment of new educational institutions. Hachette was not alone in making his fortune in this field. Armand Colin, for example, began his career in 1870 with Larive and Fleury's *Grammaire* in several different editions for the various levels of elementary-school study. Similarly, after the enactment of the Ferry Laws, Pierre Larousse expanded substantially his ventures in dictionaries and encyclopedias, which were to appear in every school library in France. According to recent estimates, educational works published between 1789 and 1959 numbered between 60,000 and 120,000 titles.[84] To this must be added an incalculable number of prize books awarded annually to schoolchildren who passed their examinations.

Like religious books produced specifically for a juvenile audience, children's stories were published by some of the most familiar names in French culture. In 1782, Arnaud Berquin established a new genre with *L'Ami des enfants*, a title subsequently republished throughout the nineteenth century by Didier, Garnier *frères*, Ardant, and Thibaut. The latter two men actually issued 23 different editions reprinted from 1875 to 1895. Similarly, Pauline Guizot's moralizing tales, "à l'usage de la jeunesse," joined Berquin's works in two series that appeared in Didier's catalog. Zulma Carraud's *Maurice* (1853) and *La Petite Jeanne* (1852), with 32 and 41 impressions respectively between 1852 and 1901, served as readers for at least two generations of schoolchildren in nearly every department in France.[85] These were only the most prominent forerunners of the comtesse de Ségur's stories in Hachette's *Bibliothèque des chemins de fer* published after 1854. Together with Jules

[83] See François Caradec, *Histoire de la littérature enfantine en France* (1977); Maurice Crubellier, *L'Enfance et la jeunesse dans la société française 1800–1950* (1979), 351–74; and HEF 3:417–43, 4:457–67.

[84] See Linda Clark, *Schooling the Daughters of Marianne: Textbooks and the Socialization of Girls in Modern French Primary Schools* (Albany, 1984), 26.

[85] See Laura S. Strumingher, *What Were Little Girls and Boys Made Of? Primary Education in Rural France* (Albany, 1983), 48–62, App. A: 155–72; and Clark, *Schooling the Daughters of Marianne*, 26–59.

Verne's science fiction, published by Hetzel in comparable editions, *Les Petites Filles modèles*, *Les Deux Nigauds*, *L'Auberge de l'ange*, and *Les Mémoires d'un âne* provided much of the reading material for French youth by the turn of the century. After World War I, children's books constituted a well-established market that would be expanded significantly only after 1950 with the development of comic books. How much of the industry was actually given over to juvenile titles, however, cannot be calculated precisely.[86]

One difficulty in assessing the child's share of the market is that statistical studies often conflate it with another feature of modern French literate culture, that is, literature itself. As discussed in more detail above, the trade in new literary works was the central concern of publishers; in time it infringed inexorably on the traditional fare of both religious and children's books.[87] For example, the average annual number of new or reprinted titles in literature rose from 544 in 1840–75 to 2,002 in 1920–25, an increase disproportionately greater than that experienced by all fields in the same period (see Table 1.2). Published in more affordable formats, literary works had far larger printings, on average, than most other publications. The remarkable expansion in their publication was interrupted only during the 1890s when publishers suffered serious commercial difficulties (two-thirds of all titles in literature published

TABLE 1.2
Titles Published, by Genre, 1840–1925

Year	Fiction		Poetry		Drama		All literature	
	Mean no. per year	% of total[a]	Mean no. per year	% of total[a]	Mean no. per year	% of total[a]	Mean no. per year	% of total[a]
1840–75	246	2.6	78	0.8	220	2.3	544	5.7
1876–85	621	4.8	139	1.1	196	1.5	956	7.4
1886–90	774	5.8	236	1.7	264	2.0	1,274	9.5
1891–99	630	4.6	249	1.8	257	1.9	1,136	8.3
1900–1905	775	6.2	241	2.7	278	2.2	1,394	11.1
1906–9	961	8.3	270	2.4	407	3.5	1,638	14.2
1910–12	1,031	8.6	345	2.9	502	4.2	1,878	15.7
1913–15	770	8.4	259	2.9	303	3.3	1,332	14.6
1916–18	360	7.4	139	2.9	104	2.1	603	12.4
1919–21	970	15.0	361	5.5	230	3.6	1,561	24.1
1922–25	1,256	12.2	378	3.7	368	3.6	2,002	19.4

Source: Otto Lorenz et al., *Catalogue général de la librairie française* (1867–1945), vols. 8, 11, 13, 17, 20, 23, 25, 27, 28.

[a] Total annual averages of all titles published.

[86] See HEF 4:461–75.

[87] Ibid., 3:369–400, 455–68, 4:147–240.

in 1891–93 had to be remaindered).[88] But this profound crisis actually made possible the transition to larger editions of less expensive new titles, such as those published by Fayard after 1900. In the interwar period, nearly one-fourth of all new editions were in literature; these led the industry's eventual return to earlier production levels, but little more progress was made.[89]

A major feature of this long-term secular rise and stagnation in literary publishing was, of course, the novel. In 1845, prose fiction constituted less than 4 percent of all new titles; eighty years later, it made up 15 percent of a vastly larger and more heterogenous group of new publications.[90] The reports of public libraries during the Third Republic indicate the overwhelming preference of borrowers for Paul Féval, Émile Chatrain, Hector Malot, and Jules Verne.[91] Only the daily newspaper and ephemeral material, like time tables, advertisements, and street posters, had more readers. The novel's domination of literature, and of the market for new books generally, which Charles Louandre had noted during the Restoration Monarchy, still held one hundred years later.[92] In 1929, the astute publisher Bernard Grasset noted somewhat ruefully the enduring importance of recent fiction to the French publishing industry, just as lycée teacher Philippe Van Tieghem learned from a survey of his students' reading.[93] Despite the growing diversity and mass circulation of other printed material that competed directly with and actually undermined the demand for literature after 1890, publishers of the novel adapted to changing commercial conditions.

Second only to literature in numbers of new publications were the categories of history and the social sciences.[94] Whereas literary works, including school manuals and children's books, occupied between 20 and 30 percent of the market—and more if their larger edition sizes are taken into account—history and social science claimed between 10 and 20 percent each. Titles in these

[88] Baillière, *La Crise du livre*, 33–35; Dreyfous, *Ce qu'il me reste à dire*, 376; and Humblot, "L'Édition littéraire au XIXe siècle," 9. Cf. Charle, *La Crise littéraire*, 27–54; and Neret, *Histoire illustrée*, 266–71.

[89] See tables in HEF 4:84–85.

[90] Cf. Charle, *La Crise littéraire*, 30; and Victor Zoltowski, "Les Cycles de la création littéraire et artistique," *Année sociologique* (1952): 193.

[91] Cf. AN F17,10737 d. 1884 (Lot-et-Garonne); AN F17,10755 d. 1890 (Morbihan); Lyons, *Le Triomphe du livre*, 180–83; and Roger Bellet, "Une Bataille culturelle, provinciale et nationale, à propos des bons auteurs pour les bibliothèques populaires (janvier–juin 1867)," *Revue des sciences humaines* 34 (1969): 453–73.

[92] Charles Louandre, "Statistique littéraire de la production intellectuelle en France depuis quinze ans," *RdDM* 20 (1847): 687–88. Cf. Marguerite Iknayan, *The Idea of the Novel in France: The Critical Reaction, 1815–1848* (Geneva, 1961), 185.

[93] Grasset, *La Chose littéraire*, 81–98; and Philippe Van Tieghem, "Ce que lisent nos élèves," *Revue universitaire* (1934): 408–15.

[94] See Brigitte Levrier, "Sources bibliographiques et statistiques concernant la production intellectuelle en France et l'exportation 1900–1950," Mémoire, Institut National des Techniques de la Documentation, Conservatoire National des Arts-et-Métiers, 1952.

subjects numbered more than a thousand per year after World War I, but rarely in editions of more than 5,000 copies. Fewer than 200 copies of theses in law and medicine ever appeared in print, compared to 166,500 copies of Louis Hémon's best-selling *Maria Chapdelaine* in 1923.[95] The remaining portion of new titles published each year was taken up by very small editions of titles in art, philosophy, science, and theology, each claiming no more than 10 percent of the total. This trend stands in sharp contrast to the more limited range of publications in the Old Regime; then, titles in history, law, and science predominated, despite a sizable underground circuit of illicit books, including philosophic works, political libel, and simple pornography.[96] Underlying the evolution of a larger, more differentiated marketplace was the enduring interest of French readers in works of mythic or imaginative qualities. Hence the influence of religion, children's literature, and above all the novel continues today.

But it is the development of the modern newspaper that exemplifies the nature and extent of the cultural changes in this period.[97] Like the *Gazette de France*, with a circulation of fewer than 5,000 readers, the most important periodicals in the Old Regime were the few officially tolerated or sponsored journals. Their content reflected the interest of the literate elite in its own affairs; their articles rarely covered more than domestic and foreign politics, cultural events, and finance. During the Restoration and early July Monarchy, the four-page papers were still deliberately aimed at a narrow range of wealthy *rentier* subscribers. Largely excluded from their attention were the sensational events depicted in the broadsides, the single printed sheets sold for a sou or less to artisans and shopkeepers in the cities. The primary news for the lower classes concerned natural disasters, horrible crimes, and curious happenings for much of the nineteenth century. The brief flurry of more than 500 politically inspired papers during the 1789 Revolution made no enduring difference in the popular press;[98] the First Empire established the administrative apparatus necessary for effective censorship right up to the Third Republic.

The range and readership of these early newspapers expanded considerably after 1836, thanks to the innovations of Girardin, Dutacq, and Millaud. With the creation of a less expensive and more widely circulating daily newspaper came a new content, more diverse and more entertaining than what had appeared in papers before the July Monarchy. Besides accounts of politics and commerce at home and abroad, the dailies now carried serial novels, like Eu-

[95] Gabriel Boillat, "Comment on fabrique un succès: 'Maria Chapdelaine,' " *Revue d'histoire littéraire de la France* 74 (1974): 223–53.

[96] See table in Darnton, *The Literary Underground of the Old Regime*, 180.

[97] See Zeldin, *France 1848–1945*, 2:540–73.

[98] See Jean-Pierre Séguin, *Canards du siècle passé* (1969); and idem, *Nouvelles à sensation. Canards du XIXe siècle* (1959). Cf. Michelle Perrot, "Fait divers et histoire au XIXe siècle," *Annales: E.S.C.* 38 (1983): 911–19.

gène Sue's *Les Mystères de Paris* in the otherwise staid *Journal des débats*. Some papers deliberately blurred the distinction between journalism and fiction by incorporating the lurid details of *faits divers* that were formerly the preserve of broadsides.[99] Many others soon made full use of illustrations and then photographs to enhance the appeal of their more simply written serious articles. The much larger number of all periodicals, some with circulations reaching the hundreds of thousands, added significantly to the amount of print available to the literate public. By the outbreak of World War II, the modern reader experienced a bewildering variety of more freely available printed matter, from the latest novel in the bookstores to the fading advertising poster on nearby drainpipes, as omnipresent as the racing sheets and crossword puzzles in the hands of commuting workers on the Paris metro.[100]

More recent production patterns indicate just how much more important periodicals are than books in the marketplace.[101] New titles issued by 319 different publishers in 1966 totaled only 247,486,000 volumes, the largest portion of which was given over to general literature—novels, essays, poetry, history, and travel. Education books, reference works, and children's literature, together constituted a smaller share, while religious titles—more than 30 percent of all production in the eighteenth century—ranked a distant third in total volumes published in 1966. But the circulation of eight leading daily newspapers far exceeded the annual publication of books. More than 4.24 million copies a day reached the hands of newspaper readers in 1967; in less than two months, news circulation equalled the total number of volumes that appeared in an entire year. The daily press represents the largest share of reading material available to contemporary French men and women. From the mid-nineteenth century onward, the lower cost, greater availability, and deliberate appeal of the press have met the needs of most readers in France.

The economic context of print must have coincided with the development of different audiences throughout the modern period. Underlying the complex history of publishing in France were certainly the needs and interests of the readers themselves, who sought out what booksellers and the press made available to them. Even though the production levels of French publishing rose rapidly in the nineteenth century to a peak achieved by the 1870s—an achievement not exceeded for the duration of the Third Republic—the manufacturing innovations and commercial instincts of several leading firms were increasingly sensitive to the demand for news and new titles. This need was well met

[99] On the Troppmann affair, Sept. 1869–Jan. 1870, for example, see Palmer, *Des petits journaux aux grandes agences*, 29–32; and Michelle Perrot, "L'Affaire Troppmann," *Histoire* (1981): 28–36.

[100] See the survey of reader interests in 1938 in Amaury, *Histoire du plus grand quotidien de la IIIe République*, 1:290.

[101] Jacques Charpentreau et al., *Le Livre et la lecture en France* (1968), 62–63, 242. Cf. Cain et al., *Le Livre français*, 96; and HEF 4:569.

by a diversity in imaginative literature. During the first four decades of the twentieth century, structural constraints on the market's further growth did not inhibit a more consistent differentiation. With the proliferation of sharply focused materials—often produced by smaller houses and journals—the link between publishers and various reading publics strengthened; different kinds of textual material appeared for a more diverse readership. Historically, the increasing differentiation of the printed word during the seventy-year pause in production growth both fostered and responded to the reading experience of literate French men and women.

Chapter 2

A LITERATE SOCIETY

"EVERYONE IS TALKING about your mysteries," wrote Ernestine Dumont to Eugène Sue, the author of *Les Mystères de Paris*, in November 1843.

> Your work is everywhere—on the worker's bench, on the merchant's counter, on the little lady's divan, on the shop-girl's table, on the officeworker's and magistrate's desk. I am sure that of the entire population in Paris, only those people who cannot read do not know of your work.[1]

Some years later, Théophile Gautier described an even larger audience, one that included the illiterate; in their fascination with Sue's novel, people had the book read to them "by some erudite doorman of goodwill."[2] The remarkable reception for *Les Mystères de Paris* evidently marked the origins of a new popular literary culture during the July Monarchy, whether or not everyone could read. If one believes Dumont and Gautier, prose fiction by 1850 had developed a national audience. The novel had become a pastime for nearly an entire society now touched more or less directly by the printed word.

To what extent was this true? How many people did indeed read in modern France? And who were they? Contemporary observers like Dumont and Gautier were wrong to assume that all social groups responded to literature before the advent of universal literacy at the end of the nineteenth century.[3] From similar sources on middle-class salon life, one learns how women constituted the primary audience for the novel.[4] But in fact, most women in France were not even literate until the Second Empire. Other evidence, such as the fan mail sent to authors about their work, indicates that males were more likely than females to read prose fiction, a genre mistakenly considered for women only. Using different sources, social historians like François Furet and Jacques Ozouf have assessed more accurately the extent of literacy and the major historical factors involved in its diffusion among different groups and regions in

---

[1] Ernestine Dumont to Eugène Sue, 24 Nov. 1843, in BHVP Fonds Eugène Sue fol. 416.

[2] Théophile Gautier, *Histoire de l'art dramatique en France depuis vingt-ans* (1858–59), 3:161. Cf. Georges Jarbinet, *'Les Mystères de Paris' d'Eugène Sue* (1932), 177–204; and Introduction, note 30, above.

[3] Cf. Edmond Werdet, *De la librairie française. Son passé, son présent, son avenir* (1860), 118; François-Florentin Bouquet, *De la moralité dans les compagnes depuis 1789* (Châlons, 1860), 25–26; and L.-E. Piette, *De l'éducation du peuple* (1859), 177–79.

[4] E.g., Germaine de Staël, *Mémoires de Madame de Staël (Dix années d'exil)* (1840), and Daniel Stern, *Mes souvenirs 1806–1833* (1877).

modern France.[5] Still others, like Antoine Prost and Maurice Crubellier, have examined the growth of French educational and cultural institutions fundamental to the definition of new reading publics.[6] But no one has examined yet the actual audiences for nineteenth-century books and newspapers. Clearly there is more to know about the effective size and composition of active readership in the recent past.

It should come as no surprise that French readers participated in the development of modern society, which grew in both size and complexity from the eighteenth century onward. Literacy, for instance, helped to define elite social groups in the Old Regime; it often distinguished the landed nobility and most urban classes, long accustomed to the world of print, from the manual worker and rural peasant, who were literally unable to sign their names. In time, this stratification by literate skills altered noticeably as French society moved from a rural hierarchy dominated by landed notables to a more urban, differentiated structure headed by new elites.[7] The small, nearly homogeneous circle of literate people in the Old Regime expanded over the course of the nineteenth century to include the whole of French society. By the twentieth century, groups once largely excluded from literacy shared in it more actively. Women, children, workers, the rural south, and non-Europeans now all responded to French printed matter to an extent they never did one hundred years earlier.

But the history of literacy is simply not identical with the history of reading. People with literate skills did not always use them. Throughout the modern period, the world of print did not concern as many women as men. Fewer old than young people read, fewer workers than notables, and fewer residents in the south than in the north. As in the past, full participation in written culture today is remarkably selective. Even though elementary education marks the historical achievement of an entire nation, active readers remain a small percentage of French society. Consequently, the diffusion of interpretive practices, as well as literacy, helped to define the historical context of a more varied print culture in France.

NUMBERS

Contemporary social scientists consider literacy to be an indicator of modernity. The historical development of literate skills is thus a topic of serious

---

[5] François Furet and Jacques Ozouf, *Lire et écrire. L'Alphabétisation des Français de Calvin à Jules Ferry*, 2 vols. (1978); and Harvey J. Graff, *The Legacies of Literacy: Continuities and Contradictions in Western Society and Culture* (Bloomington, Ind., 1987), 245–85.

[6] Antoine Prost, *Histoire de l'enseignement en France 1800–1967* (1968); and Maurice Crubellier, *Histoire culturelle de la France. XIXe–XXe siècle* (1974).

[7] Georges Dupeux, *La Société française 1789–1970* (1972), 54–151; and Fernand Braudel and Ernest Labrousse, eds., *Histoire économique et sociale de la France* (1970–82), vol. 3, pt. 1:161–238.

study, one with a sizable corpus of published research.[8] One of the first efforts to examine the matter began in 1792 when the revolutionary abbé Henri Grégoire conducted a survey of linguistic practices in the provinces.[9] After numerous local efforts to count schools and students in the First Empire and the Restoration, the baron Charles Dupin drew a map of France indicating the relative number of elementary schools and students in each department.[10] His work was continued during the July Monarchy by Adolphe d'Angeville; sharing a growing concern of many observers after 1830 with the condition of the working classes, Angeville used military records to compile a profile that included the literacy of France's conscripts.[11] During the Second Republic and Empire, surveys of industry and commerce assessed the education of French workers by trade. Victor Duruy, the Second Empire's minister of public instruction, also studied the extent of reading instruction; his work has provided machine-readable data for social historians to analyze, as have the annual editions of the *Statistique de la France* during the Third Republic.[12] Since then scholars have examined literacy's complex development.

The first comprehensive and systematic survey of literacy in France is more than a hundred years old. This is the survey compiled by Louis Maggiolo, honorary rector of the Academy of Nancy during the Third Republic, an administrator tasked to assess the extent of education prior to the Ferry Laws.[13] In 1877, Maggiolo was charged by the Ministry of Public Instruction with directing the schoolteachers in more than 30,000 communes to count the number of signatures on the marriage registers maintained by the church and the state since 1677. The result, published in 1882, consists of the number and percentage of men and women capable of signing their names in 1686–90, 1786–90, 1816–20, and 1854–77 in nearly every department in France; this survey remains a major source of data from the seventeenth century to the beginning of the Third Republic. Despite some well-known problems in Maggiolo's administration of the research and its completeness, representative-

---

[8] Cf. titles in Harvey J. Graff, ed., *Literacy in History: An Interdisciplinary Bibliography* (New York, 1981); and idem, *The Legacies of Literacy*.

[9] See Roger Chartier, *Lecteurs et lectures dans la France d'Ancien Régime* (1987), 223–44.

[10] Charles Dupin, *Forces productives et commerciales de la France* (1827), map insert.

[11] Adolphe d'Angeville, *Essai sur la statistique de la population française, considérée sous quelques-uns de ses rapports physiques et moraux* (Bourg, 1836), 330–31.

[12] Cf. Paris, Chambre de Commerce et d'Industrie, *Statistique de l'industrie à Paris . . . pour les années 1847–1848* (1851), 68; and the Duruy surveys analyzed in Patrick J. Harrigan, *Nobility, Elites, and Education in French Society of the Second Empire* (Waterloo, 1980). Statistique Générale de la France, *Annuaire statistique* (1885–1940), vols. 1–56, is now the object of a major computer study. Cf. Furet and Ozouf, *Lire et écrire*, 1:i3–58.

[13] Ministère de l'Instruction Publique, *Statistique de l'enseignement primaire*, Tome 2: *Statistique comparée de l'enseignement primaire, 1829–1877* (1880), clxvi–clxxiv. Cf. Michel Fleury and Pierre Valmary, "Les Progrès de l'instruction élémentaire de Louis XIV à Napoléon III d'après l'enquête de Louis Maggiolo (1877–1879)," *Population* 12 (1957): 71–92.

ness, and urban/rural distribution of data, historians consider this perhaps the most reliable, and certainly the most useful, assessment of adult literacy before 1882. Maggiolo's analysis of the marriage-register signatures was continued annually thereafter by the *Statistique de la France* to mark the progress of national education up to the outbreak of World War II.[14]

What these data show is a remarkable rise in the proportion of literate men and women in the population (see cols. 1–2, Table 2.1). In 1686–90, only 29 percent of the men and 14 percent of the women were literate enough to sign their names at marriage. By 1876–80, these percentages had increased to 83 and 72, respectively, indicating a nearly threefold rise for men and a fivefold rise for women in less than two hundred years. Five years before the enactment of compulsory elementary education (in 1881), male literacy rates were nearly universal, that is, 95 percent or more, in no fewer than 16 of the 87 departments listed; comparable female rates existed in no fewer than eight of the departments. The historical watershed in French literacy clearly preceded the establishment of a national educational system. Notwithstanding the disruption of the *petites écoles* in the 1790s, the cumulative impact of revolution and the educational reforms enacted by each subsequent regime made possible most of this growth.[15] The rapid development of larger cities and a more industrial economy, initially impediments to popular education, also contributed ultimately to the decline of illiteracy after the eighteenth century.[16]

These figures have at least two features particularly worth noting, one more obvious than the other. First, women remained considerably and consistently less literate than men well into the nineteenth century. Literary historians have long noted a disproportionately large role played by women in modern French letters;[17] what may have been true among urban social elites was certainly not true in the population at large. Aside from the religious imperative of learning the catechism and the litany, the educational institutions and the economic incentives necessary to the widespread acquisition of reading skills simply did not exist to the same extent for women as they did for men. After 1850, however, documented female literacy rates rose dramatically. Although French brides certainly remained less literate in every department for two centuries, they approached the ability of French grooms by the beginning of the Third Republic. Apparently, the historical forces behind the growth of literate skills

[14] Statistique Générale de la France, *Annuaire statistique. Résumé retrospectif* (1940), 56:19*–20*.

[15] See Dominique Julia and Paul Pressley, "La Population scolaire en 1789," *Annales: E.S.C.* 30 (Nov.-Dec. 1975): 16–47; Jacques Houdaille, "Les Signatures au mariage de 1740 à 1829," *Population* 32 (1977): 68–69, 76–77; Roger Chartier et al., *L'Éducation en France du XVIe au XVIIIe siècle* (1976), 93. Cf. H. C. Bernard, *Education and the French Revolution* (Cambridge, 1969), 210–22.

[16] See Furet and Ozouf, *Lire et écrire*, 1:229–69; and Raymond Oberlé, "Étude sur l'analphabétisation à Mulhouse au siècle de l'industrialisation," *Bulletin, Musée historique de Mulhouse* 67 (1959): 99–110.

[17] See Maurice Agulhon, *Le Cercle dans la France bourgeoise 1810–1848* (1977), 73–80.

TABLE 2.1
French Men and Women Signing Marriage Registers, 1686/90–1933,
and Literate Conscripts, 1832–1933

Year	Mean annual percentage		
	Men	Women	Conscripts
1686–90	29.1	14.0	—
1786–90	47.1	26.9	—
1816–20	54.4	34.7	—
1827–29	—	—	44.8
1832–35	—	—	52.6
1836–40	—	—	52.3
1841–45	—	—	55.8
1846–50	—	—	59.7
1851–55	68.4	52.6	62.4
1856–60	74.1	53.9	65.7
1861–65	74.8	57.5	70.3
1866–70	75.0	62.3	76.2
1871–75	77.8	66.3	80.5
1876–80	82.6	72.4	82.9
1881–85	86.0	78.0	85.1
1886–90	90.0	83.8	88.4
1891–95	93.0	88.6	92.0
1896–1900	94.8	92.6	93.8
1901–5	96.4	94.8	94.9
1906–10	97.5	96.3	95.5
1911–15	98.2	97.1	95.9
1916–20	98.6	97.9	95.7
1921–25	99.1	98.7	93.6
1926–30	99.3	99.0	90.8
1931–33	99.5	99.3	92.3

Sources: To 1875: Ministère de l'Instruction Publique, *Statistique de l'enseignement primaire*,
vol. 2: *Statistique comparée de l'enseignement primaire, 1829–1877* (1880), clxviii–clxix, 352–
59.
    After 1875: Ministère de l'Économie et des Finances, Statistique Générale de la France, *An-
nuaire statistique. Résumé retrospective* (1941), 19*, 20*.

in nineteenth-century France, including elementary schools for both sexes,
affected females more than males. Émile Zola, it seems, committed only a
minor historical anachronism when he portrayed Gervaise signing the *état civil*
during her wedding to the illiterate Coupeau in *L'Assommoir* (1877). By the
outbreak of World War I, women were as literate as men at rates thereafter
little affected by further political, educational, or economic change. Only the
devastating historical impact of events like the Revolution and the Great War
interrupted this steady national progress.
    The second feature of Maggiolo's survey is not so obviously indicated by

the figures, namely, the sharp difference between northern and southern France. Prior to the Third Republic, men and women in the north were far more likely to be literate than those in the south. For centuries France was cut into two different cultures bounded by a line extending from Le Havre to Besançon; below this boundary, literacy rates for both men and women were very slow to grow.[18] Even in 1876–77, the proportion of women able to sign the *état civil* lingered on at less than 50 percent in no fewer than 15 departments in Brittany, Gascony, and the Midi. Two-thirds of all women in Morbihan and Haute-Vienne, for example, were illiterate in the Third Republic. Traditionally these were regions where the Catholic Church was the strongest and the development of an urban, commercial economy the weakest, factors that historians have traditionally identified as inhibiting the spread of literate skills. Only gradually did this regional distinction, like that between the reading abilities of men and women, fade as France became more secular and its national economy more fully industrial in the twentieth century.

However revealing the patterns of evidence from Maggiolo's survey, historians have sought other sources to compensate for its numerous deficiencies. During the Old Regime, historical demographers have shown, more than 20 percent of the French population never married and therefore were excluded from the marriage registers, even though many unmarried individuals, like priests and members of religious orders, were fully literate.[19] Not all parishes kept comparable records, some of which were destroyed by simple neglect or revolutionary activity. On the other hand, social historians have found evidence of widespread migration and concubinage among urban workers, whose literacy (or, more accurately, illiteracy) also thus escaped this study.[20] Moreover, Maggiolo was unable to supervise the actual work of the schoolteachers, who were left largely to their own resources in counting thousands of signatures (Maggiolo never made clear what constituted a valid signature). Some departments had suspiciously small marriage cohorts and experienced wildly fluctuating literacy rates over time. Consequently, scholars have felt compelled to compare data from other sources.[21]

[18] On the Maggiolo line, see Roger Chartier, "Les Deux Frances: Histoire d'une géographie," *Cahiers d'histoire* 24 (1979): 393–415.

[19] D. V. Glass and D.E.C. Eversley, eds., *Population in History: Essays in Historical Demography* (London, 1965), 101–43.

[20] E.g., Louis Chevalier, *Labouring Classes and Dangerous Classes in Paris during the First Half of the Nineteenth Century*, trans. Frank Jellinek (London, 1973), 311–15; and Michel Frey, "Du mariage et concubinage dans les classes populaires à Paris (1846–1847)," *Annales: E.S.C.* 33 (1978): 801–26.

[21] E.g., Furet and Ozouf, *Lire et écrire*, vol. 2. Cf. Jean Mayeur, "Alphabétisation, lecture et écriture. Essai sur l'instruction populaire en Bretagne du XVIe au XIXe siècle," *Congrès national des sociétés savantes* 95 (1970): 333–54; Alain Corbin, "Pour une étude sociologique de la croissance de l'analphabétisation (au XIXe siècle)," *Revue d'histoire économique et sociale* 53 (1975): 99–120; and Robert Gildea, "Education in Nineteenth-Century Brittany: Ille-et-Vilaine, 1800–1914," *Oxford Review of Education* 2 (1976): 215–30.

Maggiolo's study has withstood serious scrutiny surprisingly well. Reex-
amination of registers in the most suspect departments has not invalidated the
initial efforts by Maggiolo's assistants. Nor do comparable sources do more
than refine the study's results. The data collected on men who registered for
military conscription, for instance, show similar patterns of national and regional literacy (see col. 3, Table 2.1). This more inclusive population of men
was examined for the ability to read—not just the ability to sign—during inscription for the military lottery; and this group was only marginally less literate than that of men included in Maggiolo's study. In 1827–29, 45 percent
of all males subject to military service could read; in 1876–80, 83 percent
could do so. Again the same distinction appears between the cultures on either
side of the Maggiolo line. The percentage of literate men in Brittany, Gascony, and the Midi remained far lower than that of literate men in Normandy,
Champagne, and Lorraine. The ability of school-age children examined for
reading comprehension in a study directed by Victor Duruy during the Second
Empire reflected the same differences between north and south, while it also
confirmed the historical significance of the signature as an indicator of basic
literacy. In 1866, the ability to sign one's name correlated highly with the
ability to read and summarize a simple message of at least two hundred
words.[22]

The achievement of universal male and female literacy by the end of the
nineteenth century is an accepted but ambiguous historical fact. The growth
of a literate society, if not a nation of active readers, marked the century before
World War I and created the remarkable demand for printed texts provided by
the French publishing industry in the same period. The high plateau in the
production of print, reached by the first decade of the Third Republic and
sustained with difficulty until World War II, fostered the spread of reading as
a distinctive feature of French culture. But, of course, not all sectors of the
population shared equally in the "rage to read." A distinction must be made
between simple literacy and the sophisticated ability to participate actively in
the world of print. An enormous difference, both quantitative and qualitative,
exists between deciphering two hundred words and understanding two hundred pages. Although a high percentage of the total population was literate,
not all men and women, not all age groups, not all social classes, not all
regions enjoyed comparable experiences with print for obvious historical reasons that must be examined in more detail.[23]

The first and most important of these reasons is the selective spread of ed-

[22] Furet and Ozouf, *Lire et écrire*, 1:25–27, report the high correlation between Duruy's survey
of elementary instruction and Maggiolo's survey of church-register signatures. Cf. Emmanuel Le
Roy Ladurie, *The Territory of the Historian*, trans. Ben and Siân Reynolds (Chicago, 1975), 33–
60.

[23] See Pierre Bourdieu, *Distinction: A Social Critique of the Judgement of Taste*, trans. Richard
Nice (Cambridge, Mass., 1984), 440–51; and Chapter 1, note 101, above.

ucation in France since 1800.[24] Historians have counted the number of schools and the students enrolled in them to discover the extent to which formal instruction reached the general population. The early growth of French education is impressive (see Table A.5). In 1817–20, the first years in which national figures exist, only 987,667 students attended primary school; by 1881–85, even before the full impact of the Ferry Laws, 5,364,400 did so. Here again, the creation of a national system of elementary education only ratified an already well-established trend. But this growth was not sustained. From 1882 to 1938, the total enrollments in primary school never exceeded the 5.63 million students in the years immediately preceding World War I. The number drops dramatically thereafter due to a war-related distortion in the population structure. Recovery was slow and incomplete before World War II because of severe economic problems in the 1920s and 1930s. Thus the movement of primary-school enrollments resembles closely that of book production in the same period: a rapid rise by the end of the Second Empire reaches a ceiling for the duration of the Third Republic.[25]

Statistically, elementary education reached its peak by the first decade of the twentieth century, when literacy became nearly universal. There was little more the primary-school system could accomplish other than to improve the reading skills of an already literate population. But this matter proved difficult.[26] Instructional methods emphasized rote memorization of selected passages from inappropriate texts, like wills and almanacs, that children often brought from home. Teachers remained too few, poorly trained, overworked, and inadequately compensated. Their monumental task was complicated still further by the irregular and brief attendance of children from peasant and working-class families who spoke only the local patois. In 1834, the number of students attending school dropped by 50 percent during the early summer months, when seasonal work required the supplemental labor that children provided. In 1877, attendance still dropped by 20 percent or more in the same

[24] See Prost, *Histoire de l'enseignement en France*; Pierre Chevallier and Bernard Grosperin, *L'Enseignement français de la Révolution à nos jours*, 2 vols. (The Hague, 1971); Theodore Zeldin, *France 1848–1945* (Oxford, 1973–77), 2:139–204, 243–345; Louis-Henri Parias and Michel Rouche, eds., *Histoire générale de l'enseignement et de l'éducation en France*, (1981), vols. 3 and 4; Roger Thabault, *Education and Change in a Village Community: Mazières-en-Gâtine, 1848–1914*, trans. Peter Tregear (London, 1971); Robert Gildea, *Education in Provincial France, 1800–1914: A Study of Three Departments* (London, 1983); and titles in Thérèse Charmasson, ed., *L'Histoire de l'enseignement, XIXe–XXe siècles. Guide du chercheur* (1986).

[25] Cf. Raymond Grew et al., "The Availability of Schooling in Nineteenth-Century France," *Journal of Interdisciplinary History* 14 (1983): 25–63; and J.-N. Luc, *La Statistique de l'enseignement primaire, 19e–20e siècles. Politique et mode d'emploi* (1985).

[26] See Roger Thabault, *L'Enfant et la langue écrite* (1944), 99–126; Pierre Clarac, *L'Enseignement du français* (1972), 35–118; Jean Hébrard, "École et alphabétisation au XIXe siècle," *Annales: E.S.C.* 35 (1980): 66–80; and Suzanne de Castell et al., eds., *Literacy, Society, and Schooling: A Reader*, (Cambridge, 1986), 15–58.

months. It was not until the state's provision of family allocations beginning in 1938 that this seasonal enrollment problem disappeared completely. Despite laws making primary-school attendance compulsory for ages 6–13 (after 1936, age 14), most rural students attended for no more than five years. This time was hardly sufficient to develop a critical reading competence in what was for many youths the "foreign" language of French. Again, girls attended school less often than boys, and the south lagged behind the north in primary-school enrollments, undoubtedly for the same reasons that literacy rates varied significantly by gender and region before World War I.[27]

Even more problematic was the growth in French secondary and university education, levels of schooling generally necessary for the development of fully competent readers.[28] Enrollments here were much smaller in both absolute and relative terms (see Table A.6). In 1820, 33,762 students attended a *lycée* or *collège*; in 1896–1900, this number had risen to 89,223, still less than two percent of the total population of the appropriate age group. By 1936–38, the figure had changed to 185,763, a nearly sixfold increase over enrollments in 1820, but the enrolled proportion of all youth aged 12–17 remained less than five percent. In response to the anticlerical politics of the Third Republic, enrollments in Catholic secondary schools rose unevenly in the same period, from 21,195 in 1854 to 50,800 in 1938, without altering the overall pattern of attendance. Despite a *lycée* enrollment of more than 100,000, only 4,600 *bacheliers* actually graduated in 1854. The total number of students enrolled in French universities also increased from 17,503 in 1890 to 76,405 in 1938, but very few of these students ever completed their degrees. Less than 6,500 diplomas, including both the *licence* and the *doctorat*, were awarded in 1938, and most of these were in law and medicine; only 1,818 students earned the *licence* in letters that year. From 1800 to 1940, the proportion of the population enrolled in institutions of higher education remained fairly constant.[29] University students, most of them male, constituted a truly privileged elite in France.

The limited expansion of formal instruction in France was countered somewhat by the growth of urban centers and the tertiary sector of the economy, both crucial factors in the development of a society's need and predisposition

[27] See Prost, *Histoire de l'enseignement en France*, 97–105; Gildea, *Education in Provincial France*, 222–29, 262–65; and Thabault, *Education and Change*, 52–70, 114–30.

[28] See Georges Weill, *Histoire de l'enseignement secondaire en France (1802–1920)* (1921); Paul Gerbod, *La Condition universitaire en France au XIXe siècle* (1965); Donald N. Baker and Patrick J. Harrigan, eds., *The Making of Frenchmen: Current Directions in the History of Education in France, 1679–1979* (Waterloo, 1980); Maurice Gontard, *L'Enseignement secondaire en France de la fin de l'Ancien Régime à la loi Falloux (1750–1850)* (Aix-en-Provence, 1984); and George Weisz, *The Emergence of Modern Universities in France, 1863–1914* (Princeton, 1983).

[29] Cf. John E. Talbott, *The Politics of Educational Reform in France, 1918–1940* (Princeton, 1969), 3–33.

to read regularly and well.[30] Social historians have long recognized the higher literacy rates of urban populations even in the Old Regime. In Paris on the eve of the 1789 Revolution, Daniel Roche has stated, nearly 90 percent of male servants and 80 percent of female domestics signed their wills.[31] To be sure, some social groups were less literate than others, especially those without apprenticeship in a craft or trade, but the practical necessity of reading and writing was more widespread in the city than in the countryside.[32] As the French population became increasingly urban in the nineteenth century, its literacy rates grew proportionately, despite the temporary disruption caused by exceptionally rapid industrialization in some northern cities. France was universally literate by 1920, only one decade before it was, statistically speaking, fully urban.[33] In fact, after the enactment of the Ferry legislation, the rise in elementary education parallels the rise in the percentage of the French population living in urban centers of 2,000 or more inhabitants; by law, each commune had to establish its own school. Moreover, the expansion of the service sector of the economy required ever larger numbers of competent readers to fulfill the complex literate functions its jobs demanded. The relatively slow rise of industry at the expense of agriculture in modern France was offset in part by the early rise of information-based employment in the country's older cities.[34]

Literacy's historical development demands further analysis. To what extent were French men and women able to afford the time and money to read? Although the proportion of the population that actually did read can never be known with precision, the proportion that was able to do so can and should be estimated. Data already exist not only on literacy, school enrollments, and demographic growth, but also on economic factors such as material standards of living and the relative cost of printed matter. These are known for France as a whole and for the major cities where the highest concentration of readers lived. Consequently, one can assess more precisely the size and composition of literate audiences, and therefore the extent to which the French actually read the books and newspapers published in the period.

However irregular the growth and uneven the distribution of material stan-

---

[30] Georges Friedmann, ed., *Villes et compagnes, civilisation urbaine et civilisation rurale en France* (1953); and Georges Duby, ed., *Histoire de la France urbaine* (1983), 4:357–470.

[31] Daniel Roche, *Le Peuple de Paris. Essai sur la culture populaire au XVIIIe siècle* (1981), 206. Cf. James Smith Allen, *Popular French Romanticism: Authors, Readers and Books in the Nineteenth Century* (Syracuse, 1981), 151–77; and William Sewell, "Social Mobility in a Nineteenth-Century European City: Some Findings and Implications," *Journal of Interdisciplinary History* 7 (1976): 222–24.

[32] Cf. Eugen Weber, *Peasants into Frenchmen: The Modernization of Rural France, 1870–1914* (Stanford, 1976), 232–40.

[33] See Philippe Ariès, *Histoire des populations françaises et de leurs attitudes devant la vie depuis le XVIIIe siècle* (1971), 274–311.

[34] Dupeux, *La Société française*, 30–31; and Braudel and Labrousse, *Histoire économique et sociale*, vol. 3, pt. 1:220–21.

dards of living essential to interpretive practice, these conditions generally improved from 1800 to 1940.[35] Wealthy land-owners supplemented their incomes from the primary sector of the economy by selective investments in industry, as large family firms incorporated and made their stocks available to the public. But the wealth and leisure of this privileged class of notables were only marginally affected by the growth of an industrializing economy. The professional and commercial middle classes, on the other hand, benefited enormously. They increased dramatically in size and affluence over the course of the nineteenth century. The new service sector's share of the nation's economic growth was significantly larger than that of any other social class in France. For example, the salaries of the principal white-collar positions in government administration at all levels increased on average ten times, even though real national income per capita rose only fourfold over the same 140-year period. The real daily wage of an unskilled worker, by comparison, rose less than threefold, from 2.1 francs in 1830 to 5.7 francs in 1938, a modest increase in light of those occurring among other social groups.[36] The industrial growth of the French economy did not favor the lowest portion of the social structure to the same extent that it did the middle and upper portions. But nearly every group did indeed benefit by the long-term improvements in real wages, salaries, and profits made possible by a more modern economic system, one that provided the material basis for a literate society, if not a society of active readers.

These unequally distributed material gains must also be seen in the context of other quantifiable changes in French life. While the relative cost of basic necessities such as food, shelter, and clothing decreased, the consumption of many other goods increased proportionately. The annual per capita consumption of sugar, for example, jumped ten times from 2.3 kilograms in 1830 to 23 in 1938.[37] The "relative immiseration" of the manual laborer was offset substantially by the wider range of cheaper goods available on the market—from socks to nightcaps—just as workers experienced a gradual reduction in the number of hours they were required to work for the same weekly wage. Earlier in the nineteenth century, it was common for laborers to spend twelve

[35] François Simiand, *Le Salaire, l'évolution sociale et la monnaie. Essai de théorie expérimentale du salaire. Introduction et étude globale* (1932); Jeanne Singer-Kerel, *Le Coût de vie à Paris de 1840 à 1954* (1960); Pierre Goulène, *Évolution des pouvoirs d'achat en France (1830–1972)* (1974); and Marguerite Perrot, *Le Mode de vie des familles bourgeoises, 1873–1953*, 2d ed. (1982).

[36] Jean Fourastié, *Machinisme et bien-être* (1951), 93. Cf. Jacques Rougerie, "Remarques sur l'histoire des salaires à Paris au XIXe siècle," *Mouvement social* 63 (1968): 71–108; Joan Wallach Scott, *The Glassworkers of Carmaux: French Craftsmen and Political Action in a Nineteenth-Century City* (Cambridge, Mass., 1974), 72–107; and Ira Katznelson and Aristide Zolberg, eds., *Working-Class Formation: Nineteenth-Century Patterns in Western Europe and the United States* (Princeton, 1986), 101–5.

[37] Fourastié, *Machinisme et bien-être*, 95.

hours a day, six full days a week on the job in periods of full employment. But with the legalization of trade unions in 1884 and the enactment of labor legislation after 1900, workers enjoyed more leisure time. Sunday rest became obligatory in 1906, the eight-hour day in 1919, and the forty-hour week, with three weeks paid vacation, in 1936. By 1950, the average French worker had available approximately three hours of discretionary time each day.[38] These changes in consumption and leisure surely contributed to the acquisition of reading material and the time spent on it by an ever larger portion of the French population. The real cost of a new book actually dropped from 7 francs 50 in 1820 to less than 1 franc in 1910, while that of a newspaper dropped even more, from 80 francs per year in 1820 to only 5 centimes per issue in 1863.[39] A newspaper, which cost several times the price of a two-kilo loaf of bread during the Restoration, cost considerably less than this staple on the eve of World War II.

Similarly, the general improvement in less quantifiable features of modern industrial society contributed to the growth of readership in France. Better lighting at home and in public places came about first with the introduction of gas lamps and then with electric bulbs for the wealthy middle classes before World War I.[40] Better lodging and furniture conducive to sitting for extended periods at home, if not necessarily at public libraries, also contributed to the regular reading habits of those who could afford them. Although only a small portion of the population bought optical devices before the introduction of national health care in the Fourth Republic, glasses increasingly corrected the deficiencies in eyesight suffered by as much as 40 percent of the general population.[41] The cost of making and grinding glass with precision dropped at the turn of the century. Coffee, a stimulant helpful to sustained reading habits, became a necessity at home and in public; its annual per capita consumption rose nearly fiftyfold from 1830 to 1938. Tobacco consumption rose fourfold in the same period.[42] Other idiosyncratic factors, such as more and larger public parks and more plentiful park benches, notwithstanding their self-appointed public guardians, all facilitated literate activities.

Given these considerations, from the growth of literacy and education to the improvement in material and qualitative standards of living, one might estimate the potential number of active readers in modern France. But such enu-

---

[38] Ibid., 164.

[39] Cf. Singer-Kerel, *Le Coût de vie*, 494–95 and 518–19; and HEF 3:108.

[40] Fourastié, *Machinisme et bien-être*, 95. Cf. Wolfgang Schivelbusch, *Illumination: Electric Light and the Shaping of Modern Society*, trans. Angela Davies (Oxford, 1988).

[41] There are no historical studies comparable to Jean-Claude Margolin, ''Des lunettes et des hommes, ou La Satire des mal-voyants au XVIe siècle,'' *Annales: E.S.C.* 31 (1976): 375–90. Cf. Matthew Luckiesh and Frank K. Moss, *The Science of Seeing* (New York, 1937), 249–56; and Matthew Luckiesh, *Light, Vision and Seeing* (New York, 1944), 14–19.

[42] Fourastié, *Machinisme et bien-être*, 95.

meration requires some critical assumptions. Among the more important are the differences in literacy rates between men and women, between northern and southern France, and between the various age groups in the population, especially children who had not yet learned to read. These rates can be calculated easily from the data available on the percentage of males and females, the percentage of urban and rural inhabitants, and the percentage of the people age 14 and older. More qualitative assumptions, however, concern the predispositions of different social classes to read. Although in time peasants were more literate and better educated, they were unlikely to devote very much of their leisure time or discretionary income to books. This fact appeared repeatedly in prefect reports on the literate culture of farm families all over France.[43] The same diffidence towards print existed among industrial workers in the cities. Consequently, the distinction between passive literate skills and active reading habits seems both logical and necessary, particularly in light of pervasive learning disabilities and eyesight deficiencies in any population. There were, of course, exceptions; many rural workers read actively, while many urban shopkeepers did not. But the distinctions here are deliberate approximations; their purpose is to refine even cruder categories based solely on literacy and school enrollments.

In this context, then, the number of actual book readers is surprisingly small, from less than 6 percent of the population in 1801 to little more than 38 percent in 1936 (see Table A.7). These figures constitute surely the largest portion of France ever likely to have read very much or very well on a regular basis, even though literacy and elementary education were widespread and newspaper circulation was high. Moreover, most of the growth seems to have occurred in the nineteenth century, when the literacy of females finally caught up with that of males and when French urban centers experienced their greatest expansion. Until its peak in 1881, at which time the rate actually decreased for the rest of the Third Republic, the limited growth in active readership parallels the ceilings evident in the school-enrollment figures and in the production of print. Apparently, data on literate activities reflect a "stalemated" society. Limits to actual readership appear to be another feature of a culture stalled until the multiple shocks of World War II and the later development of a postindustrial economy; it was historical events of such magnitude, together with cheap paperbacks and more extensive secondary education, that made possible another major transformation in French literate life.

While impressive in itself, the early sixfold increase in active readership hides a significant unevenness in its distribution. Not everyone shared equally in literate culture. Young people read more than adults, and white-collar pro-

---

[43] See Charles Rovert, "La Lecture populaire et les bibliothèques en 1861," *Bulletin de la Société Franklin* 45 (1872): 100–110; and Marcheville, "Notes sur l'état de la lecture populaire en France et sur la situation des bibliothèques en 1866, d'après les rapports des préfets et des inspecteurs d'Académie," *Bulletin de la Société Franklin* 50 (1872): 180–89; 52 (1872): 212–24.

fessionals more than workers and peasants. Despite newspaper and periodical circulation reaching all but 10 percent of the men and women over age 20, less than 15 percent of the population consumed more than 75 percent of all books published in 1968.[44] Numbers in themselves simply do not tell the whole story. Despite substantial absolute growth from 1800 to 1940, active readers are still a very small portion of the French population.

The exclusiveness of modern French readership appears most clearly among the changing clientele of public libraries. In response to requests from the Interior Ministry during the nineteenth century, prefects reported on the development of local library collections and their users. The earliest reports at the end of the First Empire indicate the paucity of active readers.[45] According to 24 reports sampled from a total of more than 80 filed before 1814, library users consisted primarily of students and faculty at neighboring *collèges*, *lycées*, or professional institutes. The widest range of patrons was reported in Cambray, where military officers, seminarians, attorneys, and merchants joined the students and the teachers from the local school.[46] But this was exceptional. The clientele of the public library at Clermont-Ferrand in 1833 was more typical: "some students from the *collège royal* or the school of medicine . . . , some professors, officers from the garrison, and other studious persons."[47] No mention was ever made of women or peasants, most of whom could not have survived the cross-questioning of the severe savants who often served as librarians. With titles taken from monasteries and *émigré* nobles during the First Republic, public collections were open no more than four hours a day, four days a week. Accordingly, the libraries did not suit more than "the affluent inhabitants of the city," "educated men," or "responsible persons."[48]

Seventy years and four regimes later, the reports of the University's departmental inspectors reveal a very different reading public.[49] Without specifying social groups, the reports during the Third Republic refer repeatedly to the "inhabitants of the country," "the people," and "rural families."[50] The reports actually described the population of villages whose local primary schools

[44] Jacques Charpentreau et al., *Le Livre et la lecture en France* (1968), 11.

[45] See BN NAFr 21035–54.

[46] Prefect of the Department of the Nord to the Minister of the Interior, 7 June 1813, in BN NAFr 21050 fols. 41–56.

[47] Prefect of the Department of Puy-de-Dôme to the Minister of the Interior, 20 Nov. 1824, in BN NAFr 21051 fols. 103–15.

[48] Prefects to the Interior Ministry in the Department of the Jura, ca. 1817, in BN NAFr 21045 fol. 332; of the Haute-Marne, 4 May 1813, in BN NAFr 21048 fols. 369–70; and of the Meuse, 30 Dec. 1816, in BN NAFr 21049 fols. 264–65.

[49] AN F17,10735–55.

[50] Reports of Departmental Inspector of the Pyrénées-Orientales to the Rector of the Academy of Montpellier, 26 Jan. 1884; of the Somme to the Academy of Douai, 22 Jan. 1884; Ain to the Academy of Lyon, 26 Jan. 1884—in AN F17,10737, d. 1884.

were required by law to establish public collections for the community. Occasionally, more specific reference was made to urban workers and small landowners. In 1884, for example, "the taste for reading continues to expand in the population—at least in the mountainous and industrial parts of the Vosges, for it is not solely schoolchildren who make their way to the library, but also adults."[51] The inspectors nearly all noted, however, that rural workers and peasants did not share in this otherwise pervasive literate activity. To account for this reticence, the reports often blamed the obstacles posed by Catholic clergy, parsimonious budgets, but most important, the passivity of the rural inhabitants themselves. "Work in the fields has not been interrupted," stated the inspector for the department of the Aisne. "And so the workers finding themselves tired in the evening preferred to rest rather than to stay up and read."[52] Whatever the demand for printed matter during the Third Republic, widespread literacy and elementary education did not insure either the interest or the effort to read regularly or well.

Underlying the selective growth of adequate reading skills and habits, particularly in the countryside, was the continued existence of regional languages.[53] Abbé Grégoire's survey of language use outside of Paris in 1792 had highlighted a fundamental problem for national authorities, revolutionary or otherwise, in implementing new laws where French was not even spoken, much less read.[54] In 1863, local patois still posed an obstacle to the acquisition of literacy as well as to national integration. French remained literally a foreign tongue for more than 7.4 million men and women, nearly 20 percent of the population. Breton in the northwest and Occitan in the south, for example, proved especially persistent; this linguistic particularism lingered largely because the people of Brittany and Languedoc remained economically isolated, at least until better roads, canals, and finally railroads brought these regions into a national market. The impact of free, compulsory, and secular primary education during the Third Republic anticipated that of national conscription laws on the eve of World War I; together, these factors contributed ultimately to the use of French in everyday discourse and in print. In those departments

---

[51] Report of the Departmental Inspector of the Vosges to the Rector of the Academy of Nancy, 20 Feb. 1884, in AN F17,10737, d. 1884.

[52] Report of the Departmental Inspector of the Aisne to the Rector of the Academy of Lyon, 2 Feb. 1884, in AN F17,10737, d. 1884.

[53] On local dialects, see Weber, *Peasants into Frenchmen*, 67–94, 498–501; Alain Corbin, *Archaïsme et modernité en Limousin au XIXe siècle, 1845–1880* (1975), 1:321–35; and Martyn Lyons, *Le Triomphe du livre. Une Histoire sociologique de la lecture dans la France du XIXe siècle* (1987), 25–42.

[54] See Michel de Certeau et al., *Une Politique de la langue, la Révolution française et ses patois. L'Enquête de Grégoire* (1975); Patrice Higonnet, "The Politics of Linguistic Terrorism and Grammatical Hegemony during the French Revolution," *Social History* 5 (1980): 41–69; and Martyn Lyons, "Politics and Patois: The Linguistic Policy of the French Revolution," *Australian Journal of French Studies* 18 (1981): 264–81.

with low literacy rates in Maggiolo's survey, oral traditions survived even after the war; in the Pyrenees, for example, the printed word retained its talismanic quality. But written culture, and perhaps a new mentality, developed inexorably in the rest of the country. In this way literacy encouraged (and was promoted by) the more widespread adoption of French to make possible regular literate activity for many, but not all, men and women.[55]

READERSHIP

A more detailed examination of active readership would show how pervasive were literate activities in French society from 1800 to 1940. Yet the modern reading public is extremely difficult to define. Sources of information much better than the reports on public libraries are unavailable; authors and their texts are easier to document than their anonymous readers. To compensate, most literary and intellectual historians describe a relatively narrow literate elite very much like the writers in the period.[56] In their books and other writings, authors sometimes made explicit reference to an audience and thereby suggested who their reading public was. But authors themselves were never certain of this; an intended audience was rarely realized. For instance, although Flaubert earnestly desired far larger sales than he ever achieved, he once stated that twenty intelligent readers were all he expected.[57] Numerically, Flaubert's actual audience was somewhere between his earnest desires and his cautious expectations. Relying solely on anecdotal observations like Flaubert's remarks, literary and intellectual historians cannot pinpoint precisely who was reading even in the recent past.[58]

One approach to the problem of identifying audiences lies in using a relatively neglected source: the correspondence sent to authors about their work.[59] Obviously, anyone writing to an author must at least know of his or her publications, unless of course the correspondent was merely an uninformed merchant or casual acquaintance. Relatives, friends, colleagues, publishers,

---

[55] See Roger Chartier, ed., *Pratiques de la lecture* (Marseille, 1985), 181–206. Cf. Gérard Cholvy, "Société, genre de vie et mentalités dans les compagnes françaises de 1815 à 1880," *L'Information historique* 36 (1974): 155–66; Gordon Wright, *Rural Revolution in France: The Peasantry in the Twentieth Century* (Stanford, 1964), 185–210; and Laurence Wylie, *Village in the Vaucluse* (Cambridge, Mass., 1964), 206–39.

[56] E.g., John Lough, *Writer and Public in France from the Middle Ages to the Present Day* (Oxford, 1978), 361–70, as impressionistic as René Bazin, "Les Lecteurs du roman," *Correspondant*, n.s. 262 (1900): 1148–62; and Maurice Descotes, *Le Public de théâtre et son histoire* (1964), 209–344.

[57] See George Sand to Flaubert, 2 Jan. 1876, in *The Letters of Gustave Flaubert 1857–1880*, trans. and ed. Francis Steegmuller (Cambridge, Mass., 1982), 228–30.

[58] Except for HEF 2:402–45, 498–514; 3:24–45, 470–509; and 4:528–41, 564–71.

[59] Cf. Robert Darnton, *The Great Cat Massacre and Other Episodes in French Cultural History* (New York, 1984), 215–56; Claude Labrosse, *Lire au XVIIIe siècle. 'La Nouvelle Héloïse' et ses lecteurs* (Lyon, 1985), 33–118; and Introduction, note 30, above.

and other individuals, both hostile and enthusiastic, all corresponded with writers and constituted one important audience for their texts in print, often cited by title in the letters. While letter writers are certainly not an author's entire reading public, especially for works in multiple editions of 10,000 or more copies, they do represent an active and concerned portion of it—the author's personal and professional network of readers—however atypical they may be because of their active concern. Relatively few readers take pains to write the authors of the books they read. More than likely, those who do so are deeply interested in either the author or the text, often both, in ways that shed light on the history of readers and their interpretive practices. No other source is quite so illuminating as fan mail on a topic otherwise so difficult to study.[60]

The nature of reading audiences defined by correspondence varies considerably from author to author. The more obscure the writer, for example, the less likely his or her papers are to be preserved. In most cases the letters to authors, including the most prominent, were simply discarded or lost. Few popular writers ever thought to save their early correspondence, despite its growing volume; they may never have suspected their own later fame. Like idle telephone calls today, letters often pertained to casual, trivial, or obscure matters, and so were hardly worth saving for posterity. Still others were not preserved out of carelessness or neglect, such as those from individuals unknown to the author or to the heirs of his or her papers. Unless a writer like Victor Hugo or Émile Zola developed international stature, the market value of such scraps was marginal at best. Consequently, the papers to be found in libraries and archives contain relatively few of the total number of letters that authors must have received from their readers.[61] Similarly, the principal published editions of authorial correspondence almost always reproduce the letters that authors themselves sent to others.[62] Such letters are simply inappropriate to serious historical research on readers and reading. The scholar must therefore use carefully whatever papers exist to document audiences in the period.

The actual number of fan letters, however, is substantial. In Paris and its suburbs alone, there are no fewer than three major archival collections pertaining to at least a dozen different French authors published after 1800.[63] For instance, the correspondence sent to Zola and the Goncourt brothers fills forty large folio volumes at the Département des manuscrits in the Bibliothèque

[60] Cf. the letter as a genre discussed in Charles Porter, ed., "Men/Women of Letters," *Yale French Studies* 71 (1986).

[61] Cf. letters to Renan, France, Quinet, and Hugo in the BN.

[62] E.g., F. R. de Chateaubriand, *Corr. générale*, ed. Béatrix D'Andlau et al. (1977); Charles Baudelaire, *Corr.*, ed. Claude Pichois and Jean Ziegler (1973); Gustave Flaubert, *Corr*, ed. Jean Bruneau (1973–80); George Sand, *Corr.*, ed. Georges Lubin (1964–82); *Émile Zola: Corr.*, ed. B. H. Bakker et al. (Montreal, 1978 ff.); and Marcel Proust, *Corr.*, ed. Philip Kolb (1970–).

[63] See the Selected Bibliography of Archival Sources, below.

nationale. Comparable materials exist for Jules Michelet and Eugène Sue at the Bibliothèque historique de la ville de Paris, and for Honoré de Balzac and Gustave Flaubert at the Bibliothèque Spoelberch de Lovenjoul in Chantilly. Surviving autograph letters sent to modern French authors number more than ten thousand. No one researcher could possibly mine all these sources adequately, a fact necessitating careful sampling of the correspondence to selected authors. For the present study, this selection included the correspondents of Madame de Staël, Stendhal, Balzac, Baudelaire, Sue, Flaubert, Michelet, the Goncourts, Zola, and Anatole France; their published work spans more than one hundred years in French literary history and involves ten authorial readerships defined by 1,458 different individuals.[64] It is on these particular audiences, in personal communication with selected authors, that the following description of French readers is based.

Unfortunately, this study is complicated by a paucity of documents for at least three of the audiences. Very few letters sent to Madame de Staël, Stendhal, and Balzac are extant. The same is true of other authors contemporary with them. The identification of their readers therefore requires a reasonably well-informed guess on an even weaker evidential basis: a sampling from all their correspondents known to have been alive when the authors' works were published, whether or not letters about them still exist. However imprecise an identification of actual readers among this select group, it does provide a good indication of an immediate circle of acquaintances, the audience personally known to the writer. These people constitute one public that authors had in mind when writing, even though it was a small portion of their entire readership. Literary historians have already published much of the authors' correspondence with this privileged audience; and it is not difficult, with the help of biographical dictionaries and the endnotes in scholarly editions, to establish a crude social profile of this group for comparison with the more adequate data from the letters sent to Sue, Baudelaire, Flaubert, Michelet, the Goncourts, Zola, and Anatole France.[65] The results are at least suggestive, if not definitive. One important audience at least can be studied in some detail for comparisons over time with what is already known about readers thanks to other historical sources.

The special character of these readerships is apparent from their privileged relationships to the authors (see Table A.8). In each collection of letters it is easy to discern the correspondents' prior acquaintance with the authors by the mode of address they used. Nearly 90 percent of the letters sent to Flaubert in 1857–62 preserved in Chantilly, for example, were by individuals known to the writer; they addressed him informally, frequently opening with no conventional greeting, using the second-person familiar, and closing with similarly amicable salutations, first names, sometimes just initials. The same was also

[64] See sources listed in Table A.8.
[65] See sources listed in Table A.9.

true of the correspondents with Stendhal and Balzac, whose extant communications have nearly all been published. Where some doubt exists from the internal evidence of the letters, the editorial endnotes often state in what capacity the writers knew their correspondents.[66] In all but three of the remaining cases—Sue, Michelet, and France—40 percent or more of the correspondents were previously acquainted with the authors. These were most often family members, close friends, or professional colleagues, and so they shared a broad range of interests or experiences. Clearly, then, the letter writers documented here did not represent the vast majority of readers who did not personally know the authors.

Primarily because the controversial works they published elicited a much broader response, Sue, Michelet, and France received correspondence from many more individuals they did not know, correspondence that therefore reflects more fully their actual, quite anonymous audiences. The special circumstances of Sue's collection, devoted almost exclusively to his first successful serial novel, *Les Mystères de Paris*, included anonymous individuals anxious to share their reflections on the causes of poverty in France's largest city.[67] Michelet's *L'Amour* and *La Femme* provoked similar responses about another nineteenth-century concern, the moral and social condition of French women. Like another collection that focused on his criticisms of the Roman Catholic clergy, these letters provided Michelet with material that he carefully annotated for his future work.[68] It was only in the twentieth century that the public stature of a major author was sufficient cause in itself to prompt readers to write, as Anatole France's voluminous correspondence indicates. Most of this was from a much more general audience, far more representative of his actual readers without special polemical concerns, except during World War I, when France published two controversial articles in *La Guerre sociale*.[69] The letters preserved for all the other French writers sampled here simply do not represent as fully the readers they enjoyed in their lifetimes.

Another particular feature of the letter-writing audience was its active participation in the world of print (see Table A.9). A high percentage of correspondents had published at least one book by the dates coinciding with the publication of an author's major work (in the case of the Goncourts and France, the dates vary for each correspondent according to the date of his or her first communication).[70] Thus, more than 46 percent of Baudelaire's documented readers were themselves authors by 1857, as were nearly 49 percent

[66] Cf. the editorial apparatus in *Balzac: Corr.*, ed. Roger Pierrot (1960–66); *Lettres à Charles Baudelaire*, ed. Claude Pichois (Neuchâtel, 1973); and *Émile Zola: Corr.*

[67] Cf. Jules Vinçard to Sue in BHVP Fonds Sue fols. 106, 116, 137, and 441.

[68] Cf. Jules Michelet, *L'Amour*, 2d ed. (1859), 373–406; and idem, *La Femme* (1859), i–lxv.

[69] See letters to France in BN NAFr 15439 fols. 547–95.

[70] The correspondents with the Goncourts or Anatole France who responded to any single published work were too few (less than 25) to analyze statistically. So this study used a more significant sample from all available letters sent to each author.

of those who wrote one or both of the Goncourt brothers from 1853 to 1896. Of course, writers were also readers, but few readers are writers. This percentage reflects one special quality of the social and professional network enjoyed by most authors in the period. It is certainly no accident that much of the correspondence by and to Madame de Staël, "the conscience of Europe," concerned the most prominent literati of the early nineteenth-century.[71] A century later, however, a much smaller proportion of the correspondence sent to Anatole France was from other authors. He heard from a significantly larger percentage of people who were not only unacquainted with him, but also did not share his professional interests. Unlike the correspondents of the other nine writers, France's documented audience was somewhat more a reflection of his actual readers.

It is worth noting how small was the percentage of female correspondents who had published books of their own. Even though women were indeed playing a more important role in the "republic of letters," they were not as active as men. That much is well known, and it is reflected both in the small percentage of women in the literary marketplace and in the lingering illiteracy of women in modern French society.[72] But women also seem to have shared less in the social and professional circles gathered about the major authors here (see Table A.10). One would have expected the proportion of women corresponding with Madame de Staël to have been much higher than only one-fourth of her literate network. Balzac, Sue, Michelet, and France had at least as large a proportion of women among their documented readers. The responses to *L'Amour* and *La Femme* elicited a more representative sample of the women in Michelet's audience, but this was exceptional. It was not appropriate, it seems, for a woman to write an author, unless of course she was a relative or close family friend. The bravado expressed by Balzac's anonymous female correspondents, or by Marie-Sophie Leroyer de Chantepie, who wrote several times to both Flaubert and Michelet, was not shared by many women until the twentieth century.[73] After World War I, more women wrote freely to Anatole France to congratulate him on winning the Nobel Prize for literature (in 1921), and again on the occasion of his eightieth birthday (in 1924).[74] By then, readership as well as sex roles had changed.

In the meantime, the vast majority of documented readers were men. They

[71] See the index of correspondents in *Madame de Staël, ses amis, ses correspondants. Choix de lettres (1778–1817)*, ed. Georges Solovieff (1970), 539–48.

[72] Cf. Evelyn Sullerot, *Histoire de la presse féminine en France des origines à 1848* (1966).

[73] See Marie-Sophie Leroyer de Chantepie to Flaubert, *Corr.*, 2:654 passim; and in BHVP Fonds Michelet, Tome 11, Liasse A4748 fols. 14–16. Cf. Daniel Brizenur, "Une Correspondance de Flaubert: Mademoiselle Leroyer de Chantepie," *Amis de Flaubert* 16 (1960): 3–12; 17 (1960): 3–10.

[74] E.g., J. Antoinette Norberg to France, [1921], in BN NAFr 15436 fols. 482–83; and Lilette Jean to France, 18 April 1924, in BN NAFr 15434 fol. 647.

appear to have predominated in the correspondence to all ten writers, especially to Baudelaire and Zola. The personal relationships of these two authors tended to exclude women unknown to them, the former by his often acrimonious nature with others and the latter by the reputed obscenity of his work (of which Baudelaire was also accused). That all the authors but one here were themselves male certainly skews the results, but even the correspondence of female writers like George Sand suggests at least one peculiar feature of literary life in modern France: the dominant role played by males in reading as well as writing.[75] The higher literacy rates of men and the larger percentage of males enrolled in both primary and secondary schools only serve to reinforce the perspective on reading provided by the letters.[76] For the moment, however, this insight must be qualified by the large number of correspondents who were not only writers themselves, but were also acquainted socially and professionally with the authors. The prominent place of men in the world of readers, besides that of letters generally, remains for careful attention in the light of less problematic historical sources.

Personal relationships with the writers influenced the nature of readership in other curious ways, such as in the correspondents' ages (see Table A.11). The mean ages of the letter writers, in fact, fluctuated within a fairly narrow range for 124 years. For instance, the correspondence to Anatole France was written by the youngest cohort, averaging only 32.4 years, while that to Gustave Flaubert was written by the oldest, averaging 14 years older at 46.5. This variation in the mean ages of the correspondents likely owes less to actual changes over time in the ages of audiences than to the ages of the authors at the time of the correspondence. Madame de Staël was only 34 in 1800, nearly the same age as the average correspondent in that year. Thirty years later, Stendhal was 47 years old, and his documented readers averaged nearly 43, only marginally younger than he. The greatest difference in ages between authors and their correspondents occurred in the cases of Edmond de Goncourt from 1853 to 1896 and Anatole France from 1868 to 1924, neither of whom elicited a specifically age-related response to their published work (the large standard deviation calculated in each case indicates a wide dispersion about the mean). Otherwise, the correlation between the ages of the authors and those of their documented audiences was very high, as befits the high percentages of personal acquaintance between writer and reader in these samples.

Some subtle variations in age by sex also appear among the correspondents. Despite the paucity of data here, it appears that women were more mature than

[75] Only 10 of Sand's 61 correspondents in BSL E.934–35, and only 13 of her 54 correspondents in BHVP Fonds George Sand G.5707–92, are recognizably female.

[76] See Linda Clark, *Schooling the Daughters of Marianne: Textbooks and the Socialization of Girls in Modern French Primary Schools* (Albany, 1984); Françoise Mayeur, *L'Enseignement secondaire des jeunes filles sous la IIIe République* (1977); and Maurice Crubellier, *L'Enfant et la jeunesse dans la société française 1800–1950* (1979), 273–96.

their male counterparts throughout the nineteenth and early twentieth centuries. In six of the ten cases, the mean age for female letter-writers was higher than the mean for males. In 1835, Honoré de Balzac, long believed to be the champion of *la femme de trente ans*, actually enjoyed the correspondence of women over age 43, more than seven years older than he.[77] To be sure, this was an indication of diversity in the author's personal acquaintances, but it is also a reflection of the appeal of his published work to both younger men and older women. The role played by the text in defining its audience by sex and age is also evident in the documented readership of Michelet's *L'Amour* and *La Femme* in 1859–60; here the 62-year-old historian attracted the letters of females over 25 years his junior. Sue and Zola received letters written by women much closer to them in age, perhaps because of the relatively mature nature of their published work on urban and rural poverty. (Note, however, the sample size that must qualify all inferences based on Table A.11.) Because Anatole France's novels were so popular, it could well be that his readers were in fact considerably younger than those of the nine other writers, especially among women who averaged less than 31 years of age over the course of his long lifetime.[78]

This generalization about the wide-ranging appeal of Anatole France's work is supported by the age structure of his correspondents (see Table A.12). His documented audience included the largest cohort of identifiable individuals age 20 or less, i.e., nearly 21 percent, many of them school-age youngsters writing the author for autographed copies of his novels or advice about a career in letters.[79] Nevertheless, France's readership also seems to have included a relatively large percentage of older people; nine percent were aged 60 or more. Only Michelet received letters from a significantly larger percentage of readers in this oldest age cohort, despite a considerably smaller percentage in the group of readers less than age 21. In fact, the data on the correspondents for all ten writers show a general trend towards a greater deviance about the mean: the more popular the work, the broader the appeal to readers of different ages. For example, the concentration of documented readers between 20 and 60 years old is noticeably low for Michelet's essays on love and women, whereas that for France's novels and political opinion is lower still. The international stature of the latter author partially ensured this more even age distribution, but the historical changes in readership also played an important role. With

[77] See F.W.J. Hemmings, *Balzac: An Interpretation of La Comédie humaine* (New York, 1967), 48–83; and André Maurois, *Prometheus: The Life of Balzac*, trans. Norman Denny (New York, 1965), 159–60.

[78] See Carter Jefferson, *Anatole France: The Politics of Skepticism* (New Brunswick, N.J., 1965), 237–42.

[79] E.g., Renée Chevallier to France, 21 Dec. 1919, in BN NAFr 15432 fols. 180–81; and Hélène Demouys to France, 2 Dec. 1920, in BN NAFr 15433 fols. 151–54, both clearly of school age.

higher rates of literacy and enrollments in school, Michelet's audience already included far more readers of different ages than was possible, or conceivable, in the first half of the nineteenth century.[80]

A similar trend of diversity develops in the residence patterns of the correspondents (see Table A.13); in time, Paris became less central to the audiences of French authors. One-half of the writers here received letters from people residing in the capital, the heart of French and much European literature early in the modern period.[81] Fully three-fourths of Balzac's documented readers lived in Paris, where he made both his home and his living, first as a printer and then as a writer often at the mercy of his Parisian creditors (who undoubtedly formed an interested portion of his audience). For other reasons, Stendhal, Sue, Baudelaire, and the Goncourts, also longtime residents of Paris, enjoyed a correspondence from their fellow *citadins*. Notwithstanding Madame de Staël's Europe-wide reputation in 1800, French audiences became less Parisian by the end of the nineteenth century. With the important exception of the audiences for the Goncourts and Zola, the percentage of correspondents residing elsewhere in France tended to grow as the city's book trade penetrated farther into the countryside.[82] Nearly 50 percent of Anatole France's documented readers lived outside of Paris during his literary career extending past World War I. This was especially true for the duration of the war, when most of his male correspondents were at the front. Only the Goncourt brothers and Émile Zola continued to cultivate a peculiarly Parisian network among fellow literati anxious to share in their success.[83]

That the lowest percentages of Parisians are found among the documented readers of Madame de Staël and Anatole France may well be due to the authors' various residences outside of Paris, the former often at her family home in Coppet and the latter at various villas in Île de France and Touraine. But the national diversity in their respective audiences also contributed to the large number of non-Parisian correspondents. More than 60 percent of Madame de Staël's readership lived elsewhere in Europe, naturally reflecting the distinctly European nature of her literary circle. As for Anatole France, his actual audience extended even farther than Madame de Staël's. His correspondents were drawn from no fewer than thirty different countries.[84] More than one-fourth of

[80] E.g., only one student wrote to Sue about his *Les Mystères de Paris*: Antoine Ménard (BHVP Fonds Sue fols. 32–33).

[81] Cf. François de Dainville, ''D'aujourd'hui à hier. La Géographie du livre en France de 1764 à 1945,'' *Courrier graphique* 50 (1951): 43–52; 51 (1951): 33–36.

[82] See Lyons, *Le Triomphe du livre*, 193–220; and HEF 4:76–78, 114–17.

[83] See André Billy, *Les Frères Goncourt. La Vie littéraire à Paris pendant la seconde moitié du XIXe siècle* (1954); and Jules Romains, *Zola et son exemple* (1935).

[84] Anatole France received mail from readers in North America (Canada, U.S., Mexico, Cuba), South America (Argentina, Brazil, Bolivia, Uruguay, Chile), Asia (India, Japan, Turkey), Australia, and Africa (Egypt, South Africa, and nearly all Francophone colonies), besides every major country in Europe.

his readership evidently was not even French and wrote him in languages he himself could not read. By the end of the nineteenth century, the international trade in books had finally been regulated by the Berne convention, enabling France and his publishers not only to control translations, but also to make formal arrangements for their promotion. This seems to have been the culmination of a larger historical trend evident in the growing number of non-French correspondents writing to the Goncourt brothers and to Zola after mid-century.

Finally, the correspondents' socioeconomic backgrounds deserve comparison. The letters often suggest information about social and occupational status, while bibliographies and biographical dictionaries supplement these clues for some of the more notable individuals writing the authors. The results in Table A.14 suggest long-term trends in the social composition of French readership from 1800 to 1924. One obvious feature is the decline of landed notables.[85] Over time, large landowning and independently wealthy readers nearly disappear from the correspondence, mirroring their diminished place in French society. In 1800, Madame de Staël received more than one-half of her letters from the aristocratic elite of Europe, including heads of state and their relations, an exceptional proportion due primarily to the international prominence of her own family.[86] The percentage of readers enjoying landed wealth who wrote to Stendhal, Balzac, and Sue was much lower, between 10 and 20 percent; still fewer religious, diplomatic, political, and administrative officeholders corresponded. Representatives from this latter group dropped to less than 10 percent for the remainder of the readers documented here. This is still disproportionate to their actual numbers in French society and indicates the extent to which the influence of traditional elites lingered in the world of letters. With the exception of Baudelaire's correspondents, social notables continued to make up a large portion of readers in the Second Empire and the early Third Republic, particularly for Flaubert, Michelet, and the Goncourt brothers.[87]

Later, with Zola and France, this privileged class was no longer so prominent; their share of the correspondence was more in keeping with their reduced importance in French social life, the result of more than one hundred years of political and economic upheaval and the rise of new social elites.[88] In the place

[85] On landed elites, see Jean Lhomme, *La Grande Bourgeoisie au pouvoir (1830–1880)* (1960); René Rémond, *Les Droites en France* (1982), 411–31; Braudel and Labrousse, *Histoire économique et sociale*, vol. 3, pt. 2.

[86] Cf. comtesse de Pange, *Mme. de Staël et la découverte de l'Allemagne* (Amiens, 1980); and Victor Del Litto, *La Vie intellectuelle de Stendhal. Genèse et évolution de ses idées (1802–1821)* (1959).

[87] See Lois Boe Hyslop, *Baudelaire: Man of His Times* (New Haven, 1980); Benjamin Bart, *Flaubert* (Syracuse, 1967); Lucien Febvre, *Michelet* (Geneva, 1946); and Robert Baldick, *The Goncourts* (New York, 1960).

[88] Cf. Pierre Sorlin, *La Société française*, Tome 1: *1840–1914* (1969); Georges Duby, ed.,

of aristocratic wealth appeared a much more diverse social network of correspondents. The role played by other writers, journalists especially, grew over the course of 124 years. Less than 9 percent of Madame de Staël's letters came from other writers, but nearly 41 percent of Flaubert's did. Professional authors no doubt are also voracious and interested readers, but they are represented here to an extent entirely disproportionate to their actual number in French society. Historically, as the republic of letters expanded to include many more published writers, their relationships developed; this new network resulted in more correspondence among them. Only Sue and Michelet seem not to have shared in this trend as much as the others, perhaps because of the broader appeal of their works and the special audience defined by the archival administration of their private papers.[89] Anatole France, on the other hand, also received fewer letters from fellow authors. His audience included groups far more representative of historical changes in French social structure and the definition of new reading publics from 1800 to 1940.

Among the new features in modern French society are service-sector occupations such as the professions and white-collar jobs in both business and government.[90] This development is also evident in the correspondence. Over time, physicians, lawyers, notaries, professors, and savants were more likely to write authors, as were office employees, functionaries, teachers, and librarians, whose numbers often included aspiring young writers as well as active readers. From 1830 onward, service-sector employees constituted between 20 and 40 percent of the correspondents; the highest percentage of letters from this social group was sent to Anatole France after World War I. Although they were disproportionate to their representation in the audiences documented here, white-collar occupations were a rapidly growing portion of the urban population, an important literate addition to French society. This trend appears in the correspondence from middle-class youth enrolled in secondary schools and universities. As is well known from the history of French higher education, literary study provided training most appropriate to administrative positions, and even more to middle-class social pretentions.[91] The larger place of students in literate audiences indicates their active age-related reading interests, to be sure, but also the new role of white-collar employment in modern France.

Histoire de la France urbaine, Tome 4: *La Ville de l'âge industriel* (1984); and Dupeux, *La Société française*, 152–97.

[89] The letters to Sue and Michelet maintained at the BHVP are classified by the works to which they pertain. Letters not dealing specifically with a work were not consulted.

[90] On *cadres*, see Adeline Daumard, *Les Bourgeois de Paris au XIXe siècle* (1970), 123–46; Perrot, *Le Mode de vie des familles bourgeoises*, 167–98; and Dupeux, *La Société française*, 152–59.

[91] Cf. Zeldin, *France 1848–1945*, 2:291–302; and Edmond Goblot, *La Barrière et le niveau. Étude sociologique sur la bourgeoisie française moderne*, 2d ed. (1968).

The number of letters from these more traditional bourgeois social groups regularly exceeded those sent by men (and some women) engaged in commerce, industry, and banking. The single and most notable exception to this feature of the documented readership is Balzac's correspondents, many of whom were printers, booksellers, publishers, and of course creditors. His extensive business correspondence resulted from his own unusual entrepreneurial interests.[92] Few other writers were so actively involved with the business world, which remained generally uncongenial to strictly literary activities. By the Third Republic, readers actively engaged in commerce, industry, and banking constituted only 5 percent of Zola's and France's apparent audiences. But their numbers still exceeded those of other social groups. Artisans, shopkeepers, domestics, and peasants hardly existed among the correspondents for nearly all authors. Only Eugène Sue's serial novel elicited the attention of the urban working classes; and many of these readers, like Flora Tristan and Pierre Vinçard, were extremely atypical (they had serious interests of their own in writing, as well as in social and political reform).[93] As for peasants, the largest portion of the French working population, they rarely wrote to authors whether or not they read any of their work. Even Zola's controversial novel about agrarian life, *La Terre*, failed to provoke a single response from a peasant. Only one farmer, and a wealthy one at that, extended his sympathies to Edmond de Goncourt upon reading the last volume of the aging author's journal.[94] Clearly, rural inhabitants did not share in the literate world of the urban middle classes.

These trends in audiences defined by fan mail closely resemble those evident in other sources. Using data from estate inventories, wills, and subscription lists, historians have documented the exclusive community of active readers in the Old Regime.[95] In 1750 in nine different cities, for instance, only about one-third of all inventories mentioned printed volumes. The social groups most likely to own books included writers and librarians (100 percent), professors (75 percent), and attorneys and clergy (62 percent); much less likely were merchants (15 percent), master artisans (12 percent), and journeymen (10 percent), even though the proportion of Parisian domestic servants owning books doubled between 1700 (19 percent) and 1780 (40 percent). Although comparable data do not exist for all social groups in the nineteenth

---

[92] On Balzac the businessman, see HEF 3:78–79.

[93] Besides Vinçard and Tristan, workers in Sue's audience included two journeymen type-compositors (BHVP Fonds Sue fols. 212, 220–21), a journeyman jeweler (fols. 364–65), an unskilled day laborer (fols. 378–79), a journeyman glassmaker (fols. 392–94), and a domestic servant (fols. 411–12).

[94] Armand Cabrol to France, 23 Aug. 1894, in BN NAFr 22456 fol. 9.

[95] See Robert Darnton, *The Business of Enlightenment: A Publishing History of the Encyclopédie 1775–1800* (Cambridge, Mass., 1979), 291–92; Chartier, *Lecteurs et lectures*, 166–71; and Roche, *Le Peuple de Paris*, 218.

century, studies of public-library users describe a much more diverse profile.[96] From 1865 to 1894 in six different cities, the proportion of *rentiers* never exceeded a third of the library patrons, while that of the older bourgeoisie— shopkeepers, merchants, white-collar employees, students, and profession- als—never fell below a half (except in Fontainebleau, where workers consti- tuted 45 percent of library users). The traditional landed and administrative elite of the Old Regime was largely displaced in the literate life of modern France. According to survey data collected in 1960, however, regular reading had become a feature of a still larger share of the population: 90 percent of all people at least 20 years of age.[97] A larger than average proportion of individ- uals working in agriculture (11.5 percent), earning less than 300 fr. a month (12.5 percent), or living in towns of less than 2,000 inhabitants (9.5 percent), stated that they never read. All other categories defined by occupation, in- come, and city size were remarkably uniform in their tendency to read regu- larly. In light of these other historical studies, the nineteenth century actually marked a long intermediate stage in the development of a society of active readers in modern France.

Although the social and professional networks defined by the letters were limited and the global figures on the potential audience for books imprecise, the available evidence sheds interesting light on the growth and composition of reading publics in modern French society. From 1800 to 1940, especially in the first three fourths of the nineteenth century, the number of active readers in France increased sixfold, as literacy rates rose and educational institutions developed. Like the production of printed matter, a modern society of active readers reached a plateau for the life of the Third Republic. But French audi- ences continued to diversify; more women, younger and older age groups, more non-Parisians, and new social classes participated in literate culture. As female literacy spread, women shared to a greater extent in the world of print, even if they did so less actively than men throughout the nineteenth century. State-sponsored education for all French boys and girls contributed to the growing interest of school-age children in reading activities, just as larger ur- ban centers and higher material standards of living did for the elderly. More- over, developments in the book trade made possible the geographical expan- sion of French readership no longer centered so much in Paris. While peasants and workers certainly did not enjoy the same cultural world as the urban mid- dle classes—the impact of literacy, education, and inexpensive books re- mained remarkably limited in France—the exclusive audience of a traditional

[96] Cf. prefect reports in *Bulletin de la Société Franklin* during the Third Republic, surveyed in Lyons, *Le Triomphe du livre*, 183–92; and BN NAFr 21035–54.

[97] See Charpentreau et al., *Le Livre et la lecture*, 13–50; HEF 4:569; Bourdieu, *Distinction*, 440–51; and Julien Cain et al., *Le Livre français. Hier, aujourd'hui, demain* (1972), 100.

intellectual and social elite did give way to those in new bourgeois occupations as the tertiary sector of the economy came to rival agriculture and industry. Thus the society of readers in France, like French society itself, became increasingly differentiated in ways that can be traced in the correspondence sent to various authors over a 124-year period.

Chapter 3

THE POLITICS OF RECEPTION

SOON AFTER LEARNING that the Interior Ministry had decided to prosecute *Les Fleurs du mal*, Charles Baudelaire set out to affect the trial's outcome.[1] On July 20, 1857, he wrote an obsequious letter to the minister of state, Achille Fould, a former colleague of his stepfather, to prevent his case from ever coming to court. But this flattery came to nothing, and his trial was scheduled for Thursday, August 20. Baudelaire then pleaded with C.-A. Sainte-Beuve for his political intervention, or at least for his published approval of the poet's work. Despite Baudelaire's personal visit, the powerful critic refused to help him as he had Flaubert earlier that year, even though Sainte-Beuve did sketch out a defense strategy for Baudelaire's attorney. This the poet modified and incorporated into his own instructions to Gustave Chaix d'Est-Ange, identifying the risqué verses of other poets likely to exonerate his own by apt comparison. After assembling a flattering collection of critical reviews for the court, Baudelaire had Jules Barbey d'Aurevilly contact Raymond Brücker, a close friend of the prosecuting attorney, Ernest Pinard. Baudelaire finally wrote a plaintive letter to Apollonie Sabatier, who had inspired one of the offending poems. "Flaubert had the empress working for him," he stated. "And the bizarre thought occurred to me some days ago that perhaps you could, by some possibly complicated connections and channels, get a sensible word to one of those bigwigs [the magistrates]."[2]

Baudelaire failed, of course, in all these efforts at personal intervention; he and his publisher were convicted and fined. This unfortunate case, however, suggests a key aspect to the history of reading in France: the deliberate manipulation of textual interpretation. Baudelaire's trial applied the law crudely to his carefully wrought poetry; but then, extraneous concerns pervaded the way all modern literature was read. Censorship, for example, affected reception without regard to literary achievement. Moreover, censors were themselves sensitive to influence; they were especially susceptible to the prevailing climate of official and unofficial opinion, an ideological factor for literate audiences everywhere in France. Similar constraints on the reading experience,

---

[1] See Pierre Dufay, "Le Procès des *Fleurs du mal*," *MdF* 4 (1921), 27–53; Alphonse Séché, *La Vie des Fleurs du mal* (Amiens, 1928), 153–80; and René Jouanne, *Baudelaire et Poulet-Malassis. Le Procès des Fleurs du mal* (Alençon, 1951), 30–52.

[2] Charles Baudelaire to Apollonie Sabatier, 18 Aug. 1857, in *Corr.*, ed. Claude Pichois and Jean Ziegler (1973), 1:422. Cf. Baudelaire to Achille Fould, Gustave Chaix d'Est-Ange, Caroline Aupick, and C.-A. Sainte-Beuve, 1:415–21.

such as the personal appeals that Baudelaire made so unsuccessfully, shaped the reception of texts whether or not the readers were government officials. Interpretation did not occur in isolation; it was tied to individual and group persuasion as well as more obvious legal and ideological forces. Consequently, literate politics defined yet another contextual feature of the interaction between reader and text. Just as reading publics participated in the proliferation of print and the development of a more differentiated society, French readers shared in a pervasive politics of reception.

While no aspect of interpretive practice lends itself to simple formulation—certainly no more than any other complex historical activity—the political contexts informing and informed by literate experiences deserve elucidation. A history of reading must attend to more than who read what in the past; it must also consider how these people received the printed material available to them. Among other things, this inquiry requires an examination of the way textual reception participated in the law, in systems of political ideas, and, less obviously, in the influential roles played by individuals, groups, and institutions. At the heart of interpretation lies the persuasion exerted by legal, ideological, and social circumstances, often defined by readers themselves. But careful study of this influence also reveals a remarkable continuity in the state's deliberate attempts to control interpretation, in its justification of those attempts, and in the regulating functions of various interpretive communities throughout the modern period. Historically, the politics of reception has many ruses but always the same objective—affecting the interaction between reader and text—just as Baudelaire attempted during the prosecution of his poetry in 1857.

CENSORSHIP

Legal constraints in place since the Old Regime clearly affected modern French readers.[3] In light of the political dangers posed by the stage and the press, the most restrictive measures were aimed at the theater, whose success did not require a literate audience, and at periodicals, whose ideas were easily published and cheaply distributed. Consequently, eighteenth-century officials were authorized to exercise what is known as "preventive" censorship before publication as well as "repressive" censorship afterwards. These measures also included the official *permissions tacites* required of books since the seventeenth century. As a general rule, authorities tended to be more lenient toward expensive and hard-to-transport products of the book trade, especially through the uneven and unpredictable system of the *privilèges*, thanks to the

---

[3] See Louis Gabriel-Robinet, *La Censure* (1965); Irene Collins, *The Government and the Newspaper Press, 1814–1881* (London, 1959); Albéric Cahuet, *La Liberté du théâtre en France et à l'étranger* (1902); Klaus Heitman, *Der Immoralismus-Prozess gegen die franzöische Literatur im 19. Jahrhundert* (Bad Homberg, 1970); and HEF 2:536–41 and 3:47–55.

monarchy's administrative inefficiencies. As long as C.-G. de Lamoignon de Malesherbes remained responsible for both preventive and repressive censorship as the director of the book trade from 1750 to 1763, the less controversial philosophes were reasonably free to publish what they wished. More controversial publications, like the various "editions" of Diderot's *Encyclopédie*, were smuggled into France from Switzerland. In an extremely lucrative underground trade, the Old Regime's restrictions were more an annoyance than an obstacle.[4]

Ironically, the 1789 Revolution brought a renewed concern to control the spoken and printed word.[5] Despite two years of nearly complete freedom guaranteed by the Declaration of the Rights of Man and Citizen—"the free communication of thoughts and opinions is one of the most precious rights of man"—the theater remained under close surveillance in each municipality and, like the profusion of new periodicals, continued to be the object of repressive if not preventive censorship. The First Republic created more effective controls on the press with the executive power's active prosecution of journalists on both the left and the right politically. These restrictions received considerable reinforcement from the "Law of Suspects" in 1793, a general catch-all for indiscreet dramatists and journalists alike. The stage was forbidden to all political opponents. Moreover, a deliberate policy encouraged the propagandistic use of the theater and the rewriting of classical plays to promote the new egalitarian spirit. A decree in 1793 specified the performances of politically appropriate plays, like *Brutus* and *Guillaume Tell*, while the dramatis personae of Molière's *Le Misanthrope* lost all their aristocratic titles.[6] The Old Regime rarely made the stage or the printed page in any positive context until the fall of Robespierre and the modification of the Terror's administrative apparatus in 1794.

The brief experiment eliminating preventive censorship under the Directory ended in 1797 when the police were formally charged with regulating all periodicals. This arrangement was continued and made more effective under the direction of Joseph Fouché during the Consulate.[7] In 1800, the first consul ordered the interior minister to attend to the theaters in Paris, and the prefects

---

[4] Cf. J.-P. Belin, *Le Commerce des livres prohibés à Paris de 1750 à 1789* (New York, 1962); Nicole Herrmann-Mascard, *La Censure des livres à Paris à fin de l'Ancien Régime (1750–1789)* (1968); and Robert Darnton, *The Business of Enlightenment: A Publishing History of the Encyclopédie 1775–1800* (Cambridge, Mass., 1979), 9–13, 535–39.

[5] See John Lough, *Writer and Public in France from the Middle Ages to the Present Day* (Oxford, 1978), 189–91.

[6] See Beatrice Hyslop, "The Theatre during a Crisis: The Parisian Theatre during the Reign of Terror," *Journal of Modern History* 17 (1945): 332–55; and Marvin Carlson, *The Theater of the French Revolution* (Ithaca, 1966), 169–206.

[7] See Henri Welschinger, *La Censure sous le Premier Empire, avec documents inédits* (1882); and Jean-Marie Thomasseau, "Le Mélodrame et la censure sous le Premier Empire et la Restauration," *Revue des sciences humaines* 162 (1976): 171–82.

to attend to those in the provinces. Prior authorization for the staging of all plays was officially reestablished in 1806, when a formal decree also reduced the legal number of theaters permitted to stage them. The most enduring administrative mechanisms for the monitoring of printed matter began in 1810.[8] In that year, a decree fixed the number of authorized printers and newspapers in each department. Paris, for example, was permitted only eighty printers and four newspapers, including *Le Moniteur*, which was personally directed by Napoleon I. A related measure in 1810 created the office of the Director General of Printing and Bookselling in the Interior Ministry, which was responsible for receiving from printers and booksellers the reports of all new publications. In time, this surveillance function became the basis of the *Bibliographie de la France*, the trade's first national catalog, a monument as well to the long-standing political control of books in France.[9]

Despite article 8 in the Charter of 1814, the Restoration actually tightened the imperial decrees on the printed word.[10] All titles of twenty pages or less, whether or not they were periodicals, now became subject to preventive censorship. A freer press during the Hundred Days provided the excuse for a more elaborate policing of newspapers by the Second Restoration. The duc de Berri's assassination in 1820 gave the Ultras further proof of the dangers attending even regulated newspapers, a fear expressed by the heavy fines exacted from offending periodicals that sold their excised articles as booklets (this practice had made Paul-Louis Courier infamous). But various measures before and after the coronation of Charles X failed to contain the rise of a press supporting the more liberal deputies elected in 1827. Meanwhile, the selective prosecution of prominent literary figures, like the popular songwriter P.-J. de Béranger, also discouraged the publication of political controversy in books for an elite audience.[11] The tightest controls remained on the stage, where few controversial works appeared thanks to the vigilance of the Interior Ministry's theater censors. As early romantic dramatists discovered to their dismay, almost no allusions to contemporary controversy, even the most innocuous, eluded the censors' scrutiny.

Charles X's *ordonnances* of July 1830, one of which placed severe restrictions on the press, provoked yet another revolution.[12] Both the editorial staff and the printers' workers responsible for the publication of prominent Parisian newspapers led the fight in the streets and at the Hôtel de Ville. The result was the new regime's apparent commitment to the freedom of printed opinion en-

[8] Henri Welschinger, ''La Direction générale de l'imprimerie et de la librairie (1810–1815),'' *Le Livre . . . Bibliographie retrospective* 8 (1887): 161–82.

[9] Cf. Theodore Zeldin, *France 1848–1945* (Oxford, 1973–77), 2:547–51.

[10] Cf. Claude Bellanger et al., eds., *Histoire générale de la presse française* (1969), 2:3–10; and Collins, *The Government and the Newspaper Press*, 36–52.

[11] See Béranger's legal dossier in AN BB18,1010.

[12] See Charles Ledré, *La Presse à l'assaut de la monarchie, 1815–1848* (1960), 87–124.

shrined in article 7 of the 1830 Charter. But both the press and the book trade experienced instead a more intense administrative repression. After Giuseppi Fieschi's spectacular assassination attempt against Louis-Philippe in 1835, strict preventive censorship was formally reimposed.[13] Besides the preliminary readings of periodicals, the September 1835 laws required large sums of caution money for each newspaper, administrative suspensions and fines for first and second offenses, and trials without juries for all serious press cases. In 1830, the stage was also subject to close controls for the same reasons that had justified Napoleon's decree in 1806—politically, theaters were considered more dangerous than either books or newspapers. Thus in 1835, repressive censorship of the theater gave way to preventive censorship. Of course, the text still left much to the discretion of the cast, and so some plays approved initially in manuscript were terminated after the first performance. Balzac's *Vautrin* suffered this fate in 1840 when Frédérick Lemaître, playing the leading role of a convicted thief, sported a toupée that made him look too much like the king.[14]

The 1848 Revolution freed the press and the stage from the July Monarchy's regulations.[15] Among the first acts of the Provisional Government headed by Alphonse de Lamartine was to suppress the stamp duty on newspapers; another measure ended preliminary readings and administrative penalties, reduced the amount of caution money required of all dailies, and established trials by juries for serious press offenses. By March, the 1835 press laws had been abrogated. Like other aspects central to the Revolution, however, the growth of published opinion came to an abrupt end in the wake of the June days. General Eugène Cavignac's measures against the press closed down eleven Parisian papers for their alleged incitement of civil conflict. As the Republic drifted inexorably to the right, the general's decrees against freedom of public expression were confirmed by an *enquête* in 1849. Less than a year later, the Legislative Assembly passed the so-called "law of hate" submitted by President Bonaparte to reestablish nearly all the terms of the July Monarchy's press censorship.[16] The Second Republic's measures concerning the stage traced the same pattern of initial freedom, followed by the reimposition of controls maintained by the previous three regimes. Although the 1850 law created restrictions on song and drama for only one year, they were extended by presidential decree in the last year of the Republic.

Soon after the December 2, 1851 coup d'état, the most severe limits on public expression in French history were decreed.[17] Protecting the first modern

---

[13] Bellanger et al., *Histoire générale de la presse française*, 2:111–14.

[14] Frédérick Lemaître, *Souvenirs de Frédérick Lemaître, publiés par son fils* (1880), 245–48.

[15] See Victor Hallays-Dabot, *Histoire de la censure théâtrale en France* (1862), 289–333.

[16] See the Conseil d'État, Section de Législation, Commission chargée de préparer une loi sur les théâtres, *Enquête et documents officiels sur les théâtres* (1849).

[17] Cf. F.W.J. Hemmings, *Culture and Society 1848–1898* (London, 1971), 43–76; Philip Spen-

police state, the Napoleonic "Organic Decree on the Press" of February 1852 devastated the few remaining opposition papers. It imposed heavy tax burdens, including a substantial stamp duty, that few daily periodicals could afford. Moreover, the administrative apparatus to police the press made possible the ministerial suspension of any paper after only two notices within a two-month period. Once a special decree had been issued by the president (later by the emperor), a periodical could be terminated administratively by the Sûreté Générale at any time. No parliamentary debates over the measure or court cases against it were permitted. Only laws in 1861 and again in 1868 during the Liberal Empire modified these strictures in preventive censorship, which ultimately closed four papers in Paris and another six elsewhere in the country.[18] Meanwhile, the Interior Ministry also prosecuted several authors, publishers, and printers; Baudelaire and Flaubert were only the most famous.[19] The theater experienced similar administrative and legal controls after responsibility for dramatic censorship was moved from the Ministry of the Interior to the Ministry of the Emperor's Household in 1853. Careful supervision of the Parisian stage remained, not only for the major state-supported theaters, but also in the authorization required for all private operations, at least until a decree in 1864 made the establishment of a new house far easier and less expensive.

An end to the censorship of press, book, and stage did not result immediately from the Second Empire's fall in 1870.[20] In the aftermath of the Franco-Prussian War, the Third Republic's first decade was too troubled for the establishment of free public expression, despite the easing of restrictions on the book trade in 1871. A law enacted during the Paris Commune reimposed severe penalties for authors and publishers convicted of defaming government officials. And the moral order imposed by the *république des ducs*, culminating in the *seize mai* crisis, ensured that severe administrative measures would harass the political opposition. Even before the crucial election of 1877, prefects authorized the sale of republican newspapers only in bookstores and oversaw the prosecution of papers reporting "false" news. When the royalists were finally defeated, the Republic removed the remaining legal controls on the press. On July 19, 1881, printed expression and its sale were at last declared free, subject only to restrictions of the civil law for libel and trials by juries for serious criminal offenses. Similarly, printers no longer needed to

---

cer, "Censorship by Imprisonment in France, 1830–1870," *Romanic Review* 47 (1956): 27–38; and Victor Hallays-Dabot, *La Censure dramatique et le théâtre. Histoire des vingt dernières années (1850–1870)* (1871).

[18] See "Relevé des mesures de répression administrative prises contre la presse du 17 février 1852 au 31 décembre 1863," in AN F18,294.

[19] See Alexandre Zévaès, *Les Procès littéraires au XIXe siècle* (1924), 55–174.

[20] See Josette Parrain, "La Censure et la Commune, 1881–1914." thèse de troisième cycle, Université de Paris X (1971).

declare the size of all published titles to the Ministry of the Interior. Nevertheless, this charter for the French press was amended more than thirty times in the next hundred years. In 1884, for example, a new law permitted municipal authorities to take action against all activities, including publications, that compromised public tranquility. Thanks to the wave of anarchist terrorism in the 1890s and to the obvious threats to public safety during World War I, repressive censorship for political reasons remained a feature of French journalism for much of the Third Republic.[21]

An end to theater censorship took even longer to effect, presumably because the stage posed a greater apparent danger.[22] With a law passed in 1874, the Ministry of Public Instruction and the Beaux Arts became responsible for the reading of all manuscripts at least fifteen days before staging; and the police required authorization from the censors before advertisements of a new play could be posted. Thus for the last quarter of the nineteenth century, both preventive and repressive censorship remained a brutal fact for the French theater. Officially it continued to exist, not to police morality (though in fact this remained important), but to contain political extremism, a concern debated intensely in 1891 when restrictions on the theater were again challenged.[23] By 1906, however, fears on both sides had abated in new political circumstances focused on the separation of church and state; and government funding for theater censorship lapsed, even though regulation of the cinema remained until 1913. Only with political crises, like World War I, did censorship return as an issue in French politics.[24] With the spread of literacy and elementary education, concern over the stage waned, and with it the anachronistic legal controls that had been in existence almost continuously since the Old Regime.

Censorship's impact on literate activities was obvious, both to contemporary observers and to later historians. Legal measures certainly limited the literary marketplace, hence what readers could obtain. In whatever form, preventive or repressive, restrictions on the freedom of expression also affected the freedom of reception in ways that authors have decried from the philosophes onward. Victor Hugo's statements on the subject, both literary and political, are only the most eloquent.[25] And yet protesting readers have been far fewer—the right to read has never been asserted as volubly or as forcefully as the right to express, for reasons that are not hard to imagine. Authors had

---

[21] Cf. Bellanger et al., *Histoire générale de la presse française*, 3:7–60. Cf. Zeldin, *France 1848–1945*, 2:547–51.

[22] See Neil Carruthers, "Theatrical Censorship in Paris from 1850 to 1905," *New Zealand Journal of French Studies* 3 (1982): 21–41.

[23] See Marie-Gaston Guillemet, *Rapport fait au nom de la commission chargée d'examiner les propositions de loi, de M. Antonin Proust, sur la liberté des théâtres . . . [et] de M. Le Senne tendant à obtenir l'abolition de la censure* (1891).

[24] See the *procès-verbaux* in APP BA770–73.

[25] See Odile Krakovitch, *Hugo censuré. La Liberté au théâtre au XIXe siècle* (1985), 20–21, 207–8.

far more at stake, not least of which was their livelihood. But the enforcement of censorship was so inefficient that an underground network of illicit publications provided some readers in France with precisely what they wanted, the authors' property rights notwithstanding. Moreover, the state's attempt to control the press, the book trade, and the stage often inadvertently stimulated demand for a proscribed work. Like the Catholic Church's Index of Prohibited Books, censorship can be an effective means of advertising to certain reading publics, especially those politically opposed to the regime in power. As the economic historian David Landes once noted of nineteenth-century state attempts to protect industrial innovations, intellectual "enterprise like love usually finds ways to laugh at locksmiths."[26]

How well censorship actually succeeded is very difficult to assess. In the absence of comprehensive records, historians know little about enforcement. According to calculations from the most complete catalog of proscribed publications, the number of censored books, journals, and illustrations from 1814 to 1877 varied considerably from regime to regime.[27] The Restoration and July Monarchies, the Second Republic, and the Second Empire, for example, all took legal action against approximately the same number of publications annually (25.6, 19.4, 27.3, and 26, respectively), despite their radically different political principles. On the other hand, in the early years of the Third Republic significantly fewer titles were proscribed per year, 10.4; the administrative apparatus for the repression of printed and illustrated matter had been dismantled. From 1877 to 1914, 182 court cases, less than 5 per year, succeeded against books for their contravention of "les bonnes moeurs."[28] Theater censorship followed a similarly unpredictable pattern. Using data provided by an 1891 inquiry, Odile Krakovitch calculated that fewer than 25 plays were prohibited under the Restoration, while 204 others were prohibited and more than 5 percent modified by the censors under the July Monarchy.[29] After an initial period of severity, the Second Empire banned only about 100 plays, even though more than half of all dramatic works were subject to serious modification before staging. Again the Third Republic practiced erratic surveillance; evidence exists of only 82 prohibited plays between 1871 and 1900, whereas at least 5 percent were interdicted during World War I.[30] The percentage of plays modified throughout the Third Republic was prob-

---

[26] David S. Landes, *The Unbound Prometheus: Technological Change and Industrial Development in Western Europe from 1750 to the Present* (Cambridge, 1969), 131.

[27] Fernand Drujon, *Catalogue des ouvrages, écrits et dessins de toute nature poursuivis, supprimés, ou condamnés depuis le 21 octobre 1814 jusqu'au 31 juillet 1877* (1879).

[28] Calculated from Maurice Garçon, "Les Livres contraires aux bonnes moeurs," *MdF* (15 Aug. 1931): 5–39.

[29] See tables in Krakovitch, *Hugo censuré*, 286–87, based on the author's "La Censure théâtrale de 1830 à 1850," thèse de troisième cycle, Université d'Aix-en-Provence (1979).

[30] See Krakovitch, *Hugo censuré*, 249; AN F18,I*58; and APP BA770–73.

ably extremely high, but the precise number cannot be known in the absence of adequate documentation.

Fluctuations in censorship laws are most predictable with each change of regime. The freedom to express and to receive opinion was promised in every constitutional document from 1789 onward, only to result in new laws restricting it; 1791, 1806, 1819, 1835, 1850, 1852, and 1874 are only the more important dates marking decisive shifts in preventive and repressive censorship.[31] After each period of "license," a period of rigor generally followed, hence the severity evident soon after every revolution. But abrupt changes also occurred at much less dramatic moments; often a cabinet shake-up sufficed. The new Martignac ministry in 1828, for example, meant a pause in the Restoration's concern with liberal political opposition, so long as dramatic works did not touch on religious issues.[32] Rarely was the full rigor of censorship applied evenly, much less fairly, over a sustained period. The Second Empire in particular experienced significant lapses as a consequence of conflicts between the censors and the ministers they served. And so the duc de Morny authorized the staging of *La Dame aux camélias* by Alexandre Dumas *fils*, a personal friend, despite the damning reports written by officials in his own ministry.[33] Similar political differences existed over what should be censored and how throughout the modern period.

Differences in severity also coincided with differences in emphasis. The July Monarchy, for instance, was far more concerned with the discussion of religious issues, particularly where they had political implications, than was the anticlerical Third Republic. Similarly, theater censors were extremely sensitive to the various theaters staging the plays they were assigned to read; the Théâtre français was permitted far greater moral license than the boulevard theaters, largely because of their different audiences.[34] Much of the unevenness in the censorship, of course, may be explained by the laws that almost invariably prescribed preventive censorship for the stage and repressive censorship for the book trade. This legal distinction reflects very practical enforcement considerations; there were far more books published than there were plays staged. Censorship of the press and the theater was administratively feasible in a way that censorship of the book trade was not. Moreover, given the enormous number of published works to police, legal proceedings against books were of necessity much less thorough. This fact resulted in ridiculous trials against some titles, like Baudelaire's *Les Fleurs du mal*, while

[31] Each change in censorship may be traced in J.-B. Duvergier et al., eds., *Collection complète des lois, décrets, ordonnances, et règlements depuis 1788* (1824–1908), 108 vols.

[32] See Hallays-Dabot, *Histoire de la censure théâtrale*, 244–88; and Cahuet, *La Liberté du théâtre*, 182–95.

[33] See reports on *La Dame aux camélias*, 28 Aug., 1 Sept., and 1 Oct., in AN F21,971 d. 1851; and in *La Censure sous Napoléon III. Rapports inédits et in extenso (1852–1860)* (1892), 1–13.

[34] Cf. Maurice Descotes, *Le Public de théâtre et son histoire* (1964), 248.

dozens of more salacious works went unchallenged. Authorities in the nineteenth century moved against fewer than 1,400 published items, including pictures—less than 0.3 percent of all new titles.[35]

IDEOLOGY

From its inception in the Old Regime to World War I, literary censorship has expressed well the political implications of reading in France. Indeed, the very premises on which it was based suggest the politics implicit in nearly all literate activities. Because language can always signify more than its literal meaning, it represents a major source of power in many realms besides literature, especially in France, where culture is frequently disposed to politicization.[36] From 1789 on, each regime justified its restrictions on the freedom of expression, and reception, by indicating the power of new discourses, such as socialism and anarchism, to move an unschooled, uncritical audience to revolutionary action. The perceived dangers of free speech to authority endured. Ironically, both the political left and the right expressed the same concern to control, or at least to modify, the potential impact of speech and print. Once in positions of public responsibility, republicans and socialists argued for political order with the same tenacity that royalists and bonapartists did. The result was the surprisingly widespread acceptance of repressive censorship until well into the twentieth century.

Consequently, despite fluctuations in severity and emphasis, both the principle and the practice of legal restrictions on print remained largely unchanged throughout the period. This historical continuity in attitudes and institutions existed for seven different regimes. As the baron de Pommereul, state counselor, stated in a letter to the minister of police on June 26, 1806, "The more freedom of the press spreads, the more necessary it is for a good police to survey it and to remedy promptly the excesses that legal toleration invites."[37] But more than forty years later, republicans were no less concerned with *licence*, as they stated their overwhelming commitment to some form of censorship in the wake of the 1848 Revolution. A parliamentary inquiry of 1849 reaffirmed this perspective and prepared the ground for the 1850 law on the press and the stage, one maintained and strengthened under the Second Empire.[38] Even the 1881 law freeing the press from the worst abuses of previous regimes contained provisions for the prosecution of authors and publishers for

---

[35] Calculated from Drujon, *Catalogue des ouvrages, écrits et dessins.*

[36] Cf. Ferdinand Brunot, *Histoire de la langue française des origines à 1900* (1966–68), vols. 9–10; Jean-Pol Caput, *La Langue française. Histoire d'une institution* (1975), vol. 3; François Furet, *Interpreting the Revolution*, trans. Elborg Forster (Cambridge, 1981), 81–131; and Lynn Hunt, *Politics, Culture, and Class in the French Revolution* (Berkeley, 1984), 19–119.

[37] "Rapport à Son Excellence le Sénateur, Ministre de la Police Générale de l'Empire," 26 June 1806, in AN F18,39.

[38] Conseil d'État, *Enquête et documents officiels sur les théâtres.*

libel (articles 30 and 31) and for "les outrages aux bonnes moeurs" (article 28); future court cases were based on elastic definitions of what constitutes slander and morality (and the political order they imply).[39] Throughout the Third Republic, the assumption remained that, for better or worse, print exerted too powerful an influence on the reader to go unchecked.

The apparent impact of the printed word on the reader underlies the development of a distinct ideology in modern France: the firm belief in intellectual order in otherwise rapidly changing historical circumstances. While shared by a wide range of political thought, this pervasive principle meant the extension of public authority over textual reception, despite the resulting contradictions in such an attempt by republicans and socialists alike; and it informed the interpretive predispositions of ruling elites in every regime from 1800 to 1940. The same tendency to control a presumed readership, to be sure, existed in other periods of French history—in fact, for as long as censorship existed. Nor did this particular trend disappear in the twentieth century (when there was an efficient and effective political apparatus to enforce it in periods of national emergency). But this ideological perspective was never expressed as clearly or as pervasively in interpretive practice as in the nineteenth century. The cultural hegemony of new ruling elites colored the reception of print most obviously in the law, but also in the way in which it was applied by the authorities responsible for its enforcement—the censors themselves.[40]

An ideology of political control over literary reception appears clearly in the censors' reports. Written in the government offices charged with monitoring the book trade and censoring the stage, these sources, most of them archival, express an ideological myopia even more exaggerated than the one apparent in sources concerning the press.[41] The reports seem extremely petty in their sensitivity to minor political events or issues barely mentioned even in the most detailed histories of France. One censor during the Restoration, for example, deleted mention of a popular salad known as the "monk's beard" because of its apparent attack on monastic life.[42] Similarly, every assassination attempt on Louis-Philippe's life loomed large in Interior Ministry reports.[43]

But this attention to unremarkable minutia obscures a historical trend in the

[39] Garçon, "Les Livres contraires aux bonnes moeurs."

[40] See Martyn Lyons, Le Triomphe du livre. Une Histoire sociologique de la lecture dans la France du XIXe siècle (1987), 145–68, a variation on Eugen Weber, Peasants into Frenchmen: The Modernization of Rural France, 1870–1914 (Stanford, 1976), 485–96. Cf. Hallays-Dabot, La Censure dramatique et le théâtre, 100–112, and the report on Schiller's Guillaume Tell, 17 Jan. 1828, in AN AJ13,1050, Liasse 3, d. Th. de la Gaîté.

[41] See AN F18,312–425 and 431–514. Of special significance to administrative censorship of the press are F18,412 d. RdDM, a literary review; F18,400 d. Le Pays, a political newspaper; and F18,402 d. Le Petit Républicain, a popular newspaper.

[42] See Odile Krakovitch, Les Pièces de théâtre soumises à la censure (1800–1830). Inventaire des manuscrits de pièces (F18,581 à 668) et des procès-verbaux de censures (F21,966 à 995) (1982), 34.

[43] See Krakovitch, Hugo censuré, 99–156.

censors' concerns. Whereas the Consulate and First Empire focused almost exclusively on political problems raised by the anticipated responses of readers to certain texts, later regimes broadened their attention to the religious, social, and moral problems of these responses. As long as censorship remained a fact of French intellectual life, the authorities tended to add more and more taboos in their quest ultimately to control the way in which French audiences read books and viewed plays.

Reports written during the Consulate indicate how exclusively political considerations affected reading in the Newspaper Bureau of the Prefecture of Police (see Table 3.1).[44] One title in particular generated four careful examinations, because of its treatment of recent counterrevolutionary activity in the Vendée. *L'Origine de la chouannerie*, published in 1802, portrayed the unsuccessful attempt by English and French royalists to destroy the First Republic. What saved this historical novel from prosecution was its fulsome praise for Napoleon Bonaparte's role in bringing an end to this civil unrest.[45] Similarly, *Charles, ou Les Mémoires de Mr. Labussière* skirted controversial po-

TABLE 3.1

Official Reasons for the Interdiction or Modification of Sampled Censorship Cases in France, 1799–1940

Regime	Challenges to political/ social authority		Challenges to moral order		Other reasons		Total no.
	$\%^a$	N^b	$\%^a$	N^b	$\%^a$	N^b	
Consulate (1799–1804)	92	12	0	0	8	1	13
First Empire (1804–1814/15)	84	32	8	3	8	3	38
Restoration (1814/15–1830)	66	31	34	16	0	0	47
July Monarchy (1830–48)	65	13	35	7	0	0	20
Second Republic (1848–51)	67	4	33	2	0	0	6
Second Empire (1851–70)	47	62	50	66	3	4	132
Third Republic (1870–1940)	17	20	62	75	21	25	120

Sources: AN AJ13,1050; BB18,1010/1112/1166/1742/1800–1; BB21,631; F18,39; F18,40; F18,511–555; and F21,966–995. BN NAFr 5001–5002. Anon., *La Censure sous Napoléon III. Rapports inédits et in extenso (1852–1860)* (1892). France, Commission chargée de réunir, classer et publier les papiers saisis aux Tuileries, *Papiers secrets du Second Empire* (Brussels, 1871), 1:pt. 3, 36–50. Alexandre Zévaès, *Les Procès littéraires au XIXe siècle* (1924). APP BA770–773.

[a] Percentage of all works whose censor reports were sampled within a period.

[b] Number of works whose censor reports were sampled within a period.

[44] See the dossiers in AN F18,39.

[45] Conseiller d'État, Préfet de Police au Grand Juge et Ministre de la Justice, le 10 thermidor an 11, in AN F18,39, no. 32.

litical issues by glorifying the First Consul. One police official commented, "The work is otherwise too poor to endanger public tranquility in any way."[46] Lists of other publications considered briefly by the police, many of them popular stories contained in almanacs, merited little mention despite extremely suggestive titles—*La Toilette de Vénus* and *Le Premier plaisir, ou La Curiosité des filles*, for example.[47] As for *Théophile de Solincourt, ou La Vertu sacrifiée*, another official remarked, "This novel comprises nothing that is contrary to sound moral principles"; this meant that there were no political references to affect readers.[48]

The archival sources left from the First Empire provide a still better view of relatively narrow official concerns.[49] The style of reading did not change substantially, even if the number of reports on a variety of titles did. Every reading sampled from the records of the police and the Interior Ministry concerned the political implications of literature during the Empire. Most of the 38 documented cases were censored for explicit challenges to public authority. Thirty-two of the titles included accounts of officials, the military especially, in compromising situations. Commented one reader of *Adrienne et Maurice*, a comedy whose performance was refused authorization on September 10, 1809, "To put on stage a famous man [the maréchal de Saxe], whose glory is associated with that of France, is not to depict his secret sins or to misrepresent him so by having him play such a role."[50] Four of these titles were criticized in particular for their treatment of military conscription and its consequences.[51] Similarly, a novel by Regnault-Warin, *L'Homme au masque de fer*, included a long "moral testament" by the author on the dangers of political ambition. The officials responded by authorizing the work for export, "under the custom service's lead seal," to a safer audience in the German states.[52]

The official readers of the First Empire were also troubled by specific political issues. They censored at least six works for royalist sympathies and another three for promoting civil and social disorder.[53] This response was char-

---

[46] Conseiller d'État, Préfet de Police au Grand Juge et Ministre de la Justice, le 15 vendemiaire an 12, in AN F18,39, no. 74.

[47] Conseiller d'État, Préfet de Police au Grand Juge et Ministre de la Justice, le 25 messidor an 11, in AN F18,39, no. 5.L.

[48] Conseiller d'État, Préfet de Police au Grand Juge et Ministre de la Justice, le 27 messidor an 11, in AN F18,39, no. 13.

[49] Besides dossiers in AN AJ13,1050 and AN F18,39, see others pertinent to First Empire censorship in AN F18,40; AN F21,966–95; BN NAFr 5001–02; and BN NAFr 10739.

[50] Rapport, *Adrienne et Maurice*, 10 Sept., in AN F21,966 d. 1809.

[51] See Rapport, *Le Milicien* (1809), in AN AJ13,1050 Liasse 3, d. Th. de l'Opéra; *Les Amours généreux*, in AN F21,967 d. 1809; and *Herman et Verner, ou Les Militaires*, in AN F21,966 d. 1814. Cf. the report on *Bayard à Rebec* (1814) in AN AJ13,1050 Liasse 3, d. Th. de l'Impératrice.

[52] Rapport, Bureau des Journaux au Citoyen Grand Juge, Ministre de la Justice, le 28 ventôse [an 12]; Conseiller d'État, le 22 ventôse an 12; and Rapport, le 3 germinal an 12; in AN F18,39.

[53] See reports on *Six mois d'exil, ou Les Orphelins par la Révolution*, le 17 frimaire an 13, in

acteristic of the Empire in its first years, when the regime's legitimacy remained unclear. Three verses from a play published in 1804, *Rienzi*, particularly alarmed the police for obvious political reasons. Speaking of Cola di Rienzo, the medieval Roman senator, one character states, "His superb attire is that of a monarch; / From the people, indeed the very lowest, / He has made himself a noble figure."[54] This was all too much like the French emperor. Because of changes in foreign relations, authorities also required the modification or the prosecution of six other titles, including Madame de Staël's *De l'Allemagne* in 1810, the best-known case in the period. Madame de Staël reports in her memoirs the official reasons for the banning of her book, which never even mentioned the Empire: "Do you think, said then the minister [of police], that we have been at war for eighteen years in Germany for so well known a person to publish a book without speaking of us?"[55] Less well known but no less indicative of the political fears harbored by imperial authorities is the report written by L.C.J. de Manne on *Les Beautés de Pope*. In 1813, some overly zealous official apparently felt it necessary, in light of long-standing hostilities between France and England, to have assessed the political implications of an English poet who had died in 1744.[56]

The fall of the First Empire in 1814 and its brief revival in 1815 did not alter significantly the way in which officials read. The concern with order and authority remained, especially for three censors who continued their work in the Interior Ministry under the new regime: A.-F. Villemain, P.-E. Lemontey, and J.-C.-D. Lacretelle.[57] Of 47 cases sampled from the large corpus of available documentation, two-thirds merited revision or interdiction during the Bourbon Restoration for challenges to political or social authority. The "White Terror" in the regime's first years made officials particularly sensitive to the dangers of literary license. For example, a one-act comedy proposed for the Théâtre de l'Odéon in 1814, *L'Heureux Changement*, constituted a biting satire against Napoleon Bonaparte that the theater censors could not accept; "such matter cannot be put before assembled spectators without danger; . . . the spectacle of a military coward, of a marriage made by order of the tyrant *Bataléon* [i.e., Napoléon], is not suited to avoid stirring passionate feelings."[58] The activities of political extremists alerted censors to the threats to

---

AN F18,39; and *Le Pardon généreux, ou La Lettre brulée*, n.d., in AN AJ13,1050 Liasse 3, d. Th. de Marais.

[54] Rapport, *Rienzi*, le 28 vendemiaire an 13, in AN F18,39.

[55] Germaine de Staël, *Mémoires de Madame de Staël (Dix années d'exil)* (1840), 229. Cf. duc de Rovigo to Mme. de Staël, 3 Oct. 1810, in *Madame de Staël, ses amis et ses correspondants. Choix de lettres (1778–1817)*, ed. Georges Solovieff (1970), 406.

[56] Rapport, *Les Beautés de Pope*, in BN NAFr 10739 fols. 133–34. Cf. L.C.J. de Manne's response to Brachier's *Tableau, ou Description de la Russie*, in BN NAFr 10739 fols. 110–11.

[57] See M. Berthelot et al., *La Grande Encyclopédie* (n.d.), 21:722–23, 1200.

[58] Rapport, *L'Heureux Changement*, 21 April 1814, in AN AJ13,1050 Liasse 3, d. Th. de

royalty posed by the effects of historical dramas set in earlier centuries.[59] Similarly, Béranger was prosecuted three times for his songs, which contained little more than some effective irony aimed at royalist officials and institutions. The third trial resulted in Béranger's incarceration for nine months and a fine of 10,000 francs, a sum equivalent to the interior minister's generous annual salary.[60]

In time, however, Restoration censorship's attempts to reduce civil conflict between factions broadened to include closely related religious, social, and literary issues. The first explicit directives that the theater censors received to guide their work in 1823 prohibited all allusions whatsoever to the church or its personnel, ritual, doctrine, and paraphernalia.[61] Consequently, the Interior Ministry censored at least six of the works whose cases constitute the Restoration sample. *Amy Robsart*, written by Hugo for Paul Foucher in 1827, is only one of several Restoration plays whose authorization was delayed and then suspended for its reputed profanation of faith by placing ecclesiastical figures on the stage.[62] But the official readers were perhaps less petty in their consideration of the political disruption implicit in literature; literary challenges to social authorities endangered what was considered a clear and natural hierarchy.[63] Literary works were expected to show the popular classes, youth, and women in appropriate submission to their presumed social betters, that is, to nobles, elders, and men, respectively. *Bertrain, ou Le Château de St. Aldobrand*, translated from the play by Charles Maturin in 1828, exemplifies this particular threat. Because this work's plot turns on the outrageous behavior of a young man towards a landed notable who had forced the youth's mistress to marry him, the officials found the play absolutely repugnant.

> Gathered here practically without artistic merit are plunder, murder, adultery, insanity, and suicide, that if not sanctioned are at least presented with the intention of making them interesting. . . . Indignation and disgust are the sole impressions that a reading of such extravagant acts can engender.[64]

l'Odéon. Cf. the report on *Le Siège, ou Le Maire de Rouen*, 4 Aug. 1814, in AN F21,966 d. 1814.

[59] See reports on *Henry quatre et Mayenne, ou Le Bien et le mal*, in AN F21,966 d. 1815; and on *Les États de Blois* (1814, 1820), in AN AJ13,1050 Liasse 3, d. Th. Français.

[60] Besides Béranger's legal dossier, in AN BB18,1010, see P.-J. de Béranger, *Ma biographie* (1857), 199–207; and *Le Procés fait aux chansons de P.-J. de Béranger* (1821).

[61] Cf. reports on *La Reine de Portugal*, 9 May 1823, in AN AJ13,1050 Liasse 3, d. Th. de l'Odéon; and on *Les Visitandines*, 15 June 1814, in AN AJ13,1050 Liasse 3, d. Opéra-Comique.

[62] See Rapport, *Amy Robsart*, in AN F21,967 d. 1827. Authorized initially, this play created a scandal at its only performance on 13 Feb. 1828 at the Odéon.

[63] See reports on *Louis I, ou Le Fanatisme au 9e siècle*, 30 Oct. and 3 Nov. 1824, in AN AJ13,1050 Liasse 3, d. Th. de l'Odéon.

[64] Rapport, *Bertrain, ou Le Château de St. Aldobrand*, 18 May 1828, in AN AJ13,1050 Liasse 3, d. Th. Anglais.

Generally quite circumspect, censors used such language only for the worst cases—and of course for the romantics, their literary *bêtes noires* on the eve of the July Revolution.[65]

The Orleanist Monarchy enlarged considerably this new sensitivity to the political ramifications of print. Literate audiences had to be protected even before the 1835 laws reimposed preventive censorship on the press and the stage. According to Krakovitch's thorough examination of theater censor archives left from the July Monarchy, more than 48 percent were explicitly concerned with politics.[66] Besides the issues of authority and order, the regime was particularly careful with works that seemed to question its political legitimacy.[67] This trend appears in thirteen of the twenty items sampled for the present study. The authors of *Le Testament*, for example, had to change a passage in which the king became a mere "monsieur."[68] In 1836, the theater censors requested substantial modifications in another comedy based on the reluctant transfer of political power in an anonymous Swiss canton. For Florent, Haussmann, and Perrot, who signed the report, "This play . . . contains some sarcasms against men in power," not in Switzerland but in France. "The names are those of honorable men who could complain of seeing themselves thus given up to ridicule on the stage." And so in deference to this very special audience, all the names had to be changed.[69] Another play submitted in 1842, *Les Prétendants, ou Les Glinets de 1840*, ridiculed functionaries loyal to the regime and seemed likely to cause a scandal. It was accepted only after the author had modified the language and moved the setting to Scotland.[70]

But the principal innovation of official reading in the July Monarchy was not so much the interest in attacks on the regime's political legitimacy; this had been important in both the First Empire and the Restoration. Rather, it arose from the authorities' increasing moral scruples. Officials especially feared unrest among easily excitable audiences—for instance, at the Odéon, which was frequented by unruly students from the nearby schools of law and medicine. Thirty-five percent of the sampled reports thus impugned the "morality" of literary works challenging established social institutions and conventional behavior.[71] Using a plot resembling that of Beaumarchais's *Le Mariage de Figaro*, a play submitted to the Théâtre français in 1838 presented a licentious aristocrat, "a blond woman with bare arms, / A hundred times more

[65] See Hallays-Dabot, *Histoire de la censure théâtrale*, 287–88.

[66] See Krakovitch, *Hugo censuré*, 69–204, 286–87.

[67] See the reports on *Une Nuit de Cromwel* [sic], 3 Mar., and on *Sardanaple*, n.d., both in AN F21,967 d. 1843.

[68] Rapport, *Le Testament*, 24 Dec., in AN F21,966 d. 1835.

[69] Rapport, *Les Adieux au pouvoir*, n.d., in AN F21,967 d. 1836.

[70] Rapports, *Les Prétendants, ou Les Glinets de 1840*, 15 and 16 April 1842, in AN F21,967 d. 1842.

[71] E.g., reports on *Le Camp des croisés*, 25 Jan., in AN F21,967 d. 1838; on *L'Hôtel d'Alban*, 27 Oct., in AN F21,967 d. 1843; on *Bianca Capello*, 8 Feb., in AN F21,967 d. 1842.

ardent than Madame Venus, / Mad for pleasure otherwise destroyed by moral scruple.'' Commented the report on the play signed by all four censors, ''The boldness of the details, in each case, aggravates what is in essence merely suggestive in the action.''[72] The ostensible reason for refusing authorization was its view of an irresponsible social class in England remarkably similar to Louis-Philippe's supporters in France. Although Krakovitch found a far larger proportion of such reports in her survey, the same relationship between morality and social order was apparent. Any threat to established convention, even a literary one, earned the censors' disapprobation—hence the well-documented problems that the censors posed to the staging of plays by romantic authors. Like Alfred de Musset, they were often accused of ''fairly improper scenes, very embarrassing plots, and some suggestive passages'' likely to provoke a public scandal.[73]

Unrest on the eve of the 1848 Revolution meant a return to politics per se; the regime's last censor reports simply responded to the new political climate and the new ways in which audiences could be influenced. But the Revolution itself brought an end to official readings of literary works during the Second Republic until the 1850 law reinstated legal controls on expression and reception. The few reports that exist from the last year of the Republic, however, reflect the same ideological predispositions expressed by authorities during the previous regime. Unfortunately, the archival sample is too small for more than a few glimpses of this trend. Four of the six reports censored literary works for their more or less explicit challenge to political and social authority, while the two other works were objectionable because of their violation of the prevailing bourgeois moral order.[74] The reading of *Une Fille de France*, a play proposed for the Théâtre français in August 1850, is an apt illustration. This account of the curious intrigue between the duchesse de Berri and the chevalier de Riom annoyed four censors; they demanded that the chevalier's liaison with another woman, the marquise de Mouchy, be suppressed, just as they insisted on a new title: ''By its general nature, [the title] projects on all women of royal blood the odium that history attaches to the duchesse de Berri's exceptional character.''[75] For these readers, the dangers of royalism were far less important than were those of improper behavior on the part of a prominent social class.

By the beginning of the Second Empire, political authority, social order, and literary morality had become inseparable in the minds of officials respon-

[72] Rapport, *Le Ménestrel*, 15 July 1838, in AN F21,966 d. 1838.

[73] Rapport, *Un Caprice*, 26 Nov., in AN F21,966 d. 1847. Cf. Krakovitch, *Hugo censuré*, 15–26.

[74] On politics, see the report on *Les Batons crottans, ou L'École du pouvoir*, 2 Nov., in AN F21,966 d. 1850; on social conflicts, *Le Paysan aujourd'hui*, 8 Jan., in AN F21,967 d. 1851; and on morality, *La Dame aux camélias*, whose dossier is cited in note 33 above.

[75] Rapport, *Une Fille de France*, 26 Aug., in AN F21,966 d. 1850.

sible for preventive and repressive censorship.[76] This broadened sensitivity seemed to mark the establishment of the implicit ideology of audience control that had developed since the Consulate more than fifty years earlier. As stated in the report on Émile Augier's *Le Fils de Giboyer* in 1862,

> A play's interdiction finds its rationale, generally, in four different concerns: (1) the interest of public morality; (2) the interest of social order and government policies; (3) the interest of religion; (4) finally, propriety and taste in allusions to persons and things.[77]

For the first time, after five different regimes, the administrative guidelines for one form of censorship had been set down clearly. But the sources of objection now included immorality.[78] Consequently, exactly one-half of the 132 cases sampled for the Second Empire represented challenges to the established moral order. For Second Empire censorship, politics touched nearly all aspects of literary creation, from almanacs for peasants to poetry for Parisian literati.[79] All genres were reviewed by an impressive bureaucracy of surveillance and control that left extensive records of its official responses in the new political climate.

Besides the censor reports on play manuscripts submitted for authorization—many of them published during the Third Republic—the better-known prosecutions of the Goncourts, Flaubert, and of course Baudelaire reflect this larger ideological context assumed by both the state and the audiences affected by it. For example, Jules and Edmond de Goncourt were tried for an article reproducing five lines by Jacques Tahureau, a sixteenth-century poet. Sensing the futility of a rigorous argument, the defense attorney never questioned the legal or literary grounds of the prosecution; instead, he pleaded the extenuating circumstances of the authors' extreme youth.[80] Similarly, the attorneys defending both Flaubert and Baudelaire actually argued from the same ideological perspective as the prosecution. The works, they contended, were use-

---

[76] Besides the dossiers in AN F21,966–95 and AJ13,1050, see *La Censure sous Napoléon III*; Commission chargée de réunir, classer et publier les papiers saisis aux Tuileries, *Papiers secrets du Second Empire* (Brussels, 1871), vol. 1, pt. 3:36–50; Commission du colportage, 1852–60, AN F18,551–55; AN BB24,494–99 d. S.56.4409 on Montépin's *La Fille de plâtre*; and AN BB18,1742 d. 6006 on Veuillot's *Les Ordures de Paris*.

[77] Rapport, *Le Fils de Giboyer*, 3 Oct., in AN F21,966 d. 1862, no. 6456. Cf. Rapport, *Corr. du baron Grimm*, 2 April 1813, in BN NAFr 5002, item 39.

[78] On politics, see reports on *Ne parlons pas politique!* 5 Mar., in AN F21,996 d. 1868; on social disorder in *Diane de Lys*, 10 Jan., in AN F21,973 d. 1853 (also in *La Censure sous Napoléon III*, 37–38); and on morality in *L'Étrangère*, 8 Oct., in AN F21,973 d. 1864 (also in *La Censure sous Napoléon III*, 251–53).

[79] See AN F18,551–55 for similar concerns expressed by the Second Empire's Commission de Colportage, in Jean-Jacques Darmon, *Le Colportage de librairie en France sous le Second Empire. Grands Colporteurs et culture populaire* (1972), 296–98.

[80] See Edmond and Jules de Goncourt, *Journal. Mémoires de la vie littéraire*, ed. Robert Ricatte (Monaco, 1956–58), 1:89–101.

ful illustrations of the implicit political danger inherent in all challenges to middle-class morality. Both men were serious and upstanding citizens; far from indulging in scandalous situations or images for their own sake, they had created serious intellectual works aimed at the moral instruction of their readership.[81] Asked Chaix d'Est-Ange during Baudelaire's trial, "How is it a mistake and above all how can it be a crime, if in order to stigmatize evil [the poet] exaggerates it, if he paints vice in vigorous and striking tones, because he wants to inspire in you a more profound hatred?"[82] The poet's conviction is owed, in part at least, to the difficulty of basing such an argument on imagery as protean as Baudelaire's. His poetry did not resemble Flaubert's apparently more straightforward "morality tale" of a young woman tragically deluded by her reading into adultery and suicide. For readers in Second Empire France—and elsewhere for that matter—poetry was more problematic than fiction.[83]

The ideological implications of official (and unofficial) reading during the Second Empire are perhaps less obvious than its rampant hypocrisy. What the censors considered safe for bourgeois audiences at the Théâtre français was too dangerous for a more plebeian clientele at the boulevard theaters. A long published report on Victorien Sardou's *La Poudre d'or*, proposed for the popular Théâtre de La Gaîté, suggests the political implications of literary morality, at least as the censors perceived them. Posing as "a man of the world," the central character Pougnasse

> jests over theft, he banters about murder, he sports with blood; in a word, this is an odious fellow, all the more revolting when he is cynically accepted and when it would be dangerous for us to put him back on the popular stage, after Robert Macaire has been chased from it and where Chopart is only tolerated with regret.[84]

This literary challenge to political, social, and moral order posed too great a threat to the regime's authority, as did many other works read by officials within the Second Empire's ideological context. The Empire's failure to police as effectively the works intended for other audiences simply points up the allegiance it claimed from these other social classes, an allegiance it would lose by 1870.[85]

---

[81] See Maxime Du Camp, *Souvenirs littéraires* (1892), 2:139–55; and the trial briefs in Gustave Flaubert, *Madame Bovary*, ed. Edouard Maynial (Garnier frères edition, n.d.), 325–99. Cf. André Pasquet, *Ernest Pinard et le procès de Madame Bovary* (1949). On Baudelaire's case, see notes 1 and 2 above; the court briefs in Baudelaire, *Oeuvres complètes: Les Fleurs du mal*, ed. Jacques Crépet (1930), 330–56; and Baudelaire's dossier in AN BB21,633.

[82] Cited in Baudelaire, *Oeuvres complètes*, p. 337.

[83] Cf. Dominick LaCapra, *"Madame Bovary" on Trial* (Ithaca, 1982), 15–22; AN F18,411 d. *Revue de Paris* (9); and Ernest Pinard, *Mon journal* (1892), 1:48–59.

[84] Rapport, *La Poudre d'or*, n.d., in AN F21,977 d. Th. de la Gaîté.

[85] See J. M. Thompson, *Louis Napoleon and the Second Empire* (New York, 1955), 224–54; Theodore Zeldin, *The Political System of Napoleon III* (New York, 1958), 135–42; and Sanford

The motives of the Third Republic's censorship are much more difficult to document. From 1866 onward, the officials responsible for preliminary readings of plays staged in Paris preferred to speak directly with playwrights and theater directors rather than to record their responses to the manuscripts. Even though at least 82 plays were interdicted from 1871 to 1900, few records of them exist.[86] More than 25 of these interdictions occurred before 1874 and reflected a predictable political sensitivity to the aftermath of the Franco-Prussian War and the Paris Commune. But the prosecution of published titles provides ample evidence of new emphases in official readings. All ten sampled cases dealt explicitly with literary immorality. Their moral concerns were often far removed from the political implications evident in the official readings recorded during the previous regime. For example, the excessive touchiness of the "Moral Order" resulted in the ludicrous prosecution of Jean de La Fontaine's stories in 1875. After 1881, despite the provisions of article 28 in the new press law, prosecution of immoral literature faded somewhat.[87] The link perceived between morality and politics seems to have weakened (the number of censorship cases dropped off remarkably towards the end of the century), only to revive on the eve of World War I. At no time, however, did the freedom of reception become an ideological principle acceptable to the *nouvelles couches sociales.* In France's historically most enduring constitutional compromise, from 1870 to 1940, the political context of reading may have changed, but not the predisposition of public authorities to control reception.

The Great War marked an illuminating exception to the paucity of records on censorship after 1870.[88] Notwithstanding the obvious threat to the French state posed by the German invasion in 1914, the principal motives for the preventive measures taken against plays and songs were not political or even war-related, but moral. In 75 of 110 sampled cases, the police censors focused on the problems posed by obscene language and action, such as those indicated in the reports on the bawdy vaudeville *Vous n'avez rien à déclarer?* by Maurice Hennequin and Pierre Weber. This work had first been staged in 1906 at the Théâtre des Nouveautés, but was prohibited in 1915 at La Gaîté until the authors modified the play's offending dialogue and indecent situations. The only ostensible connection between this modest pornography and the French war effort appeared in a letter to the prefect of police written by the

---

Elwitt, *The Making of the Third Republic: Class and Politics in France, 1868–1884* (Baton Rouge, 1975), 19–52.

[86] These figures were compiled from AN F18,I*58; and Krakovitch, *Hugo censuré*, 245–66.

[87] See Zévaès, *Les Procès littéraires au XIXe siècle*, 175–80; and the prosecutor's reading of Jean Richepin's *Les Caresses*, 7 Mar. 1877, in AN BB18,1800–1 d. 497–A.77.

[88] Note the law of 5 Aug. 1914, in Émile Mermet et al., eds., *Annuaire de la presse* (1915), 37. Hence the procès-verbaux on plays, songs, newspapers, and letters in APP BA770–73; APP BA697–736; APP BA744–48; APP BA755–64; AMG 7N 952; and AMG 7N 979–1001.

director of the *Correspondance d'union républicaine*: "At this tragic hour in which we live, it is scandalous to see brothel scenes specially offered at our theaters. . . . What must foreigners think of us?"[89] It is clear, at least from the concern with public morality expressed by the police censors, that the free reception of literary expression, even in wartime, stopped at obscenity. Ironically, World War I saw the end of a century-long trend in the ideology of modern French censorship; in effect, wartime censorship marked the triumph of concern with moral order over, or perhaps as a disguise for, the interests of political authority.

COMMUNITIES

The legal and ideological setting of reading in modern France was complemented by another aspect of literate politics: interpretive communities.[90] No less important for its relative obscurity, this third political feature of reception was the influential role played by the social groups and institutions to which readers belonged. French readers responded to literature in a manner appropriate to the milieu informed by changing laws and climates of political opinion; they also responded within another milieu shaped by networks of officials, authors, critics, publishers, schools, churches, friends, and family. Few readers experienced print as isolated atoms. In place of the well-defined roles played by public authorities in the Old Régime, modern communities of reception tended to be less formal, but also more numerous and more pervasive; an individual reader may have participated in many different, loosely connected, overlapping networks. The resulting influences and their accommodation constituted a form of politics, one no less real for its conflicts and relative diffusion, as Baudelaire's efforts to affect the outcome of his trial indicate. Here the historical context of the interaction between reader and text worked at a more particularistic level that was no less important to the way in which many new readers shared in a rapidly growing literate culture.

Censors formed one of the more obvious interpretive communities in the nineteenth century. Not only were their ideological concerns reflected in their sensitive readings over a long period; but they also constituted a relatively stable and homogeneous group of men. Censors often survived from regime to regime. It was common practice for new governments to retain lower-level

[89] Rapport, 22 April 1915, *Vous n'avez rien à déclarer?* in APP BA770, item 669. Cf. Rapport, "Le Beau Grenadier, ou Mon fusil," 30 Mar. 1915, in APP BA697 d. 1; and Rapport, *La Cigale rechantée*, 18 April 1919, in APP BA773, item 3786.

[90] See Stanley Fish, *Is There a Text in This Class? The Authority of Interpretive Communities* (Cambridge, Mass., 1980), 1–17. Cf. Maurice Agulhon, *Le Cercle dans la France bourgeoise 1810–1848. Étude d'une mutation de sociabilité* (1977), 73–80; Elihu Katz and Paul F. Lazarsfeld, *Personal Influence: The Part Played by People in the Flow of Mass Communications* (New York, 1955), 1–133; and Morris Rosenberg and Ralph H. Turner, eds., *Social Psychology: Sociological Perspectives* (New York, 1981), 66–93, 320–43, 653–82.

functionaries in many ministries, including the theater censors in the Ministry of Justice during the Consulate and First Empire, in the Ministry of the Interior from the Restoration to the Third Republic, or in the Ministry of the Emperor's Household during the latter half of the Second Empire. Jacques-Louis Florent, for instance, served almost continuously in the Interior Ministry for no fewer than three different regimes, from the July Monarchy to the Second Empire. Despite dramatic political change, his persistence resembled that of other ministerial personnel in the same period, whose positions remained so long as their functions remained.[91] The roster of censors throughout the nineteenth century numbers less than 50 men loyal to different conceptions of political, social, and moral order. Thus the bureaucratic structure itself defined one reading network as it implemented the policies of very different regimes.[92]

For whatever reason, however, censors resigned and new personnel were hired, a fact that in time changed their community. Literary censors under the First Empire and the Restoration, for example, differed considerably from those of subsequent regimes. The former were literary figures in their own right, often with their own well-developed sense of critical judgment. Early in the Bourbon Restoration, L.C.J. de Manne and A.-F. Villemain, among other imposing figures, read officially in the Interior Ministry; and their intelligent reports often show shrewd literary insight.[93] Their opposition to the romantics, for instance, stemmed from a rigorous classical education reflected in the Latin marginalia that they inscribed on several reports. They were quite unlike L.-T. Perrot, J.-L. Florent, and their colleagues in the July Monarchy, who were much more obsequious bureaucratic figures with no substantial literary standing of their own. Their successors in the Second Empire and Third Republic remained minor figures, however influential in the literary world because of their administrative responsibilities. The aggressively apologetic tone of two books by Victor Hallays-Dabot, an official reader during the Second Empire, suggests the kind of men who enforced censorship after 1850.[94] In light of these changes in the community of public functionaries, one can understand why censorship grew more moralistic and less critical by the end of the nineteenth century.

The censors were not alone as a social group sharing common textual predispositions. An even better known community certainly existed among Pari-

[91] Note that no article on Florent appears in the standard biographical dictionaries in or on the nineteenth century.

[92] See Michel Crozier, *The Bureaucratic Phenomenon* (Chicago, 1964), 213–93; and idem, *The Stalled Society* (New York, 1973), 77–107.

[93] L.C.J. de Manne wrote at least one book and edited another by the end of his life, according the BN catalog. See Gabriel Vauthier, *Villemain, 1790–1870. Essai sur sa vie, son rôle et ses ouvrages* (1913).

[94] See Hallays-Dabot, *Histoire de la censure théâtrale*; and idem, *La Censure dramatique et le théâtre*.

sian authors. Like the correspondence discussed in Chapter 2, most sources on literate life in modern France underscore its relatively small and centralized republic of letters. The journals and memoirs written in the nineteenth and twentieth centuries nearly all indicate to what extent professional networks affected the reading of French literature. During the First Empire, Madame de Staël and Benjamin Constant collected around them the leading literati of Europe in opposition to Napoleon. The intimacy of their literary activities is reflected in their accounts of life shaped by a common social background as well as by a common political outlook.[95] Similarly, Stendhal noted the small circle of writers closely intertwined with polite Parisian society during the Empire and the Restoration. Much of his ambivalence towards a career in literature appears in the limited success of his works, but also in his marginal social standing in the leading literary salons of his day.[96] Chateaubriand's famous memoirs, on the other hand, indicate a much larger and more prominent circle of social acquaintances, as many as thirty-five of whom appeared regularly at the readings of his work-in-progress at Madame Récamier's salon at the Abbaye-aux-Bois. While the fawning attention of these acquaintances may not have been as intense as Sainte-Beuve described it, this contemporary perception certainly owed much to an extensive personal network during the Restoration and July Monarchies.[97]

Years later, as if to counter this social intrusion into literary reception, Flaubert retreated into a far smaller circle of friends and family who appreciated his meticulous attention to creation. At times he seemed to have been writing for a private audience of one, his look-alike alter ego, Louis Bouilhet, who each Sunday heard Flaubert read successive drafts and who suggested revisions with a candor possible only among close personal relations.[98] Similarly, for the Goncourt brothers, literature was the occasion for personal interaction with others in Parisian cafés, restaurants, salons, and clubs. Their snide, often bitter remarks about fellow writers and their relative success, however, reflect the influence of their direct acquaintance with a rapidly growing literate world.[99] The society of Parisian authors had expanded, and with it the networks of textual interpretation. The more controversial issues arising from

[95] See Germaine de Staël, *Mémoires de Madame de Staël*; *Madame de Staël, ses amis, ses correspondants*; Benjamin Constant, *Journaux intimes*, ed. Alfred Moulin and Charles Roth (1952); and the fictionalized relationship presented in Benjamin Constant *Adolphe* (1965), 51–176.

[96] See Stendhal, *Oeuvres intimes*, ed. Henri Martineau (1955), 1:64–65, 2:447–52.

[97] Cf. C.-A. Sainte-Beuve, "Poètes modernes de la France. XI. Chateaubriand. Mémoires," *RdDM* (15 April 1834): 209–12; and Chateaubriand, *Mémoires d'outre-tombe*, ed. Maurice Levaillant and Charles Moulinier (1946–48), 1:445–47.

[98] On Bouilhet, see Benjamin Bart, "Louis Bouilhet, Flaubert's 'accoucheur,'" *Symposium* 17 (1963): 183–202.

[99] E.g., the Goncourt dinners at Magny's recounted in their *Journal*, 5:204, 217; 6:36, 42, 120, 125, passim.

literary experimentation in the period moved still more writers into tighter circles of like-minded literati. The romantic *cénacles* gathered around Nodier, Hugo, and Gautier were replicated under new circumstances by the parnassians, the naturalists, and the symbolists, a development often resulting in the founding of literary periodicals of extremely short duration. By the time André Gide had written most of his journal, authors associated with *La Nouvelle Revue française* had come and gone to suit the changes in friendships as well as literary styles.[100]

A related group of readers, literary critics, formed perhaps an even more important interpretive group in France.[101] Over the course of the nineteenth and twentieth centuries, criticism moved rapidly from the margin of literary creation to the center of literary reception. The reviews written in response to specific texts by selected authors—the same authors whose correspondence was studied in Chapter 2—appeared within a definable circle of critics and journalists; these men in their turn were responsible for the direction of periodicals with well-established editorial policies. The storm of criticism raised by prose fiction throughout the modern period, from Stendhal to Sartre, thus resulted in nearly uniform patterns of published response: any experimentation in style or substance almost always generated resistance. The early realists encountered just as much opposition as the naturalists and some symbolists did later.[102] While not entirely predictable, the reviewers employed many of the same terms or phrases in their consideration of a text. Émile Zola's *La Terre*, for example, was accused of obscenity by fifty-one of the sixty reviews published within a year of its publication. As Henri Peyre noted in his history of criticism, critical misunderstandings stemmed from a relatively narrow range of immediate concerns having less to do with the work than with the critics considering it.[103]

Social profiles suggest the kind of interpretive community that reviewers actually constituted. A nearly exhaustive list of critical reviews of texts by selected French authors indicates that more than 96 percent of them were written by men, entirely disproportionate to the place that males played in all literate activities. Even though this tendency declined somewhat over time, most critics also had published at least one book by the year of their review. Fewer reviewers in the twentieth century were themselves published authors; like

[100] Cf. Roméo Arbour, *Les Revues littéraires éphémères parasissant à Paris entre 1900 et 1914* (1956); and Lina Morino, *"La Nouvelle Revue Française" dans l'histoire des lettres* (1939).

[101] Cf. the list of critics in Irving Babbitt, *The Masters of French Criticism* (Boston, 1912), 395–419; with Jean Hébrard and Anne-Marie Chartier, *Discours sur la lecture (1880–1980)* (1989), 465–91.

[102] See Bernard Weinberg, *French Realism: The Critical Reaction, 1830–1870* (New York, 1937); Michel Raimond, *La Crise du roman. Des lendemains du naturalisme aux années vingt* (1985); and Roger Fayolle, *La Critique* (1978), 111–71.

[103] Henri Peyre, *Writers and Their Critics: A Study of Misunderstanding* (Ithaca, 1944), 81–136.

other writers, critics became increasingly specialized as a professional group. Moreover, reviewers were usually the same age, varying little from the mean between 35 and 40, except for the noticeably younger romantic generation in the first half of the nineteenth century. The residence patterns of modern French critics are also distinctly Parisian; more than 70 percent of literary reviews were written and published in Paris, despite the growth of literate activity in the provinces. And finally, the occupational structure of the critics remained remarkably homogeneous and stable throughout the period. The vast majority of reviewers were professional writers, journalists especially, the rest of whom supplemented their income in business or the professions by turning out occasional reviews for a newspaper or literary journal. By the turn of the century, critics seem to have shared a common professional outlook that clearly distinguished their style of reading new works.[104]

As publishing grew more complex, the relationship between authors and most readers attenuated and was subject to new pressures. Like Alfred de Vigny in his poetic advice to a poet, authors very reluctantly threw their work to the fate of anonymous readers, so difficult did writers find it to accept the workings of the literary marketplace. This much the otherwise commercially astute Balzac recognized during the July Monarchy; he resorted frequently to personal self-promotion through the dedication of his works to influential acquaintances. His flattering praise of Geoffrey Saint-Hilaire at the beginning of *La Comédie humaine*, besides his handwritten inscription in the copy he sent to the famous naturalist's son, did not save it from either the hostility of the reviewers or its relatively disappointing sales. Instead, like other writers living by their pen, Balzac supplemented his extensive personal and social network with the more effective means of promoting his novels by appropriate business practices detailed in his publishing contracts.[105] Thus by the time Baudelaire had completed the poems for his first collection in 1857, the poet was expected to advise his publishers on how it should be advertised. But this appeared as an afterthought in a letter that detailed which of his friends and personal acquaintances should receive free copies of the work, including five men in the Interior Ministry (more than likely to forestall its prosecution for obscenity).[106] Not until late in the nineteenth century did writers cease to circumvent the market and resign themselves to the limited impact that their acquaintances could make on the reception of their literary production among thousands of readers.[107]

---

[104] Data on critics were taken from a study: James Smith Allen, "Critics in Search of a Text: Book Reviewers as an Interpretive Community in Modern France," *Proceedings of the Annual Meeting of the Western Society for French History, 1990*, vol. 18, forthcoming.

[105] *Balzac: Corr.*, ed. Roger Pierrot (1960–66), 4:33–37.

[106] See Baudelaire to Eugène de Broise, 13 June 1857, in Baudelaire, *Corr.*, 1:406–8.

[107] See Priscilla Parkhurst Clark, *Literary France: The Making of a Culture* (Berkeley, 1987), 78–96.

This stoicism did not mean that authors forgot entirely their friends and professional relations. At the beginning of the twentieth century, the personal manipulation of reviews had been developed into a fine art, one that Marcel Proust used to ensure favorable treatment of *Du côté de chez Swann* in 1913.[108] He prevailed on no fewer than five friends to place positive critiques in appropriate periodicals and thereby enlarged his circle of appreciative admirers. This ruse had been a common but more discreet practice throughout the modern period.[109] Despite the relative anonymity of authorship in a vast and diverse literate culture, French authors continued to rely on personal networks to promote their work, albeit in less formal or more profit-oriented settings. Until recently, small shops dominated the commercial distribution of books; like publishers, they were closely associated with specific writers. Bookstores (and neighborhood libraries) often served as recognized locations for the gathering of literati and their audiences.[110] As a result, few book buyers remained untouched by the interpretive community of an author, even in the most overt commercial setting. Well after World War I, personal acquaintance continued to affect the acquisitions and responses of readers. Booksellers still recommend books and thereby predispose people to them on the basis of personal relationships.

The most formal interpretive communities in modern France were schools and churches. Clearly, these institutions made possible remarkably uniform responses to both new and old literary works. Since its establishment, the Catholic Church had attempted to control the way the faithful viewed the scriptures. But with the Counter-Reformation, its influence was extended to the way in which other texts were read. The church's close coordination with the state to control publishing, as well as the Index of Prohibited Books for the laity, were only the most obvious instances of this concern, especially during the Restoration, when religious and public officials cooperated to ban a wide range of works.[111] Similarly, the clergy made clear in homilies at mass and in the instruction of church-sponsored schools how secular books should be considered from a Catholic Christian perspective. They therefore exerted a pervasive and enduring influence well into the modern period. Michelet was not alone in decrying the role played by the church in shaping many personal

---

[108] Douglas Alden, *Marcel Proust and His French Critics* (Los Angeles, 1940), 8–20; and George Painter, *Marcel Proust: A Biography* (Harmondsworth, 1977), 2:195–200.

[109] See Constantin Hilbey, *Venalité des journaux. Révélations accompagnées de preuves* (1845).

[110] See HEF 4:471–509; and Pierre Nora, ed., *Les Lieux de mémoires* (1984), 1:323–51.

[111] French titles on the Index of Prohibited Books also appear in Drujon, *Catalogue des oeuvres, écrits et dessins*. Cf. the editor of *Romans-revue* (1908–39) and church spokesman, abbé Louis Bethléem, *Romans à lire et romans à proscrire. Essai de classification au point de vue moral . . . (1880–1920)* (1922); with Hébrard and Chartier, *Discours sur la lecture*, 13–74, esp. 45–74.

activities besides reading.[112] In spite of themselves, the radical anticlericals of the Third Republic actually intensified the church's interpretive intrusion by forcing readers to take sides on political issues that eventually became of passionate interest to all French men and women. Only with the growing indifference to religious life made possible by secularization in the twentieth century did the church become less important as an interpretive community, however cohesive it may have become to the smaller number of the faithful. The same can be said of the roles played by Protestant and Jewish institutions in the period.

The development of secondary and university education, albeit slow before World War II, also helped to define responses to literature. For example, scholars taught students their interpretive predispositions. Early in the nineteenth century, literature per se was not a separate field of study; rather, it was either subordinated to the related study of rhetoric, or it was treated as an illustration of social and moral verities.[113] Those literary instances which could not be so clearly classified, such as modern drama and prose fiction, earned the disdain of serious readers deeply imbued in the Greek and Roman classics, or more often in the French classics of the seventeenth and eighteenth centuries. Not until the establishment of the *explication de texte* as a pedagogical method during the Third Republic (under the influence of the German school of textual exegesis) did the study of more contemporary literature become a scholarly activity.[114] In time, the historical-critical method employed by Ernest Renan in the study of Biblical scripture also seemed applicable to literature and fostered the literary histories written by Ferdinand Brunetière and Gustave Lanson.[115] Consequently, schools and universities established curricula in various literary genres and appropriate approaches to them that ultimately shaped the critical responses of scholars and students alike. By 1900, they constituted a community even more influential than censors, authors, publishers, and priests.

Family and neighbors made up a less definable and perhaps waning interpretive force. Unfortunately, the historian of reading is handicapped by a paucity of adequate sources. But some insight is again provided by the personal letters sent to authors about their work. Approximately one percent of more

[112] Cf. Jules Michelet, *Le Prêtre, la femme et la famille* (1881), 270–72; BHVP Fonds Michelet, Tome 10, Liasse A4745, fols. 1–136; Tome 12, Liasse A4751, fols. 1–133; and "Instruction pastorale de Mgr. l'évêque de Troyes pour le carême . . . 1859," in Darmon, *Le Colportage de librairie en France*, 306–7.

[113] Cf. Capelle, *Dictionnaire de morale, de science et de littérature* (1810), 1:9–16, 121–22; and AN F17,1547 d. Procès-verbaux . . . 1831, Séance 1 Sept. 1831.

[114] See titles listed in Introduction, note 32, above. On the school as an interpretive community, see Hébrard and Chartier, *Discours sur la lecture*, 179–234.

[115] See Fayolle, *La Critique*, pp. 111–35; René Wellek, *A History of Modern Criticism, 1750–1950* (New Haven, 1965), 4:58–79; and Antoine Compagnon, *La Troisième République des lettres. De Flaubert à Proust* (1983), 174–81.

than 1,400 identifiable correspondents mentioned oral readings within the family. For instance, one man wrote Michelet in 1859 about reading *L'Amour* aloud to his wife, thereby informing her response to the book by his poignant inflections and pauses.[116] This practice remained common in middle-class French households before the intrusion of electronic media in the twentieth century. Other correspondents indicated that they learned of the work they read from friends who thought it likely to be of interest.[117] The extensive personal network of the authors (whose acquaintances constituted more than one-third of the total sample) contributed significantly to the predisposition of their readership defined by the correspondence. The participation of neighbors in an individual's predisposition to read a particular work or to interpret it in a predictable way, however, cannot be studied systematically in the letters; too little mention is made of it.[118] As modern urban life permitted greater anonymity and autonomy from traditional social relations, the absence of neighborhood influence is not surprising. This dimension to the politics of reading diminished in time as the historical context of reception grew more diffuse.

And so political influences appear in the documented responses of different audiences. Censor reports, letters, reviews, journals, and memoirs all indicate how the law, ideology, and communities shaped and were in turn shaped by literate activities. The most profound historical forces were not limited solely to preventive or repressive censorship. They included as well an enduring ideology of control and a network of various social groups. Each of these factors imposed severe limitations on what people did with texts. On the other hand, literate audiences themselves created these restrictions. Readers prohibited literary works, readers justified their prohibitions, and readers formed communities that made these actions possible. Literate people thus negotiated a multitude of influences, many of their own making, in ways that ultimately circumscribed their responses to printed matter. In this way, then, modern French men and women defined yet another contextual feature of reading in the past, namely, the politics of reception.

---

[116] E.g., A. Guépin to Jules Michelet, 29 or 30 December 1859, BHVP Fonds Michelet, Tome 11, Liasse A4750, fol. 41. Cf. the much denser networks studied by Alan Spitzer, *The French Generation of 1820* (Princeton, 1987), 3–34, 283–97.

[117] E.g., Charles Alexander to Michelet, n.d., BHVP Fonds Michelet, Tome 11, Liasse A4750, fol. 6.

[118] E.g., Fanny Dénois to Eugène Sue, 19 April 1843, BHVP Fonds Sue, fol. 146, expresses the concerns that Dénois's neighbors had about talking with the author; they feared he might portray them as objectionable characters in his ongoing serial novel, *Les Mystères de Paris*.

Chapter 4

CULTURAL MENTALITIES

LIKE OTHER MODERN FRENCH AUTHORS, Anatole France received mail from readers who expressed an enthusiastic appreciation of his work, of course, but who also defined a peculiar predisposition to the printed page. In 1891, for example, a student at the École normale d'institutrices in Périgueux, Yvonne Ethève, wrote a long letter on her responses to France's novels.[1] While reading his books in a little park near home, she often daydreamed about the natural beauty around her. In so doing, she said, she created "the spritely visions of a world that I explored alone," a mental universe she peopled with classical gods and described with allusions to Greek and Latin works. Hardly a useless fantasy, Ethève stated, this detachment from the text provided her a perspective on life far wiser than the dogmatic self-righteousness of a fellow student also discussed in the letter, even though her professors failed to understand this higher knowledge derived from literature. Thanks to her reading of France's work, the student exclaimed, "I have a full head like an old chest, but I think, without false modesty, that it is not filled topsy-turvy." The letter closed with a request that the author continue writing for her edification: "I await the pretty stories that you will tell me perhaps remembering your old affection for benevolent sprites." Ultimately the young woman and others like her, whether or not they wrote to Anatole France, were more concerned with themselves than they were with the books they claimed to read.

Otherwise unremarkable, Yvonne Ethève's letter suggests the complex cultural context of modern French literary response. One obvious feature, for instance, was the pervasiveness of neoclassical norms that were so deeply rooted in readers' expectations that they constrained even the romantic; classical allusions intruded on Ethève's daydreams, it would seem, in spite of her immediate surroundings or the contemporary text before her. A second cultural dimension evident here was the useful reality evoked by the work she was reading. Her abstract sensibility owed little to either her senses or the literary text, though it retained a remarkable personal utility. Ethève's imagination provided her a basis for comparison with other worlds besides her own, while ironically it also kept her in touch with peers and teachers at school. Finally, the letter documents a common assumption among readers that literature is knowledge, however it may have been conceived by different people.

---

[1] Yvonne Ethève to Anatole France, 27 Nov. [1891?], in BN NAFr 15433 fols. 417–20.

For Ethève, the novel illuminated the inner recesses of the self, the profound depths of human nature, indeed, the solitary infinitude of the cosmos.

Consequently, there were at least three different assumptions in this woman's reading experience—order, utility, and principle—each assumption representing one aspect of a "constitutive rule" in the reception of literary works.[2] For French audiences like Yvonne Ethève at the turn of the century, the closely related conceptions of ordered norms, useful reality, and principles in knowledge clearly informed their responses to texts.

This particular context to reading is as deserving of careful examination as the economy of print, the literate society, and the politics of reception discussed in earlier chapters. The number and kinds of texts proliferated, the habits of active reading appeared among new social groups, and political networks increasingly pervaded the literate activities of French men and women. This much is evident. But the "culture" of reading also affected reception.[3] The anthropological side to interpretive practice is no less important for its apparent obscurity in modern society. The cultural implications of literary history at least appear in the communities formed by critics, correspondents, and schools, audiences that exerted independent historical forces of their own. These groups often defined the role that reading played in economic growth, social change, political conflict, and intellectual achievement. Above all, however, these three readerships also defined textual predispositions by a specific conception of norms, reality, and knowledge, i.e., the elements of a particular cultural mentality at the heart of interpretive practice in modern France.

NORMS

From the eighteenth century onward, the size and influence of one interpretive community, literary critics, grew in direct proportion to the development of publishing, literacy, and free expression.[4] Criticism at one time had been largely indistinguishable from authorship; in the Old Regime, writers like d'Alembert and Diderot considered their creative and evaluative roles to be nearly interchangeable. But this functional unity broke down as authors increasingly specialized. After establishing their reputations as novelists, prose realists rarely published comments on the work of poets or dramatists. Moreover, newspapers expanded the range of their content to include literary re-

---

[2] On constitutive rules, see Richard A. Sweder and Robert A. LeVine, eds., *Culture Theory: Essays on Mind, Self, and Emotion* (Cambridge, 1984), 88–119.

[3] See Jack Goody, *Literacy in Traditional Societies* (Cambridge, 1968), 1–19; Clifford Geertz, *The Interpretation of Cultures* (New York, 1973), 3–30, 193–233; and Mary Douglas, ed., *Essays in the Sociology of Perception* (London, 1982), 120–31.

[4] See René Wellek, *A History of Modern Criticism, 1750–1950* (New Haven, 1955–86), 1:12–78, 2:1–72, 3:216–58, 4:1–96, 433–63; Pierre Moreau, *La Critique littéraire en France* (1960), 96–202; and Roger Fayolle, *La Critique* (1978), 75–171.

views written by staff journalists, many of whom never published a creative work of their own. And yet critics (and subsequent literary historians) were responsible for defining literary movements, at times even coining the terms used to characterize them, like romanticism and symbolism. No matter how inappropriate or misleading, these labels have informed cultural discourse ever since. Contemporary reviewers agreed notably in their use of categories and expressions, a fact that underscores this cultural group's substantive influence on the history of reading.

As critics responded to texts by specific authors from Stendhal to Sartre, they revealed the values implicit in modern French literary perception—the values of order, balance, unity, and tradition. Each aspect of a work had to be part of an integral whole, and each whole part of an enduring cultural heritage. As René Wellek aptly defined it, this critical neoclassicism sought ''to discover the principles or the 'laws' or 'rules' of literature'' always at work in the indissoluble alliance of the True, the Beautiful, and the Good that were so apparent in the literature of ancient Greece and Rome (and seventeenth-century France)—hence the critics' close attention to eternal verities, distinct genres, deliberate craftsmanship, moral instruction, aesthetic pleasure, clarity, and concision.[5] Such were the assumptions made by hundreds of book reviewers and their assessments of recently published novels. Notwithstanding the personal relations among critics and authors that affected the reception of nearly all new works, radical experiments in style and substance, by definition, violated the long-standing and widely respected virtues of French classicism. The result was a determined resistance to literary innovation. This cautious spirit remained true of French criticism, from romanticism in the early nineteenth century to existentialism on the eve of World War II.

Stressing originality, imagination, and spontaneity, the romantics were among the first to clash with this pervasive conservatism.[6] Prominent reviewers before 1850, like Armand de Pontmartin, Gustave Planche, and Alfred Nettement, excoriated romantic experimentation. For their part, Victor Hugo, Émile Deschamps, and Stendhal attempted to counter these attacks, but it was the decisions made by dozens of romantic imitators and thousands of their readers that ultimately established the movement as a fact of French intellectual life. There were some apparent defections among writers long associated with the romantics; Alfred de Musset's amusing satire of two imaginary provincial men of letters, Dupuis and Cotonet, did not persuade the critics of his neoclassical purity. They continued to accuse him of the wrong literary sympathies long after his denunciation of romanticism, so strong was the prevailing prejudice against stylistic elaboration in any genre. Labelled early in their

[5] Wellek, *A History of Modern Criticism*, 1:12. Cf. René Bray, *La Formation de la doctrine classique en France* (1951), 114–39.

[6] See Charles Desgranges, *Le Romantisme et la critique. La Presse littéraire sous la Restauration (1815–1830)* (1907).

professional careers, Musset and creative spirits like him fell victim to lingering values of critical reception.

In the first half of the nineteenth century, the conservative world of criticism was reflected in the published responses to the earliest prose realists: Stendhal, Balzac, and Sue. When *Le Rouge et le noir* appeared in December 1830, the reviewers most often noted the author's interest in portraying aspects of contemporary reality antithetical to French classicism. Jules Janin, for one, accused Stendhal of an important literary sin when he decried the novelist's "invincible need to depict everything as ugly."[7] Like the works of other writers in the movement, the novel glorified the hideous, indeed the immoral, especially in its apparently cynical presentation of Julien Sorel's activities and motivations. Even Balzac, who was accused later of much worse, stated that Stendhal "has just wounded the human heart."[8] The literary virtues of Stendhal's unpretentious prose went unnoticed in the reviewers' concern with attacking the author's cold-blooded skepticism and his frank portrait of modern French manners and morals. As for the defects of his style, the critics were nearly unanimous; it violated their sense of deliberate form: "Calm without being measured, the style of it is young, fresh, and full of color, too full sometimes, for it is vermilion that dominates"—a typical response in the guise of a back-handed compliment, one suggestive of more overt condemnations of the romantics.[9] Stendhal's critics here expressed a neoclassical resistance that must have been exacerbated by the relative success of other works still more representative of romanticism.

Balzac's *La Peau de chagrin* (1831) came in for similar critical treatment. Although his reviewers were uniformly more pleased with his views of contemporary society, praising especially the novelist's treatment of Raphaël's dilemma in the work, they sharply criticized Balzac's apparent materialism and immorality. "Religious indifference and philosophical skepticism lead minds to fatalism," warned an anonymous critic in the *Revue européenne*.[10] For Amédée Pichot, the novel was "quite simply a fantastic story without any morality."[11] Even more neutral assessments tended to stress the work's exaggeration of situations and details that implicitly denied the author's thematic

---

[7] [Jules Janin], " 'Le Rouge et le noir,' " *Journal des débats* (26 Dec. 1830): 3–4, cited in Bernard Weinberg, *French Realism: The Critical Reaction, 1830–1870* (New York, 1937), 11. Cf. Jean Mélia, *Stendhal et ses commentateurs* (1911), 78–82; and Adolphe Paupe, *Histoire des oeuvres de Stendhal* (1903), 75–79.

[8] Honoré de Balzac, "Lettres sur Paris," in *Oeuvres diverses*, ed. Marcel Bouteron and Henri Longnon (1938), 2:115.

[9] [Anon.], " 'Le Rouge et le noir.' Chronique du XIXe siècle. Par M. de Stendhal," *Figaro* (20 Dec. 1830): 2.

[10] [Anon.], " 'La Peau de chagrin,' roman philosophique, par M. de Balzac," *Revue européenne* (Sept. 1831): 93. Cf. David Bellos, *Balzac Criticism in France, 1850–1900: The Making of a Reputation* (Oxford, 1974), 1–15; and Weinberg, *French Realism*, 32–81.

[11] X.X.X. [Amédée Pichot], " 'La Peau de chagrin,' " *Revue encyclopédique* (Aug. 1831): 328.

intentions. "M. de Balzac has observation, style, some dazzling pages, light and blithe jesting, dash, but here and there, exaggeration and affectation," commented another anonymous critic, who preferred the more serious reflections of the novel where they appeared.[12] Expressed in nearly every review of *La Peau*, these reservations were mild in comparison to those published on Balzac's later novels; a British Balzac scholar, David Bellos, remarks that these criticisms irrelevant to Balzac's literary achievement were libelous.[13] As some reviewers readily admitted, critics knew the author and his extravagances too well to treat his work fairly. But conservative values made it especially difficult for all innovative authors, despite romanticism's diminishing influence on them, to escape the critics' ire entirely.

In the published criticism of Eugène Sue's *Les Mystères de Paris* (1842–43), the same collective predisposition against literary experiment appears in defense of established formal convention. The extravagance of romanticism, however, was not the issue; the deliberate portrait of offensive poverty and crime was. The new material was too vulgar to merit proper literary treatment. For example, Sainte-Beuve characterized the work's inspiration as "an essence of debauchery: stench circles about it everywhere, even when the author hides it in would-be fragrances."[14] Other conservative critics objected to the novel's depiction of cutthroats, prostitutes, and thieves, "this descent to the underworld of crime, this species of reviewing all the sewers that a major city can contain."[15] But the serialized novel's deliberate appeal to a large, socially undistinguished audience alarmed reviewers at least as much as its attention to the underside of Parisian society. For Sue's critics, this combination of a new subject matter and a new readership was nothing less than an outrage to literary propriety. Asked the indignant Alfred Nettement, "Would you find it appropriate that young men and women frequent the 'Tapis Franc' *estaminet* in the rue aux Fèves?"[16] Of course, some reviewers like George Sand and Désiré Laverdant found the work's appeal precisely in its attempt to bring social problems to the attention of a broader public. But they still had reservations about the author's handling of the vicious underclass that could be confused with the honest and upright poor. In a scathing assessment of the novel, Karl Marx identified this problem in particular, despite his cultural distance as a recent German immigrant.[17]

[12] N., " 'La Peau de chagrin,' roman philosophique; par M. de Balzac," *Journal des débats* (30 Aug. 1831): 4.

[13] Bellos, *Balzac Criticism in France*, 1.

[14] C.-A. Sainte-Beuve, *Chroniques parisiennes (1843–1845)*, (1876), 169. Cf. Georges Jarbinet, *'Les Mystères de Paris' d'Eugène Sue* (1932), 159–204; and Jean-Louis Bory, *Eugène Sue. Le Roi du roman populaire* (1962), 243–95.

[15] Evariste, "Lettre de Paris," *Mode* (15 Jan. 1845): 3.

[16] Alfred Nettement, *Études critiques sur le feuilleton roman* (1845), 305–6.

[17] Cf. Eugène Faure [George Sand], " 'Les Mystères de Paris' par M. Eugène Sue," *Revue indépendante* (25 May 1843): 186–96; D.[ésiré] L.[averdant], " 'Les Mystères de Paris,' " *Dé-*

In time, Parisian critics became less hostile to prose realism. Their reviews of works by Stendhal, Balzac, and Sue actually mark a critical nadir. Similar novels appeared and provided critics a much larger basis for comparison. By the Second Empire, the rigid neoclassical principles used to critique the romantics had given way to more flexible criteria by which to judge the relative success of subsequent novels on contemporary manners and morals. A sense of order, balance, unity, and tradition was adapted to the realistic narrative and its literary conventions. Consequently, a controversial work like Flaubert's *Madame Bovary* (1857) found a surprisingly large number of reviewers to praise its formal plot and scrupulous style, even when writers continued to object to the subject matter and the author's detachment from the immoral situations of the main character.[18] Increasingly, it took significant variations on this particular genre to elicit outcries from the interpretive community of Parisian critics. For this reason, innovations in the subsequent work of Flaubert and the Goncourt brothers provoked a chorus of disapproval; these authors pressed the limits of recently established novelistic conventions. Though colored by social and political conflict, neoclassical cultural values were tailored to suit a new genre and thereby retained their importance at mid-century.

For example, Flaubert's *Salammbô* elicited a profound sense of collective betrayal when it was published in 1862. Perhaps because critics had resigned themselves to the realistic novel, they could not accept an apparent throwback to the exoticism of the romantics. Opposition to *Salammbô*'s eccentricities was nearly universal. For example, Guillaume Froehner condemned the novel's archeological fantasy: "[There is] nothing natural in these flights of a feverish and overexcited imagination; all is affected, forced, and strained in the extreme."[19] The work, set in ancient Carthage, was nothing but an historical novel perverted by the author's penchant for detached realism. Flaubert's detail thus seemed excessive, irrelevant, superficial, ugly, and horrible. Stated Pierre-Paul Douhaire, "One finds there only frightful war scenes, hideous massacres, abominable human butchery."[20] To this Eugène Delaplace added a sharp critique of the work's style, which to him was exaggerated, forced, and bombastic: "M. Flaubert's prose resembles [Auguste] Barbier's

---

mocratie pacifique (13 Aug. 1843): 1–2, (20 Aug. 1843): 3–4; and Karl Marx and Friedrich Engels, *The Holy Family, or The Critique of Critical Criticism*, trans. Richard Dixon and Clemens Dutton (Moscow, 1975), 65–91.

[18] See René Dumesnil, " 'Madame Bovary' et son temps (1857)," *MdF* (16 Nov. 1911): 291–316, (1 Dec. 1911): 466–91; "Opinion de la presse sur *Madame Bovary*," in Gustave Flaubert, *Oeuvres complètes: Madame Bovary* (1930), 527–37; and Weinberg, *French Realism*, 159–73. Cf. Marguerite Iknayan, *The Idea of the Novel in France: The Critical Reaction 1815–1848* (Geneva, 1961), 182–84.

[19] Guillaume Froehner, "Le Roman archéologique en France," *Revue contemporaine*, 2d ser. (31 Dec. 1862): 855.

[20] P. Douhaire, "Revue critique," *Correspondant*, n.s. 21 (Dec. 1862): 802.

Iambes.''[21] Accusations of immorality resulted predictably from the narrative's impersonality; the author's apparent cynicism implied a cruel and sensual skepticism. To Sainte-Beuve, who had respected *Madame Bovary* only five years earlier, *Salammbô* was "much stranger and more bizarre than original.''[22] Half realistic, half romantic—rather, half history, half fiction—its literary innovation violated the critics' taste for distinct genres.

Three years later, in 1865, the Goncourt brothers published *Germinie Lacerteux*, and the critics seemed almost relieved to read a purely realistic work. While they continued to attack the prose realists' meticulous attention to the underside of French society, they accepted the form more readily for what it meant to the development of the French novel. Critical opinion about this work was more evenly divided between those who condemned it primarily for its subject matter and those who willingly ignored this aspect of the novel to praise its formal achievement. The work, it seems, did not innovate sufficiently to confuse (or to irritate) the reviewers. The harshest attacks centered on the authors' apparent calumny of the honest lower orders, who were nothing like the lascivious and dishonest Germinie. Summarized Jules Claretie, the novel consisted "of slang, a scent of cheap brandy and of bad places, of vices and still more vices, the municipal pawn shop, the sludge, the hospital, and these are the masses! There are other things besides vice in the people.''[23] But this disdain for the work's wretched character, plot, and setting was challenged by fellow practitioners of the novelist's craft, most particularly Émile Zola: "In principle [the author] can know no limit here in the study of truth," a principle Zola would more or less maintain years later in his own novels.[24]

In fact, the critical debate over naturalism remained essentially the same as the one over realism. From romanticism onward, the issue was the continuity of neoclassical values, of refined taste and defined form. The vast majority of critics were thus hostile to the novelistic innovation of Zola's *L'Assommoir* when it appeared in 1877. They refused to accept its apparent claim to empirical description. Arthur Ranc, for instance, criticized Zola for his unscientific use of secondhand sources, namely Denis Poulot and Maurice Roret. Because of the author's especially heavy debt to Poulot's *La Sublime*, an anonymous review in *Le Télégraphe* accused Zola of plagiarism. Still other reviewers denied the author's pretense to scientific truth in an imaginative genre. Mocked Henry Houssaye, "Finally the Truth is drawn from the well where for thirty centuries neither Homer, nor Shakespeare, nor Molière had been able to ex-

---

[21] E. Delaplace, "Le Roman contemporain," *Revue contemporaine*, 2d ser., 38 (15 Mar. 1864): 159. Cf. Max Bach, "Critique et politique: La Réception des *Misérables* en 1862," *PMLA* 77 (1962): 595–608.

[22] C.-A. Sainte-Beuve, " 'Salammbô,' " *Nouveaux lundis* (1865), 4:83.

[23] Jules Claretie, "Romanciers du XIXe siècle. Edmond et Jules de Goncourt," *Revue de Paris* 10 (1865): 172. Cf. Weinberg, *French Realism*, 185–90.

[24] Émile Zola, *Mes haines: Causeries littéraires et artistiques* (1923), 81.

tract it.''[25] The ''duc de Guise'' of French letters, Jules Barbey d'Aurevilly, doubted the sincerity of the author's intentions; despite its preface, the work focused deliberately on obscene details for the sake not of truth but of sales. ''Displayed initially in a newspaper, all this vileness has had its offensive success. It was cried aloud, and perhaps still louder cries can begin, now that it is no longer raised up, this filth, by the shovelful, in a serial, but mounted *en bloc* in a book.''[26] Consequently, for most reviewers, *L'Assommoir* had failed as science, but even more as art; however much the author's friends and associates defended it, the work seemed neither orderly, balanced, nor organic.

Ten years later, when Zola's *La Terre* appeared, the cultural values of Parisian reviewers had not changed. The political atmosphere leading to the Daniel Wilson affair was tense, and it affected the reception of Zola's new novel, just as the moral order earlier in the Third Republic must have affected the reception of *L'Assommoir*: conservatives resisted both political and literary modernism. *La Terre*, however, was attacked even more vehemently by self-proclaimed intimates of the author. Before *Le Bien public* had finished its serialization of the work, Paul Bonnetain, J.-H. Rosny, Lucien Descaves, Paul Margueritte, and Gustave Guiches published a manifesto repudiating the father of naturalism:

> Zola, in effect, has perjured his program with each passing day. Incredibly lazy in his *own* experimentation, armed with bales of documents amassed by others, full of Hugo-like bombast, all the more enervating in how eagerly he preached simplicity, sinking to tiresome repetitions and perpetual clichés, he has disconcerted the most enthusiastic of his disciples.[27]

This open letter to the author itself became the inspiration for the attacks on naturalism that made the critical corpus on *La Terre* far larger than that on *L'Assommoir*. For hostile critics, this rift within the ranks of the ''faithful'' added another excuse to denigrate the author's literary achievement, even though the young men, thanks to their obscurity, failed to destroy the new trend in prose fiction. The basis of their criticism—Zola's inadequate science, implicit romanticism, immoral subject, and aesthetic flaws—merely highlighted a long-standing resistance to literary exploration. Whether or not *La*

[25] Henry Houssaye, ''Variétés. Le Vin bleu littéraire,'' *Journal des débats* (14 Mar. 1877): 3. Cf. Léon Deffoux, *La Publication de 'l'Assommoir'* (1931), 58–134; and Auguste Dezalay, *Lectures de Zola* (1973), 9–57.

[26] Jules Barbey d'Aurevilly, *Le XIXe siècle. Des oeuvres et des hommes*, ed. Jacques Petit (1966), 2:277.

[27] Paul Bonnetain et al., '' 'La Terre'. À Émile Zola,'' *Figaro* (18 Aug. 1887): 1–2 (emphasis in the original). Cf. Maurice LeBlond, *La Publication de 'La Terre'* (1937), 75–89; and Robert Pageard, ''*La Terre* vue par la presse d'Eure-et-Loir lors de sa publication (1887–1888),'' *Cahiers naturalistes* 40 (1970): 177–85.

Terre represented the creative bankruptcy of the naturalistic novel, as Ferdinand Brunetière argued, it elicited the expression of persistent critical values.[28]

Just as a more cohesive community of Parisian critics began considering new literary developments, Anatole France wrote one of the more important reviews of *La Terre*. His criticisms of Zola are revealing, for they suggest what subsequent critics would seek in France's own novels, and eventually in those of Marcel Proust. Although he later retracted his harshest remarks, France disliked Zola's brutish view of peasants; it was typical of the approach that naturalists took to all their subjects. Moreover, France was offended by the language Zola gave to the peasants. "M. Zola does not show us the peasants clearly. What is still more serious, he does not have them speak properly. He lends them the loquaciousness of workers in the cities."[29] But the vulgarity of the novel's characters was exceeded only by the vulgarity of Zola's own language in the work. "I regret to add that when M. Zola speaks on his own account, he is ponderous and flabby. He tires the reader by the crushing monotony of his formulas."[30] This was a sin that critics would never accuse France or Proust of committing, despite their own offensive subject matter. The symbolists' love of language, often for its own sake, encountered markedly less hostility from reviewers, who for decades had been critical of innovation in prose fiction.

The reasons for this shift in criticism are not hard to discern. By the turn of the century, the world of letters in Paris had become sufficiently specialized to permit at least one more coherent interpretive community to develop. The newspapers turned over their review columns less frequently to creative writers, and the many smaller literary journals received new works with a greater appreciation of formal experimentation within some neoclassical limits. Critical opinion varied less because practicing critics themselves, increasingly distinct from serious scholars and leading literati, were a more homogeneous group of readers than ever before.[31] Despite the divisive political and social issues in the aftermath of the Dreyfus Affair, reviewers continued to share a broad range of cultural values about what constituted good fiction. The specialization among critics only served to reinforce their conservative values. Literary criticism as a distinct genre ensured the critical importance of form and language to literary creation. Fiction remained a subject of controversy, of course, but the debate was tepid compared to the earlier furor over roman-

---

[28] Ferdinand Brunetière, "Revue littéraire. La Banqueroute du naturalisme," *RdDM* (1 Sept. 1887): 213–24. Cf. Michel Raimond, *La Crise du roman. Des lendemains du naturalisme aux années vingt*, 2d ed. (1985), 25–43.

[29] France, " 'La Terre,' " in *Oeuvres complètes illustrées* (1926), 6:208.

[30] Ibid., 210. Cf. Annette Antoniu, *Anatole France. Critique littéraire* (Paris, 1929).

[31] See Alexandre Belin, *La Critique française à la fin du XIXe siècle* (Paris, 1926); and Fayolle, *La Critique*, 137–71.

ticism, realism, and naturalism.[32] In this context, the formal elegance of fiction by France and Proust, among other subsequent literary innovators, experienced a more predictable critical favor.

The uniformly warm reception of France's *Le Lys rouge* in 1894 illustrates well this development in the critical community of Paris. Although most reviewers were uneasy with the plot, concerning Mme. Martin-Bellème's adulterous loves, all but one of them praised the work's exquisite language. Remarked Émile Verhaeren in *Art moderne*, "If not for the literary sauce which is by a rare cook, one sees, it would only be a very meager affair, a fungible adultery. But the sauce, the sauce, ah! how tasty it is!"[33] This aspect of the author's writing appealed to reviewers less given to culinary figures of speech, including the young Léon Blum, who summarized the most enduring literary virtues still honored by critics at the turn of the century.

> M. Anatole France is the principal writer of our time. One rediscovers in him all the classical beauties of language; he unites the richest currents of the French spirit: the fluidity of Renan, the sure and difficult taste of the Parnassians, the courageous freedom and natural sensuality of Diderot, the precise and delicate elegance of Fénelon or Racine, at times the brusque force of Retz or Saint-Evremond, always the abundant and sustained irony of Montaigne or Rabelais.[34]

This extravagant praise places France's work among his culture's literary glories, largely on the strength of its elegant style and refined taste, which all reviewers noted approvingly, even when they objected to its subject matter or to the precious social world it represented. Charles Arnaud expressed most forcefully these minor reservations: "M. France does nihilistic philosophy, as Molière's pedants did Greek, for the pleasure and the amusement of a small coterie in mutual admiration [of one another]."[35] But most critics found this exclusiveness easy to forgive; they perceived too much of their cultural heritage in France's work.

Critical opinion now focused somewhat more on the literary achievements of a novelist than on the political, social, and moral implications of a work. These latter considerations became less and less important in Parisian book reviews, unless of course they appeared in periodicals like the *Action française* with well-defined nonliterary interests. Accordingly, when Proust's *Du côté*

---

[32] See Jacques Lethève, *Impressionistes et symbolistes devant la presse* (1959); and Raimond, *La Crise du roman*, 60–105.

[33] Émile Verhaeren, "Anatole France. 'Le Lys rouge,' " *Art moderne* 14 (30 Sept. 1894): 308. Cf. Drehan Bresky, "Cinquante ans de la critique francienne," *Nineteenth-Century French Studies* 7 (1979): 245–57; and Albert Gier, *Der Skeptiker in Gespräch mit den Leser. Studien zum Werke von Anatole France und zu seiner Rezeption in der französischen Presse 1879–1905* (Tübingen, 1985).

[34] Léon Blum, "La Revue de Paris," in *L'Oeuvre de Léon Blum . . . 1891–1905* (1954), 85.

[35] Charles Arnaud, " 'Le Lys rouge,' de M. Anatole France," *Polybiblion* (Feb. 1895): 114.

de chez Swann was published privately in 1913, the critics were receptive to its radical stylistic experimentation.[36] The author left little to chance in this; his correspondence reveals how hard he worked to influence the work's reception. Before the novel appeared, Proust had several notices placed in leading newspapers and journals. And after the publication of reviews by professional critics, he paid *L'Écho de Paris* to print a flattering response written by his friend Jacques Émile Blanche to counter whatever reservations had appeared. The difficulties for critics were few; like André Gide, the reviewers did not take the author very seriously.[37] They naturally objected most to the work's formlessness, its complicated style, and its appeal to an exclusive social elite. But the reviews balanced their account of these problems with their appreciation of the book's poetry, its empathy, and its evocation of everyday life. Despite, or perhaps because of, Proust's publicity campaign, professional critics accepted a different literary talent; his innovation was easily located within the formal discipline of French symbolist literature.

A similar uniformity of critical response greeted Sartre's first novel in 1938, *La Nausée*. The opinion of most reviewers was that the philosopher had overwhelmed the novelist. Albert Camus lamented the author's misdirected talent: "The novelist's affecting gifts and the play of the cruelest and most lucid of minds are here both squandered and wasted." Especially flawed in its form, the book was not a novel but a monologue. Camus also objected to the work's thin tragedy centered on Roquentin's misery.[38] Similarly, Paul Nizan found intrusive "the spiritual consequences of solitude. They are analyzed with a rigor of thought and expression that will undoubtedly appear intolerable to a majority of readers."[39] This reservation was put more politely by Armand Robin, who otherwise believed that the book well represented French culture, despite "slight traces of a labored, methodical, nearly academic origin."[40] Within the context of twentieth-century criticism written by literary specialists clearly more accepting of formal experimentation, Sartre's novel seemed an anachronistic *roman à thèse* whose first-person narrative bored rather than enlightened. As André Thérive noted in *Le Temps*, "If *La Nausée* had appeared thirty years ago, what excitement in the world of letters, what an uproar probably! Today the novel appears perfectly normal. Its importance comes from

[36] See Douglas Alden, *Marcel Proust and His French Critics* (Los Angeles, 1940), 8–20. Cf. Eva Ahlstedt, *La Pudeur en crise. Un Aspect de l'accueil d'À la recherche du temps perdu de Marcel Proust, 1913–1930* (Paris, 1985).

[37] Gide refused to read Proust's manuscript, according to Eugen Weber, *France, Fin de Siècle* (Cambridge, Mass., 1986), 244.

[38] Albert Camus, " 'La Nausée' de Jean-Paul Sartre," in *Essais*, ed. R. Quillot and L. Faucon (1965), 1417. Cf. Joseph Juret, "La Réception du roman par la critique de l'entre-deux guerres," *Oeuvres et critiques* 2 (1977–78): 65–74.

[39] Paul Nizan, " 'La Nausée,' un roman de Jean-Paul Sartre," in *Pour une nouvelle culture*, ed. Susan Suleiman (1971), 285.

[40] Armand Robin, "Les Lettres. Jean-Paul Sartre: 'La Nausée,' " *Esprit* (July 1938): 574.

how it embodies several tendencies in contemporary literature and psychology.''[41] The same was true of modern French criticism and its slowly evolving values expressed by an identifiable community of critical reception.

REALITY

Like the conservative norms in book reviews, interpretive predispositions appeared in another historical source: the letters sent to authors. As noted in Chapter 2, correspondents constituted an informal network focused on the authors who received the letters. But the letter writers also expressed a second feature of reading's cultural context in modern France, namely, a particular conception of reality, one that informed perception of the printed page.

Just as book reviews assumed neoclassical criteria in their judgment of literary value, the letters considered reading matter a social commodity, a vehicle perhaps, appropriate to cultural exchange within a complex web of family, personal, and collegial relations.[42] As a consequence, French readers conceived of their world and its texts both empirically and practically. Their literary reality was preeminently useful, since literature made possible the patronage practiced by professional writers; it fostered the pursuit of knowledge, consolation, and escape; indeed, it was at the heart of all social occasions and organizations devoted to literate activities. Moreover, this special reality tended to confuse authors with narrators, actual people with literary characters, and more generally the world of the text with that of the reader. In order to give immediate meaning to the abstraction of a printed page, the correspondents projected a personal world view onto the text and thereby revealed another aspect of the important cultural context of reading.[43]

In the minds of the correspondents and other readers like them, literature was a real and quite useful medium of exchange.[44] This belief was especially evident before the Second Empire, when the economy of print had yet to make books and newspapers inexpensive goods available to all social groups in France. Accordingly, in the heyday of the lending library, gifts and loans of books actually supplemented the literary marketplace. Letters to Madame de Staël, Stendhal, and Balzac, all written before 1850, requested volumes far more frequently than the later letters written to Flaubert, Zola, and Anatole

[41] André Thérive, "Les Livres. Jean-Paul Sartre, 'La Nausée,' " *Temps* (14–15 July 1938): 3.

[42] See Roger Chartier, *Lectures et lecteurs dans la France d'Ancien Régime* (1987), 165–222; Roger Chartier, ed., *Pratiques de la lecture* (Marseille, 1985), 181–206; Anne-Marie Thiesse, *Le Roman du quotidien. Lecteurs et lectures populaires à la Belle Époque* (1984), 15–35; and HEF 4:529–41.

[43] See Michel Vovelle, *Idéologies et mentalités* (1982), 5–17.

[44] Using anthropological work on exchange (esp. Mauss, Firth, and Weiner) is Natalie Zemon Davis, ''Beyond the Market: Books as Gifts in Sixteenth-Century France,'' *Transactions of the Royal Historical Society*, 5th ser., 33 (1983): 69–88.

France—except during World War I. Then soldiers begged for things to read at the front, where books and newspapers were scarce because of military operations and political censorship. But the network of exchange among readers had another function; it also stimulated the market for print. Again, Balzac was not alone in dedicating his novels, including each volume in *La Comédie humaine*, to respected friends or colleagues. Zola, too, sought to curry favor among important readers ambivalent in their attitudes towards the naturalistic novel. Théodore Duret recommended that Zola take an inscribed copy of *L'Assommoir* to the appropriate official in the Interior Ministry responsible for authorizing the book's sale in railway stations everywhere in France.[45] Whether or not Zola did so, the ministry refused to permit such work "to affect too keenly the anonymous clientele of rail-station bookstores," a faceless public who bought their books rather than receiving them as gifts.[46]

Underlying the exchange of printed matter was the expectation of reciprocity. Every gift represented for the recipient an obligation to the donor, a personal responsibility resented by some people and enjoyed by others. Balzac's touchy brother-in-law, Eugène Surville, reminded the author of this cultural assumption in explicit terms. Upon hearing that Balzac had sent a book to his wife, Surville wrote, "If Laure accepts your gift, it will be, I'm sure, by right of friendship on her part and mine. It is only thus that you can hope to see it accepted. If you are our debtor [in this], we hope to remain creditors for the rest."[47] Surville would not be obliged to his wife's brother no matter how well intended Balzac's gesture. On the other hand, Alphonse Daudet responded very differently to an inscription in the copy of Zola's *La Terre* that was sent to him: "It touches me, this dedication, because it proves that you have forgotten what others had attempted to put between us, the slander that for a moment you appeared to believe I had inspired."[48] This gift thus served to dispel a misunderstanding rather than to create one between two writers with different conceptions of prose fiction. Evidently, within well-defined relationships among family members, colleagues, friends, and acquaintances, reading was a social act fraught with cultural implications that came with books passed from hand to hand even after print had become a cheap commodity in the market.

This practical reality, well represented by the exchange of reading material and the mutual obligations it entailed, appeared in some correspondents' quest for patronage and advice from established writers. The receipt of a volume certainly put reviewers in awkward positions, as Léon Blum stated diplomat-

---

[45] Théodore Duret to Zola, 13 Jan. 1877, in BN NAFr 24518 fols. 252–53.

[46] See Henri Mitterand and Jean Vidal, eds., *Album Zola* (1963), 153.

[47] Eugène Surville to Balzac, 2 Dec. 1834, in *Balzac: Corr.*, ed. Roger Pierrot (1960–66), 2:586.

[48] Alphonse Daudet to Zola, [18 Nov. 1887], in BN NAFr 24517 fol. 306. Cf. Huysmans to Zola, [20 Aug. 1887], in EZRP Coll. LeBlond A152.

ically to Anatole France. After the author had sent him *Le Puits de Sainte Claire* in 1895, the critic wrote, "I am very happy to have such a book, and even happier if my article truly did not displease you."[49] More common were annoying manuscript offerings from aspiring authors; their gifts arrived with often plaintive appeals for help in writing and publishing their work. A provincial poetaster, Fanny Dénois, virtually pestered Eugène Sue for more than a year with various installments of her interminable poem inspired by *Les Mystères de Paris*, though it is unclear whether or not Sue had a hand in its eventual publication.[50] Similarly, Hippolyte Lucas wrote to Balzac, "I will be happy if this slight work I am sending you procures for me the advantage of knowing you and of initiating me into the secrets of your craft."[51] Anatole France received more than 175 such letters from writers, their work also enclosed for his perusal and approval. But some correspondents resorted to flattery for other reasons; nearly every tale of woe soliciting for the letter writer an autograph or a favor was prefaced by extravagant praise for the author's latest books. This was true as well of requests for loans and jobs that every writer here received in the period.

The utility of reading was especially evident in the consolation and escape that correspondents sought in literature. Nearly timeless in this function, books provided solace for loneliness, boredom, homesickness, worry, grief, even physical pain. Stendhal's sister Pauline once lamented the ennui and lethargy of adolescent life; to resolve this problem, she stoutly declared, "I must choose between reading and a pistol."[52] Peyranne de Candolle managed to forget the pain he suffered from gout with Rabelais's *Pantagruel* and Balzac's *Contes drolatiques*. Like Ernest Lemarié, who wrote to Flaubert from Madrid, travelers far from France read to forget their intense longing for home.[53] World War I in particular forced both men and women to allay their anxiety for loved ones, or themselves, by reading. Carlos Blacker wrote Anatole France repeatedly how the novelist had provided him release from deep concerns over his sons at the front. "I am reading your books indefatigably," he said in 1915. "They are my *sole* consolation"—as France's work proved to be for others as well.[54] The panacea of literature was expressed, albeit ironically, by another correspondent thanking France for the book that the author had sent; "accord-

[49] Léon Blum to France, [1895], in BN NAFr 15430 fol. 427.

[50] Fanny Dénois to Eugène Sue, in BHVP Fonds Sue fols. 36–78, 142–43, 146–47, 187, 201–2, 243, 244–45, 420–22. Cf. Fanny Dénois *Les Mystères de Paris* (1843).

[51] Hippolyte Lucas to Balzac, [Dec. 1834], in *Balzac: Corr.*, 2:585.

[52] Pauline Beyle to Henri Beyle, [5 Dec. 1805], in *Stendhal: Corr.*, ed. Henri Martineau and Victor Del Litto (1967–68), 1:1151.

[53] See Peyranne de Candolle to Balzac, [27 Dec. 1833], in *Balzac: Corr.*, 2:290; and Ernest Lemarié to Flaubert, 20 Dec. [1862], in BSL H.1364 (B.IV) fols. 194–95.

[54] Carlos Blacker to France, 10 Sept. 1915, in BN NAFr 15430 fol. 354 (emphasis in the original). Cf. Loring Baker Walton, "Anatole France and the First World War: The Correspondence with Carlos Blacker," *PMLA* 77 (1962): 471–81.

ing to Rabelais's directives in one of his prefaces, I immediately placed it on my lung, and I was cured. If I am still in bed, it is to satisfy the doctors' incurable manias."[55] The cure offered by a text was more effective than medicine.

Literature meant more than diversion, however necessary to existence; it also meant knowledge, often of profound importance to the attentive reader. Characters in a novel served as models from which lessons for life could be drawn, as Zulma Carraud reminded Balzac in a letter warning him of his extravagant personal expenditures: "Have you measured the shagreen talisman since you redecorated your apartment?" she asked, in an explicit reference to the fate of the main character in *La Peau de chagrin*.[56] Correspondents frequently mentioned how much they had learned from their reading. Father Damourette of Châteauroux, for one, told Eugène Sue that he had been moved to found a house for orphan girls, one modeled after a rural utopia described in *Les Mystères de Paris*, to redeem the virtuous poor in his department.[57] Other correspondents noted the wise counsel, the sage advice, the soothing philosophy apparent to them in literature. Besides moral attitudes for upright behavior, readers acquired substantive knowledge of art, society, and politics, especially in the realistic novel after 1850. But prose fiction, realistic or not, offered very practical insight into the self; one Frenchwoman explained her realization of this literary truth at length in a letter to Zola: "As I read, I feel my self-esteem rising again in my own eyes. I understand that I am merely subject to a general law, the first law in fact, of nature."[58] Her reading (and that of other letter writers) made possible perhaps the most profound knowledge of all, that of her own being.

This practical understanding of the self, however, almost always existed within a specific social setting. For the correspondents, reading took place within a network of personal relations of varying intensity and duration. For example, books were an important topic of conversation and gossip among family and friends. And so the relative merits of Aeschylus and Voltaire were heatedly discussed at a dinner attended by Stendhal's close associate Louis Crozet.[59] Literary works in fact constituted a convenient excuse to talk about their authors at similar social occasions. Apt quotations from books that guests had read added sparkle and wit to otherwise dreary provincial drawing-rooms. Moreover, tags from Latin authors studied in school and long passages from an author's most recent production littered the letters by correspondents anxious to impress the recipients, while news of the latest publications in Paris filled the letters to Stendhal written by Adolphe de Mareste, Sophie Duvaucel,

[55] S. Burnet to France, 29 Oct. 1919, in BN NAFr 15431 fol. 201.

[56] Zulma Carraud to Balzac, 10 Sept. 1832, in *Balzac: Corr.*, 2:115.

[57] Damourette to Sue, 24 Oct. 1843, in BHVP Fonds Sue fol. 486.

[58] Carole to Zola, Jan. 1887, in EZRP Coll. LeBlond A39.

[59] Louis Crozet to Beyle, 26 brumaire an 14, in *Stendhal: Corr.*, 1:1137.

and Astolphe de Custine.[60] But nearly every correspondent here saw reading as actually engaging the author of the text in dialogue; literature became a personal communication from the writer to the reader, little different from a letter. Sometimes a book was mistaken for a proper social introduction. Wrote one woman, Octavie de B., to Eugène Sue, "My happiness would be complete if I had given myself to know the man who wrote such ravishing pages. Could you, Monsieur, . . . spare some time from inspiration to devote it to the most sympathetic of your woman readers? I am at home every evening."[61]

The social dimension to literate activities in modern France usually had more innocent implications. Because many letter writers were close friends of the author, they sometimes served as privileged auditors of work in progress or recently completed. Félix Faure listened to Stendhal's manuscripts, as did Zulma Carraud to Balzac's, Alfred Baudry to Flaubert's, and William Busnach to Zola's. This intimate context of reading among writers occurred as well among family members. Jules Troubat told Zola how amused his household had been one night by the flatulent antics of "Jesus Christ" in *La Terre*; during the reading *en famille*, the children could bearly stifle their giggles, while the servant split her sides in laughter.[62] Despite the character's grotesque vulgarity, the group's merriment prevailed, the text transformed by the mutual trust felt by the family members. Other social occasions outside the family also informed literate activities. Most frequently, correspondents mentioned reading in salons, clubs, and schools where literature was prominently featured. Stendhal, Balzac, Sue, and Flaubert were invited to literary dinners with friends and colleagues; Zola was asked what formal organizations held meetings devoted to literature; and Anatole France was informed of schools that used his work for class dictation.[63] In each case, people shared textual experiences for practical public purposes—entertaining, promoting, studying.

Defined by expectations of literary exchange, patronage, consolation, knowledge, and activity in relationship with others, the reader's social reality was indeed profound enough to alter the immediate experience of literature itself. Literary characters, for example, became textual representations of actual people the correspondents claimed to know. Among Madame de Staël's

[60] See letters to Beyle from Adolphe de Mareste, [8 Mar. 1818], in *Stendhal: Corr.*, 1: 1254–56; Sophie Duvaucel, 10 Oct. 1834, in *Cent soixante-quatorze lettres à Stendhal (1810–1842)*, ed. Henri Martineau (1947), 2:86–94; and Astolphe de Custine [Feb. 1838] in ibid., 2:153.

[61] Octavie de B. to Sue, 23 June 1844, cited in Bory, *Eugène Sue*, 277. Cf. Marie to Balzac, n.d., in BSL A.318 fol. 104.

[62] Jules Troubat to Zola, 9 Dec. 1887, in BN NAFr 24524 fols. 307–8.

[63] See letters from Custine to Beyle, [10 Sept. 1838], in *Cent soixante-quatorze lettres à Stendhal*, 2:161; Delphine de Girardin to Balzac, [16 Mar. 1836], in *Balzac: Corr.*, 3:43; Annette Lefort to Sue, 13 May 1843, in BHVP Fonds Sue fol. 168; Edmond About to Flaubert, [1857], in Flaubert, *Oeuvres complètes: Madame Bovary*, 525–26; Jan ten Brink to Zola, 12 July 1877, in BN NAFr 24512 fol. 8; and Gabriel Jean to France, 26 May 1923, in BN NAFr 15434, fol. 645.

personal acquaintances there was almost universal agreement that the heroine of *Corinne* was Germaine herself. *"Corinne* will never be a book for me," declared her lover, Prosper de Barante. "It was always you I heard."[64] Madame de Staël, of course, had made no secret of her fictional alter ego. Other readers were less pleased to believe themselves portrayed. Jules Sandeau scolded Balzac for the unflattering depiction of Lucien de Rubempré and his relationship to Madame de Bargeton in *Illusions perdues*; they were too much like the hapless Sandeau and the more experienced George Sand, his former mistress.[65] At the invitation of the author, correspondents asked Eugène Sue to have their personal situations recounted in his novel serialized in the *Journal des débats*. Henry Monnier saw much of himself in Homais, the philistine pharmacist of *Madame Bovary*, and half seriously asked Flaubert for the role if the novel should ever become a play.[66] Similarly, both Zola and France were questioned about the people behind the characters with the same name as the correspondents. Queried André Manchon to France in 1918, "Did you know this Colonel Manchon [in *La Révolte des anges*]? Does he really exist or was his name merely a creation of your imagination?" The correspondent himself did not know "this honorable representative of my family."[67]

The social reality of reading also made actual people out of literary characters. Correspondents frequently referred to Oswald in *Corinne*, to Julien in *Le Rouge et le noir*, to Vautrin in *Le Père Goriot*, to Emma in *Madame Bovary*, to Françoise in *La Terre*, and to Sylvestre in *Le Crime de Sylvestre Bonnard* in the same way they would to family members, friends, or neighbors. Even more remarkable were the correspondents who believed in the actual existence of a principal character, like Prince Rodolphe of Gerolstein in Eugène Sue's *Les Mystères de Paris*: "You give him so many accolades, it is impossible that he will not help me in something," wrote one desperate reader in quest of charity from a most unlikely source.[68] Years later, the publisher Yves Guyot suggested that Zola draw up a genealogical tree for the Rougon-Macquart family, the main characters in Zola's novel cycle: "I am sure that their family affairs would interest our readers" in light of their sincere concern for the fate of these people.[69] Although most letters written to France tended to identify characters with the novelist, they also spoke of them as trusted companions who kept excellent company, just as an actual person could have done. The world of prose fiction here was not at all fantastic, but substantive and

[64] Prosper de Barante to Germaine de Staël, 19 May 1807, in *Madame de Staël, ses amis, ses correspondants. Choix de lettres (1778–1817)*, ed. Georges Solovieff (1970), 218.

[65] Jules Sandeau to Balzac, [17 Mar. 1837], in *Balzac: Corr.*, 3:267–68.

[66] Henry Monnier to Flaubert, 30 Dec. 1857, in Flaubert, *Oeuvres complètes: Madame Bovary*, 524.

[67] André Manchon to France, 10 May 1918, in BN NAFr 15436 fol. 49.

[68] E. Bazire to Sue, 4 Sept. 1843, in BHVP Fonds Sue fol. 378.

[69] Yves Guyot to Zola, 19 Dec. 1877, in BN NAFr 24519 fol. 464.

populated with recognizable personalities whether or not they were based on people of the author's acquaintance. Some correspondents, in fact, considered certain literary characters their best friends.

For many readers, the author was the most prominent figure in a text. Friends and colleagues long familiar with a novelist could not avoid noting his or her resemblance to a particular narrative voice. For instance, Henri Latouche wrote to Balzac about *Le Dernier Chouan*: "I have seen no one, because I wanted to hear your voice in peace."[70] Close acquaintances with Jules Michelet also claimed to hear the writer speaking in *La Femme*, but much less clearly. No matter how well Michelet's correspondents thought they knew him, the man apparent in the text eluded them, perhaps because the work itself was impossible to classify. Michelet was responsible for what letter writers called variously "science," "natural morality," "a practical manual," "a gospel," "thoughts," and "dreams." Few readers knew with certainty, some preferring even vaguer references to the "work," the "book," the "creation," or more general still, the "production."[71] Outside a writer's private circle, people were often more decided about the figure in the text. Exclaimed the baron Galvagna about Balzac, "I have known some works by celebrated writers, but the morality that appears through his writings is not of the nature to inspire in me an ardent desire to make his personal acquaintance."[72] Most documented readers, however, found Balzac's narrative persona far more appealing, and the women among them especially sought to make his acquaintance. As one anonymous female wrote to Balzac in 1836, "I do not distinguish the man from the author"—nor did readers of texts by other writers in the period.[73]

If the conception of an immediate, deeply personal reality fostered a certain interchangeability of people and characters, voices and narratives, it also helped create the correspondents' deification of the author. The author's divine nature, as perceived by readers from the romantic period onward, was expressed frequently in the letters sent to every French novelist studied here. Women readers called Balzac "everyone's hero," "God's revelation," "like these celestial souls of Dante," while a glassworker wrote Eugène Sue, "You are the truth, and the truth is God."[74] After World War I, fans made a virtual cult of Anatole France; dozens of them appealed each year for autographs,

---

[70] Henri Latouche to Balzac, [26 Nov. 1828], in *Balzac: Corr.*, 1:352.

[71] See letters in Jules Michelet, *Oeuvres complètes—L'Amour—La Femme*, ed. Paul Viallaneix et al. (1985), 625, 627, 628, 629, 631, 634, 639.

[72] Baron Galvagna to comtesse Clara Maffei, 10 Mar. 1837, cited in *Balzac: Corr.*, 3:263 n.

[73] Anon. to Balzac, 13 Feb. [1836], in *Cahiers balzaciens, No. 2*, ed. Marcel Bouteron (1924), 22.

[74] See letters to Balzac from C. [before 26 April 1832], in *Cahiers balzaciens*, 2; anon., n.d., in BSL A.318 fol. 91; and comtesse Potocka, 14 Mar. [1834], in *Balzac: Corr.*, 2:478. Cf. Goguilly to Sue, 7 Sept. 1843, in BHVP Fonds Sue fol. 392.

photographs, and assorted relics from the reigning deity of French letters—
"God of light and of goodness," as one correspondent put it.[75] Adolescents
especially developed a passionate devotion for the author of the books that
were passed surreptitiously in class from student to student. In 1920 a schoolgirl, Hélène Demouys, wrote

> Since—and with the years—from *Thaïs* to *Petit Pierre*—the company of "Ana-
> tole"—has become familiar to me—as we called him then among initiates and
> fans—and with what unequalled admiration—what youthful enthusiasm—nearly
> with devotion—the celebrated man who enchanted us.[76]

Other readers sought out writers as oracles to request their views of recent
events. Unhappy women went to Balzac, socialist sympathizers to Sue, fellow
naturalists to Zola, and ardent pacifists to France, all for confirmation of their
faith in the authors' infinite wisdom. In this context, the writer was no longer
a voice in the narrative, but the text itself.

Readers thus tended to combine the realities of text and of life. Characters
in the novel became people on the street, acquaintances became literary figures, authors became narratives. The correspondents frequently confused the
fictional and nonfictional genres they claimed to have read; the writer's carefully crafted creative imagination was thus appropriated by the reader's less
structured everyday world. According to Jules Gaulthier, for instance, the
comtesse Clémentine de Tascher mistook Stendhal's novel, *L'Abbesse de Cas-
tro*, for a love letter intended for her.[77] Balzac's letter writers remarked the
author's careful observation of detail more appropriate to history than to prose
fiction. One reader, in fact, corrected minor details in *La Peau de chagrin* that
had placed the action of two chapters in Aix-en-Savoie: "Savoy is not in Italy,
it is still French. Aix has no casino."[78] One of Sue's readers was even less
sophisticated, mistaking installments of a serial novel for news articles in the
Journal des débats. With the development of literary realism and naturalism,
however, this misconception became far more common in the letters sent to
Flaubert and Zola. The prose narrative's careful attention to detail misled readers who likened the novel to a painting, an actual picture of the world in which
they lived. For Henry Morel, *Madame Bovary* became a map of Rouen that
permitted him to trace Emma's course through the city.[79] For others, *Salammbô* presented still another reality no less palpable. "After reading it, I
pinched my thighs to convince myself that I still exist," wrote Charles-Ed-

---

[75] Isa Sion [Danesti Vaslin] to France, n.d., in BN NAFr 15439 fols. 215–16.
[76] Hélène Demouys to France, 2 Dec. 1920, in BN NAFr 15433 fols. 151–54.
[77] Jules Gaulthier to Beyle, [9 Feb. 1839], in *Cent soixante-quatorze lettres à Stendhal*, 2:167.
[78] Ernest de Blosseville to Balzac, 19 Mar. 1832, in *Balzac: Corr.*, 1:683.
[79] Henry Morel to Flaubert, 1 Mar. [1857], in BSL H.1365 (B.V) fols. 38–39.

mond Chojecki, "then I went to the mirror over the fireplace, and I was surprised to see that I was not wearing a Carthaginian hairdo."[80]

From all the evidence at hand, then, it would seem that French readers had a distinct conception of reality, one that was at once useful and personal, practical and immediate. The letters sent to authors repeatedly defined literate activity as a social good within networks of exchange, patronage, knowledge, and organization; books shared in the relationships that the correspondents had with their family, friends, and others. This much of the reader's world gave literature a vital utilitarian function. Similarly, the letters revealed how much textual meaning owed to individual experience within a web of social relations; literary characters became real only when they resembled the reader, a loved one, or a close acquaintance. Although the voice of the text remained entirely the author's, the everyday life of the reader transposed the literary imagination of the writer. In this way, audiences rendered the abstract meaning of print understandable, indeed tangible. Otherwise, the text would have been opaque, at least for the letter writers and their literate experiences documented here. Their specific cultural context by and large existed unchanged over the course of the nineteenth century. The notion of what was real remained basically the same for the readers of Anatole France as it had been for the readers of Madame de Staël 125 years earlier. Romantic, realist, naturalist, and symbolist texts alike appeared in a comparable guise, both immediate and personal, subject of course to minor variations apparent among the correspondents. But the conception of reality was the same, as unaltered as the conservative literary norms of the reviewers in the same period. For modern French readers, literature was an eternal truth—of a very special sort.

KNOWLEDGE

To the extent that both teachers and students regarded texts as a source of knowledge, the school constituted still another interpretive community. Educational institutions were even more cohesive than book reviewers or correspondents. In fact, French education from the First Empire to the outbreak of World War II made fundamental assumptions about learning in general and reading in particular.[81] Among other things, instruction was intended to instill moral principles in all literate French men and women through a rationalistic approach to problems, a cartesian habit of mind. These implicit educational objectives demanded rules, order, and discipline in schools established by

---

[80] Charles-Edmond Chojecki to Flaubert, n.d., in BSL H.1361 (B.I) fols. 348–49.

[81] See H. C. Rulon and Philippe Friot, *Un Siècle de pédagogie dans les écoles primaires (1820–1940)* (1962); Pierre Giolitto, *Histoire de l'enseignement primaire au XIXe siècle* (1984), vol. 2; Clément Falcucci, *L'Humanisme dans l'enseignement secondaire en France au XIXe siècle* (Toulouse, 1939); Paul Foulquié, *Dictionnaire de la langue pédagogique* (1971); and Guy Avanzini, ed., *Histoire de la pédagogie du 17e siècle à nos jours* (1981).

church and state alike. Accordingly, French pedagogical methods reflected this rigid formalism, breaking apart every problem into its constituent elements and studying each one from the simplest to the most complex in relation to the whole. On the primary-school level, for example, the teacher most often resorted to the statement and illustration of truisms that the students were to accept at face value, however far removed such *leçons de choses* often were from personal experience. Children rejected or distorted the lesson to fit what they already knew of the world, but they fully internalized the deductive thought underlying the instruction they received.[82] In this way, French education, from primary school to the university, developed another collective predisposition to the text (as a cultural code) in a rationalism that pervaded interpretive practice throughout the period.

Cartesian thinking was even at the heart of elementary reading instruction. Despite the rise of competing approaches, the "synthetic" method based on principles of phonetic decoding remained the most common in France until quite recently.[83] In strict order, students learned to pronounce letters, syllables, words, and in some cases whole sentences before they learned what these sounds meant when put together. "The first attention one must pay," stated N.-A. Viard in *Les Vrais Principes de la lecture*, an extensively used text since 1763, "is to determine the proper sound of each letter."[84] As a consequence, young children were forced to memorize the many sounds that these signs made, an especially challenging task in a language as phonetically irregular as French. A. Peigné acknowledged this fact in his text, *Méthode de lecture* (1832): "The countless difficulties that a child encounters in learning to read come almost solely from the multitude of exceptions that burden our writing system."[85] So long as proper pronunciation remained the bedrock of reading instruction, teachers resorted to various mnemonic devices to facilitate the relatively sophisticated phonetic deciphering required of young children. Flash cards, sound tables, appropriate illustrations, and songbooks appeared early on in primary-school classrooms for the affluent; but such tools came much later to the rural poor who recited texts, conned without any substantive understanding of their meaning. And so for the entire Third Republic, reading instruction in French proceeded logically from the simplest to the most com-

---

[82] See Jules Masson, *Le Livre de lecture des petits garçons* (1880), 61–62. Cf. Jean Hébrard, "Apprendre à lire à l'école en France: Un Siècle de recommandations officiels," *Langue française* 80 (1988): 111–28.

[83] See Ferdinand Buisson, ed., *Dictionnaire de pédagogie et d'instruction primaire* (1887), 2:1534–49.

[84] Nicolas-Antoine Viard and Luneau de Bois-Germain, *Les Vrais Principes de la lecture, de l'orthographe et de la prononciation française* (Avignon, 1830), 3 (in no fewer than 24 editions, 1763–1830).

[85] A. Peigné, *Méthode de lecture, ouvrage adopté par la Société pour l'instruction élémentaire* (1832), v–vi.

plex elements of language, even though cognitively this proved too difficult for one-fourth of all first-year students.[86]

Strictly formal instruction continued in the study of grammar. Even before reading and writing were taught together—a reform instituted only after the Ferry Laws of the 1880s—grammatical rules were memorized and applied in yet another rationalistic procedure, one derived from traditional conceptions of the humanities (grammar, rhetoric, and dialectic). Larive and Fleury's widely used textbooks, for example, moved from principles of orthography (year one) and sentence construction (year two) to composition (year three) based on classical French models of language use. Each step emphasized the rhetorical and logical elements of grammar to promote a proper writing style with "*nobility, precision, simplicity, clarity, harmony*, and *concision*."[87] By the end of the third year of study, these books assumed that students would recognize (and adopt) the features of language modeled on seventeenth-century French texts. As G. Belot stated explicitly in 1911, "Elementary-school teachers know that the chief end of their efforts must be to prepare good students in grammar classes, that is to say, to form good minds to study classical culture" in the broadest sense of the word.[88] The less capable children would, of course, share in that preparation whether or not they continued their studies beyond the elementary-school level. Because reading exercises were an important part of grammar study, interpretive practices shared the same humanistic assumptions; the frequent oral readings in class reinforced the rhetorical character of modern French discourse and its reception outside as well as inside the classroom setting.

A heavy moralizing quality characterizes the reading materials that schoolchildren used to practice their newly acquired skills. One purpose of primary education, since the Counter-Reformation at least, had been the inculcation of religious belief; this the Catholic Church's *petites écoles* promoted by carefully selected texts, such as those Viard enclosed in his primer: the catechism, the Lord's Prayer, the Hail Mary, the Confession of Sins, and the Ten Commandments.[89] Practical information was a secondary concern of early reli-

---

[86] See J. Downing, ed., *Comparative Reading* (New York, 1973), 319–41. Cf. compensation in Abria, *Méthode de lecture sans épellation* (Valenciennes, 1835); P. Néel, *L'École. Méthode Néel, lecture, écriture, leçons de choses* (1873); and Eugène Cuissart, *Méthode Cuissart. Enseignement pratique et simultané de lecture, de l'écriture et de l'orthographie* (1882). Cf. Ségolène LeMen, *Les Abécédaires français du XIXe siècle* (1984), 111–98.

[87] Larive and Fleury, *La Deuxième Année de grammaire* (1872), 126 (emphasis in the original), 126–29, 150–52, and idem, *La Troisième Année de grammaire* (1879), 230–40. On the distribution of these and other texts, see Laura S. Strumingher, *What Were Little Girls and Boys Made Of? Primary Education in Rural France, 1830–1880* (Albany, 1983), 155–72.

[88] Louis Liard et al., eds., *Instructions concernant les programmes de l'enseignement secondaire (garçons et filles)* (1911), 64. Cf. Gérard Genette, "Enseignement et rhétorique au XIXe siècle," 21 *Annales: E.S.C.* (1966): 292–305.

[89] See Viard and Luneau de Bois-Germain, *Les Vrais Principes*, Table of Contents, 173.

gious education. When the state assumed responsibility for elementary education, however, it replaced religious dogma with heavy doses of moral virtue and patriotism, especially after the French defeat in the Franco-Prussian War. In 1835, one textbook admonished young readers: "Use this first learning that you have just acquired only to improve yourself and to make your heart moral and upright."[90] Among the most widely used primary-school readers in the Third Republic, Zulma Carraud's *La Petite Jeanne, ou Le Devoir* (for girls) and *Maurice, ou Le Travail* (for boys) praised obedience, work, and family, just as G. Bruno's *Le Tour de France par deux enfants* extolled love of one's country.[91] Whether religious or secular, a more or less explicit normative principle underlay these and other texts used in French elementary schools; their instruction followed a set procedure of statement and demonstration for every lesson or exercise. In the nineteenth-century grammar school, reading always had a well-defined purpose.

These *a priori* pedagogical concerns for rule, order, and discipline were well expressed by a state commission to select texts for use in primary schools. Begun in the last months of the Restoration, the commission did not receive clear guidelines until September 1831. Only then did the minister of public instruction and cults, the comte de Montalivet, state explicitly the cartesian nature of elementary education in modern France.

> First of all, what we want taught must be well understood; this is a necessary condition. For that, one must begin with true principles [and] become capable of appreciating their implications, of applying them. The best method in this respect is therefore that which conforms to the nature of things, which reflects their principle and follows faithfully from the coordination [between theory and practice].[92]

For the next seventeen years, the commission followed the minister's advice closely, reporting their reasons for classifying books submitted for their approval according to their audience, subject matter, style, and morality. For instance, one reader's report on Pascal de Lodève's *Méthode pour apprendre à lire en très peu de temps* remarked, "It is impossible to tie it down to a logical order, and the difficulties cannot be graduated."[93] It therefore was not recommended for use in French primary schools, because it violated the rationalistic assumptions of proper elementary instruction. As for Miss Edge-

---

[90] Abria, *Méthode de lecture sans épellation*, 32.

[91] Zulma Carraud, *La Petite Jeanne, ou Le Devoir* (1852), reprinted 40 times, 1852–1901; idem, *Maurice, ou Le Travail* (1853), reprinted 31 times, 1853–97; and G. Bruno, *Le Tour de France par deux enfants, devoir et patrie* (1877), reprinted 29 times, 1877–1910 (8 million copies). Cf. Pierre Nora, ed., *Les Lieux de mémoire* (1984), 1:291–322; Aimé Dupuy, "Les Livres de lecture de G. Bruno," *Revue d'histoire économique et sociale* 2 (1953): 27–49; Dominique Maingueneau, *Les Livres d'école de la République, 1870–1914. Discours et idéologie* (1979), 195–217.

[92] AN F17,1547 fols. 40–41.

[93] AN F17,1549, item 1501.

worth's *Éducation familière*—a manual for the moral education of children in wealthy families—it was "a model of its type," not just in the Orleanist Monarchy but throughout the modern period.[94] The pedagogical principles remained largely the same for both school and family.

This formal manner of knowing, and teaching, continued to inform the study of texts in secondary schools. The objectives, methods, and means of education here were the same as in primary school, only now imaginative literature came to play a far more important role. Latin and French literary classics, the curricular core at most collèges and lycées before World War II, were used to perpetuate the humanistic ideals of ancient Greece and Rome; these values were adapted first to a Catholic Christian context and then to that of a secular nation-state.[95] The focus, however, was not on the texts themselves, but on their timeless truths and the cultured individual who understood and quoted them. "It is commonly accepted," stated one prominent educator in 1883, "that only literature instruction is efficacious in education, in that literature alone clarifies, develops, and informs the emotions—in other words, it speaks to the heart."[96] Consequently, for most of the nineteenth century, secondary-school students studied carefully selected extracts, brief aphoristic passages usually taken from seventeenth- and eighteenth-century monuments of French classicism. For example, in 1810 Capelle entitled his schoolbook *Dictionary of Morals, Science, and Literature, or A Selection of Ingenious and Sublime Thoughts . . . In Order to Provide Relaxation, to Inform the Heart, to Ornament the Mind, and to Sustain the Memory of Young People.* In 1853, Louis Baude stated, "Literature has the purpose of embellishing useful things with the grace of language," a sentiment substantiated by his text's attention to genre and style appropriate to poetry and oration.[97]

It is within this pedagogical context that the debate over Latin study occurred at the turn of the century. The controversy centered on the educational utility of dead languages, even though the same methods of instruction applied to reading selections in either French or Latin. In 1902, the noted historian Ernest Lavisse complained of his early education, "The true end of study then was rhetoric, where the best students spent two years. In rhetoric everything was given over to speeches. We composed two of them each week, one in Latin and the other in French," each one based on a situation derived from the reading of a brief text.[98] Accordingly, reading and rhetoric were inextricably

---

[94] AN F17,1547, item 43.

[95] Avanzini, ed., *Histoire de la pédagogie*, 303–10. Cf. Ralph Albanese, Jr., "Lectures critiques de Molière au XIXe siècle," *Revue d'histoire du théâtre* 36 (1984): 341–61.

[96] Buisson, ed., *Dictionnaire de pédagogie*, 2:1599.

[97] Louis Baude, *Cahiers d'une élève de Saint-Denis* (1853), 11:1.

[98] Ernest Lavisse, "Souvenirs d'une éducation manquée," *Revue de Paris* (15 Nov. 1902): 17. Cf. Edmond Goblot, *La Barrière et le niveau. Étude sociologique sur la bourgeoisie française moderne*, 2d ed. (1967), 81–86.

related, even confused, in Lavisse's mind long after his student days. But in 1873, Mgr. Dupanloup had responded to earlier charges against the utility of Latin by posing and answering a single question: "What is the end of the highest literary instruction? The end is to embrace not the empty and banal word, but the true, replete, and strong word, the lively expression of thought, the word of great minds." Just as the ancients specialized in certain timeless rhetorical forms, so must students study them. "True culture and great education" constituted "a new, more noble and elevated form" than the primitive natural idiom of vulgar French.[99] Although after 1902 students could choose a course of study without Latin, few of them did; most continued to learn the French language's Latin roots and its considerable debt to classical stylistic forms.

Literary instruction changed in 1880, when literary history officially replaced rhetoric in the secondary-school curriculum; but this move actually reinforced long-standing pedagogical concerns. In the *Instructions officiels* of 1890, Minister of Public Instruction Léon Bourgeois called for the study of whole works, in lieu of the abstract summaries and illustrative snippets that generally appeared in most secondary-school textbooks.[100] The purpose of this attention to French literature—increasingly at the expense of rhetoric and Latin study—was to promote the development of the individual, just as it always had been, only now in a more contemporary perspective. With further ministerial instructions to the same effect in 1902 and again in 1911, literary study in French collèges and lycées came to include a new subject matter (nineteenth-century texts) and a new method of reading it (the *explication de texte*). For students, literature thus became less "the living thought of a person separated from us in time and space" and more "a noble commerce with the elites of our race" in recent texts.[101] Clearly, well-focused instruction in French literature alone was most cogently defended in 1892 by the dean of literary studies, Ferdinand Brunetière. To ensure continuity in both curriculum and pedagogy despite the loss of Latin, he called for three conditions: effort from the students, perfection from the texts they read, and a sense of history from their teachers. Such were "the exigencies . . . of a purely French and yet classical secondary education."[102] Despite the reforms, the conception of literature as knowledge remained intact.

As a ministerial official stated in 1911, "Explicated reading remains the

---

[99] Mgr. [Félix] Dupanloup, *Second Lettre . . . sur la circulaire de M. le ministre de l'instruction publique relative à l'enseignement secondaire* (1873), 51.

[100] Léon Bourgeois, in Ministère de l'Instruction Publique, *Circulaires et instructions officielles relatives à l'instruction publique*, Tome 11: *Juin 1889–décembre 1893* (1894), 300–304.

[101] Cf. Alexandre Vessiot, *La Récitation à l'école et la lecture expliquée (Cours moyens et supérieurs)* (1888), 208; and Bourgeois, *Circulaires et instructions*, 11:301.

[102] Ferdinand Brunetière, *Essais sur la littérature contemporaine* (1892), 313. Cf. Julien Bézard, *De la méthode littéraire. Journal d'un professeur* (1911), 733–40.

foundation of literary instruction.''[103] The close analysis of texts had been implicit in grammar and recitation exercises throughout the nineteenth century. But it was not until the reforms of 1902 that this style of reading displaced the time-honored *discours* (a speech composed on imaginary situations taken from classical texts) as the most prominent pedagogical feature of French secondary education. The formality of literary instruction remained the same, however, as a resourceful teacher in the decade before World War I, Julien Bézard, explained: textual explication was ''the symbol of the principle which must above all direct us in our studies; it represents the *love of order*.''[104] Although Bézard sought to develop his own students' taste, sentiment, and imagination, his less-conscientious colleagues made close reading yet another formulaic exercise, a veritable rite, that has endured in French schools to this day. The basic elements have changed little since Gustave Rudler formulated them, one by one, in 1910:

1. We present all historical clarifications. . . .
2. We read [the passage] aloud.
3. We situate it within the larger work. . . .
4. We state . . . the theme, the dominant sentiment of the selection.
5. We disentangle from it the composition's general plan, the division into parts, the movement and the structure of the whole, if it is in prose; if it is in poetry, the rhythm and melody in general.
6. We highlight the work's literary qualities or salient moral character.
7. If contextual information remains for presentation that appeared inappropriate under item 1, it finds its natural place here.[105]

While Rudler's claim to scientific objectivity and precision was not widely shared, his cartesian method was: ''Form and content are counterparts, the verification of one another, in the same way as the whole and its parts.''[106] Like many other subjects, textual analysis required rationalistic instruction.

Students responded remarkably well to the persistent pedagogical principles in French secondary education. Their notebooks and journals record the precise reading skills they learned in school. In 1815, during the Napoleonic Hundred Days, Émile Bary, for instance, brought to bear the moralistic concerns of his teachers on a reading of Rousseau's *La Nouvelle Héloïse*; ''All young

[103] Liard et al., eds., *Instructions*, 44.

[104] Julien Bézard, *La Classe de Français. Journal d'un professeur* (1908), 18. On the transition from *discours* to *explication de texte*, see Antoine Prost, *Histoire de l'enseignement en France 1800–1967* (1968), 52–53, 246–49.

[105] Gustave Rudler, *L'Explication française. Principes et applications* (1902), 44. Cf. Eugène Cuissart, *Premier Degré de lectures courantes (Troisième livret)* (1884), 3–4; Vessiot, *La Récitation*, 5; and Liard et al., eds., *Instructions*, 83.

[106] Rudler, *L'Explication française*, 4. Cf. W. M. Frohock, *French Literature: An Approach through Close Reading* (Cambridge, Mass., 1964), 105–9.

people can draw from it a useful lesson," he noted in his journal. "With vice, there can be no happiness," quite aside from the tears he shed over the fate of Julie de Wolmar and Saint-Preux.[107] School-age youths over the course of the next hundred years were equally adept at applying the rules of literary instruction. Classroom dictations, grammar exercises, formal compositions, but especially imaginary speeches to famous literary figures in French and Latin texts required the attention of collège students before the Third Republic's reforms. Beginning in the 1880s, however, *explication de texte* exercises appear frequently in classes devoted to literature, even among primary-school children. Bernard Derouelles in the first year of study at the École primaire supérieure in Thouars dutifully copied out the specific questions from his textbook that had guided his reading of Balzac's *Eugénie Grandet*.[108] Apparently, little had been left to his imagination in the analysis of the text. Summarized another student in her outline of a composition on why she should study literature, "Literature study = work of textual reading, of reasoning, of meditation. . . . One must want it and love it for itself but also and especially because it teaches you to live," a sentiment little different from that expressed by Émile Bary a century earlier.[109]

There were, however, significant differences in the teaching of literature to boys and girls.[110] Throughout the period, significant lacunae in female instruction were derived from (and contributed to) the most conservative principles of French education. Not only did the few girls who attended school study different subjects, but they did so for very different purposes. Secondary schools for females did not offer Greek or Latin, and therefore denied girls the opportunity to sit for the *baccalauréat* examination and thus to enter the university for further study. This deficiency in their education had to be made up by private tutors or by the *khâgnes* in letters that were required for entrance to the École normale supérieure. Most young women achieved little more than the *certificat d'études primaires* after it was instituted during the Third Republic. Moreover, all girls' schools, not just the convents operated by the church, emphasized religious and moral training that reinforced subservience to men, domesticated sex-roles, and male authority in general. Such was the secondary

[107] [Émile Bary], *Les Cahiers d'un rhétoricien de 1815* (1890), 20. Cf. Noël Vaulcin, *Les Mémoires d'un instituteur français* (1896), 23–25.

[108] Bernard Derouelles, "Cahier de lecture expliquée," E.P.S. garçons, Thouars (1936–37), in MNE 3404/82 557(4). Cf. Edmond Devesly, "Cahier d'explication littéraire," École Normale d'Evreux (1902), in MNE 3405 02/82 1453(2); Annette Léon, "Cahier de Français," Lycée Molière, Paris (1920–21), in MNE 3404/37 507(2); and Jean-Paul Léon, "Cahier d'explication de textes," Lycée Janson de Sailly, Paris (1926), in MNE 3405 02/37 601(2).

[109] Thérèse Labussière, "Devoirs de rédaction," Angers (1915), in MNE 3405/86 1440(2).

[110] See Linda Clark, *Schooling the Daughters of Marianne: Textbooks and the Socialization of Girls in Modern French Primary Schools* (Albany, 1984), 5–25; Françoise Mayeur, *L'Enseignement secondaire des jeunes filles sous la Troisième République (1867–1924)* (1977); and Maurice Crubellier, *L'Enfance et la jeunesse dans la société française 1800–1950* (1979), 273–94.

education remembered by independent-minded girls like George Sand and Simone de Beauvoir, who described with distaste the tightly disciplined and moralistic instruction they received. In both principle and practice, girls were expected not to study serious subjects in depth or to develop analytical skills, but to imitate the models of attitude and comportment they observed in their mothers and teachers.[111] These models also appeared in the religious texts they read in class. And so girls were taught, sometimes quite effectively, to study literary works accordingly.

What held true for females also held for the inhabitants of rural areas.[112] According to Robert Gildea, teaching methods in the primary schools of three departments in the north remained archaic well into the Third Republic. Formal, mechanical, and ritualistic, provincial reading instruction often required students to copy out passages of texts, to commit them to memory, and to recite them aloud in class (more or less imperfectly). It is no wonder that the progress of literacy was in some areas so uncertain and unsteady. In the first twenty years of the nineteenth century, the department of the Nord actually witnessed a regression. Roger Thabault found elders in his village in the Gâtinais who recalled the colporter books they had read aloud as schoolchildren in the July Monarchy: *Simon de Nantua*, Fénelon's *Télémaque*, and the catechism. The message of these books, which were conned sentence by sentence, was barely understood, and their assumptions went unchallenged. By the Third Republic, Noel and Chapsal's grammar book was taught by the tried-and-true method of old; each rule was still read aloud, memorized, and recited.[113] In rural collèges and lycées, literary instruction saw a similar exaggeration of formalistic pedagogy and a comparable delay in curricular reform. Student notebooks written in literature classes mostly contained résumés of literary texts, copies of famous passages, and transcriptions of favorite poems.[114] By World War II, provincial instruction celebrated the same ideals, in the same schools, with the same texts, and in the same way that rural students had for the previous 140 years.

While far more sophisticated than primary and secondary instruction, urban or otherwise, university training in literature also honored cartesian principles. Universities as they are today in France did not exist for most of the nineteenth

[111] See Bonnie Smith, *Ladies of the Leisure Class: The Bourgeoises of Northern France in the Nineteenth Century* (Princeton, 1981), 165–86.

[112] On rural education, see Robert Gildea, *Education in Provincial France, 1800–1914: A Study of Three Departments* (Oxford, 1983), 222–29, 262–65; and Roger Thabault, *Education and Change in a Village Community: Mazières-en-Gâtine, 1848–1914*, trans. Peter Tregear (London, 1971), 52–70, 200–228.

[113] Cf. Rémond, "Cahier de dictée et d'analyse" (1829), BIPN 2R-C-2439; and Thabault, *Education and Change*, 60–62, 127–29.

[114] E.g., "Cahier d'un élève du Collège Bourbon en 1836," in BIPN 1R-158600; Louis Boudry, "Cahier," Collège de Confolens(?) (1846), in BIPN 1R-75252; and Andrée Labussière, "Cahier de résumés et de textes" (1913), in MNE 3404/86 1467(1–2).

century: their faculties were dispersed and their curricula ill-defined, despite the Napoleonic reorganization.[115] Therefore, study for the *licence* differed little from that for the *baccalauréat*. It was not until the Third Republic that the faculties of letters prescribed a program of study and research; an 1880 decree defined specific competencies required for the *licence, agrégation,* and *doctorat* in letters. But with the rising interest in literary history as it was taught by Ferdinand Brunetière and Gustave Lanson, scientific truth became the new ideal. "Such is actually the spirit of the Faculties," stated Lanson at a conference at the University of Brussels in 1909.

> There can be no greater concern than to read the text exactly, to bring great rigor to the observation of facts, to reason according to the rules of a scrupulous logic, in short, to apply to our studies, in the appropriate manner, the methods that conform best to the exigencies of the scientific mind.[116]

Here the formal moralistic concerns of textual study at the primary and secondary levels finally gave way to another rationalistic concern: scientific rigor. Instruction, however, remained largely what it had been for centuries: a formal method of reading a text for the purpose of demonstrating an essentially non-literary principle. At the university, be it the Sorbonne or the École normale supérieure, the cultural conception of reading as knowledge attained its most erudite but still recognizable form.

The history of French instruction thus marks a very slow change, if any, in one important contextual feature of reading in the modern period. Primary schools taught literate skills just as Descartes had approached problems: analytically, from the simplest to the most complex parts of a larger whole. Secondary schools presented literary texts as illustrations of rhetorical rules and moral truths best studied by the formal *explication de texte* that in time became a pedagogical ritual. Universities, once established, applied the positivist methods of scientific inquiry to the history of literature, its texts and sources. These institutional objectives and methods resisted curricular and pedagogical change, in the same way French education continued to identify and instill in social elites, usually urban, male, and middle class, the same humanistic conception of literature as general culture. The result was, in part at least, a perpetuation of a distinct French mentality vis-à-vis the printed page, a mentality at once rationalistic, formalistic, and deductive in its interpretive practices, one entirely appropriate to the conservative society of the Third Republic.[117] Together with the period's enduring norms of literary value and perceptions of

---

[115] See George Weisz, *The Emergence of Modern Universities in France, 1863–1914* (Princeton, 1983), 18–54; and Robert Smith, *The École Normale Supérieure and the Third Republic* (Albany, 1982), 5–18, 56–78.

[116] Paraphrased in Bézard, *De la méthode littéraire*, 372. Cf. Gustave Lanson, *Essais de méthode, de critique et d'histoire littéraire*, ed. Henri Peyre (1965).

[117] See Chapter 1, note 48, above.

empirical reality, long-standing definitions of knowledge in both language and literature informed the predispositions of French teachers and students. It is, of course, no accident that these cultural predispositions to the printed page continue to shape, in one way or another, reading activities in France today.[118]

Cultural mentalities, at least those evident in French conceptions of norms, reality, and knowledge, constituted but one historical circumstance in modern interpretive practice. As the last four chapters have demonstrated, people also encountered texts within a matrix of economic, social, and political forces, namely, the economy of print, the literacy of society, the politics of reception, as well as the mentalities of order, utility, and principle. Nearly all intellectual life, and not just reading, occurred within the boundaries defined by these factors. This much is obvious. But far less apparent is the important role played by readers themselves in defining those boundaries. Literate individuals provided the demand for printed matter, they structured society, they censored texts or influenced their reception, and they conceived their own neoclassical, utilitarian, and rationalistic values. Readers were active agents, especially in interpretive communities, whether as critics, censors, educators, or just friends and family of published authors. Moreover, their contextual horizons evolved very slowly over the course of the nineteenth and twentieth centuries; change in the rise of modern publishing, in the growth of active literacy, in the ideology of control, and in the mental ''equipment'' of French men and women took much more time than most events in history. They were no less significant for such slowness. This long historical moment in French literate culture, in fact, set the stage for the specific interpretive practices studied in the following chapters. Within their particular milieus, people left records of both the art and the act of reading—artistic images, novels and memoirs, personal letters and literary reviews—all in response to a variety of texts. What these documents say about reading itself now becomes the focus of this book.

[118] See Laurence Wylie, *Village in the Vaucluse: An Account of Life in a French Village* (New York, 1964), 55–97. Cf. Jean Foucambert and J. André, *La Manière d'être lecteur. Apprentissage et enseignement de la lecture, de la maternelle au CM2* (1976); and G. Mialaret, *L'Apprentissage de la lecture* (1975).

PART II

Historical Interpretive Practices: The Art of Reading

Chapter 5

ARTISTIC IMAGES

MORE THAN ANY OTHER ARTIST, Honoré Daumier was intrigued by the different kinds of readers in modern French society.[1] When he died in 1879 after fifty years of work, Daumier left images of literate activity in all its variety among both men and women, rich and poor, young and old, at work and at play. One can find portraits of lawyers reading briefs to clients, parents reading stories to children, actresses reading scripts to other players, and many other less singular individuals simply reading a book or newspaper to themselves. Wherever literate people were in nineteenth-century Paris, Daumier portrayed them—in cafés, parks, and libraries, at home in the parlor, the bedroom, the kitchen, even the bathtub. Approximately two percent of his enormous output (at least 162 of some 8,000 lithographs, sketches, and paintings) depicted readers in almost every conceivable situation. Although hardly a preoccupation of Daumier's, the reading experience pervaded his artistic practice, perhaps because literate culture had come to pervade the very society he sought to portray. Historical circumstance and personal fascination together conspired to make Daumier the greatest French artist of readers and reading.

Daumier was not the only artist of literate life; no fewer than eighty others worked in France between 1800 and 1940.[2] Collectively they produced more than 500 images of reading in every available medium and format. Moreover, their work is every bit as varied in subject matter as that of Daumier's. Nineteenth-century art encompasses literate figures in nearly every social class—aristocrats, notables, priests, merchants, lawyers, shopkeepers, artisans, and peasants. Even though the upper ranks of society predominate, women, children, and the aged among them appear in disproportionate numbers with the spread of public education and modern publishing. The props used in portraits also changed; there came to be as many newspapers and magazines as books

---

[1] On Daumier's life and work, see Jean Adémar, *Honoré Daumier* (1954); Oliver W. Larkin, *Daumier: Man of His Times* (Boston, 1968); Karl Eric Maison, *Honoré Daumier: Catalogue Raisonné of the Paintings, Watercolors, and Drawings* (London, 1968), 2 vols.; and Roger Passeron, *Daumier* (New York, 1981).

[2] See, e.g., Loÿs Delteil, *Le Peinture-graveur illustré (XIXe–XXe siècle)*, 32 vols. (1906–1926) (hereafter Delteil); François Courbon, *Histoire illustrée de la gravure en France*, pt. 3: *XIXe siècle* (1926); John Rewald, *The History of Impressionism*, 4th ed. (New York, 1973); Francis Carey, *From Manet to Toulouse-Lautrec: French Lithographs, 1860–1900* (London, 1978); and Beatrice Farewell, *French Popular Lithographic Imagery 1815–1870*, 5 vols. (Chicago, 1981–86).

in the hands of sitters. Naturally, as public patronage waned and as new salons and galleries developed, artists focused more on the interpretive experiences of their clientele, especially urban bourgeois families. Images of reading among parents and children, and occasionally among more distant relations, servants, and friends, proliferated in the nineteenth and early twentieth centuries. For these subjects, the domestic setting was most appropriate, but literate culture appeared in other social contexts as well, such as libraries, schools, offices, assemblies, churches, cafés, and estaminets. Thus, a sizable corpus of artistic evidence provides the historian a remarkable opportunity to recapture the past's different textual experiences.[3]

Despite the bewildering diversity of such imagery, historically significant patterns did emerge with the evolution of interpretive practices. In fact, artistic form and content changed at roughly the same time that literate life changed. What had been an exclusive culture in the Old Regime developed rapidly after 1789 into a commonplace among new and different social groups. That much is obvious from the subjects that artists chose to portray as well as from other historical evidence.[4] But more than the circumstances of literate life altered; so did its habits. Once a collective and public activity, reading became an individual and private concern—in both artistic image and social reality. By the end of the nineteenth century, in life as in art, reading within groups and in pairs gave way to men and women reading by themselves. Similarly, the eighteenth century's extraordinary absorption became the twentieth century's everyday routine.[5] People today receive texts self-consciously and alone, separated and often alienated from others who may or may not be close by. Art here reflected history in the development of modern reading activities. It makes sense, then, to follow this artistic reflection in France from 1800 to 1940.[6]

---

[3] Cf. the historical use of artwork in A. Hyatt Major, *Prints and People: A Social History of Printed Pictures* (New York, 1971); Michael Baxandall, *Painting and Experience in Fifteenth-Century Italy: A Primer in the Social History of Pictorial Style* (Oxford, 1972); Carl E. Schorske, *Fin-de-Siècle Vienna: Politics and Culture* (New York, 1980), 208–78; Theodore K. Rabb and Jonathan Brown, eds., "The Evidence of Art: Images and Meaning in History," in *Journal of Interdisciplinary History* 17 (Summer 1986): 1–6, 203–32; Simon Schama, *The Embarrassment of Riches: An Interpretation of Dutch Culture in the Golden Age* (Berkeley, 1988), 9–10, 565–76; and Peter Paret, *History as Art: Episodes in the Culture and Politics of Nineteenth-Century Germany* (Princeton, 1988).

[4] Cf. the problem of iconology, with implications for the meaning of books in portrait art, according to Erwin Panofsky, *Meaning in the Visual Arts: Papers in and on Art History* (Garden City, N.Y., 1955), 26–55.

[5] Cf. Michael Fried, *Absorption and Theatricality: Painting and Beholder in the Age of Diderot* (Berkeley, 1980); and Jean Hébrard and Anne-Marie Chartier, *Discours sur la lecture (1880–1980)* (1989), 427–63.

[6] Cf. the history of reading by inference from images in the text: Meyer Schapiro, *Words and Pictures: On the Literal and the Symbolic in the Illustration of a Text* (The Hague, 1973); Richard Altick, *Paintings from Books: Art and Literature in Britain, 1760–1900* (Columbus, 1986);

GROUPS

For much of the nineteenth century, the art that depicted reading most often showed multiple figures gathered around a single, prominently featured text.[7] Artistically, with the important exception of portraiture, literate culture originally meant a collective activity. The text itself was at the center of the composition, a position that highlighted its importance to the group as well as to the artist's conception. Whatever the setting, be it familial, educational, religious, or political, intellectual life in art subsumed the reader within a larger social context. Evidently, interpretive practice remained a public rather than a private interest at the height of realism in French art. This trend before the 1850s appears clearly in the artistic sample of works portraying three or more figures with a text, at least until the Second Empire, when another emphasis begins to appear.[8]

Reading groups were a common feature in nineteenth-century French art. P. L. Debucourt's "The Visitation" (c. 1800), for instance, satirizes the pretentious Incroyables and their grisettes during the Consulate, an oral reading completely ignored by the misbehaving young men and women. French intellectual life had changed and with it the artist's conception.[9] Reading also appears in public spaces, such as in Louis Bacler d'Albe's "The Tuileries Garden" (1822): a Sunday afternoon crowd of bourgeois families nearly engulfs three newspaper readers. Serious discussion of political issues during the Restoration would have died quickly within this more familiar, almost domestic context. Later in the century, collective literate activities retreated into smaller, more professional groups. Henri Fantin-Latour's "At the Table's Corner" (1872) and Théo van Rysselberghe's "The Reading" (1903) depict serious literati attending to a close colleague's work-in-progress (see Ill. 5.1).

Claude Labrosse, *Lire au XVIIIe siècle. La 'Nouvelle Héloïse' et ses lecteurs* (Lyon, 1985), 209–39; and Martyn Lyons, *Le Triomphe du livre. Une Histoire sociologique de la lecture dans la France du XIXe siècle* (1987), 221–48.

[7] Cf. Old Regime images in: L. G. Lemonnier, "Première lecture de l'*Orphelin de Chine* de Voltaire, en 1755, dans le salon de Madame Geoffrin" (1755) in the Musée des Beaux Arts, Rouen; Carle Van Loo, "La Lecture espagnole" (1761) in the Hermitage, Leningrad; J. A. Meissonier, "La Lecture d'un texte de l'*Encyclopédie* chez Diderot" (c. 1770) reproduced in HEF 2:398; anon., "Les Plaisirs de Chaville" (c. 1785) reproduced in Howard C. Rice, Jr., *Thomas Jefferson's Paris* (Princeton, 1976), 97; J.-B. Greuze, "Le Grandpère mourant" (1779) in the Louvre, Paris; anon., "La Lecture du soir" (1778), illustration in N. E. Restif de la Bretonne, *La Vie de mon père* (Neufchatel, 1779); and anon., title page to *La Feuille villageoise* (1790).

[8] Gabriel Weisberg, *The Realist Tradition: French Painting and Drawing 1830–1900* (Cleveland, 1980), 1–38.

[9] Cf. Daumier's rich visual satires on bourgeois intellectual life: "Des victimes de la Révolution" (1830) in Delteil 20: no. 14; "Je crois que mon cinquième acte fera beaucoup d'effet" (1838) Delteil 21: no. 473; "Nouvelles diverses" (1842) Delteil 22: no. 985; "Lecture du *Moniteur*" (1843) Delteil 22: no. 1020; "Dussent-ils maudire ces barbares parens" (1844) Delteil 23: no. 1256; and "Le Bas-bleu déclamant sa pièce" (1844) Delteil 23: no. 1242.

5.1 Théo van Rysselberghe, "The Reading" (1903). Copyright A.C.L.-Bruxelles

While the artist's treatment of the subject remains formal, even stiff, the actual details of the setting had become more recognizable and plausible. By World War I, the Third Republic's portrait realism had largely displaced the Old Regime's institutional idealism.[10]

This did not mean that artists ceased idealizing certain social institutions. Literate families especially remained the subject of much sentimental art in the nineteenth century.[11] Louis Léopold Boilly's "Reading the Bulletin of the Grande Armée" (c. 1810) presents an oral reading *en famille* in the Greuze tradition, for obvious propagandistic purposes appropriate to the artist's drawing. Similar nostalgic treatment appears in Jean Platier's "A Family Reading of *Les Mystères de Paris*" (1842), less to promote a national policy than to sell a serial novel. But in family portraiture generally, the nineteenth-century artist rendered the figures more distinctly, as in Gustave Courbet's "Portrait of P. J. Proudhon and His Family" (1865–67) where the socialist's youngest daughter is carefully shown with a picture book. Jacques Tissot's "A Widow" (1868) and Edgar Degas's "The Rehearsal" (1873) take a similar view of familial readings. The Tissot contrasts the young widow's pensive boredom with her guardian's rapt attention to an open book; the lush garden scene underscores the conflict between human passion and social conventions (including reading). Similarly, the Degas depicts a domestic drama, the histrionics of husband and wife playing roles far removed from their everyday selves. While portraying each figure distinctly, Degas still renders the exaggerated theatrical gestures as expressions of both the text and the relationship between the players. Historically altered since the Old Regime, the family and its dramatic reading are here transformed artistically.

In his lithographs especially, Daumier contributed to the artistic rendition of family reading. His earliest work follows in the sentimental tradition exemplified by O. Tassaert, D.-M.-A. Raffet, and H. de Montaut, some of Daumier's undistinguished contemporaries.[12] His "Reading the Newspaper" (1835), for example, pictures an extended family attending to a paper read aloud by the family patriarch. Except for the text, the setting recalls a motif

---

[10] Cf. artistic and historical changes discussed in T. J. Clark, *The Painting of Modern Life: Paris in the Art of Manet and His Followers* (Princeton, 1984), 205–58.

[11] See C. Constans, after Louis Léopold Boilly, "... Et l'ogre l'a mangé" (1820) in the Musée Carnavalet, Paris; title page to J. N. Bouilly, *Contes à ma fille* (Bruxelles, 1821), vol. 1; L. L. Boilly, "La Lecture du roman" (1828) in BN Oa 22, 340–59 "Soirées en famille"; title page to Charles Perrault, *Conte de fées* (n.d.); Bertall, untitled illustration in *Paul et Virginie* (1846); Moynet, "La Mérite des femmes" (1846) in BN Kb matières 1 (595) "Scènes de lecture"; title page, *Le Coin de feu* (Paris, 1855); after M. Brion, "La Lecture de la Bible" (1868) in BN Oa 22, 340–59; and Charles Clérice, "L'Île en feu" (1897) in BN Oa 22, 340–59.

[12] See O. Tassaert, "La Lecture de la Bible" (1851) in the Musée Fabre, Montpellier; D.-M.-A. Raffet, "Le Billet de contentement" (1835) in Courbon, *Histoire illustrée de la gravure en France*, 3: no. 1205; and H. de Montaut, "Une Lecture chez la portière" (1855) in BN Oa 22, 340–59.

common since at least the Old Regime. In time, however, Daumier developed a more comic approach to this subject: his ''Advantages of Italian Terraces'' (1846) shows a bourgeois couple, seated in a large garden, reading a newspaper together while enduring the mosquitoes that swarm around them. The child swinging a hat to chase the insects away is as much a distraction as the insects themselves. In 1847, Daumier again depicted the untimely interruptions created by children; ''The Pleasures of Paternity'' has a newspaper-reading father ambushed by his four offspring, one grabbing his head, another holding his legs, still another pushing his stomach, and the last pulling his robe. In this lithograph, the familial context is actually enriched by the diversions from literate activity; playful irreverence toward the text as well as toward parental authority is the natural (and logical) source of the viewer's amusement. In creating his visual satire, Daumier moved from the implausible to the typical; in so doing, he was at once more original and more accurate in his treatment of an otherwise hackneyed theme.[13]

Another important nineteenth-century subject evident in artwork is reading instruction. Early in the century, most children began learning to read at home, a tradition captured by the age-old stock image of a mother teaching her children the alphabet. Nearly every illustrated *abécédaire*, whatever the format, includes this familiar situation in the frontispiece or on the title page.[14] The same crude and anonymous woodcut often serves as many as five different primers, the scene invariably set within a comfortable bourgeois household, the young children as attentive as they are appreciative of their capable and loving mother. When older children appear in these situations, a father will occasionally attend to their instruction—for his sons, rarely if ever for his daughters. Throughout the nineteenth century, reading within the family was gender-specific in image and in fact.[15] The title page to Marcelline Desbordes-Valmore's *À mes jeunes amis* (1830), for example, depicts a little boy reading aloud to a brother or friend, while a little girl looks distractedly to the right. Mastered by the males outdoors, this text is not hers. Instead, she will memorize another text at home within a more intimate milieu. The catechism remains essentially a female text in most bourgeois families, both real and imagined, as suggested by nineteenth-century book illustrations.[16]

After the Guizot Law of 1833, a new location for reading instruction ap-

[13] Cf. Auguste Renoir, ''Déjeuner à Berneval'' (1898) in a private collection; and Georges Domergue, ''Victimes du pessimisme'' (1915) in BN Oa 22, 340–59. Note the discussion of Daumier's satire in Larkin, *Daumier*, 31–63, 108–33.

[14] See the numerous illustrations of mother-child teaching imagery in Ségolène Le Men, *Les Abécédaires français illustrés du XIXe siècle* (1984), 64–71.

[15] Note the division of domestic responsibility in an anonymous, untitled lithograph, ''L'Éducation commencée'' (1845) in BN Kb matières 1 (no. 1567), in which a mother teaches the child while the father tends the fire.

[16] See also Paul Thomas, ''La Bonne Éducation'' (c. 1890) in the BN, Paris.

pears more frequently in French art: the public school. Eighteenth-century artists had, of course, portrayed religious instruction, but instances of this faded from the work of nineteenth-century artists.[17] What had also been an upper-class activity guided by parental tutors became a popular necessity taught by public officials. In later images of reading instruction, the school replaces the home, the teacher takes over from the parent, the text and the children stay the same.[18] Early versions place the school scene in rustic habitats, such as C. Motte's "The Village School" (1830–40), where the harried teacher does what he can with the rural roustabouts who have invaded his home. The beleaguered instructor persists even when the setting has shifted into a schoolroom provided by the commune; an anonymous "The Schoolmaster" (c. 1840) reveals a crowded, poorly equipped class of inattentive youngsters. Only during the Third Republic, after the Ferry Laws, do artists (and photographers) render more faithfully the actual learning that must have occurred among millions of French boys and girls. Accordingly, Léon Lhermitte's "A Schoolroom" (c. 1900) presents a provincial class in which a child is reciting a text, his companions more or less attentive to the task at hand within a functioning formal institution (see Ill. 5.2). The dozing student is the exception to the rule within the strict discipline and established routine of the modern school.[19]

Reading in other public institutions received similar detailed treatment.[20] In

[17] Cf. J. C. Richard de Saint-Non, after François Boucher, "La Leçon de lecture à la ferme" (1756) in the Louvre, Paris; Boisseau, "Le Grand Maître d'école" (c. 1780) in HEF 2:469; and Milient after Doublet, "La Petite École" (c. 1790) in the Institut National des Recherches Pédagogiques, Rouen.

[18] Cf. Delannois, "L'École de filles sous la Restauration" (c. 1820) in the BN, Paris; Raquenthal, "Le Maître d'école" (1825–30) in the Institut National des Recherches Pédagogiques, Rouen; anon., "Salle d'école dans une étable" (c. 1840) in the Institut National des Recherches Pédagogiques, Rouen; anon., "L'École de village" (c. 1850) in Institut National des Recherches Pédagogiques, Rouen; François Bonvin, "L'Ecole des frères" (1865) in Museo de Arte de Ponce, Puerto Rico; and A. Truphême, "La Dictée" (c. 1900) in the Musée Granet, Palais de Malte, Aix-en-Provence.

[19] Note images of examinations, established institutional rituals in the Third Republic: Claverie, "Examen de fin de cours des aspirantes aux places du service télégraphique, au Ministère des Postes et Télégraphes" (c. 1890) reproduced in Françoise Mayeur, *Histoire générale de l'enseignement et de l'éducation en France* (1981), 3:49; and P. Grenier, "Une Séance d'examen pour le baccalauréat ès sciences, à la Sorbonne" (c. 1890) in the BN, Paris. Cf. Daumier's views of classroom reading: "Un Service d'ami" (1845) Delteil 24: no. 1438; "Rappelez-vous que l'élève Cabassol" (1846) Delteil 24: no. 1469; and "Je ne m'étonne plus si celui-là se tenait tranquille" (1846) Delteil 24: no. 1459.

[20] See library readers in anon., "Caricature parisienne" (1821) in the Musée Carnavalet, Paris; Daumier, "Une Visite à la bibliothèque" (1853) Delteil 26: no. 2358; the masthead of *Le Cabinet de lecture* (1835); Félix Regamey, untitled lithograph of a lending library (c. 1840) reproduced in Robert Escarpit et al., "La Lecture" in *La Vie populaire en France du Moyen Âge à nos jours* (1965), 2:299; Claverie, "Bibliothèque populaire, rue de la Chapelle" (after 1850) in the BN, Paris; and Édouard Vuillard, "La Bibliothèque" (1911) in the Musée d'Orsay, Paris.

5.2 Léon Lhermitte, ''A Schoolroom'' (c. 1900). Courtesy Phot. Bibl. Nat. Paris

the nineteenth century, artists painted literate activity during religious services with special care. Gustave Courbet's stunning "A Burial in Ornans" (1849–50) positions a duly solemn priest reading the burial service among the distracted mourners and attendants. The dignity of the occasion is actually heightened by the public reading as well as by Courbet's profound understanding of the many faces at the grave site. A comparable dignity appears in Jules Breton's work, a more conservative realism both artistically and politically. Although the treatment is more sanctimonious than in Courbet's funeral, Breton's "The Benediction of the Wheat" (1857) and "The Placement of a Calvary" (1858) demonstrate an equally keen eye to the responses of the faithful to religious texts. The profound spirituality at the heart of these paintings is genuine, just as religion was generally for devout French Catholics in the nineteenth century. The same mood of textual devotion receives close attention in Isidore Pils's "Prayer in the Hospice" (1853), Alphonse Legros's "St. Francis's Vocation" (1861), and François Bonvin's "The Poor People's Pew. A Memory of Brittany" (1864). Despite their place within the realist tradition, these works express a quiet power derived from their dignified settings, meditative figures, and traditional rites focused on sacred texts.[21]

French artists were less awed by secular rituals. Readings at civil wedding ceremonies, for instance, earned their share of lighter treatment. In this Daumier was not alone. His "Before the Mayor" (1845) and "At City Hall" (1854), amusing satires of the nervous bride and groom, accentuate an occasion that was also depicted by Henri Gervex's "Mathurin Moreau's Marriage" (1881: see Ill. 5.3). In the latter work, a festive yet dignified air surrounds the erect couple and proud parents; the guests behind them are relaxed, smiling, and chatting while the mayor leads the official ceremony. The party listens not to the word of God but to the rhetoric of the state, a fact that alters considerably the work's mood. Daumier struck a more amusing tone in his treatment of political speeches during the Second Republic. In four different lithographs from 1850, he portrayed the indifferent responses to empassioned pronouncements before the Legislative Assembly, the texts obviously of greater interest to the speakers than to their audiences.[22] Unlike the reverent responses to religious services depicted by other artists, the impact of the secular word here

[21] See Vuillard, "La Chapelle du château de Versailles" (c. 1910) in the Musée d'Orsay, Paris; Gustave Doré, "Le Néophyte" (c. 1860) in Courbon, *Histoire illustrée de la gravure en France*, 3: no. 1070; and Henri de Toulouse-Lautrec, "Au pied de l'échafaud" (1893) reproduced in Eugen Weber, *France, Fin de siècle* (Cambridge, Mass., 1986), 43.

[22] See Daumier's lithographs: "M. L.P.F. Esquirou de Parieri" (1850) Delteil 25: no. 1874; "Eugène Rouher" (1850) Delteil 25: no. 1878; "Pendant une suspension de séance" (1850) Delteil 25: no. 1972; and "Quand un orateur ennuyeux est à la tribune" (1850) Delteil 25: no. 1961. Cf. Daumier, "Jacquinot-Godart" (1833) Delteil 20: no. 180; and idem, "Le Ventre législatif" (1834) Delteil 20: no. 131.

5.3 Henri Gervex, "Mathurin Moreau's Marriage" (1881). Courtesy of the Mairie du 19e Arrondissement, Paris

is weakened, though not lost, as printed matter, like political power, becomes more widely distributed in modern France.

In the nineteenth century, then, images of reading together, whether on public or private occasions, centered on the text.[23] Everyone in the composition responded to what was more or less a common interest in the salons, families, schools, churches, and assemblies that provided the natural loci for this activity. By mid-century, however, artists shifted the focus of their attention; they tended more and more to move the text off-center, literally or figuratively, from a public to a private concern. In this way the reader was increasingly isolated from other people in the image; reading, even in groups, became less privileged, but also more alienating. Oblivious to his or her surroundings, the literate figure appears self-contained and detached, like the text itself, from the rest of the composition. Before representational subjects begin to disappear from French art at the turn of the century, images of reading in groups capture an important new feature in literate experience.[24]

Instances of alienated readers increase markedly after 1850. Daumier's "Interior of a First-Class Carriage" (c. 1862) places four complete strangers in a compartment together; one of the passengers, a young woman, reads a newspaper, while the others gaze out the window or straight ahead, as unmindful of each other as they are of the text they cannot share (see Ill. 5.4). To be sure, public conveyances are not an appropriate setting for oral readings. There were plenty of other distractions, as Maurice Delondre's "In the Omnibus" (1890) suggests: a top-hatted bourgeois neglects a newspaper in his hands to eye an attractive woman on his left. But even more congenial moments do not necessarily promote collective reading. Two outdoor scenes of friends and family attending a regatta, one by Henri Michel-Lévy (1878) and another by M. Moller (1879), seat a woman apart from the rest of the party. In each case she is intently reading a book, completely unmindful of the boat race and its excitement for everyone else around her. Gustave Caillebotte's "Portraits in the Country" (1885) and Degas's "Reading *Le Petit Journal*" (1888) treat readers in a similar fashion. Caillebotte placed four women in a small garden; three of them in the foreground and middle ground are knitting, the fourth behind them to the right is reading. The reader is detached, visually and mentally, from the other women in the painting. Degas's newspaper reader is separated still further from the ballet dancers practicing in the large hall. The literate dancemaster, who is cut off by the frame in the foreground, is completely out of place.

---

[23] E.g., Daumier, "Politics" (c. 1860) in Maison, *Honoré Daumier: Catalogue Raisonné*, no. 326.

[24] Note that in the development of modern art, impressionists and their successors tended to emphasize light and color at the expense of composition. It could well be that the displacement of the reader was a function of this new artistic interest. See Rewald, *History of Impressionism*, pp. 547–87.

5.4 Honoré Daumier, "Interior of a First-Class Carriage" (c. 1862). Courtesy of the Walters Art Gallery, Baltimore

Even more telling is Auguste Renoir's "The Children's Afternoon in War-gemont" (1884: see Ill. 5.5).[25] A young girl perusing an open book is seated to the left, while her older sister sits to the right, sewing and attending to another little girl holding a doll in the young woman's lap. The viewer's attention is drawn away from the dark colors on the left by the bright reds and whites in the right-center of the painting; the richly decorated tablecloth and curtains complement the older girl's light summer attire. The blue of the littlest girl's dress, however, highlights the blues of the reading girl's clothes, sofa seat, and book. It is this color relationship that keeps the latter figure from fading out of the composition completely. For whatever reason, Renoir must have wanted to show the fully engaged reader's detachment from her companions.[26] Only one person here is attending to the text; the painting's composition makes this clear. Evidently, by the end of the century, in Renoir's work and elsewhere, the reading experience had become private, almost insular; increasingly, the literate individual's isolation from others was as common in French life as it was in French art—and nowhere more tellingly than in other images featuring only one or two figures.

PAIRS

Images of only two reading figures are much less formal than those of larger reading groups. By its very nature, the double portrait is more immediate, indeed more intimate. And so the domestic setting predominates. More than one-sixth of all the artwork sampled here presents two people related to each other. The most common subject is reading by married couples, a marvelous source of social satire as well as serious portraiture in the nineteenth century. Other familial pairs, such as parent and child, brother and sister, master and servant, also constitute an artistic concern. Outside of the household, friends and neighbors are frequently paired in literate activity, while reading among complete strangers appears much less often. No more than one-eighth of the sample has unacquainted figures reading together, and for a very obvious reason: in time the modern experience with texts became a deeply personal activity. Today, only at well-defined occasions does reading serve a public purpose; literate people tend to experience texts alone. Consequently, it seems odd to see total strangers reading together, either in life or in imagery. The art that depicts reading between pairs of people who know each other well reflects this historical fact.

In light of this artistic and historical trend, it is paradoxical that pairs of literate individuals appear so isolated from one another in modern French art. Artists often portrayed individual readers curiously detached from their por-

[25] For more on this painting, see Anne Distel et al., *Renoir* (1985), 238–41.

[26] Note the resemblance of the girls' faces on the right to that of the doll. By her very distance from the doll—and the other girls—the reading figure wears a less doll-like "mask."

5.5 Auguste Renoir, "The Children's Afternoon in Wargemont" (1884). Courtesy of the Staatliche Museen Preussischer Kulturbesitz, Nationalgalerie, Berlin (West)

trait partners, as if their activity were not a joint endeavor at all. The text appears variously as either an obstacle or a medium of exchange between the two figures, at least after 1800. In Old Regime art, this paradox rarely arose. The most common scenes of reading were of instruction, such as J.-H. Fragonard's "The Virgin's Education" (1748–52) or J.B.S. Chardin's "A Girl Recites the Gospel" (c. 1740). Detachment between teacher and pupil seems most implausible.[27] Hubert Robert's "The Reading" (c. 1760) portrays Madame Geoffrin alone at table while her servant stands to the right reading a book, his other domestic tasks interrupted for the sake of the text they share together. Their poses and placement in the painting alone suggest the enormous social distance between them.[28] Not even the fervor of revolution could isolate literate individuals entirely from one another. An anonymous aquatint, "The Reading" (c. 1790), has an elegant sansculotte mother holding the Declaration of the Rights of Man and Citizen before her child; they are evidently reading this famous document to each other, a special source of bonding in a world otherwise given over to divisive political conflict.

The imagistic link between reading pairs continued into the nineteenth century; a strong artistic tradition portrayed lovers declaring their affection in and through the texts they shared with each other.[29] Becquet's "The Novels" (1838) presents a fashionable couple reading an open book, presumably a novel whose story reflects the pair's own relationship. Another elegantly dressed couple reads a newspaper on the train in Devambez's untitled lithograph (1910). The text here is certainly more important to the pair than the woman's splendid hat, which the artist features so prominently. Again, lovers examine a letter together in Henri de Toulouse-Lautrec's "Yvette Guilbert" (1894), one of his illustrations to Gustave Geffroy's biography of the noted singer (see Ill. 5.6). In fact, Yvette turns away from the page before her to read the missive in her lover's hands. Binding yet another couple, literate life in Grandville's "New Scene from Paris" (J.I.I. Gérard, 1840) makes a critic's task much easier; he has given the job to the mistress at his feet, who is writing the review to appear under his name. Their lives, like those of other lovers depicted in the nineteenth century, are enriched (and complicated) by reading.[30]

---

[27] See J.B.S. Chardin, "Leçon de lecture" (c. 1730) in private collection; and idem, "The Young School Mistress" (1731–32) in the National Gallery, London.

[28] Cf. Jean-Honoré Fragonard, "La Lecture" (c. 1780) in the Louvre, Paris.

[29] E.g., Fragonard, "Les Souvenirs" (1765–72) in the Frick Collection, New York; and idem, "L'Amour et l'amitié" (1771–73) also in the Frick Collection, New York.

[30] Note the close relations between reading friends in Paul Cézanne, "Une Lecture chez Zola" (1864), a drawing reproduced in Henri Mitterand and Jean Vidal, eds., *Album Zola* (1963), 61; Daumier, "Vieux Garçons" (1847) Delteil 24: no. 1565; idem, "Les Buveurs de bière" (c. 1850) in the Nathan Collection, Zurich; Camille Corot, "Le Repos des philosophes" (1871) Delteil 5: no. 25; C. Léandry, untitled lithograph (1897) in BN Kb matières 1 (D.08509); Vuillard, "Sous la lampe" (1892) reproduced in Jean Vergnet-Ruiz and Michel Laclotte, *Great French Paintings*

5.6 Henri de Toulouse-Lautrec, ''Yvette Guilbert'' (1894). Courtesy of the Fine Arts Library, University of Oklahoma

These exceptions notwithstanding, the connective nature of reading is attenuated in nineteenth-century art. Reading does not always strengthen marital relations, for instance. There were many urban bourgeois husbands and wives

from the Regional Museums of France (New York, 1966), 183; Pierre Bonnard, ''La Lettre'' (1925) reproduced in Francis Bouvet, *Bonnard: The Complete Graphic Works* (New York, 1981), 244; and Pablo Picasso, ''Lecture de la lettre'' (1920) in the Musée Picasso, Paris.

who actually used texts to distance themselves from their spouses.[31] Degas's "Sulking" (1873–75) brings the viewer into a domestic squabble at a point when the husband has retreated from his wife by pretending to examine the papers on his desk (see Ill. 5.7). She is not fooled by this ruse and appeals directly to the viewer. Leaning over the desk as if the texts there had played a role in the quarrel, she looks out indignantly from the painting. Herman Paul satirized bourgeois marriage with far less sympathy in "Do Not Speak to Them of a Beach Where a Casino Would Be" (1875). The husband is seated at a table and reading a newspaper; his back is turned toward his wife. He is clearly not sharing the paper with her, the distance between them exaggerated as much by his reading as by her sleeping. Moreover, Caillebotte's "Home Life" (1880) shows a married couple attending to two completely different texts: the husband is engrossed by a book, his wife by a magazine, the space between them as empty as their relationship. In each case the text is at least emblematic, if not the cause itself, of the distance between husband and wife.

More than any other artist, Daumier realized the comic possibilities of the text in married life.[32] A lithograph in *Le Charivari*, "The Reading Husband" (1839), depicts the man in bed reading a romantic novel to his coyly attentive wife. Literary imagination here contrasts sharply with conjugal reality. In images of older couples, the divisiveness represented by the text is even greater. The husband in Daumier's "Here's One of an Agreeable Sort" (1842) attempts to amuse his wife by reading to her at all times of the day. What must have started as an innocent domestic amusement had become a tiresome marital chore. His wife now only feigns interest. Daumier also created a series of family situations in which books interfere with the wife's household responsibilities, as in "Well Good! . . . There She Is . . . Pouring Wax in My Chocolate" (1844). To the husband's chagrin, the wife finds the novel far more engrossing than the preparation of an evening snack. "O misery!" cries another wife left alone on a riverbank, book in hand, by her husband the fishing enthusiast (1844). The caption continues, "To have dreamed throughout my girlhood of a spouse who adored divine poetry as much as I, and to have

[31] E.g., Gustave Caillebotte, "Intérieur" (1880) in a private collection; idem, "Les Orangers" (1878) in the Museum of Fine Arts, Houston (Kirk Varnedoe, *Gustave Caillebotte* [New Ha-1987], 109); Aimé Perret, "Noël des vieux" (1896) in BN Oa 22, 340–59 (no. 177); Ulet, untitled lithograph (c. 1900) in BN Oa 22, 340–59 (no. 5749); A. Guillaume, untitled lithograph (c. 1900) in BN Kb matières 1; Bonnard, "Le Figaro" (1903) reproduced in Bouvet, *Bonnard*, 187; and Jean Frilaut, "Lecture sous la lampe" (1923) Delteil 21: no. 228.

[32] See Daumier's lithographs: "Je me fiche bien de votre Mme. Sand" (1839) Delteil 22: no. 629; "Le Mari—Bobonne veux-tu . . ." (1840) Delteil 22: no. 644; "Un Article louangeur" (1845) Delteil 23: no. 1133; "Il parait qu'on vient de revoir le serpent de mer" (1846) Delteil 24: no. 1496; "Un Bon mari, qui pour distraire son épouse" (1847) Delteil 24: no. 1530; "Bourgeois se faisant lire, après diner, quelques chapitres" (1847) Delteil 24: no. 1532; "Un Oasis au milieu de la plaine St.-Denis" (1847) Delteil 24: no. 1651; and "Une Lecture intéressante et rafraichissante" (1854) Delteil 26: no. 2583.

5.7 Edgar Degas, "Sulking" (1873–75). Courtesy of the Metropolitan Museum of Art, the H. O. Havemeyer Collection, Bequest of Mrs. H. O. Havemeyer, 1929

fallen on a husband who loves only gudgeons. . . . That man was born to be a pike!'' Not necessarily symptomatic of domestic problems, books can be a source of personal solace. But the difference between reader and spouse remains.

A much closer relationship naturally arises in images of reading mothers and their children. And in most elementary texts intended for a child's first lessons in reading, the bond between parent and offspring is well signified by their common endeavor. From these images it was long assumed that nearly all children learned the alphabet at their mothers' knees.[33] This impression, deepened by dozens of frontispieces and title pages, is hard to escape.[34] But when older children are depicted with their parents, a new distance appears. For instance, Édouard Manet captured well a mother's solitude in the presence of her reading child: ''Home Life at Arcachon'' (1871) sets Madame Manet at home with her son, the two figures separated in the composition by a large window and Léon's pensive gaze, evoked by an open book before him. The painting places them in two different worlds (see Ill. 5.8).[35] Even Berthe Morisot's well-known ''The Artist's Sister Edna and Their Mother'' (1870) implies a distance between parent and child. The mother is intently reading and her daughter only vaguely listening. The latter is preoccupied with her own thoughts, whether or not they are suggested by the text. Whatever the affective tie between generations (or between members of the same sex), the book plays an ambivalent role.

A similar distance occurs in images of siblings. Except for the sentimental treatment of little children learning to read together—a stock motif for elementary texts[36]—the depiction of older literate brothers and sisters expresses an ambiguity; a text attenuates their relationship in one way or another. Morisot's ''Eugène and Julie Manet'' (1868), a drawing of the famous painter's two children, seats the lad engrossed in a magazine to the left; the girl is standing to the right, looking out through a large window with her back to both the

---

[33] According to François Furet and Jacques Ozouf, about 20 percent of those who were literate in the nineteenth century owed their literacy to some form of home instruction. See *Lire et écrire. L'Alphabétisation des Français de Calvin à Jules Ferry* (1977), 1:306.

[34] See illustrations in Le Men, *Les Abécédaires français illustrés*, 63–71; and title page to Bouilly, *Conseils à ma fille* (1812), vol. 2; title page to Mme. de Courval, *Les Jeunes Orphelins, ou Les Contes d'une grand'mère* (1825); anon., ''La Lecture de la Bible'' (1843) in BN Kb matières 1 (no. 1041); anon., ''L'Heureuse Mère'' (1844) in BN Kb matières 1 (no. 3766); anon., ''La Leçon de lecture'' (c. 1875 and 1880) in BN Kb matières 1 (nos. 205 and 2551); and A. Marie, ''La Leçon de lecture'' (1886) in BN Kb matières 1.

[35] See also Édouard Manet, ''La Lecture'' (1865–73) in the Galeries du Jeu de Paume, Paris; idem, ''Le Chemin de fer'' (1872–73) in the National Gallery, Washington, D.C.; and idem, ''Sur la plage'' (1873) in the Galeries du Jeu de Paume, Paris. Cf. Françoise Cachin et al., *Manet: 1832–1883* (1983), 258–60, 340–42, 344–45.

[36] Besides illustrations in Le Men, *Les Abécédaires français illustrés*, 80, 22, 32, see the title pages to Pierre Blanchard, *Félix et Félice, ou Les Pasteurs du Jura* (1824), and to Hans Christian Andersen, *Contes danois* (Tours, 1853).

5.8 Édouard Manet, ''Home Life in Arcachon'' (1871). Courtesy of the Sterling and Francine Clark Art Institute, Williamstown, Massachusetts

viewer and Eugène. There is no indication that he is reading to her. Again, Renoir's portrait of a close friend's children, "Martial Caillebotte's Children" (1895), implies a minor rivalry between Jean and Geneviève, who are seated on a divan looking at a picture book together. Guarding the open book in her lap and the others to her left, the little girl gazes off into the distance, while her brother leans forward, straining to look at the brightly colored text. It is clear that Geneviève is controlling their joint activity, whether or not Jean is even aware of it. Older siblings are still more detached in Pierre Bonnard's curious "Portrait of the Bernheim Brothers" (1920: see Ill. 5.9). Although their desks are adjoining, the two figures are distinctly separated in the painting's composition. The elder Bernheim is reading a letter in the foreground, his back partially turned on the younger man seated behind him. The distortion

5.9 Pierre Bonnard, "Portrait of the Bernheim Brothers" (1920). Courtesy of the Musée d'Orsay, Paris (copyright Photo R.M.N.-SPADEM)

5.10 Honoré Daumier, "Lawyer with a Woman Client" (c. 1860). Courtesy of the National Museum of Wales

in perspective makes the background figure appear much farther away than he is, but the desk littered with papers is a still greater obstacle to their common effort in the office. Only the work's title assures the viewer that the men are even related.[37]

Similar contrasts in textual response appear in Daumier's lithographs and watercolors, especially those depicting unrelated pairs. For example, the shifty lawyer and his plaintive victim in "Lawyer with a Woman Client" (c. 1860) are at odds (see Ill. 5.10). The attorney, of course, would like to prolong the case, the woman would like to bring it to a swift conclusion. Their difference is therefore focused on the significance of the latest legal document in the lawyer's hands: does it mean an end of their business or not? The poor woman is unlikely to see a timely resolution to her legal difficulties. A text also represents divided interests in Daumier's "A Bookseller in Ecstasy" (1844); a dealer in used books flips happily through a 1780 edition of Horace, while the customer watches anxiously. Their common concern with the book is undermined by their divergent conceptions of its worth; one's loss is another's gain. Contrasting assessments of a text's value arise in Daumier's "The Slender Manuscript" (1845), where a young dramatist tries to convince a theater director of his work's merits. "I believe that Mr. le Directeur is going to be satisfied with the reading of my melodrama. . . . I am sorry, though, for having written only six acts!" From the impassive look on the director's face, the author's work will remain in manuscript. In everyday literate life, strangers, no less than family members, found texts a source of difference, even conflict. The pairs in Daumier's lithographic satires are no exception.[38]

Daumier was especially sensitive to conflicting responses to the political press. In 1848 and again in 1871, he recognized how often the news divided bourgeois and worker, social classes who were at times bitter enemies during the nineteenth century. Their encounters touched on more than the petty annoyances of unpaid bills ("An Encounter with the Tailor," 1853) or insults exchanged at work ("The Concierge on the Day After," 1867); in each case a newspaper serves as a barrier between the two parties. But more telling are Daumier's images of the workers' political challenge to bourgeois interpretive authority. At times, the working-class type claims the printed page for himself, as in "Worker and Bourgeois" (1848): a man in his smock stands in the street intently reading a newspaper, while the fat middle-class gentleman has

---

[37] Note the different versions of this motif in oils by Henri Fantin-Latour. Besides "Les Deux Soeurs" (1859) in the Saint Louis City Art Museum, see "La Lecture" (1870) in the Fundaçao Calouste Gulbenkian, Lisbon; and "La Lecture" (1877) in the Musée des Beaux Arts, Lyons. Cf. Edward Lucie-Smith, *Henri Fantin-Latour* (New York, 1977), and idem, *Fantin-Latour* (Oxford, 1977), 11–37.

[38] See Daumier, "Une Charge déplacée" (1845) Delteil 23: no. 1398; idem, "Sur les boulevards de Paris" (1848) Delteil 25: no. 1760; and idem, "Je suis reçu!! . . . Refusé! . . . Les crétins!" (1859) Delteil 27: no. 3139.

eyes only for the food display in a shop window. In another lithograph, it is the worker who reads to the bourgeois the political posters in the street ("The Proclamation Reading," 1848). A kiosk tender also flaunts his politics, represented by an 1870 issue of *La Liberté*; a customer is surprised to see this paper available to the "wrong" hands in Daumier's "Peekaboo! Here It Is Again!" (1870). Textual experiences can mean more than detachment between two strangers; they can also lead to revolution.[39]

Such images of reading pairs suggest well the rise of individual interpretive practice. What had been for much of the Old Regime a binding activity became in the nineteenth century a more ambivalent occasion, at times even a divisive one. Reading tends to create distance between husbands and wives, parents and children, masters and servants, as well as propertied and working classes. This alienating force in modern life represented by the printed text appears in the more intimate art of reading that features only two figures, an art ranging from serious double portraits to light-hearted satirical lithographs. As in the images of groups examined earlier, the modern literate experience of the individual is implicit over time in each successive instance. Consequently, detachment within an otherwise personal artistic motif acquires a historical dimension, one indicative of a larger development in how individuals read and how they interpreted what they read from 1800 onward.

INDIVIDUALS

Like images of groups and pairs, French portraiture developed a greater concern for realism in the nineteenth century.[40] The idealization of purpose and institution that had been so common in eighteenth-century art made room for more mundane themes and motifs. (Ordinary people serving no public function actually seem to be reading the books given to them as props.[41]) A certain

[39] Note the sociohistorical view of Gustave Courbet's work during the Second Republic in T. J. Clark, *Image of the People: Gustave Courbet and the 1848 Revolution* (Princeton, 1982) and idem, *The Absolute Bourgeois: Artists and Politics in France, 1848–1851* (Princeton, 1982).

[40] Cf. the Old Regime's "realism" in Fragonard, "La Liseuse" (1773–76) reproduced in Georges Wildenstein, *Fragonard* (1960), no. 387; Chardin, "L'Instant de méditation. Portrait de Mme. Le Noir tenant une brochure" (1747) in Georges Wildenstein, *Chardin* (1951), no. 537; idem, "Portrait de jeune garçon tenant un livre" (c. 1746) in Wildenstein, *Chardin*, no. 629; Greuze, "Un Écolier qui étudie sa leçon" (1757) in the National Gallery, London; and idem, "Le Tendre Ressouvenir" (c. 1763) in the Wallace Collection, London.

[41] E.g., Courbet, "Liseuse" (c. 1865) in the National Gallery of Art, Washington, D.C.; Corot, "Liseuse" (1869) in the Metropolitan Museum of Art, New York; Renoir, "Femme au chien noir" (1874) in Distel et al., *Renoir*, 131; Claude Monet, "Femme dans le jardin—printemps" (1875) in the Walters Art Gallery, Baltimore; Mary Cassatt, "Woman Reading" (1876) in the Museum of Fine Arts, Boston; Jacques Joseph Tissot, "Le Journal" (1883) in Christopher Wood, *Tissot* (Boston, 1986), 126; Albert Besnard, "La Liseuse" (1885) Delteil 30: no. 40; Toulouse-Lautrec, "Au café" (1886) reproduced in Maurice Joyant, *Henri de Toulouse-Lautrec* (1926), 2:n.p.; Georges Seurat, "La Jeune Fille dans l'atelier" (1887) reproduced in Rewald, *History of*

unadorned reality appears, for example, in the portraits painted by Henri Fantin-Latour during the Second Empire, exemplars of spare artistic style at its height. "The Reading" (1863) seats the artist's fiancée, Charlotte Dubourg, in a simple chair partially hidden by the woman's expansive but somber-colored dress (see Ill. 5.11). She is holding an open book with both hands in her lap, her setting otherwise indistinctly rendered in order to focus the viewer's attention on the reading figure. However detailed the portrait, it is unclear whether the painter's subject is the figure or the reading. Fantin-Latour must have wanted to portray as faithfully as possible his attractive fiancée, but in so doing he also introduced a second feature, the literate experience.[42] Realistic portraiture had more than one artistic interest; other artists besides Fantin-Latour suggested the same ambiguity of subject, whether or not they developed the same forthright style.[43] In nineteenth-century art, one can identify portraits of reading as well as of readers.

It is this attention to literate activity that makes some modern portraiture more intense. The subject is not a passive or idle sitter, but an actively engaged reader, especially after the Old Regime. Until the development of French expressionism, portrait art tended to focus increasingly on the dialogic relationship between reader and text. The subject's engagement with print actually seemed to grow. In place of the eighteenth century's daydreamer with a book, generally a young woman in love, came the nineteenth century's citizen of the world, a man or woman intent upon the literate task at hand. In short, knowledge of a text became at least as important as its emotional evocations. At the same time, a new historical context evolved rapidly after 1789, and with it a new artistic vision. The result was, in part at least, a new subject matter appropriate to the changes in literate culture.[44] Once again the rise of individual interpretive practice can be traced in the history of French portrait art from the eighteenth century onward.

Old Regime art marks a point of departure. Pierre-Antoine Baudoin's "The Reading" (c. 1760), for instance, seats an attractive woman in her boudoir; she is gazing rapturously into space, her hand resting on an open book. Her reading experience is nothing short of a voluptuous moment. In the same Old

Impressionism, 158; Anders Zorn, "La Liseuse" (c. 1890) Delteil 38: no. 38; Eugène Carrière, "La Lecture" (1896) Delteil 8: no. 29; Jean-François Raffëlli, "La Lettre" (1898) Delteil 16: no. 47; Bonnard, "La Lettre" (1906) in the National Gallery of Art, Washington, D.C.; Henri Matisse, "Liseuse au guéridon, en vert, robe rayée rouge" (1923) in Kunstmuseum, Bern; and Picasso, "Jeune Fille lisant" (1935) in the Musée Picasso, Paris.

[42] Cf. Fantin-Latour, "La Lecture" (1861) in the Musée d'Orsay, Paris.

[43] See also Frédéric Bazille, "Edmond Maître" (1867) in the National Gallery of Art, Washington, D.C.; Manet, "Le Liseur" (c. 1870) in the Saint Louis City Art Museum; Daumier, "Homme lisant au jardin" (c. 1854–56) in the Metropolitan Museum of Art, New York; and Auguste Toulmouche, "La Liseuse" (1870) photographed in BN Kb matières 1 (no. 1201).

[44] Cf. E. H. Gombrich, *Art and Illusion: A Study in the Psychology of Pictorial Representation* (Princeton, 1969), 3–30.

5.11 Henri Fantin-Latour, ''The Reading'' (1863). Copyright A.C.L.-Bruxelles

Regime context, other women are similarly moved not so much by the text itself as by its suggestiveness.[45] The females in Fragonard's ''Memories'' (1773–76), Chardin's ''The Amusements of Private Life'' (1747), and Rob-

[45] See also Augustin de Saint-Aubin after Greuze, ''Une Jeune Fille qui envoie un baiser par la fenêtre, appuyée sur des fleurs, qu'elle brise'' (c. 1769) in the BN, Paris; and the works by Fragonard: ''Girl Crowned with Rose'' (1773–76) in the Metropolitan Museum of Art, New York; ''Study, Portrait of a Girl'' (1773–76) in the Wallace Collection, London; and ''Sultana Seated on a Sofa'' (1765–72) in Wildenstein, *Fragonard*, no. 335.

ert's "Shame on Him Who Thinks Evil of Others" (1775) all swoon, apparently in response to a book or letter, its intimacy strong and immediate. With the principal exception of Chardin's "A Philosopher Occupied by His Reading" (c. 1735), scholars and intellectuals also appear particularly affected by their reading, as in Fragonard's "Plutarch's Dream" (1748–52), where the great biographer, deep in thought, looks up from his books. The painting celebrates erudition in a striking fashion. Only when reading touches on everyday life does it merit strict attention; an account book in Chardin's "Economy" (1747) evokes no flights of introspection in the prim bourgeoise attending to her household expenses. This was hardly one of portraiture's glamorous moments. In the eighteenth century, artists were more generally given to portraying their subject's rich personal world.[46]

These Old Regime images were explicitly emblematic, a tendency that continued to flourish under the influence of romanticism.[47] The romantics stressed, among other things, the imagination and its creative force. So one is not surprised to see images featuring this artistic element in the nineteenth century. The lithographer Francis's "Meditation" (c. 1835) is typical of the genre; a woman seated by a stream ponders dreamily the closed book beside her. Nevertheless, a more realistic impulse intrudes. Daumier's "The Novel" (1833) depicts the book reader's actual dream; the characters from the novel in her lap are acting out their assigned roles at her feet. An anonymous illustrator contemporary with Daumier drew a female reader in medieval garb for the title page to Madame de Renneville *La Galerie des jeunes vierges* (1834). Attention to a romantic text has transformed her dress in an appropriate fashion. Similar motifs appear later, as in Eugène Grasset's "The Romantic Bookstore" (1887), the florid poster ad for a reedition of Victor Hugo's *Notre Dame de Paris*. The cathedral itself is placed in the background, a prop more relevant to the book's title than to the reader's experience with the text. Later, Pablo Picasso's "The Dream" (1932) will even obscure the textual source of the sleeping reader's dream.[48]

As a general rule after 1800, however, most artists depicted more serious readers.[49] Attentive females actually predominated in nineteenth-century portraiture. At least three appear in Renoir's work, for example. His "Young

---

[46] Cf. the figure in Lempereur after Greuze, "Retour sur soy même" (c. 1775) in BN Kb matières 1 (no. A.09761).

[47] See Hugh Honour, *Romanticism* (New York, 1979); Kenneth Clark, *The Romantic Rebellion: Romantic versus Classic Art* (New York, 1973); and Pierre Courthion, *Romanticism* (Geneva, 1965).

[48] Note the obvious use of books as props in Seurat, "Femme nue étendue" (1888) reproduced in John Russell, *Seurat* (New York, 1965), 246; and Matisse, "La Séance de peinture" (1919) in the Scottish National Gallery of Art, Edinburgh.

[49] Some interesting exceptions to the rule: Achille Deveria, "Les Heures du jour" (1829) in the Musée Renan-Scheffer, Paris; Delarue, "La Lecture" (1876) in BN Kb matières 1 (no. 598); and Jules Goupil, "Nos aïeules. Le Livre d'images" (1895) photographed in BN Kb matières 1—all of them female fashion plates.

Woman Reading an Illustrated Newspaper'' (1880–81), "The Woman Reader'' (1886), and "Gabrielle Reading'' (1890) portray, amid much light and color, young women fully engaged in the texts before them.[50] Not long afterwards, Toulouse-Lautrec portrayed three others, each of them seated alone and intent upon the text in hand (see Ill. 5.12). That the latter artist's subjects are obviously married, older, and wealthier in no way detracts from

5.12 Henri de Toulouse-Lautrec, "Portrait of the comtesse A. de Toulouse-Lautrec in the Parlor at Malromé'' (1887). Courtesy of the Musée Toulouse-Lautrec, Albi

[50] See Distel et al., *Renoir*, 186–87; Phoebe Pool, *Impressionism* (New York, 1969), 241; and Heinrich Haerkötter, *Deutsche Literaturgeschichte* (Darmstadt, 1978), 94.

their careful attention. Their social status actually contributes to the gravity of their literate activity. Toulouse-Lautrec's formal titles are revealing: "Portrait of the comtesse A. de Toulouse-Lautrec in the Parlor at Malromé" (1887), "Madame Aline Gilbert" (1887), and "Madame Marthe X . . ." (1900).[51] Whereas Renoir's women are busy with illustrated magazines, Toulouse-Lautrec's attend to either a book or a newspaper, the symbols of more intensive reading habits. Other artists followed this realistic portrait tradition in the nineteenth century; intent female readers are at last featured prominently.

This did not mean that artists forgot literate males; portraits of serious men reading continued to appear. In 1840, for instance, Benjamin Roubaud caricatured Charles Nodier, the appointed librarian of the Arsenal, seated on a stack of books and surrounded by the ostensible tools of his trade.[52] Besides the text he is reading, there are others in his pockets and scattered about on the floor. Similarly, Cham [Amédeé de Noé] depicted an ardent bibliophile, Trottman, closely examining the defective copies of Balzac's work published in Belgium.[53] Literate activity was a central feature of his business, just as it was for the many writers portrayed in the nineteenth century. Manet's "Portrait of Stéphane Mallarmé" (1876) and Degas's "Edmond Duranty" (1879) are only two of several such studies of French intellectuals (see Ill. 5.13). These figures are not solely the creators but also the receivers of texts. Consequently, Antonin Proust, Anatole France, and Pierre Reverdy all appear as shrewd critical minds intent upon the works before them.[54] Perhaps a more striking instance is Eugène Carrière's untitled etching in which a scholarly figure reads a large open book highlighted by the light focused on the man and the text.[55] The difficulty of identifying the scholar at work lends a curious intensity to his activity.

But nonliterary figures also appeared with books. Artists portrayed each other as readers, however inappropriate the props may have been. In this particular tradition, Renoir's "Portrait of Claude Monet" (1872) belongs with Paul Gauguin's "Meyer de Haan" (1889), Marcellin Desboutin's "Edgar Degas Reading" (1884), and Claude Monet's "Alfred Sisley" (c. 1880). These men were not particularly well known for their serious literate interests. Similarly, in 1906, Anders Zorn presented a French diplomat, the baron Estournelles de Constant, in a pensive literate pose, even though the figure is not

---

[51] For more on this artist's work, see Douglas Cooper, *Henri de Toulouse-Lautrec* (New York, 1966), 57.

[52] Benjamin Roubaud, "Charles Nodier" (c. 1840) in the Musée Balzac, Paris.

[53] Cham, "Les Contrefaçons belges" (c. 1835) in the Musée Balzac, Paris.

[54] See Zorn, "Antonin Proust" (1889) Delteil 4: no. 33; idem, "Anatole France" (1906) Delteil 4: no. 205; and Picasso, "Portrait de Pierre Reverdy" (1922) in the Museum of Modern Art, New York.

[55] See also Carrière, untitled etching (1898) in BN Kb matières 1. Cf. Manet, "Portrait d'Émile Zola" (1868) in the Galeries du Jeu de Paume, Paris. Cachin et al., *Manet*, 280–85.

5.13 Edgar Degas, "Edmond Duranty" (1879). Courtesy of the Metropolitan Museum of Art, Rogers Fund, 1918 (19.51.9a)

actually reading the text before him on the desk.[56] By contrast, the female domestic standing and reading before a large bookcase in Bonnard's "The Reading" (1905) has at least as much claim to erudition as Zorn's privileged official. The servant's quiet moment with a book is conducive to literate contemplation, as are many of the accoutrements important to interpretive practice among ordinary people. Léon Cogniet's "The First Letter from Home" (1817) introduces eyeglasses, Cézanne's "Portrait of the Artist's Father Reading" (1866) a good chair, Georges Seurat's "Portrait of the Artist's Mother" (1883) a table lamp, and Alphonse-Léon Noël's "Portrait of Madame V. Noël" (1830) a heating stove. In each case, as in Armand Guillaumin's portrait of Pissaro's friend Martinez, the setting contributes to the reader's preoccupation (see Ill. 5.14).

Whatever their places in life, modern portrait subjects became more self-conscious readers. In time, artists developed a better sense of the reader's deliberate isolation from others. Fragonard's "Study" (1769) has an upper-class woman, open book in hand, appealing to an unseen audience. She is not alone, but in relationship with other people interested in the text that she is sharing with them. At the end of the next century, however, there are fewer suggestions of oral readings. Albert Besnard's "The Reading" (1892) portrays a woman looking up from her text, but it is unclear whether there are

[56] See Zorn, "D'Estournelles de Constant" (1906) Delteil 4: no. 202.

5.14 Armand Guillaumin, ''Pissaro's Friend Martinez in Guillaumin's Studio'' (1878). Courtesy of the Iris and B. Gerald Cantor Collection

people elsewhere in the same darkened room (see Ill. 5.15). More than likely, she has been interrupted by the viewer. The presence of another individual actually means a momentary intrusion upon the reader's mental space. While the entrance of another person is a distraction from the literate experience, it can also be a welcomed relief from a tedious text—hence Maurice Jacquet's untitled painting in 1907.[57] A young décolleté female looks enticingly at the

[57] Maurice Jacquet, untitled painting (1907), photographed in BN Kb matières 1.

5.15 Albert Besnard, "The Reading" (1892). Courtesy of the Bibliothèque d'Art et d'Archéologie (Photo S.A.B.A.A., Paris)

viewer, the book completely forgotten in her alluring pose. Clearly of no serious concern to her, reading is an idle interlude between more interesting activities. Thus by 1900, French portraits assume that books are private concerns, be they profound or trivial, quite apart from the social relations of ordinary life.[58]

Curiously, reading's self-contained nature in portraiture poses a problem: it appears to contradict the remarkable sociability of French readers evident in other historical sources.[59] Thousands of letters sent to authors suggest the important social networks among family, colleagues, and friends. On the basis of this evidence, the French literate experience was closely tied to collective

---

[58] Cf. D. Reyolros, untitled painting (1907) photographed in BN Kb matières 1; and anon., untitled drawing (1898) in BN Kb matières 1.

[59] See Chapter 4, pp. 122–26.

activity. How could artists have missed this social dimension? Why were readers in portraits so detached from others? An obvious answer is the nature of the artistic genre.[60] Single subjects pose alone, and the suggestion of other people off canvas is a relatively unusual technical device. A more intriguing answer, however, lies in the distinction between reading and interpretation. Focused largely on external appearances, portraits can easily capture the readers' circumstances. But interpretive practice is not so easily rendered, because the artist depends upon a mute medium of expression. What subjects actually did with the texts before them defies all but the most sophisticated artistic treatment, just as what artists mean in their work often defies the most insightful reader. Portraiture cannot reveal the collective side to reading any better than it can interpretation. The contradiction between conclusions drawn from two different and problematic sources is therefore not surprising.

Apart from portraiture, book illustrations suggest another conundrum: What influence did images accompanying texts have on the reading experience? To date, all historical answers have been based on inference, if not outright speculation. Indeed, there can be no satisfactory historical answer to this question. The most common illustration technique, wood engraving, appeared long before the eighteenth century, but it graced only the most expensive products of the book trade until the Second Empire.[61] When art did appear pervasively in literary works, there was a marked disjuncture between image and text. Artists had creative inspirations of their own to develop. Moreover, less-sophisticated illustrators of serial novels during the Third Republic employed a limited range of stock images—dying bodies, kneeling suitors, pleading women, all borrowed from early modern broadsides—for the most dramatic moments in the narratives. Many illustrations were used indiscriminately from one novel to the next, and still others were misplaced in the text. Often, more than one artist had a hand in each illustration.[62] Trends in the popular press's type and page design also opened the text up to a larger, less attentive audience, creating a more accessible product. But this development did not ensure any particular interpretation, either; like the images themselves, this development had no discernible historical impact. Correspondents and reviewers rarely if ever mention art or page design in the works they read. For them, Gérard Genette's paratexts did not exist.[63]

[60] Cf. John Pope-Hennessy, *The Portrait in the Renaissance* (Washington, D.C., 1966), 3–63, 233–39; and Heinrich Wölfflin, *Principles of Art History: The Problem of the Development of Style in Later Art*, trans. M. D. Hottinger (New York, 1950), 226–37.

[61] On illustrations, see HEF 3:286–363 and 4:344–475.

[62] On roman-feuilleton illustrations, see M. E. Warlick, "Max Ernst's Collage Novel, *Une Semaine de Bonté*: Feuilleton Sources and Alchemical Interpretation," doctoral dissertation, University of Maryland (1984), 34–68; and Jean-Noël Marchandiau, *L'Illustration, 1843–1944. Vie et mort d'un journal* (1987), 41.

[63] See Gérard Genette, *Seuils* (1987). Cf. discussion of type and page design as paratexts in Lyons, *Le Triomphe du livre*, 223–31; and Richard Terdiman, *Discourse/Counter-Discourse: The*

Of course, no historical source is perfect. Perhaps more than any other "document," art has a tradition of its own that alters significantly its utility to another discipline. Certain motifs and techniques, such as historical subjects and classical models, affect the way an artist represents the world. Pictorial realism is most certainly not photography. This much art historians like E. H. Gombrich know.[64] Similarly, the models that artists used did not need to be literate to pose with a book or newspaper. In most cases, print was just a prop. In time, as expressionism developed after 1900, the model did not have to exist at all except in the artist's imagination. Eventually, the complete stylization of subject matter meant that readers would disappear from art altogether, while a growing literate population remained as preoccupied as ever with a more varied print culture. In the twentieth century, the "art of reading" does indeed wane; and it tells the historian less about interpretive practice than it does about new artistic interests. The images of literate activity earlier in the period are thus suspect as empirical evidence of any historical development other than what artists were doing. The world of art is not necessarily historical.

Given the enormous archive available, however, the historian may begin with the least problematic images of readers in groups, in pairs, and in portraits. Documenting how this large body of work changed over a 140-year period illuminates the history of reading. More and different kinds of literate experiences appear in art as well as in fact. More and more figures read alone, detached and even alienated from their surroundings and the other people around them. Clearly, texts in modern art were obstacles as much as they were vehicles to personal and social relationships. New literate social groups arose, and with them the appropriate images; young women, for example, predominate in portraiture after 1850. Art increasingly focused on the act of reading itself until the waning of impressionism. Thereafter, the subject practically disappears from art. As the circumstances of interpretive practice evolved, so too did the products of artistic practice, whether they were used to illustrate a text or to portray a reader. Despite the interpretive and documentary problems such images pose, some aspects of reading in modern France and its history are here rendered both visible and beautiful.

Theory and Practice of Symbolic Resistance in Nineteenth-Century France (Ithaca, 1985), 117–27.

[64] Cf. Gombrich, *Art and Illusion*, 359–89; Bates Lowry, *The Visual Experience: An Introduction to Art* (Englewood Cliffs, N.J., 1965), 9–121, 239–65; M. Mespoulet, *Images et romans, parenté des estampes et du roman réaliste de 1815 à 1865* (1939), 154; and David Scott, *Pictorialist Poetics: Poetry and the Visual Arts in Nineteenth-Century France* (Cambridge, 1988), 38–70.

Chapter 6

IN THE NOVEL

A KEY SCENE in Marcel Proust's *Le Temps retrouvé* (1922) illustrates well the complex role of reading in modern character development. The author's alter ego, Marcel, is in the Guermantes family library where he finds a copy of George Sand's *François le Champi*. Suddenly, Marcel recalls details of his childhood in Combray, and he ponders their origins in the text.

> Things—a book in a red cover like any other—as soon as we perceive them become in us something immaterial, of the same nature as our preoccupations or our sensations at a particular moment, and meld indissolubly into them. . . . A name once read in a book contains among its syllables the fresh wind and brilliant sunshine at the time we first read it.[1]

A special object, Sand's text evokes Marcel's memory of the past so sharply that he himself is transformed by the experience, even though a prolonged reading can actually hamper the much-desired remembrance of things past. In the rush of recollection, the reader forgets the book and consequently the source of memory's stimulation. "I know too well how these images left by the mind are easily erased by the mind. In the place of the old, it substitutes the new that does not have the same power to resurrect [the past]."[2] And so Marcel feared that his impressions of the present would displace completely his memories of the past and obliterate any recall of the child he once was.

This interesting moment in Proust's long novel suggests the important function of the life cycle in literate activity.[3] As Marcel acquires deeper insight into himself and his relations with others, he reflects more fully upon his experiences with texts. As an adult, the narrator self-consciously reads the same book he had first encountered as a child. The difference in his experience is obviously a result of age and the perceptions of the world that come with it; the main character's maturation from childhood to adulthood provides a new

---

[1] Marcel Proust, *À la recherche du temps perdu*, ed. Pierre Clarac and André Ferré (1954), 3:885.

[2] Ibid., 3:887–88. Cf. Jean-Yves Tadié, *Proust et le roman* (1971), 17–60; J. M. Cocking, *Proust* (Cambridge, 1982), 183–90; and Edward J. Hughes, *Marcel Proust: A Study in the Quality of Awareness* (Cambridge, 1983), 57–124.

[3] Studies in cognitive development appropriate to reading over the life cycle are Jean Piaget, *The Origins of Intelligence in Children* (New York, 1963); William G. Perry, Jr., *Forms of Intellectual and Ethical Development in the College Years: A Scheme* (New York, 1970); and Eleanor J. Gibson and Harry Levin, *The Psychology of Reading* (Cambridge, Mass., 1975), 225–482.

perspective on the text and the nature of reading. In its consideration of literate life over time, however, Proust's novel is hardly unique. Prose fiction in modern France is filled with similar reflections. The *roman de formation* in particular treats the development of a main character whose reading changes in appropriate ways. At each stage in the central figure's quest for identity and love, books occupy a special place well-suited to his or her age. It is as if texts were an indispensable feature of growing up. Like the art studied in Chapter 5, literature mirrors historical experience.[4]

In life as well as the novel, momentary impressions inform interpretive practice. This truism merits closer examination in the history of prose realism in France from 1800 onward.[5] For the purposes of exploring the modern reader's life cycle, it makes sense to examine the French variation of the *Bildungsroman*.[6] From instance to instance, characters read as children at home and at school (before age 15), as youths in quest of love and career (ages 15–30), and as adults with responsibilities for others (after age 30).[7] These activities in the novel are thus models of actual interpretive practice in the lives of individuals like the characters who appear in prose fiction. But even more important is the growing awareness, in literature as in life, of the incredible power of print to shape people's lives. At the proper moment, texts deeply move readers as children, youths, and adults throughout the nineteenth and early twentieth century, when a progressive disenchantment with the world changed the literary experience for individuals of all ages. As the life cycle changed historically, so too did the art of reading in the modern novel.[8]

CHILDHOOD

Formal reading instruction at home or at school is an inconsequential event in most modern narratives. Despite the importance of literate activity in later life, a character's learning to read rarely appears in prose fiction, perhaps because

---

[4] See Lionel Trilling, *The Liberal Imagination: Essays on Literature and Society* (Garden City, N.Y., 1953), 199–215.

[5] See Harry Levin, *The Gates of Horn: A Study of Five French Realists* (New York, 1966); John Porter Houston, *Fictional Technique in France, 1802–1927: An Introduction* (Baton Rouge, 1972); Michel Raimond, *Le Roman depuis la Révolution*, 8th ed. (1981); and Christopher Prendergast, *The Order of Mimesis: Balzac, Stendhal, Nerval, Flaubert* (Cambridge, 1986).

[6] Cf. Maurice Beebe, *Ivory Towers and Sacred Founts: The Artist as Hero in Fiction from Goethe to Joyce* (New York, 1964), 175–96, 232–59.

[7] For useful surveys of age-cohort study, see Henri Peyre, *Les Générations littéraires* (1948), 7–44; Julián Marìas, *Generations: A Historical Method*, trans. Harold C. Riley (University, Ala., 1970); Alan B. Spitzer, "The Historical Problem of Generations," *American Historical Review* 78 (1973): 1353–85; and idem, *The Generation of 1820* (Princeton, 1987), 3–34.

[8] Cf. the critical discussion of prose fiction as an historical source in James Smith Allen, "History and the Novel: *Mentalité* in Modern Popular Fiction," *History and Theory* 22 (1983): 233–52; and idem, "Obedience, Struggle, and Revolt: The Historical Vision of Balzac's *Father Goriot*," *Clio* 16 (1987): 103–19.

such an event is of no interest in itself.[9] Rather, the earliest experiences with print are presented only if they shed light on a figure or situation, such as the patriarchal values expressed in Rétif de la Bretonne's *La Vie de mon père* (1779). There, as in Greuze's emblematic paintings, reading is a collective act carefully directed by the father, the priest, or the schoolmaster, traditional Old Regime authorities (at least as Rétif conceived of them). No one read alone in Rétif's fictional world, and certainly not outside the context of family, church, or school.[10] And this social control of literate life continued to appear in novels after 1800. Balzac's Louis Lambert, Flaubert's Frédéric Moreau, Jules Vallès's Jacques Vingtras, and Roger Martin du Gard's Jacques Thibault, among other fictional figures, all study texts in school and respond in ways appropriate to their personalities. Occasionally, family readings serve a similar function, as in the Goncourt brothers' *Germinie Lacerteux* (1864), in which Mlle. de Verandeuil, as a young girl, translates Giorgio Vasari's great study of painters under her father's supervision.[11] Individuals have their first taste of intellectual life in such familial settings, whether or not these scenes are depicted in prose fiction.

But such formal contexts do not shape character as fully as more private, individual reading experiences do. In fact, the novel most often portrays the central figure reading alone in revolt against institutional constraints. His or her extracurricular reading merits a good deal more attention, and for good reason: character can best be defined in contrast to already well-established and widely accepted social values.[12] School and family often serve this counterfunction. Emma Bovary, for example, first learns of the romantics as an impressionable adolescent in a convent school. At first she actually enjoys the assigned reading, such as the résumés of religious history by Bishop Frayssinous and the apostrophes to nature in Chateaubriand's *Le Génie du Christianisme*.[13] Her attention naturally turns to the medieval romances of Sir Walter Scott and his French imitators; Emma adopts their characters as models for her own sensibility and even for some of her subsequent behavior. The stern

---

[9] The most common literary-critical approach to readers in texts is to study not images of reception, such as characters learning to read, but the structure of narrative, e.g., Wayne C. Booth, *The Rhetoric of Fiction* (Chicago, 1961), 89–148; Tzvetan Todorov, *The Poetics of Prose* (Ithaca, 1977), 234–46; Jonathan Culler, *On Deconstruction: Theory and Criticism after Structuralism* (Ithaca, 1982), 31–83; and Peter J. Rabinowitz, *Before Reading: Narrative Conventions and the Poetics of Interpretation* (Ithaca, 1987), 15–169.

[10] See N. A. Rétif de la Bretonne, *La Vie de mon père* (1970), 8–9, 29, 131–32. Cf. Émile Guillaumin, *La Vie d'un simple (Mémoires d'un métayer)* (1904), 144–45.

[11] See Jules and Edmond de Goncourt, *Germinie Lacerteux* (1979), 44. Cf. Lazare Prajs, *La Fallacité de l'oeuvre romanesque des frères Goncourt* (1974), 13–124.

[12] Cf. E. M. Forster, *Aspects of the Novel* (New York, 1927), 43–64.

[13] Gustave Flaubert, *Oeuvres*, ed. Albert Thibaudet and René Dumesnil (1951), 1:324. Cf. Maurice Bardèche, *L'Oeuvre de Flaubert* (1974), 163–212; and Michal Peled Ginsburg, *Flaubert Writing: A Study of Narrative Strategies* (Stanford, 1986), 82–107.

moral discipline of the school, like that imposed on many other children in the nineteenth century, is ultimately ignored in favor of a more immediate literate experience.

And so it is the reading outside of family and school settings that defines youth best. Octave's early reading experiences in Alfred de Musset's *La Confession d'un enfant du siècle* (1836), for instance, certainly bear this out. As a child of the First Empire, Octave reads the German and English romantics; their literary angst is a formative influence on his generation. "When English and German ideas thus passed through our heads," Musset writes, "it was like a dismal and silent disgust followed by a terrible convulsion." Byron, Goethe, and later Chateaubriand are the impressionable Octave's favorite writers until he inherits a chest of lascivious novels from his aunt. The youth then throws himself into their world of debauchery, hypocrisy, and corruption. The resulting moral anguish, deepened by his subsequent reading of the Bible, tortures him beyond belief. "I rushed to the open window: 'And so is it true that you are empty?' I cried looking at the great pale sky which was spread out overhead. 'Answer! Answer! Before I die, will you put something else but a dream here in these two arms?' " It is no accident, therefore, that with this notion of love defined by his reading—"the revels of his childhood"—Octave's relationship with Brigitte turns so perverse and so disastrous for them both. Early experience with texts actually shapes later life.[14]

In Balzac's *Louis Lambert* (1832), youthful reading leads to more than difficult love affairs; it causes insanity. Despite the novel's unreliable narrator, one can discern the central place of literate life in Louis's later mental breakdown. The work's third sentence mentions a decisive event in the story: "The Old and New Testament had fallen into Louis's hands at the age of five; and this volume in which so many books are contained, had decided his destiny." On one level at least, the novel demonstrates the influence of these works on Louis. His knowledge of the world is mediated through the printed word, his images of reality derived almost exclusively from the books he read. "A man of ideas, he needed to slake the thirst of his brain that had wanted to assimilate all ideas. Hence his reading, and from his reading, his reflections that gave him the power to reduce all things to their simplest expression." Later at the Collège de Vendôme, Louis spurns the schoolboy exercises in Latin and grammar to plumb the depths of Swedenborgian mysticism and other religious systems. Reading in fact becomes for him a form of prayer, one discovered by his patron Madame de Staël, resulting in his profound if quirky meditation on the human will. By the end of the novel, however, Louis is the victim of his

[14] Alfred de Musset, *Oeuvres complètes en prose*, ed. Maurice Allem and Paul Courant (1960), 74, 105. Cf. Ronald Grimsley, "Romantic Emotion in Musset's *Confession d'un enfant du siècle*," *Studies in Romanticism* 9 (Spring 1970): 125–42; and Anthony Rizutto, "Octave in Alfred de Musset's *La Confession d'un enfant du siècle*," *Kentucky Romance Quarterly* 24 (1977): 83–94.

intense study. He withdraws from the world completely and utters aphorisms incomprehensible to everyone but his devoted wife. Tragically, serious early reading here creates an insane oracle.[15]

Perhaps a more benign influence is traced in Flaubert's *L'Éducation sentimentale* (1869). For much of the novel, Frédéric Moreau's youthful experiences with texts merely intensify his proclivity for dreaming.[16] In order to highlight the differences between Frédéric and his more realistic companion Deslauriers, Flaubert describes their favorite literate activities. Charles as a youngster took particular interest in Plato, Jouffroy, Cousin, Laromiguière, Malebranche, and the Scottish philosophers. Frédéric, on the other hand, took up less serious works: "After medieval dramas, he launched into memoirs: Froissart, Comines, Pierre de l'Estoile, Brantôme. The images that this reading introduced to his mind obsessed him so forcefully, he evinced a need to reproduce them. He aspired to be one day the Walter Scott of France." Frédéric preferred to the vast philosophical systems that fascinated Charles the suggestive, dreamlike qualities of the romantics. Similarly, Louise Roque, Frédéric's provincial sweetheart, also falls victim to her reading. After hearing Frédéric's rendition of Shakespeare's *Macbeth*, she suffers a nightmare derived from Lady Macbeth's vision of unwashable bloodstains. Accordingly, the rest of the novel develops the characters initially defined by these childhood differences in literary response.[17]

Still more positive influences of reading appear in Vallès's *L'Enfant* (1879), the first volume of the Jacques Vingtras trilogy. A key feature of the novel is the freedom that the main character finds in his first books. Otherwise beaten and abused at home and at school, Jacques discovers liberation in Daniel Defoe's *Robinson Crusoe*. A copy of this work belonging to a classmate occupies him for hours of blessed forgetfulness that recur at various points in his development.

> From this moment, [Jacques remarks,] there was in my imagination a blue corner, in the prose of my battered childhood a poetry of dreams, and my heart set sail for countries where one breathes, where one works, but where one is free. How many times I read and reread this *Robinson*![18]

---

[15] Honoré de Balzac, *La Comédie humaine*, ed. Pierre-Georges Castex et al. (1980), 11:589, 643. Cf. Pierre Citron, "Les Lecteurs de roman dans *La Comédie humaine*," *Année balzacienne, 1967* (1968): 111–24.

[16] Cf. Bardèche, *L'Oeuvre de Flaubert*, 269–314; Victor Brombert, *The Novels of Flaubert: A Study of Themes and Techniques* (Princeton, 1966), 125–85; idem, *The Hidden Reader: Stendhal, Balzac, Hugo, Baudelaire, Flaubert* (Cambridge, Mass., 1988), 130–35; and Deana Knight, *Flaubert's Characters: The Language of Illusion* (Cambridge, 1985), 85–93.

[17] Flaubert, *Oeuvres*, 2:44–45, 127.

[18] Jules Vallès, *Jacques Vingtras 1: L'Enfant* (1973), 148. Cf. Victor Brombert, *The Intellectual Hero: Studies in the French Novel, 1880–1955* (Philadelphia, 1960), 43–51; and Max Gallo, *Jules Vallès, ou La Révolte d'une vie* (1988), 389–417.

Of course, Jacques already had a propensity for daydreaming to escape the misery of his childhood. But reading deepened his reverie and provided for it a particular social setting, whether it was at home, in school, or among his comrades. In Nantes, he turns to *La France maritime*, whose accounts of voyages on the open seas he incorporates into his other reading "where birds swirl over the ocean." "In Nantes I will be able to escape when I want."[19] By the end of the term, he is delighted to have the novels of Walter Scott read to him by the indulgent Professor Larbeau, a sharp contrast to his severe parents, who had never read him anything. Until the end of the novel, reading represents the only freedom that Jacques and other children like him would ever know.

But reading also offers an important dimension to self-understanding. Initially, Jacques conceives the world through books, in much the same way that Louis Lambert and Emma Bovary had done. His rich imagination is fed by each encounter with a text. As he grows older, however, Jacques learns to divert his reading into a purposeful reality. In time, Jacques's dreams turn to action. He does not merely envisage himself as the heroic Alexander the Great at Arbelles or the valiant Captain Lelièvre at Mazagran—"We had translated yesterday the story of Arbelles in *Quinte Curce*"—he actually throws stones at his schoolyard enemies. He does not merely sell the ridiculous prize books that he had won at the end of the school year; he defies his father's wishes for the sake of a popular Parisian paper still smelling of the printers' workshop. "I would have kept them," he explains to his mother, "if I had found in them what bread cost and how it was earned." The result of this act for Jacques is a cold, wet night spent in the street, because thanks to his reading he preferred his own judgment to that of his father. Books gave Jacques sufficient self-confidence to do more than dream of escape from the tyranny of authority; he now resists it. By the end of his childhood, like those of other rebellious types in nineteenth-century France, Jacques is already *l'insurgé* of Vallès's third volume in the Vingtras trilogy.[20]

A similar but much more subtle awakening to interpretive self-consciousness is depicted in Proust's work. Like the famous madeleine and tea, books also evoke sensations worthy of young Marcel's attention. One night, after his mother had tucked him into bed and given him his long-awaited goodnight kiss, she paused to read. At first, Marcel saw the bedtime reading as a ruse to keep her for himself. But he soon realized that this literate experience and its evocations had more important implications. This new book was "not like an object having much else similar to it, but like a unique individual having a reason to exist in itself." In time, Marcel became aware of the reader's independent function. The text was not truly sufficient in itself; it had to be inter-

[19] Vallès, *L'Enfant*, 242.

[20] Ibid., 135, 398. Cf. the use of texts by the narrator in Alphonse Daudet, *Le Petit Chose* (1887).

preted. And so, as his mother read *François le Champi*, Marcel noticed holes in the plot, gaps that he himself had created by inattention, but also gaps that his mother had made by leaving out all allusions to love in the novel. "If my mother was an unfaithful reader, she was also for the works where she found the accent of a true emotion, an admirable reader in the respect and simplicity of her interpretation, in the beauty and sweetness of her voice." She lent to the text the resulting mystery of literature that Marcel experienced, but also the generosity and moral distinction that she had learned from her own mother. Self-conscious interpretation of texts as well as of sensations thus became by the turn of the century a feature of modern intellectual development.[21]

Other people besides Marcel's mother play influential roles in his early reading experiences. The books that his mother read to him had been gifts from a grandmother who enjoyed literature and wanted to share it with Marcel. This decisive woman could not tolerate anything utilitarian or vulgar; everything she gave him had to be worthy of appreciation in and for itself. While traveling to Balbec, for example, the old lady gave Marcel her copy of Madame de Sévigné's letters.

> My grandmother who had come to this book from within, by the love for her own, for nature, had taught me to appreciate its genuine beauty that was of another order. . . . [Madame de Sévigné] presents to us things according to our perceptions of them instead of explaining them according to their causes.[22]

None of the text's peculiar idioms, mannerisms, or conventions appealed to Marcel. These evoked common, undistinguished responses. Instead he acquired from his grandmother a taste for what he later called the Dostoyevski side of Madame de Sévigné's letters, that is, for their description of characters as landscapes. Marcel would later refine this taste in his infatuation with Bergotte's writing. In the meantime, he had become aware of the reader's own creative sensibility.[23]

The influence exerted by Bloch, Swann, and Norpois soon replace that of Marcel's mother and grandmother. Each of these figures, in one way or another, contributes to Marcel's developing identity. But in his disillusionment with Bergotte, i.e., Anatole France, he comes to a sense of his own interpretive practice. Marcel first learns of Bergotte from Bloch, a chum at school, and Bloch's extravagant enthusiasm for the author's lyricism easily convinces his young friend. Marcel is particularly impressed by the poetic passages, whose meaning he never bothers to explore. When Bloch is discredited by his insincerity and banned from the house by Marcel's anti-Semitic grandfather, the

[21] Proust, *À la recherche du temps perdu*, 1:41, 42.

[22] Ibid., 1:653.

[23] Cf. J.-F. Revel, *Sur Proust* (1960), 193–217; Jeffrey Mehlman, *A Structural Study of Autobiography: Proust, Leiris, Sartre, Lévi-Strauss* (Ithaca, 1974), 20–64; and Janet Varner Gunn, *Autobiography: Towards a Poetics of Experience* (Philadelphia, 1982), 90–117.

older and more experienced Swann offers Marcel assurance that Bergotte is a writer worth knowing personally. But neither he nor anyone else ever considers Bergotte a great writer. The most Marcel can elicit from Swann is that he knew him and that he still considers him "a charming wit." Marcel's suspicions grow still more after the marquis de Norpois expresses contempt for the author. "Bergotte is what I call a flute player," Norpois remarks; "one must recognize for the most part that he plays it pleasantly, albeit with much affectation and mannerism. But in essence it is only that." So Marcel is well prepared for his disappointment when he actually meets Bergotte and discovers that all his reservations about the man's work are confirmed. "Just as the human word is related to the soul, but without expressing it as the style does, Bergotte had an air of speaking nearly the opposite [of what he meant]." Thus Marcel comes to trust his own literary judgment.[24]

This precious but pervasive literate experience is at once celebrated and satirized in André Gide's *Les Faux-Monnayeurs* (1925). In the first scene of the novel, the schoolboy Bernard Profitendieu discovers letters written to his mother by an unknown lover, and the texts confirm what Bernard had come to believe in his adolescent revolt, that Albéric Profitendieu is not actually his father. With the most incriminating letter in hand, Bernard asks himself,

> Is it becoming to question my mother? . . . Let us give her good taste credit. I am free to imagine that he is a prince. It would hardly be to my advantage if I learn I am the son of a poor wretch! Not to know who one's father is will surely cure the fear of resembling him. All knowledge complicates. Consider this ignorance a blessing. Do not probe any further. Besides, I have had enough of it for today.[25]

No longer sure of who he is, Bernard fabricates a persona of his own, one little different from the Proustian aesthete, in order to embark on a series of adventures. In this way, the identity and development of one character in Gide's complex novel is based on a self-conscious interpretation of a text appropriate to the theme of personal and literary counterfeit. True literature, like true relations between people, requires a closer tie between author and reader, self and other, than is evident in the reading of either Bernard or his Proustian model.

Perhaps more typical of modern reading response is Daniel de Fontanin's discovery of Gide's *Les Nourritures terrestres* in Martin du Gard's *Les Thibault* (1922–40). Daniel had already suffered from the embarrassing revelation of his influence on Jacques Thibault that opens the novel sequence. But in time, relations between Daniel and Jacques cool. The young Fontanin retreats to a more private literary fascination. Despite Jacques's disapproval of Gide, Daniel chances to read a few enticing phrases of *Les Nourritures* in a

---

[24] Proust, *À la recherche du temps perdu*, 1:99, 473, 550.
[25] André Gide, *Romans*, ed. Maurice Nadeau et al. (1958), 933.

train, and as soon as he returns home, he buys a copy for himself. Daniel immediately reads the novel and stays up all night to peruse it a second time. The result is an epiphany: "This mania for moral judgment that his education had taught him, he understood, was in one stroke shaken off. The word 'sin' had changed its meaning." The next day Daniel felt liberated from the familial constraints of his childhood. "That night, in a few hours, the scale of values that he had believed immutable since childhood had been turned upside down." The discovery of this text and its apparent challenge to conventional morality, Gide's complex irony notwithstanding, leads Daniel to a new stage in life, to a new self-awareness that is an important feature of the *roman de formation*. Reading actually makes possible this literary transition to adulthood.[26]

In several French novels from Balzac to Martin du Gard, then, early reading experiences are central to the first stage of character development. The principal figures encounter life at least partially through books that can either facilitate or impede the quest for identity. School texts are often disdained, almost always neglected in favor of contemporary literature's challenge to institutional authorities. Ultimately, independent reading represents the freedom to be. But even more important is the self-discovery that these early texts actually foster.

In life as in fiction, the novel was indeed read in the context of social and emotional maturation, in a process that became increasingly deliberate in the nineteenth century. The child grew into adulthood with literate experiences to match. By 1900, childhood interpretive practice, in keeping with other life experiences, had become more directed and more purposeful. Direction and purpose were especially marked among the offspring of social and intellectual elites in the early twentieth century. In time, boys and girls developed an awareness of both the self and its relationship to the other, including texts. Modern French children matured and learned to read self-consciously, thanks to the experiences of powerful texts well portrayed in prose fiction.[27]

YOUTH

In the lives of young people, reading towards a career constitutes yet another stage of personal development. The quest for identity in the first stage continues, of course, but in a more complex fashion. Moreover, this search is no longer as rebellious as it is accommodating; the principal figure does not seek to undermine established authority but to join it, to become a part of the soci-

---

[26] Roger Martin du Gard, *Oeuvres complètes* (1956), 1:581–88. Cf. René Garguilo, *La Genèse des Thibault de Roger Martin du Gard* (1974), 394–422; and Peter M. Cryle, *Roger Martin du Gard, ou De l'intégrité de l'être à l'intégrité du roman* (1984).

[27] Cf. Carla L. Peterson, *The Determined Reader: Gender and Culture in the Novel from Napoleon to Victoria* (New Brunswick, N.J., 1986), 1–36, 227–34; and HEF 3:470–509.

ety that had at one time seemed so antithetical to childhood. And so it is not
surprising to see how novels like Flaubert's *L'Éducation sentimentale* define
character maturation in terms of texts. Each of Frédéric's Parisian comrades
appears with a book or newspaper appropriate to his future role in the Second
Republic. Early in the novel, Regimbart grumbles over a news account about
a dismissed schoolmaster, Sénécal looks through a volume of Louis Blanc,
and Hussonnet attacks the romantic school as un-French. Their roles after the
revolution evolve accordingly: Regimbert becomes an alcoholic café-sitter,
Sénécal turns Napoleonic policeman, and Hussonnet administers press and
theater censorship in the new regime. For the novel, reading becomes increasingly important after childhood; adolescence and its ambitions are of necessity
literate. To the extent that professions depend upon reading skills, novelists
incorporate this feature of adolescent life into their narratives.

Stendhal's *Le Rouge et le noir* (1830) makes particularly good use of Julien
Sorel's interest in books. One first sees Julien in the family sawmill absorbed
in reading Las Cases's *Mémorial de Sainte-Hélène*, his favorite text. This
work, Rousseau's *Les Confessions*, and a collection of bulletins from the
Grande Armée serve as Julien's secular bibles to guide his behavior for much
of the novel. Under their influence, he refuses to eat with M. de Rênal's servants and later plans a Napoleonic campaign to win the love first of Louise de
Rênal and then of Mathilde de la Mole. Each time Julien needs courage to
advance his interests, he recalls accounts of the emperor's exploits. Only after
Julien meets the comte Altamira, an Italian revolutionary, does he question
these literary mentors: "He spent the rest of the night reading the history of
the revolution." Moreover, reading his employers' books is the principal
source of unmitigated happiness for him in each household. First introduced
into the marquis's splendid library, Julien exclaims, " 'I will be able to read
all that. . . . How could I be unhappy here? . . .' He became mad with joy on
finding a complete edition of Voltaire." Mathilde avails herself of the same
edition and thereby suggests to Julien a common rebelliousness worthy of his
ambitions. And when Mathilde finally declares her love for Julien, her letter
"lent him the size and stature of a hero."[28]

Texts thus suggest the course of adolescent growth in the novel. But this
literate dimension to Julien's professional quest appears most clearly in established social settings. For example, Julien acquires the reputation of a learned
man because he has memorized the entire Vulgate Bible. "With a soul of fire,
Julien had one of those astounding memories so often associated with stupidity." He conned scripture like the calculating seminarians at Besançon who

---

[28] Stendhal, *Romans et nouvelles*, ed. Henri Mitterand (1952), 1:234–35. Cf. Maurice Bardèche, *Stendhal romancier* (1947), 159–225; Henri Martineau, *L'Oeuvre de Stendhal* (1966), 337–
74; and Geoffrey Strickland, *Stendhal: The Education of a Novelist* (New York, 1974), 126–64.

"liked better to earn their bread by reciting some Latin words than by digging in the dirt." Consequently, Julien recites long passages to impress guests at social gatherings or to win over important allies to his personal cause, even though he also knows by heart Molière's *Tartuffe*. After performing at M. de Rênal's, Julien earns the respect of the mayor's children, who from then on address the carpenter's son as "monsieur." Later, the marquis de la Mole asks Julien to exercise his memory for the purposes of a reactionary political plot; the text matters little to the young man, be it the first page of *La Quotidienne* or a secret message to a foreign ambassador. And yet Julien fails to see the significance of one key text in the narrative, namely, the newspaper article on Louis Jenrel, who had murdered his mistress in church. (Julien would attempt to do the same by the end of the novel.) This selective style of reading, entirely in keeping with Julien's character, illustrates well the literate youth's ambition to climb the social ladder in nineteenth-century France.[29]

Eugène de Rastignac in Balzac's *Le Père Goriot* (1835) also reads selectively. Early in the novel, Rastignac writes his family for more money, but without saying that he needs it to buy new clothes; he wants to keep secret his quest for a rich and socially prominent mistress. When his mother responds, she chides Rastignac for the sacrifices he had requested of his family for no clear purpose. At first, Rastignac sees how little better were his ambitions than those of the self-centered Anastasie de Restaud. But after reading his sister's letter, Rastignac thinks differently of his demands for money. In light of Laure's selfless simplicity and grace, Rastignac's ambitions return. " 'Oh! yes,' Eugène told himself, 'yes, a fortune at any price! Whole treasures would not repay this devotion.' " His responses to the two letters all too conveniently match his own desires to succeed in Parisian society. In time, Rastignac's interpretive style develops with his worldly education. When he receives an invitation for both himself and Delphine de Nucingen to the vicomtesse de Beauséant's ball, he notes a conspicuous omission. " 'But,' Eugène told himself on rereading the note, 'Madame de Beauséant tells me quite clearly that she does not want the baron de Nucingen.' " Without a deeper understanding of social relations in aristocratic Paris, he would never have made such an observation. Reading and experience here coincide neatly.[30]

Of course, a more conflicted life with texts is possible. In another Balzac novel, *La Peau de chagrin* (1831), Raphaël de Valentin begins studies towards a career in the law. But when his father dies and leaves a small estate, Raphaël devotes himself instead to drama and philosophy. For three years the young man lives a monkish existence given exclusively to his study.

[29] Stendhal, *Romans et nouvelles*, 1:235, 383–84, 240, 715–30.

[30] Balzac, *La Comédie humaine*, 3:130, 235. Cf. Félicien Marceau, *Balzac et son monde* (1970), 60–70; Pierre Barbéris, *Le Père Goriot de Balzac* (1972); and David Bellos, *Honoré de Balzac: Old Goriot* (Cambridge, 1987).

> I rejoiced in thinking that I was going to live on bread and milk, like a hermit in
> the Egyptian desert, immersed in the world of books and ideas, in an inaccessible
> realm in the middle of tumultuous Paris, a sphere of work and silence where, like
> a chrysalis, I would build a tomb in order to be reborn brilliant and glorious.[31]

For this material sacrifice, Raphaël enjoyed the scholar's life to which "study lends a sort of magic." The result, however, was a deeper dissatisfaction with his state and an unrequited love for the woman without heart, Foedora. His years of patient reading had merited little attention; Raphaël developed a new social ambition, one that proves empty of all human emotion. In his despair, Raphaël saves himself only by a strange wager with a shagreen skin reputed to have once belonged to King Solomon. Raphaël's reading of the inscription in Arabic prolongs his life just long enough for him to realize his dreams of love and wealth. With each wish that Raphaël makes and the magic skin grants, both the talisman and the young man's life shrink. In the end, the skin with its inscription disappears, and Raphaël dies as the realization of a very peculiar text, that of modern adolescent ambition.[32]

A related theme in Martin du Gard's *Les Thibault* is the quest not for success but for control of one's destiny, a mastery sought by nearly all young people and well represented by their reading. Antoine, for instance, uses his books to achieve a sense of self-sufficiency. When he establishes an office to meet with patients, he begins with his texts and fills a bookcase with lecture notes, dictionaries, and medical manuals. Each time he consults his references, he feels the power of both his knowledge and his authority as a physician. Like his father, leery of relationships out of his control, Antoine resorts to books whenever women frustrate his plans. Antoine later extends his command to others, most notably to his brother Jacques and their father, by studying their writings. Jacques's long story in an avant-garde literary journal becomes for Antoine a means to discover why the writer had fled so precipitously to Switzerland and how he might be induced to return. Similarly, after Oscar Thibault's painful death, Antoine reads through his papers, only to learn from them who his father actually had been.

> Since Antoine had touched these papers, raised this corner of the veil, suspected
> matters, he thought with a kind of agony that beneath these majestic appearances,
> a man—a poor man, perhaps—had just died, that this man was his father, and that
> he had never really known him.[33]

---

[31] Balzac, *La Comédie humaine*, 10:133. Cf. the perspective in Brombert, *The Hidden Reader*, 37–47; and Marceau, *Balzac et son monde*, 70–72.

[32] See Claude Duchet, ed., *Balzac et La Peau de chagrin* (1979), 25–42; Pierre Bayard, *Balzac et le troc de l'imaginaire* (1978); and Samuel Weber, *Unwrapping Balzac: A Reading of La Peau de chagrin* (Toronto, 1979). Cf. the cynical practice of reading in Guy de Maupassant, *Bel ami* (1885).

[33] Martin du Gard, *Oeuvres complètes*, 1:1344. Cf. Musset, *Oeuvres complètes en prose*, 156.

After years of conflict, it took this reading for Antoine to know his father and, in part, himself. By perusing the text of his father's life, Antoine at long last gains control over their relationship, and ultimately over his own fate as well.

But the second stage of character development in the novel requires more than self-definition in one's chosen work; it also means the realization of love. Sexual ties are more often than not the subject of the novel, and here reading plays an interesting role. In the *roman de formation*, love transforms the literate experience; no lover regards certain texts indifferently. Moreover, reading itself shapes the course of courtship and marriage; as Flaubert once quipped, the novel teaches one how to love. And in a century before electronic communication and rapid transportation, the written text, the letter especially, was fundamental to amorous activity, at least among the educated classes.[34] French fiction is replete with the influence of intense emotion on interpretation; fictional texts affect sexual relationships, just as the personal nature of letters shapes interpretive practice. Reading and love are thus also closely related in the maturation process.

Benjamin Constant's *Adolphe* (1816) features clearly love's transformation of the written text. From the outset, one learns of the distraught narrator's desultory reading in the publisher's note: "He read a lot, but never very attentively." Some terrible event has affected him, one presumably detailed in the first-person narrative. In this way, the novel introduces reading as an index to the narrator's state of mind. The main character shares his enthusiasm for the English romantic poets with Ellénore, and he writes to her under their influence. Her response, however, is less intense, and she tells him so in a letter. "This response upset me. My imagination, stimulated by obstacles, became the master of my whole existence. An hour earlier I had congratulated myself on feigning the love that I now believed I had to prove with a fury." Ellénore's letter induces the young man's passion. But when his emotion has cooled and he writes her an equivocal letter of his own, she then reads with an unexpected ardor.

> Ellénore had read, in my writing, my promises about abandoning her, promises that had been dictated only by the desire to remain longer with her. . . . The indifferent eye of M. de T—— [on the other hand] had easily discerned the irresolution that I had disguised by these protestations, reiterated in each line, by the ruses of my own incertitude.[35]

[34] See Janey Gurkin Altman, "The Letter Book as a Literary Institution 1539–1789: Toward a Cultural History of Published Correspondence in France," *Yale French Studies* 71 (1986): 17–62. Cf. Martin Turnell, *The Rise of the French Novel* (London, 1979), 3–28.

[35] Benjamin Constant, *Oeuvres*, ed. Alfred Roulin (1957), 11, 23, 73. Cf. Ian Welach Alexander, *Benjamin Constant: Adolphe* (London, 1973), 50–57; and Martha Noel Evans, "*Adolphe*'s Appeal to the Reader," *Romantic Review* 78 (1982): 302–17.

In each case, for both Adolphe and Ellénore, their interpretive practice suits well all lovers' changing emotions.

A tortured love results in a comparable reading style in Musset's *La Confession*. Octave is given to experiencing the world first in and through texts, especially during his soirées with friends who are also devoted to the romantics. "How many times one of us, at the moment when the flagons were emptied, took in hand a volume by Lamartine and read in an emotional voice! One must see how all other thoughts disappeared!" Consequently, when Octave falls in love with Brigitte, he cannot refrain from seeing her in romantic terms. In fact, a perverse libertine character, Degenais, immediately comes to Octave's mind once Brigitte denies him access to her diary. "I kept my eyes on the book, and I felt vaguely in my memory I know not what forgotten words, which I had heard once before, but still gripped my heart." Doubt poisons his increasingly perverse love and leads to the couple's eventual separation. Towards the end of the novel, Octave recalls a story by Diderot in which a jealous woman, hoping to rekindle his interest, tells her lover that she no longer loves him. Misunderstanding her intentions, the man leaves her. "This bizarre scene that I had just read too young had struck me like an amazing presence, and the memory that I had kept of it made me smile suddenly. 'Who knows,' I told myself, 'if I have done the same?' " For once, Octave sees reality more clearly through the refraction of a literary text.[36]

Human passion also alters Julien Sorel's reading experience in *Le Rouge et le noir*. At first Julien relies upon Rousseau, Napoleon, and the Bible for his knowledge of women, but they prove altogether inadequate for his affair with Mme. de Rênal. "He owed to Madame de Rênal a whole new way of understanding books." Even the work on insects that Julien and Louise read together is transformed. But when he is forced to leave Verrières, Julien returns to Rousseau in order to flirt with a barmaid in Besançon: "In ten minutes he recited portions of *La Nouvelle Héloïse* to the enthralled mademoiselle Amanda; he was happy with his bravura." He repeats this experiment with Mathilde de la Mole, though with less immediate success. Mathilde is much more given to texts from the sixteenth century, which Julien shrewdly examines with her in mind. But the letters they write to each other prove more important and lend their affair the character of an epistolary novel, as Julien cynically remarks. Letters and their privileged interpretation are even more deliberate features of Julien's campaign for the affection of Mme. de Fervaques. Thanks to the Russian Prince Korasoff, he has an entire sequence of letters at his disposal. These empty, bombastic missives convince both the countess and Mathilde of his love. Julien's last letter, however, is his most

[36] Musset, *Oeuvres complètes en prose*, 136, 190, 262. Cf. Margaret Walker, "*Cherchez la Femme*: Male Malady and Narrative Politics in the French Romantic Novel," *PMLA* 104 (1989): 141–51.

sincere—the newspaper account of his execution that he knows Louise will read. For Julien and his women—indeed, for nearly all youthful elites his age—reading is an essential ingredient to love.[37]

In Flaubert's *L'Éducation sentimentale*, lovers read texts differently. This time the man, not the woman, is a victim of novels. Under the influence of the romantics, Frédéric conceives an impossible attachment for Marie Arnoux. "He esteemed passion above all; Werther, René, Frank, Lara, Lélia, and others more mediocre than they enthused him almost equally." Never a particularly discriminating reader, Frédéric resorts to Musset for the phrases necessary to declare his love for Marie. "A volume by Musset was found by chance on the bureau. He turned some pages of it, then began to talk of love, of its despairs and of its transports. All this, according to Mme. Arnoux, was criminal or factitious." Frédéric responds to Marie's more dispassionate approach to texts with examples of suicides drawn from Racine, Virgil, Shakespeare, and Prévost, but Marie remains unconvinced. In sharp contrast to her young lover, Mme. Arnoux reads history, and with rapt attention. She is not given to the romantic dreams of Mme. Dambreuse, whom Frédéric later courts for her money and title (even that impressionable woman finds Frédéric's soulful poetry reading tedious). During one emotional meeting, Marie seeks release in her knitting, while Frédéric turns the pages of an illustrated magazine. Without a text to follow in his own interpretive fashion, Frédéric is lost.[38]

Emotions develop and interpretive practices change, especially in Proust's work. Swann is still deeply enamoured of Odette when he receives an anonymous letter enumerating her various affairs with both men and women. Still secure in his passion, Swann is not jealous; the letter only moves him to identify its author among his many acquaintances. Who could it be? M. de Charlus? M. des Laumes? M. d'Orsan? "As for the substance of the letter, he was not concerned, for not one of the accusations formulated against Odette had even a shadow of probability. Swann like many people had a lazy mind and lacked any inventiveness." In short, he believes what he wishes from this text. In very different circumstances, however, Marcel also reads what he wants into a letter. This time it concerns evidence of Albertine's infidelity that Marcel cannot dismiss so easily; she has left him, and everything that reminds Marcel of her is painful, including overstated newspaper prose. When Aimé writes to him about Albertine's behavior in the bathhouse at Balbec and again with a laundress in Nice, Marcel consoles himself with the thought that he had never known her entirely, that his love for her had been incomplete. The news "made her still more of a stranger to me, proved that what I had had of her, what I carried in my heart, had only been a small part of her." Like lovers in

---

[37] Stendhal, *Romans et nouvelles*, 1:306, 372.
[38] Flaubert, *Oeuvres*, 2:46, 230.

real life, Swann and Marcel adopt an interpretive style appropriate to their particular passions in Belle Époque France.[39]

The interpretive function is therefore central to yet another phase of character development. In many novels, the literary experience responds to but also shapes a youth's love, in much the same way it does his career choice. The more characters read, the more texts participate in their sexual and professional maturation. This is as true in fact as it is in fiction. From 1800 onward, an increasing proportion of French men and women in quest of mates and jobs were literate; their reading certainly helped in their decisions. Gide's characters in *Les Faux-monnayeurs*, for example, are not at all atypical of French middle-class youths whose reading shaped their love lives and defined their professions, whose loves and vocations in turn affected their interpretive practices. It is surely no accident that a character like Édouard and his writings touch every figure in search of both relationship and occupation. The precociously literate men and women in Gide's novel, as in the other works examined above, thus highlight effectively a widespread cultural phenomenon in modern France: sex, work, and reading were increasingly bound together not just in prose fiction, however powerful its influence, but also in the everyday life of youth since the eighteenth century.

MATURITY

In Gide's *Les Faux-monnayeurs*, Édouard's former piano teacher, La Pérouse, asks an interesting question:

> Why are old people so rarely the subject of books? . . . That comes, I believe, from the fact that old people can no longer write about themselves and that young people are not concerned with them. An old person interests no one. . . . All the same, there would be some very curious things to say about them.[40]

Though the paranoid La Pérouse is perhaps not a very good example, older figures in prose fiction do indeed merit more critical attention, especially as readers. They are the logical culmination of character development from childhood onward, and their reading experiences match their personal maturity as well as their function in the narrative. Fully responsible for themselves and others, these individuals are portrayed as reading to instruct, to empower, to distract, and to understand. They are accordingly more deliberate interpreters of text and life. Consequently, they suggest as no other characters can the

---

[39] Proust, *À la recherche du temps perdu*, 1:359, 527. Cf. reading in Anatole France, *Oeuvres complètes illustrées* (1927), 9:290.

[40] E.g., Gide, *Romans*, 1025–26. Cf. Wallace Fowlie, *André Gide* (New York, 1965), 85–97; Albert J. Guerard, *André Gide*, 2d ed. (Cambridge, 1969), 139–83; and G. W. Ireland, *André Gide: A History of His Creative Writings* (Oxford, 1970), 340–76.

meaning of reading as a literary motif highlighting the merits and dangers of one's own perception and judgment. In the French novel, older readers demonstrate the interaction of books and the lives they touch. Both embody well the subjective reality of actual interpretive practice.[41]

Clearly, reading in the *roman de formation* represents more than the reality of interpretive practice throughout the life cycle. Literate activity is at least one literary device among many that authors have at their disposal to reveal character, to promote action, and to structure the narrative. But reading in the novel is also a suggestive metaphor for the relationship between literature and life. The different meanings of the verb "to read" in the figurative sense, as in "to divine" or "to ascertain," occur frequently in the modern novel. In Constant's *Adolphe*, for instance, the shrewd ambassador, M. de T——, claims to read the narrator's soul, to discern that the young man is no longer in love with Ellénore despite the power she still has over him.[42] And the ambassador is right; his reading of Adolphe's situation is accurate. In Balzac's *Le Père Goriot*, when Mme. de Beauséant is left by her Portuguese lover for a younger woman, she teaches Rastignac an important lesson. "Although I had read much in this book of the world, there were pages that remained unknown to me. Now I know everything."[43] The older woman then advises the law student in terms little different from those of Vautrin, the escaped convict, who also claims to read the world correctly. Proust's Marcel notes how one's social personality is a creation of other people's thought, just as a book is defined by the reader.[44] In these and other instances, the literary significance of reading is enlarged to include more than the conning of a literal, printed text. Rather, it is also a figurative understanding of reality beneath the surface of everyday life.

The subjective nature of human experience is one theme well illustrated by readers in the novel. For example, when Musset's Octave discovers his deceased father's papers, he finds as well a remarkable calm and clarity. "In the first pages I read, I felt at heart this freshness that enlivens the air around a tranquil lake; the sweet serenity of my father's soul exhaled like a perfume from the powderous pages as I turned them before me." Here, in an image borrowed from Lamartine's "Le Lac," the older and somewhat wiser Octave dispels the deep emotional ambivalence of his love for Brigitte. That personal conflict disappears completely. In its stead Octave calls up the dreamlike purity of his feelings for the man whose papers he is examining.

---

[41] Cf. Norman N. Holland, *Five Readers Reading* (New Haven, 1975), 1–12, 113–29; David Bleich, *Subjective Criticism* (Baltimore, 1978), 10–37; and Stanley Fish, *Is There a Text in This Class? The Authority of Interpretive Communities* (Cambridge, Mass., 1980), 1–17.

[42] Constant, *Oeuvres*, 55.

[43] Balzac, *La Comédie humaine*, 3:116.

[44] Proust, *À la recherche du temps perdu*, 1:19.

The journal of his life reappeared before me; I could count day by day the beating of his noble heart. I began to bury myself in a sweet and profound dream, and despite the firm and serious character that prevailed everywhere, I discovered an ineffable grace, the peaceful flower of his goodness. As I read, the memory of his death mingled incessantly with the story of his life. I cannot say with what sadness I followed the limpid stream that I had seen fall into the Ocean.[45]

At this point Octave realizes the difference between his feelings for Brigitte and those for his father. Only upon reading his father's papers does Octave learn that these differences derive not from the two objects of his affection, but from himself. The Ocean is Octave's memory as well as his father's life, an insight made possible by a special text. In Musset's novel, as in historical experience, reading and maturing are inseparable.

Despite its irony and sentimentality, Anatole France's *Le Crime de Sylvestre Bonnard* (1881) presents a comparable style of reading. The main character is an elderly scholar, more at home in the past than in the present, whose whole life is devoted to historical documents. The novel opens on his discovery of the existence of a rare manuscript from the abbey of Saint-German-des-Prés, the culmination of forty years of scholarly work on the abbey itself. " 'Why,' I said to myself, 'why have I learned that this priceless book exists if I must never possess it, never even see it? . . . I shudder to think that perhaps its torn pages are covering some housekeeper's pickle jar.' "[46] Tracking the manuscript first in a catalog and then in various sites in Sicily and Paris, the old man finally acquires it, thanks to a wealthy woman who remembers an earlier kindness of his at a time of personal distress. The rest of the novel follows the scholar's attention to a close friend's library until he is distracted by the daughter of a childhood sweetheart. When he manages to save her from a horrible convent school, he is confronted with the Napoleonic Code: he has unwittingly broken a law whose medieval text he knows by heart but whose modern version he does not know at all. It is not until the end of the novel that he realizes the depth of his emotional life aside from scholarship.

Until then, for Bonnard and others in the nineteenth century, reading is all. Bonnard exists only in his library. Despite the bibliophile's fitful efforts to escape the City of Books, he is consumed by his passion for texts. "For me there are only words in the world, so much am I a philologist. Everyone dreams his life in his own manner. I dream mine in the library." Of course, the narrative moves the old pedant out from his selfish concerns with books to deep involvement in the lives of other people. But Bonnard never escapes from his own Book of Life. "We are our passions," he remarks to himself. "I am my precious books. I am as old and as shriveled as they." Consequently, when he sells his personal library to provide a dowry for Clémen-

---

[45] Musset, *Oeuvres complètes en prose*, 156.
[46] France, *Le Crime de Sylvestre Bonnard* (Calmann-Lévy edition, n.d.), 20.

tine's orphaned daughter, he is not turning a page in his scholarly career. Rather, Bonnard is expressing the intimate relationship between those books and his life now centered on the happiness of another. "I had already deciphered these old texts with a high-minded ardor. So what had I hoped to find in them? . . . For sixty years I sought without finding this something . . . that having no substance had no name and yet without which no earthly intellectual work would be undertaken." Humanity is thus not at odds with scholarship, but the essence of it.[47]

A similar link between text and experience is established more fully in Proust. Despite the tears she sheds over newspaper accounts of human suffering, Françoise is singularly implacable in her dealings with an ailing kitchen maid. The young woman's illness and pain are real, but Françoise can summon no sympathy for her. What genuine compassion Françoise experiences for others exists only in her reading. "Beyond those people related to her, human beings and their miseries excited her pity the farther they were from her."[48] And so Françoise's concern for the young woman, a feeling derived from a medical reference, changes to indignation once she sees the woman again. There is nothing left to her imagination but the cause of the illness, the kitchen maid's sexual adventure. Similarly, the baron de Charlus expresses his marked preference for Balzac's novels suggestive of homosexual relations, a veritable *idée fixe* for this figure, covertly acknowledged by other characters in the novel. When Marcel publishes an article in *Le Figaro*, the Guermantes are finally moved to read something, for the sake of a personal acquaintance. Otherwise they would have never seen it, even though they subscribe to the paper. As it does Proust's theory of reality, the subjective element determines the Guermantes's literate habits and their social existence.[49]

This particular understanding is especially important in the twentieth century. Despite the romantic movement, self-conscious perception of the world largely disappears from nineteenth-century prose realism, only to reappear and develop more fully in the modern psychological novel and its variations.[50] Gide, like Proust, is concerned with the different interpretations individuals can have of the same character, event, or text. As Édouard notes in his journal, "We live on accepted emotions and how the reader imagines himself to feel, because he believes everything in print; the author speculates on this, as he does on the conventions that he believes are the foundations of his craft."[51] This bit of posing on Édouard's part is a deliberate attempt to counter a con-

---

[47] Ibid., 80, 149, 218.

[48] Proust, *À la recherche du temps perdu*, 1:122.

[49] Cf. Gérard Genette, *Figure III* (1972), 41–63; and Gilles Deleuze, *Proust et les signes* (1964), 9–124.

[50] See Leon Edel, *The Modern Psychological Novel* (New York, 1964), 104–22.

[51] Gide, *Romans*, 1198. Cf. Germaine Brée, *André Gide. L'Insaissible Protée* (1970), 251–312; and Alain Goulet, *Fiction et vie sociale dans l'oeuvre d'André Gide* (1985), 497–552.

temporary literary trend that uses art to deceive. Even though artistic devices often ring false, they also make possible sincere expression; they can promote genuine understanding of the self and others, and ultimately, they constitute a surer reality than experience itself. Repeatedly in Gide's *Les Faux-monnay-eurs*, characters read themselves and others into various letters, journals, and books. Their substance is not what the author writes but what the reader makes.

Two other subjective readers appear in Jean-Paul Sartre's *La Nausée* (1938). One of them, Antoine Roquentin, is an historian writing the biography of the marquis de Rollebon, an eighteenth-century intriguer. Several times the narrator struggles with his sources, especially the marquis's own testimony, which lacks "resolution, consistency." Other witnesses, such as Tcherkoff and Ségur, not only disagree, but are no more reliable, leaving large gaps for the historian to fill. "I am beginning to believe that one can never prove any-thing," Roquentin remarks to himself. "I have the impression of writing a work of pure imagination." Later he ponders Rollebon's two writings, *Le Traité de stratégie* and *Les Réflexions sur la vertu*, to conclude that he would be better off writing a novel about the marquis. The result for Roquentin is still more existential malaise. Sartre's other older reader is the Autodidact, who is systematically studying the books in the Bouville public library. His reading plan, however, is idiosyncratic in the extreme: he chooses his books not by subject matter but alphabetically, by the author's last name. "He read everything; he ranged in his head most of what is known about parthenogen-esis, most of the arguments against vivisection. Behind him as before him, there was a whole universe." For both Roquentin and the Autodidact—mod-ern French readers incarnate—texts mediate their conception of reality, but also define their very existence.[52]

But the significance of self-conscious reading is especially well explored by Sartre's existential hero. After five years of silence, Roquentin receives a note from Anny, a former lover. His first impulse is not to read, but to examine the envelope. The careful detail of his description suggests a disassociation of the words from their emotional context. Roquentin is too surprised to respond to the text immediately. It is, however, an invitation to see her in Paris. "I slipped Anny's letter into my briefcase: she gave me what she could; I cannot call up the woman who took the letter in her hands, folded it, and put it into the envelope. Is it possible only to think of someone in the distant past?" Even though he still considers his biography of the marquis de Rollebon the sole justification of his existence, he can think only of the coming rendezvous and the life that he and Anny had shared together many years earlier. His personal

---

[52] Jean-Paul Sartre, *La Nausée* (1938), 25, 26, 49. Cf. Naomi Segal, *The Banal Object: Theme and Thematics in Proust, Rilke, Hofmannsthal, and Sartre* (London, 1981), 94–116; and Clayton Kolb and Susan Noakes, eds., *The Comparative Perspective in Literature* (Ithaca, 1988), 179–94.

reading here differs substantially from his research, because the absurdity of his existence is less obvious to him, at least until he finally sees his old lover again. Meeting her in Paris, without passion or meaning, Roquentin encounters the problem of defining his essence as powerfully as ever. "Yesterday I still had so many questions to ask her. . . . But that interested me only to the extent that Anny had given herself with her whole heart. Now I am no longer curious." Like the letter she had written, neither her life nor his contains a meaningful text for him to read.[53]

Sartre's first novel actually culminates the development of a profound historical "intertextuality."[54] On one level of philosophic and literary analysis, Roquentin's initial problem as a reader is to define existence and its essence. His task as an historian was to understand texts left by the dead, a job that makes print an object like any other. Early in the novel, Roquentin even contemplates a scrap of classroom dictation in terms no different from those he uses to characterize a stone. "One must not *touch* objects, since they do not live. One feels them, one puts them in place, one lives among them: they are useful, nothing more. As for myself, they touch me, insupportably so. I am afraid to enter into contact with them all, as if they were living beasts." Accordingly, books, too, are agents of their own existence but without substance. It is not until the end of the novel that Roquentin learns to consider meaning, including that of the written page, not as an object in itself but as an active subject of his own making. Instead of Rollebon's biography, Roquentin must write a book that will force the reader to realize "that one discerns behind the printed words, behind the pages, something that would not exist, that would be above existence." It may not exist in fact, but it will be for both the writer and the reader the essence for which Roquentin has been searching. In this way, an individual must create the text of a life that is authentically his own and not someone else's.[55]

The modern French novel thus introduces, indeed creates, a new subjective reality at the heart of modern interpretive practice. Older figures in French fiction read to instruct, to empower, to distract, but ultimately to understand the implications of their own perception and judgment. *La Nausée* is neither the first nor the last work to demonstrate this complex interplay between reading and living. But like many other narratives written in the modern period, it provides an insightful perspective on the literate experience over a lifetime.

Again and again, reading appears in the novel, the *roman de formation* in particular, as an element of each stage in personal development, namely, a child's self-definition, a youth's career and love, and an adult's responsibility

[53] Sartre, *La Nausée*, 94, 214–15.

[54] See Gerald Prince, "Roquentin et la lecture," *Obliques* 18–19 (1979): 67–73. Cf. the intertextual subjectivity in Georges Bernanos, *Oeuvres romanesques*, ed. Albert Béguin and Michel Estève (1961), 1037, 1043, 1045.

[55] Sartre, *La Nausée*, 22, 248.

in the world. To the extent that authors observe as well as imagine, the novel depicts one feature of historical reality, especially that of reading appropriate to the entire life cycle, from childhood through youth to maturity. The intertwining of text and life is a natural aspect of growing up, in fact as it is in fiction. As people read, they pattern their lives on that experience and in turn become themselves a continuously evolving book for others to read. It would seem from modern French prose fiction, then, that literate activities are more than an idle cultural pastime in the development of fictional characters; they are as well an important dimension to the lives of actual readers like them.[56]

Reading experiences in prose fiction not only change over the life cycle; they also change historically. Clearly evident in the history of *roman de formation* is a rise in the individual's self-conscious power to interpret. Early in the nineteenth century, characters encounter texts imaginatively, emotionally, idiosyncratically, but most often in a manner appropriate to romanticism. Constant's Adolphe, Stendhal's Julien, and Musset's Octave are, in fact, models of the romantic reader. A hundred years later, however, the novelistic hero interprets texts far more deliberately. Literate life becomes subjective most obviously in the symbolist tradition represented by Proust's Marcel, Martin du Gard's Jacques, and Sartre's Roquentin. These figures appear disenchanted with the empirical world and retreat into a private interpretive space of their own making. Whether or not French men and women at the turn of the century actually followed suit—though the artistic evidence in Chapter 5 suggests that they did—the reading experience in the novel evolved over the course of the nineteenth century, and with it the interpretive models for literate audiences to copy.[57] In this way, the art of reading in and out of texts changed from 1800 to 1940.

[56] Cf. Maurice Crubellier, *L'Enfance et la jeunesse dans la société française 1800–1950* (1979).

[57] See Chapters 7 and 8. Cf. Lionel Trilling, *Sincerity and Authenticity* (Cambridge, Mass., 1972), 53–133.

Chapter 7

JOURNALS AND MEMOIRS

In March 1821, Chateaubriand was guest of honor at a ball at Sans Souci, the palace of Frederick William III in Potsdam. Soon after, an article about the event appeared in the *Berliner Morgenblatt*. According to Chateaubriand's memoirs, the article's author, Madame la baronne de Hohenhausen, described the celebrated author and minister in unusually flattering terms.

> The beautiful women of Berlin have continued to esteem the author of *Atala*, that superb and melancholy novel in which the most ardent love succumbs in a struggle against religion. . . . M. de Chateaubriand is rather short, and yet well proportioned. His oval face expresses piety and melancholy. He has black hair and black eyes that shine with the fire of his mind so pronounced in his features.[1]

Madame la baronne saw similarities between the writer and his work, and she stressed them in her description perhaps too enthusiastically. Many years later Chateaubriand noted,

> I have white hair: I am more than a century old—and more I am dead: so excuse Madame la baronne de Hohenhausen for having sketched me in my younger days, even though she had already conceded me some years. The portrait is otherwise very pretty; but I must say in all sincerity that it is not a good likeness.[2]

Apparently Madame de Hohenhausen had exaggerated the author's youth because it seemed so appropriate to her idea of the novel.

This curious anecdote suggests another historical source on the art of reading. Chateaubriand, and others like him, left copious accounts of literate activity. Their personal journals, memoirs, and autobiographies are rich historical documents that define still more dimensions to the history of interpretive practice.[3] Chateaubriand's recollection of Madame la baronne de Hohenhausen, for example, provides useful information about how non-Parisians read. Not everyone does so like a native; here a Prussian expresses a remarkable interest in the French novel. Similarly, the author's famous memoirs show

---

[1] F. R. de Chateaubriand, *Mémoires d'outre-tombe*, ed. Maurice Levaillant and Georges Moulinier (1946–48), 2:38–39.

[2] Ibid., 2:39. Cf. Emmanuel Beau de Loménie, *La Carrière politique de Chateaubriand de 1814 à 1830* (1929), vol. 2.

[3] Cf. Paul Eakin, *Fictions in Autobiography: Studies in the Art of Self-Invention* (Princeton, 1985), 181–278; Philippe Lejeune, *Le Pacte autobiographique* (1975), 13–48, 311–44; and Georges May, *L'Autobiographie* (1984).

how a distinct social class, the aristocracy, responds to texts. Like people from various regions of France and Europe, social groups have their own styles of reading that are often very different from one another. In this regard, if one is to believe the article, the elites of Berlin and Paris have much in common. Chateaubriand also writes of how men and women interpret the same work. For the novelist, the baronne's literary enthusiasm is more typical of females than of males. But other men and women express similar interpretive differences. In similar personal writings from Stendhal to Sartre, one can make comparable discoveries about reading experiences.

Despite the difficulties of using literary sources in empirical studies, journals and memoirs suggest these particular insights into modern interpretive practice.[4] Over time, dozens of readers indicated the variety of their approaches to texts thanks to at least three socially defined predispositions: as residents of France, as representatives of various social classes, and as gender-conscious men and women. These tendencies within French society, in fact, made possible a plurality of reader responses among different interpretive communities. This trend towards diversity developed in the nineteenth century, but it was especially apparent after 1900. By then, nationalism, social status, and gender identity obviously shaped reading habits in France; as a general rule, readers were informed ever more fully by nationalistic sentiment, ideological prejudice, and acquired sex-roles. Like the attention given to the work of artists and novelists in Chapters 5 and 6, close study of autobiographies and diaries reveals just how powerful these social factors in the art of reading became after 1800.[5]

REGION

Besides its politics, Paris is well known for texts of all sorts. Observers throughout the period remarked the ready accessibility of print in France's largest city. In 1789, the Englishman Arthur Young was astonished by the flood of material on all topics that he could afford only to sample on his limited budget.[6] Posters were prominent as early as the Second Empire when Baudelaire wrote of his "immense nausea from such texts."[7] Their pervasiveness

---

[4] Cf. Dominick LaCapra, "Rethinking Intellectual History and Reading Texts," *History and Theory* 19 (1980): 245–76; and L. E. Shiner, *The Secret Mirror: Literary Form and History in Tocqueville's "Recollections"* (Ithaca, 1988), 1–12, 139–47, 199–206.

[5] Note the use of journals and memoirs in Jean Hébrard and Anne-Marie Chartier, *Discours sur la lecture (1880–1980)* (1989), 401–26. Cf. the rich reading experiences discussed in Maurice Barrès, *Mes cahiers* (1929–38); and Paul Valéry, *Les Cahiers*, ed. Judith Robinson (1973–74), neither of which is discussed in this chapter.

[6] Arthur Young, *Travels in France during the Years 1787, 1788 and 1789*, ed. Jeffrey Kaplow (Garden City, N.Y., 1969), 104, 232.

[7] Charles Baudelaire, *Oeuvres complètes*, ed. Y.-G. LeDantec and Claude Pichois (1961), 1213.

was at least as obnoxious to him as their content, or their lack of it. In time, most Parisians became immune to public notices; by 1910, when Jules Renard's latest work was prominently displayed on many city walls, he went unrecognized on the tramways.[8] But Paris also offered books and newspapers peddled on the streets and even at construction sites, according to Martin Nadaud, the stonemason-turned-politician during the Second Republic. "The bookstore porters passed through the work sites and sold us a brochure history of the Bastille and a multitude of other writings."[9] Xavier-Édouard Lejeune would later note the numerous lending libraries over whose books he frequently passed whole nights, at least until his mother rationed his candles. As a youth Lejeune haunted second-hand bookstores and stalls along the Seine, monuments to the large population of university students and their literate interests in the Latin Quarter.[10] If not always a city of light, Paris was most certainly a city of print.

Most of this printed matter was produced and consumed in town. Paris naturally brought writers and readers together in ways possible only in a large metropolitan area. Literate life appeared in salons, cafés, and clubs as well as in the streets, lending libraries, and schools already mentioned. In 1800, Stendhal listed the literary gatherings that he attended weekly *chez* madames Cardon, Rebuffel, Sorel, and above all, Daru. "Such a society is only possible in the country of Voltaire, Molière, Courier," and their Parisian readers.[11] Literate culture so imbued urban life, Stendhal later claimed, that children spoke like the comte de Salvandy, preferring the poetic *coursier* to the prosaic *cheval*. A large number of writers lived in the French capital to inspire their readers. As a young man, Chateaubriand encountered François de Bassompierre's seventeenth-century account of a beautiful young woman in the rue aux Ours. Nearly two hundred years later, this story moved the arch-romantic to visit the same street himself.[12] Jules Michelet also enjoyed the literate privileges of Paris. While a student during the Restoration, he kept an accurate record of his reading, much of it done on sunny days in streets and parks with his schoolboy friends.[13] Nineteenth-century Paris was as congenial to readers as it was to writers.

A very different world appears in accounts of reading in the provinces. To be sure, the contrast between Paris and the rest of the country was often ex-

---

[8] Jules Renard, *Journal 1887–1910*, ed. Léon Guichard and Gilbert Sigaux (1960), 1262.

[9] Martin Nadaud, *Mémoires de Léonard, ancien garçon maçon* (1976), 306–7.

[10] Xavier-Édouard Lejeune, *Calicot* (1984), 120.

[11] Stendhal, *Oeuvres intimes* ed. Henri Martineau (1955), 2:521, 930. Cf. Victor Brombert, *The Hidden Reader: Stendhal, Balzac, Hugo, Baudelaire, Flaubert* (Cambridge, Mass., 1988), 164–82, 183–90.

[12] Chateaubriand, *Mémoires d'outre-tombe*, 1:126–28.

[13] Jules Michelet, *Écrits de jeunesse: Journals de 1820–1823. Mémorial. Journal des idées*, ed. Paul Viallaneix (1959), 157. Cf. Michelet, *Le Peuple* (Lausanne, 1945), 36–43.

aggerated. But the evidence is striking and abundant. Complained Young in 1789,

> The whole town of Besançon has not been able to afford me sight of the *Journal de Paris*, nor of any paper that gives a detail of the transaction of the States [General]; yet it is the capital of a province, as large as a dozen English counties, and containing 25,000 souls.[14]

There was the same paucity of print everywhere Young traveled outside of Paris. As a consequence, he concluded that the Revolution itself proceeded "from a want of intelligence being quickly distributed."[15] On the eve of his departure for Paris, Stendhal found the intellectual interests of Grenoble equally moribund; "the reigning taste then in Grenoble tended to reading and to citing the letters of a M. de Bonnard."[16] By the Second Empire, non-Parisians still had to struggle against isolation and boredom. According to the Goncourts, Théophile Gautier considered life at George Sand's estate in Nohant "like a Moravian convent."[17] Such a remark is too cute to be altogether accurate. Louise Michel's memoirs describe more intellectual activity among the villagers of Vroncourt, Audeloncourt, and Chaumont where she grew up and was educated. Her great-uncle had bought a whole library of eighteenth-century novels and shared them with family and friends.[18] Similarly, some village women were ardent consumers of serial novels.[19] But the circulation and sophistication of the texts available to non-Parisians left much to be desired by the standards of the contemporary urban bourgeois.

French peasants read even less. Until the Third Republic, at least, their access to printed matter was difficult and their local patois pervasive. In 1789, according to Young, most of rural France was bereft of newspapers. "I might as well have demanded an eggplant," he complained in disgust.[20] This was still the situation in 1849 when Nadaud ran for the Legislative Assembly in the Creuse. For reasons that are not hard to fathom, he campaigned there from Paris by correspondence, his fellow construction workers helping out with the writing. News of his election came in its turn by mail, in a letter from his wife. At the time, papers in the region did not exist, evidently because there was so little demand for them. Most peasants still spoke and read French poorly be-

[14] Young, *Travels in France*, 159.

[15] Ibid., 160.

[16] Stendhal, *Oeuvres intimes*, 2:724.

[17] Jules and Edmond de Goncourt, *Journal. Mémoires de la vie littéraire* (Monaco, 1956–58), 6:121.

[18] Louise Michel, *Mémoires* (1979), 51. Cf. Edith Thomas, *Louise Michel, ou La Velléda de l'anarchie* (1980), 31–64.

[19] See "Femme née en 1890" and "Femme née en 1896," in Anne-Marie Thiesse, *Le Roman quotidien. Lecteurs et lectures à la Belle Époque* (1984), 61–63.

[20] Young, *Travels in France*, 171. Cf. Gordon Wright, *Rural Revolution in France: The Peasantry in the Twentieth Century* (Stanford, 1964), 185–208.

fore the introduction of free, compulsory, secular education. Nadaud's mother, for example, knew only the dialect in the Creuse.[21] Before World War I, Pierre-Jakez Hélias recalled, Breton remained the preferred language in his village. When the local priest said Mass in Latin, he confused his younger parishioners with the "Kyrie Eleison"; it sounded too much like "kirri eleiz 'so," Breton for "there are many wagons."[22] These personal anecdotes, one senses, exaggerate historical reality, but the perceptions of contemporaries are worth noting. In the nineteenth century, literate culture was in fact much slower to spread among French peasants than it was among urban workers.

The rural French were remarkably reluctant to read anyway. Before 1850, peasants resisted sending their children to schools; they needed the extra hands on the farm, and their own illiteracy had made no difference to their lives. Agricol Perdiguier mentioned that during the Restoration, local schoolmasters charged families 1 franc to teach each child to read, and another 1 franc 50 to teach him or her to write.[23] For many peasants the expense seemed an invitation to unnecessary complications. Nadaud's grandfather complained to his son, the stonemason's father, about reading the Napoleonic bulletins: "I always told you, this printed trash that came from the war . . . and that you bought at the Saint-Jean market, would end up causing you trouble."[24] Years later, in 1909, the obtuse unlettered peasant was still a stock figure in Renard's journal, embodied by his farmgirl domestic troubled by life in Paris: "She is bored here. She wants to return to the country, to find a place on a farm, and to dance every Sunday."[25] When literate skills had reached the Gâtinais, Roger Thabault noted, old grandmothers cherished the letters they received from far-off sons and daughters. "And they would then carefully hold the edges of the magic paper that had brought them—black on white—the news of absent ones and that had permitted them to call up their image."[26] The written word in the countryside was not a personal communication so much as a symbol whose meaning was decided by oral rather than literate tradition.

This rural resistance to reading remained after most French men and women were literate. Elementary schooling actually contributed to habits of face-to-face exchange. Besides their notorious inefficiency—a succession of inept teachers took a whole year to teach Nadaud the alphabet—village schools emphasized the dictation and memorization of texts, exercises more appropriate

[21] Nadaud, *Mémoires de Léonard*, 366, 370, 184.

[22] Pierre-Jakez Hélias, *Le Cheval d'orgueil. Mémoires d'un Breton du pays bigoudon* (1975), 133.

[23] Agricol Perdiguier, *Mémoires d'un compagnon* (1982), 40–41.

[24] Nadaud, *Mémoires de Léonard*, 69.

[25] Renard, *Journal*, 1223.

[26] Roger Thabault, *Mon village. Ses hommes—ses routes—son école, 1848–1914. L'Ascension d'un peuple* (1945), 180.

to oral than to written culture.[27] A prolific reader all her life and a graduate of an *école normale*, Louise Michel was deeply affected by a bookstore's display, just as she had been in Bourmont when an unlettered peasant girl.[28] Her awe of the printed word resembled that of Marcel Pagnol's father, a schoolteacher himself, who long believed that older books were wiser books.[29] Such an adage no doubt came to him by word of mouth. Renard noted how long traditional folkways lingered in the countryside: "The people of Chaumot . . . would approve and even like what I said, if it were in songs."[30] For the peasants in Brittany before World War I, according to Hélias, church bells still communicated important news.[31] And in Mazières-en-Gâtine during the Third Republic, girls ordered from sales catalogs only what they had first seen or handled, their literate imaginations restrained by the immediacy and concreteness of oral tradition.[32] Throughout the modern period, reading in rural France was subject to strong cultural constraints.

In time, however, these conditions gave way, or at least adapted, to the growing circulation of printed matter. As provincial towns were drawn into a national network of bookstores, especially by the railroad, rural inhabitants expressed increased interest in print. Like a number of other peasants, Michel's Uncle Georges had already made considerable sacrifices at home and at work to read regularly; he spent many hours with books in a dimly lit flour mill.[33] Pagnol's grandfather was ashamed of his illiteracy and ensured that all his children would not only learn to read but also teach others to do so.[34] Because literate skills in French were essential to bourgeois status, Hélias's grandfather encouraged the child's precocious efforts in school, despite his family's aversion to the anticlerical Third Republic.[35] Similarly, in 1889, Renard recalled ironically,

> I know a man who is twenty years old, who manages three farms, who drives his men hard and loves only his animals, who mates a bull or a stallion each time he can, who helps cows give birth with his bare arms, sleeves rolled, who reaches far into the womb for his lambs when they fall, who knows by heart all the unseemly aspects of his job, and who said to my wife with a shy and embarrassed air: "Don't go and tell my mother that I am reading *La Terre!*"[36]

[27] Nadaud, *Mémoires de Léonard*, 69, 70, 74. Cf. Antoine Sylvère, *Toinou. Le Cri d'un enfant auvergnat* (1980), 32–36; and Ephraïm Grenadou and Alain Prévost, *Grenadou, paysan français* (1966), 28.

[28] Michel, *Mémoires*, 94.

[29] Marcel Pagnol, *Le Château de ma mère. Souvenirs d'enfance II* (1958), 218.

[30] Renard, *Journal*, 898.

[31] Hélias, *Le Cheval d'orgueil*, 46.

[32] Thabault, *Mon village*, 173.

[33] Michel, *Mémoires*, 52.

[34] Marcel Pagnol, *La Gloire de mon père. Souvenirs d'enfance I* (1957), 20.

[35] Hélias, *Le Cheval d'orgueil*, 100.

[36] Renard, *Journal*, 23.

It is interesting to note that this man's embarrassment came from the reputed immorality of Zola's novel, and not from the fact that he spent time reading. By the end of the century, peasants increasingly shared in literate culture.

With rural France more disposed to the world of print, how did readers there differ from their Parisian counterparts? Did responses vary from region to region? These questions are not readily answered in personal journals and memoirs; their accounts of rural interpretive practice are few and scanty. But the more loquacious Parisians, books in hand, traveled in France (and elsewhere) and amply described their literate experiences on the road. While far from Paris, these individuals read for at least two reasons: to pass the time and to remember home. Travel by coach or boat was very slow. Madame Récamier took Chateaubriand's *Le Génie du Christianisme* with her on board a ship to The Hague; and Stendhal read a biography of his favorite Italian poet, Alfieri, in a coach through the German states.[37] But with the introduction of the railroad, travelers tended to read even more thanks to the relative convenience and comfort of modern transportation. André Gide was a particularly avid reader on trains, according to his accounts.[38] Once they had arrived at their destinations, Parisians continued to pass the time with books. Few French men and women, it seems, could leave home without reading and thinking of home. The countryside was rarely as interesting as a text and its familiar evocations.

No one traveled without seeing the printed page with different eyes. In Italy, for example, Stendhal, Chateaubriand, and Gide all responded to various texts with that country foremost in their mind. On his first trip to Milan, Stendhal noted how Shakespeare had "italianized" the characters in *Romeo and Juliet*, set in Verona. He quoted Romeo's lines to Friar Lawrence, only to wonder why he had recorded them in his journal—"in order to be able to read in Italy, in the most beautiful nature in the world, verse by the greatest *of the bards*."[39] Italy and Shakespeare were thus linked in his mind. Otherwise, Stendhal was easily bored without books during his Italian travels. The same country conjured up for Chateaubriand passages from its foremost poet, Dante. While in Rome, the French aristocrat could not refrain from thoughts of other great writers who had visited there; he reviewed texts by Montaigne, Goethe, and Schiller to compare their impressions with his own. Similarly, a trip to Venice called up Villehardouin and Byron.[40] One hundred years later, when Gide reached Italy, he fell into the same habit: "I am seeing Rome with Stendhal's eyes, despite myself."[41] Gide would have preferred more imme-

[37] Chateaubriand, *Mémoires d'outre-tombe*, 2:171.
[38] E.g., André Gide, *Journal* (1948), 132.
[39] Stendhal, *Oeuvres intimes*, 1:670 (emphasis in the original).
[40] Chateaubriand, *Mémoires d'outre-tombe*, 2:228, 250, 790–95.
[41] Gide, *Journal*, 65.

diate contact, but texts continued to mediate his perceptions. For him as for others, travel was an interpretive experience.

Change in venue often affected reading more explicitly. Even though he rarely traveled very far from home, Joseph Joubert described his interpretive practice in an elaborate metaphor. "When I read Mr. de Beausset," he wrote, "I imagine traveling by boat on a nice day, in good weather, in a pleasant country, and on a beautiful river, where I see charming islands full of flowers, inscriptions, and monuments."[42] This figure of speech was more than an idle daydream; for Joubert, Beausset's book was a boat, his story a river, his country the reign of Louis XIV, his climate the seventeenth century and the author's clarity, and his islands the citations and carefully chosen words in the text. Others who actually lived in such settings thought of reading in similar dreamlike terms. As a young man, on a trip with Maxime Du Camp in Brittany, Gustave Flaubert read Chateaubriand's *René* seated at the foot of an oak in a lovely bucolic setting: "As shadows fell across the book's pages, the bitterness of the language prevailed upon our hearts, and we dissolved in delight from something I know not what that was large, melancholy, and sweet."[43] Thus for Flaubert and Du Camp, reading was less a figure of speech than it was a moving personal experience. Later in life, whether or not on a trip, Flaubert would still consider reveries as the natural response to good literature.[44] Equally hostile to romanticism, Charles de Rémusat also found himself associating books with his immediate surroundings. His first encounter with Bernardin de Saint-Pierre's *Paul et Virginie* took place appropriately in a small garden enclosure.[45]

French readers occasionally ventured to encounter foreign authors; and when they did so, their responses were characteristic. Perhaps the most extensive records of such encounters were left by Gide. As a youth he developed facility in at least two languages other than French. Gide enjoyed works by Browning and Shakespeare in the original, and felt compelled to correct errors in Hippolyte Taine's history of English literature. In time, as he read more widely, Gide claimed that he learned the least from French authors: "And how would it be otherwise? I have them in the blood, in my head; even before reading them, I was one of them." During World War I, despite his close acquaintance with the literature of other countries, this natural affinity led to strong nationalistic preferences. In 1916, Gide actually criticized Romain Rolland for the German influences he saw in *Jean Christophe*. "Everything French tends to individualize," he wrote, "everything German tends to diminish or submit." In 1924, Gide complained of a critic's overtly nationalist

---

[42] Joseph Joubert, *Les Carnets*, ed. André Beaunier (1938), 819–20.

[43] Gustave Flaubert, *Oeuvres complètes* (1927), 324–25.

[44] Flaubert to Louise Colet, [26 Aug. 1853], in Flaubert, *Corr.*, ed. Jean Bruneau (1973–80), 2:417.

[45] Charles de Rémusat, *Mémoires de ma vie*, ed. Charles Pouthas (1958–67), 1:94–95.

sentiments, his irritation derived not from the writer's chauvinism but from "a truth so evident . . . that this morning it appeared to me quite new." Only when his attention turned to the Soviet experiments under Joseph Stalin did Gide accept other literatures again more freely. Nevertheless, it seems that readers, including Gide, expressed insular impulses peculiar to the French and, for that matter, to other Western cultures.[46]

When foreigners approached native authors, French readers were quick to admonish them. Chateaubriand doubted whether literary works in translation could ever be appreciated properly:

> In a living literature, no one is a competent judge except of those works in his own language. You believe in vain that you possess instinctively a foreign idiom, someone else's breastmilk. . . . The more intimate, individual, national the talent, the more its mysteries elude the mind that is not a *compatriot* to this talent. . . . Style is not cosmopolitan like thought: it has a native land, a sky, a sun all its own.[47]

Similarly, Stendhal was amused by the literate hypocrites he found in Rome; he often heard notorious Italian women remark "such a *truly immoral wit*" that was apparent to them in his books.[48] When Nadaud was exiled to England during the Second Empire, he was surprised at the alacrity with which he was hired to tutor French literature and history, subjects he had never studied. His qualifications for the post unchallenged by his English host, he soon acquired the rudiments and the foolhardiness necessary for expertise in his new profession.[49] Edmond de Goncourt remarked more critically the reading habits of a young man he discovered holding a woman's hand one day in the Bibliothèque impériale. "It was a German couple," he wrote. "No, it was Germany!"[50] Although his comments reveal as much about the French bachelor as they do about the German couple, Goncourt assumed a national peculiarity in this interpretive practice.

Whichever commentator one examines, the art of reading varied considerably from place to place in modern France. For most of the nineteenth century, Paris was the center of literate culture, and nearly every journal and memoir reflected this fact. Parisian readers expressed a remarkable cultural centralization each time they picked up a newspaper or book unavailable to their provincial counterparts. In time, however, there were more and more readers in the rest of the country. By the outbreak of World War I, Paris's monopoly on intellectual life had weakened. The French reading experience was increas-

[46] Gide, *Journal*, 1277, 674, 780. Cf. accounts of Gide's reading in Jean Delay, *La Jeunesse d'André Gide* (1956–57), 1:390–94, 409–13, 441–44; 2:77–101, 155–61, and 214–19.

[47] Chateaubriand, *Mémoires d'outre-tombe*, 1:412–13 (emphasis in the original).

[48] Stendhal, *Oeuvres intimes*, 2: 804 (emphasis in the original).

[49] Nadaud, *Mémoires de Léonard*, 432.

[50] Goncourts, *Journal*, 7:159.

ingly national—and nationalistic. With changes in the book trade, literacy rates, rail transportation, and national politics, interpretive practice changed, as well. According to much personal testimony, literate culture was self-consciously regional and its interpretive impulses appropriate to the new locations open to it. In this new context, it is not surprising to find Sartre writing on his wartime reading of Heidegger near the Maginot Line, "In this way I can rediscover this assumption of his German destiny in the wretched Germany after the war in order to help me assume my own destiny as a Frenchman in the France of 1940."[51] Few statements express better the historical implications of literate life as it moved from Paris to the rest of France.

CLASS

Not only was interpretive practice regional; it was also self-consciously social. The reader's place in French society shaped his or her reading experience in ways that journals and memoirs show clearly. Such personal records testify to this fact of French literate life, especially in the nineteenth and early twentieth centuries. With the development of republican politics and industrial capitalism, class consciousness intensified; ultimately, status affected reception within France's rapidly changing social structure.

After the Revolution of 1789, aristocrats in particular felt keenly the destruction of their legal privileges, and they expressed their loss whenever texts reminded them of their new condition. During the Directory, Stendhal recalled the high regard in which M. de Saint-Gervais held Madame de Genlis's *Veillées du château*, "a model of *all these little things that are forgotten*."[52] But no documented reader in the nineteenth century was more sensitive to his noble lineage than Chateaubriand. In England during the Revolution, he responded to the news of Louis XVI's flight to Varennes as only a true noble could have: "A sudden conversion occurred within me," Chateaubriand wrote years later. "I abruptly interrupted my journey and told myself: 'Return to France.' " As a blueblood himself, the romantic noble was charmed by Montlosier's theory of blue as the color of life. Towards the end of his life, after rereading his journal, Chateaubriand warned his audience, "If you continue right to the end of these *Mémoires*, you will see that in rendering justice to what seemed beautiful to me, at various times in our story, I think that in the end the old society is finished."[53] During the Second Empire, the same

[51] Jean-Paul Sartre, *Les Carnets de la drôle de guerre. Novembre 1939–mars 1940* (1983), 229–30. Cf. Eugen Weber, *Peasants into Frenchmen: The Modernization of Rural France 1870–1914* (Stanford, 1976), 3–22, 485–96; and Theodore Zeldin, *France 1848–1945* (Oxford, 1973–77), 1:365–92.

[52] Stendhal, *Oeuvres intimes*, 1:342 (emphasis in the original).

[53] Chateaubriand, *Mémoires d'outre-tombe*, 1:268, 482. Cf. Maurice Levaillant, *Chateaubriand, Madame Récamier et "Les Mémoires d'outre-tombe" (1830–1850)* (1936).

aristocratic prejudices underlay the response of princesse Mathilde to the Goncourts' *Germinie Lacerteux*. "What revolted her in it," Edmond noted, "was that she was condemned to make love the same way as these wretched women."[54]

In turn, the French middle classes developed prejudices of their own. Again Chateaubriand noted the leveling effect created by Samuel Richardson's *Clarissa* in France; the sensibilities of its bourgeois readers were elevated while those of its aristocratic readers were lowered.[55] It was Stendhal, however, who had a more intimate acquaintance with the intellectual pretensions of the French middle classes. For example, his family "believed itself nearly among the nobility . . . reading all the newspapers, following the king's trial as it would follow that of an intimate friend or relative." Stendhal also mocked the would-be gentleman scholar, M. Faurial, reading Dante's work: "It would be speaking *Chinese* that he does not know." In hindsight Stendhal realized the vulgarity of the Daru's salon, "a family of Louis XIV's courtiers just as Saint-Simon depicted them."[56] Like Stendhal's neighbors in Grenoble who frowned on reading as entertainment, the Goncourts' stockbroker friends in Paris regarded realism as the ultimate in literary art. Edmond could not convince one of them that a character he had created was not at all drawn from life.[57] In 1894, Renard would encounter a similar difficulty: " 'For, in short, you too are a bit of an artist, in your own way, since you are a journalist,' M. D. . . . told me, the construction engineer for collapsible and portable houses."[58] Such bourgeois interpretive practice appears tightly circumscribed by class experience.

Not all bourgeois readers were pretentious fools. Professional writers themselves constituted a self-consciously literate group. They knew and depended upon each other for intellectual exchange, notwithstanding their mutual antagonisms. Joubert in his notebooks, for example, could not conceive of a writer without a reader. "When an individual capable of producing a great thought is born in a nation, another one capable of comprehending and admiring him is also born there."[59] In light of Joubert's obscurity, his thoughts on the dialogic relationship between author and audience may have been as wishful as they were profound. Du Camp certainly sensed an enormous distance from the manuscript that his close friend Flaubert had read to him and Louis Bouilhet in 1849. "Contenting ourselves to exchanging occasional glances, Bouilhet and I stayed to listen to Flaubert; those silent hours have remained very painful

[54] Goncourts, *Journal*, 7:100.
[55] Chateaubriand, *Mémoires d'outre-tombe*, 1:410.
[56] Stendhal, *Oeuvres intimes*, 2:632, 625, 907.
[57] Goncourts, *Journal*, 12:103.
[58] Renard, *Journal*, 197.
[59] Joubert, *Carnets*, 55.

in my memory.''[60] The work was so bad that Du Camp and Bouilhet had to screw up their courage to respond honestly. But respond they did, and the author soon abandoned his project. A more positive reading of Chateaubriand's *Les Martyrs* by Augustin Thierry inspired the famous medievalist to adopt a romantic vision of the past.[61] Fellow historian Michelet concluded a journal of his youthful reading in the belief that scholarship required his acquaintance with a narrower range of texts. "My historical work had forced me to read the special books that concerned themselves with the period I was then studying.''[62]

Working-class readers and their interpretive practices are much more difficult to document. Relatively few workers recorded their literate lives in any detail, and observers from other social classes were often vague about them. In 1789, Young referred generally to "the people," by which he meant the men and women in the streets of Paris, but he would have been hard put to describe them any more precisely as readers.[63] Chateaubriand bragged about the wide circulation that *Atala* enjoyed among the lower orders.[64] He haunted an estaminet incognito to overhear the comments about his book, though he failed to indicate what the clientele had to say. Michelet had a better claim to knowing artisans and journeymen, an acquaintance he used to advise workers not to betray their class with the wrong kind of reading.[65] But the actual habits of workers remained a mystery to him. Over time, as class lines were more sharply drawn, the bourgeois knew less and less about the worker's interest in books. In 1916, Gide discovered what he considered a worker's hostility to literate culture; in a passageway to the Paris metro he remarked a young woman intently reading a large format book when "a big worker" deliberately knocked it from her hands. Enraged, Gide admonished the man: " 'Ah! that was clever, what you did there.' . . . 'Clever' was welcomed by a big, sly laugh, repeated in a tone that pretended to imitate my voice; then the man [said] with a stroke of the hand: 'As for me, that is more amusing than reading.' ''[66] In such encounters, accounts of the worker's literate interests were distorted by the enormous distance between social classes in modern France.

But when people speak for themselves, a different impression of their literate activity emerges. Unlike the peasant, the urban worker was on occasion an avid reader. Perdiguier noted the literary enthusiasms he acquired from his fellow woodworkers on the tour of France. While in Bordeaux, a companion by the name of Devigne loved to read and shared his books with Perdiguier.

---

[60] Maxime Du Camp, *Souvenirs littéraires* (1892), 1:313–14.

[61] Augustin Thierry, *Récits des temps mérovingiens* (1840), 1:xvii–xxii.

[62] Michelet, *Écrits de jeunesse*, 331.

[63] Young, *Travels in France*, 163.

[64] Chateaubriand, *Mémoires d'outre-tombe*, 1:445.

[65] Michelet, *Le Peuple*, 159–61.

[66] Gide, *Journal*, 563.

"I was enraptured with them. . . . We especially loved dreadful, somber plays; and I swear, the more dead bodies there were at the end of the tragedy, the more sublime, magnificent, perfect we found it."[67] The stonemason Nadaud also found widespread interest in print among workers during the July Monarchy. "Every morning," he wrote later, "I was asked at the wine merchant's shop to read aloud Cabet's *Le Populaire*."[68] After work for ten years, from 1838 to 1848, he would teach dozens of workers eager to acquire literate skills, a common practice during the *enseignement mutuel* movement. Similarly, Jules Vinçard, the Parisian *chansonnier*, gathered with others to read letters addressed to them by fellow Saint-Simonians.[69] By the end of the century, reading pervaded more fully the everyday lives of ordinary people. At the heart of their experience was a collective enjoyment of an essential distraction from the burdens of work and home. Noted one Parisienne born in 1900, "My father bought *Le Petit Journal*, in the morning, before going to the factory; he read it in the evening before supper. As for me, I read the serial to my mother at night."[70] Although their motives and tastes may have mystified or annoyed the bourgeois, some workers were active readers.

Defined in this way by social class, interpretive practice tends almost unavoidably to the ideological. It is not hard to find readers with marked political preferences appropriate to their class interests. Stendhal, for instance, noted the predispositions of a conservative landowner in Grenoble: "M. Raillane, like a true ministerial newspaper in our day, knew us to speak only of freedom's many dangers."[71] A committed royalist, Chateaubriand found his works heavily censored by officials of the First Empire, including Napoleon Bonaparte himself.[72] When Chateaubriand saw the appeal that Napoleon had made to the prince regent of England in 1814, he could not restrain his own political prejudices; the letter, he stated, was bereft of all sincerity and any regard for the future of France. (This long-standing political animus, however, did not prevent Chateaubriand from noting the glory of the emperor's career.) Equally incisive was Baudelaire's ironically ideological reading of Molière's *Tartuffe*: "An atheist, if he is simply an upright man, will conclude from this play that certain serious questions must never be raised with the rabble."[73] Religion aside, political considerations prevail. The Goncourts had firsthand knowledge of this tendency soon after the December 1851 coup d'état. Their printer insisted that the authors excise certain political allusions from the gal-

---

[67] Perdiguier, *Mémoires d'un compagnon*, 185.

[68] Nadaud, *Mémoires de Léonard*, 140–41.

[69] Jules Vinçard, *Mémoires épisodiques d'un vieux chansonnier saint-simonien* (1878), 153–55.

[70] "Femme née en 1900," in Thiesse, *Le Roman quotidien*, 66.

[71] Stendhal, *Oeuvres intimes*, 2:608.

[72] Chateaubriand, *Mémoires d'outre-tombe*, 1:637, 659, 661.

[73] Baudelaire, *Oeuvres complètes*, 1227.

ley to *En 18..*, even though the manuscript had been completed long before the coup.[74] No reading can be entirely free of politics.

In time, literate activity among workers became equally ideological. When Perdiguier acquired a taste for Racine and Voltaire during the Restoration, illiterate *compagnons* were still fighting each other in the streets.[75] Apparently, workers had yet to develop a consciousness of themselves as a class with collective interests to protect, a consciousness highly correlated to widespread literacy. But Perdiguier's example suggests the origins of a literate working-class identity. Not long afterward, Nadaud claimed that educated workers had a higher self-esteem and asserted their interests more actively. "It seems to me that I grew in my own eyes," wrote Nadaud. "In effect, I had discovered in myself a force of will and obstinacy for intellectual work that I had not recognized before."[76] Louise Michel was herself profoundly moved by Lamennais's *Les Paroles d'un croyant*; from that moment onward, Michel wrote, she belonged to the masses. That commitment would endure a lifetime of political activity, including the reading of Baudelaire on the barricades of the Paris Commune.[77] By 1900, workers read socialist newspapers no less deliberately than had the early founders of the labor movement. Working men in particular favored leftist publications.[78] So long as the printed word addressed certain vital concerns—politically or socially—literate culture engaged the working class.

No less a polemical concern was religion. Religious passions created very similar interpretive predispositions, especially during the clerical controversies of the Third Republic. Pagnol remembers his uncle admonishing him as a child for failing to understand the metaphor of the grape in a story by Lamennais. Pagnol's father also failed to understand it, but refused to be persuaded by his brother that Lamennais was anything but a canting parson.[79] Renard reports in his journal how the aumônier de Corbigny responded to *Poil de carotte*, Renard's fictionalized account of childhood: " 'From a literary point of view, it is absolutely worthless. . . . This is a dangerous man: he has such religious ideas.' "[80] A more sympathetic religious reader, Gide was sensitive to how Charles du Bos's conversion to Catholicism had affected his treatment of Keats. Du Bos preferred *The Fall of Hyperion* to *Hyperion*, according to Gide, because "he found there traces of a spirituality that would permit him to include in Catholicism a poet whom he admired above all and who he felt

[74] Goncourts, *Journal*, 1:44–45.
[75] Perdiguier, *Mémoires d'un compagnon*, 186–87.
[76] Nadaud, *Mémoires de Léonard*, 152.
[77] Michel, *Mémoires*, 29, 166.
[78] Cf. newspapers in Thiesse, *Le Roman quotidien*, 61–72.
[79] Pagnol, *La Gloire de mon père*, 163–70.
[80] Renard, *Journal*, 719.

might otherwise elude him.''[81] Later, Gide likened the power of Marxism to that of Catholicism; both beliefs required a careful initiation of their followers into the mysteries of sacred texts. As a youth, the historian Philippe Ariès respected the Catholic Church's Index of Prohibited Books until Pius X condemned Charles Maurras's Action française in 1926, at which point Ariès finally ''discovered the cursed poets who had long been hidden from us.''[82]

Just as religious sentiments often cut across class boundaries, so too did literate activities within the family. Ideological lines among readers blur remarkably whenever other commitments compete with social status. Chateaubriand, for example, noted the routine of his entire household—relations and servants alike—to join in prayer every evening. Similarly, when Napoleon was exiled, his valet went too and read to him for two or three hours every morning, their responses to the text shaped by their common experiences despite the enormous social differences between them.[83] Families gathered to read in every social class. Besides the aristocratic habits of the Chateaubriands, there were readings among workers in Louise Michel's family and among the bourgeois in Stendhal's.[84] The domestic locus for literate activity was so important that the Goncourts worried about its demise during the Second Empire. ''I see women, children, servants, families in [the] café. Home life is disappearing. Life threatens to become public. The club for the upper classes, the café for the lower, that is what society and the people are coming to.''[85] But this apparent trend does not seem to have prevented family members from reading to each other. Years later, André Gide recalled his many relations, including his grandfather, coming together to hear selections from the Bible. During a moment no less solemn, Gide read with the Blanche family the latest news leading to World War I in *L'Écho de Paris*.[86] In nearly every journal and memoir, whatever the social milieu, reading began and continued within the home.

Literary salons, clubs, and academies all served similar interpretive functions. Rarely were these groups so exclusive that only one social class or ideological tendency was represented. For example, Chateaubriand listed a surprisingly heterogeneous group of men attending Madame de Beaumont's evenings during the First Empire, ''men who occupied a place in literature or business.''[87] C.-A. Sainte-Beuve once described the embarrassed silence that resulted from Étienne Délécluze's account of the revolutionary Terror in Ma-

---

[81] Gide, *Journal*, 974.

[82] Philippe Ariès, *Un Historien du dimanche* (1980), 39. Cf. the long list of biblical citations in Paul Claudel, *Journal*, ed. François Varillon and Jacques Petit (1968–69), 2:1337–60.

[83] Chateaubriand, *Mémoires d'outre-tombe*, 1:24, 1015.

[84] Michel, *Mémoires*, 23–24; and Stendhal, *Oeuvres intimes*, 2:621–22.

[85] Goncourts, *Journal*, 4:112.

[86] Gide, *Journal*, 445.

[87] Chateaubriand, *Mémoires d'outre-tombe*, 1:449–50.

dame Récamier's salon; even though many in his audience had lost relatives to the guillotine, they listened politely to the end.[88] When Nadaud was arrested during the December 1851 coup, he shared a cell with a remarkable collection of opponents to the new regime, though their reading was restricted to religious books and histories by François Guizot.[89] Another confusion of social types appeared at princesse Mathilde's literary parties at Saint-Gratien, where government officials sat at table with authors whose books they had just prosecuted for obscenity. At times, even the various "immortals" of the Académie française agreed on precious little. The Goncourt brothers related how Alfred de Vigny alienated his fellow academicians whenever he sought their approval. Thanks to his enthusiasm, the Académie delayed awarding a prize to Hippolyte Taine's book on Livy.[90] The many dinners enjoyed by Parisian literati throughout the nineteenth century included rivals and in some cases bitter enemies.

Social status and ideological positions conflict within age groups as well. Beginning with the romantics, the French became increasingly aware of generational differences that shaped more than just the reading experience. Stendhal, for one, knew that the books celebrated during the Restoration would be ridiculous by 1860.[91] Despite his loathing for the First Empire, Chateaubriand found himself deeply moved by accounts of Napoleon's death because he was a contemporary. The romantic could feel sympathy for few other age groups, except for the young: "Youth alone was sincere, because it was close to its cradle."[92] Much later in the century, Renard would claim that the most influential book in his life was one he had read as a child: "We have had our education, formed our taste, with the books whose first page was torn. . . . It was an old, tattered novel that was read forty times on the sly."[93] Others who had not read the same work in precisely the same circumstances would, of course, never understand. Sartre sensed the power of his age when he wrote, "My period, my situation, and my freedom all decided my encounter with Heidegger."[94] Not long before Sartre, Beauvoir had felt the same influence at work on her adolescent intellectual crisis: "Barrès, Gide, Valéry, Claudel: I shared the pieties of the new generation's writers. . . . Every young man in print was anxious."[95] At that moment in her life, neither class nor politics played the same role as age in her reading.

Nevertheless, class and ideology had an impact on interpretive practice. As

---

[88] C.-A. Sainte-Beuve, *Nouveaux lundis* (1865), 3:88–90.

[89] Nadaud, *Mémoires de Léonard*, 403.

[90] Goncourts, *Journal*, 6:12, 126.

[91] Stendhal, *Oeuvres intimes*, 2:906.

[92] Chateaubriand, *Mémoires d'outre-tombe*, 1:925.

[93] Renard, *Journal*, 1199.

[94] Sartre, *Les Carnets de la drôle de guerre*, 229.

[95] Simone de Beauvoir, *Mémoires d'une jeune fille rangée* (1958), 193–94.

republican politics and industrial capitalism redefined the relations between the aristocracy, the bourgeoisie, and the proletariat, social-class consciousness informed the reading experience in clearly discernible ways. In time, interpretation was politicized; the responses of sensitive individuals evinced the polemic appropriate to their place within French society. But this historical trend encountered serious resistance from other important social groups defined not by class but by religion, family ties, institutions, and generations. The interpretive practices of these elements often cut across class lines and immeasurably complicated ideological responses. Class remained important throughout the period, but it was certainly not the only social factor at work in the modern French reading experience. Some groups, like literary critics, responded apolitically to texts and thereby earned the opprobrium of other professional writers, who felt betrayed by them. As the Goncourt brothers noted somewhat ruefully, Parisian critics did not fall neatly into any social class or espouse any well-defined ideology; the interpretive impulse of these literate pariahs was often too personal to admit such grand but ultimately simplistic sociological formulations.[96]

GENDER

Another important factor, gender, informed literate life every bit as much as did region and class. Indeed, men and women responded to texts differently for reasons that are not hard to discern; sex roles are particularly well defined in modern French culture, and they have had an obvious impact on reading. In journals and memoirs, one can easily see how men and women were socialized to interpret texts in ways appropriate to public conceptions of their sex.

This process resulted in some specifically female attitudes about reading. George Sand once noted the most common reasons why women read: "We learned in order to become capable of talking with educated persons, in order even to read the books we had in the cupboard, and to kill time in the country and elsewhere."[97] Obviously, literacy was a domestic skill. But female interpretive practice had other, more social advantages. Long after Sand wrote, André Gide observed that a conventional message could serve more than one purpose. When Madame Walckenaër left her calling card to congratulate the Widmer family on the birth of a baby, she did so six weeks late, in fact after

[96] See Goncourts, *Journal*, 5:13, 6:125, 195, and 8:195 on the critic Sainte-Beuve. Cf. Georges Dupeux, *La Société française 1789–1970* (1972); and Zeldin, *France 1848–1945*, 1:11–282.

[97] George Sand, *Oeuvres autobiographiques*, ed. Georges Lubin (1970–71), 1:801. Cf. Simone de Pétrement, *Simone Weil: A Life*, trans. Raymond Rosenthal (New York, 1976), 12–14, 19, 21, 69, 141–42; Elizabeth A. Flynn and Patrocinio A. Schweickart, eds., *Gender and Reading: Essays on Readers, Texts and Contexts* (Baltimore, 1986), 267–88; and Sally McConnell-Ginet et al., eds., *Women and Language in Literature and Society* (New York, 1980), 258–73.

the infant had died. But all was not lost, another woman suggested, because the unsigned card had automatically become an expression of condolence instead.[98] These women thus situated reading within the context of female social convention, one that pervaded other literate activities. Wives, for example, took their interpretive cues from their better-educated husbands at various times in Beauvoir's memoirs.[99] In working-class circles, women read almost exclusively within the household; working daughters and wives at home enjoyed feuilletons especially, because the installments suited best their brief moments of rest from the day's domestic chores.[100] Like their bourgeois counterparts, these women adapted their literate activity to the specific roles they played in French society.

Females were not free to read everything. As adults and as girls, they suffered close supervision by their family relations. The constraints began even before they left for school, but intensified as they grew older and more curious. In her memoirs, Mme. de Rémusat remarked how her serious intellectual interests shocked the mixed company at a salon in 1802: "What audacity! What prodigious erudition!"[101] Similarly, Daniel Stern noted the limited curriculum at the convent of the Sacred Heart, which she attended in Paris. Stern's course of study, established by Jesuits, contained nothing of substance.[102] The Belgian-born feminist Céline Renooz recalled as well the attitude of her brother during the Second Empire when he claimed their deceased father's library for himself, because, as he stated, it was the man's responsibility to provide books for his family.[103] Simone de Beauvoir's parents carefully monitored her reading long after she had finished the Cours Désir and entered the Sorbonne. Her mother no longer pinned the pages of books to prevent young Simone from encountering the wrong material. But both mother and father made scenes over her reading whenever they disapproved of it, and they continued to suggest works they thought more suitable to a young bourgeoise. "My father considered Anatole France as the greatest writer of the century; he had me read *Le Lys rouge* and *Les Dieux ont soif* towards the end of vacation."[104]

Most literate women internalized these strictures. For much of nineteenth-century society, women were regarded as the guardians of moral values, whether or not they were in fact. An intelligent schoolgirl, Geneviève Bréton

---

[98] Gide, *Journal*, 116.

[99] E.g., Beauvoir, *Mémoires d'une jeune fille rangée*, 38–39 (Uncle Gaston broadens his wife's intellectual horizons) and 108 (Beauvoir praises her father's intellect).

[100] See Thiesse, *Le Roman quotidien*, 21.

[101] Comtesse de Rémusat, *Mémoires* (1957), 110.

[102] Daniel Stern [Marie d'Agoult], *Mes souvenirs 1806–1833* (1877), 181.

[103] Céline Renooz, "Mémoires," in BHVP Fonds Bouglé. Boite 16 d. "Souvenirs d'enfance et de jeunesse," fol. 69.

[104] Beauvoir, *Mémoires d'une jeune fille rangée*, 82–83, 188–89.

wrote about popular novels in 1868, "It is not bad to show girls brutal and repulsive evil [so that] they fear it. To spiritualize love and sensuousness like Madame Sand, now there's the danger."[105] A form of passive constraint, such self-righteousness on the part of female readers struck the Goncourt brothers as absurd, or worse, hypocritical. Edmond related an incident in a café where Émile Zola and Georges Charpentier, his publisher, stopped for a drink. Near them sat a *cocotte* with the latest issue of *Le Voltaire*, which was serializing Zola's *Nana*. The men were surprised to overhear the woman exclaim, " 'Merde! Isn't this one dirty. I'm not going to read it.' "[106] Mothers of inquisitive children like the young André Gide had their hands full. In his autobiography, Gide recalls the careful attention his mother paid to his books; she forced him to read aloud, and when he arrived at an objectionable passage, she would tell him how many pages to skip before he could start again.[107] It is interesting to note the scrupulous abhorrence that working-class women developed for the detective novel, a genre that presumably threatened feminine sensibilities.[108] "Self-respecting" matrons did not violate socially accepted virtues.

Whatever their moral values, women often shared their reading experiences with other women. As part of sex-role socialization within the family, mothers taught their daughters literate skills. Sometimes it was a grandmother, as in George Sand's case: "Perceiving my melancholy, my grandmother sought to distract me with work. She gave me lessons."[109] For Louise Michel, it was a collective effort on the part of her mother, grandmother, and an aunt "around the table . . . one reading aloud, the others knitting or sewing."[110] Beauvoir actually claimed to have instructed her younger sister: "Teaching my sister reading, writing, arithmetic, I knew from the age of six the pride of efficacy."[111] But once learned, literate activities remained important to female family members; women tended to read together so long as they were in the same household. Chateaubriand mentioned his grandmother staying up late at night to hear her maid read a novel.[112] A century later, working-class women regularly read to each other installments of the latest serial novel in the local newspaper. Recalled one woman, "At the time when we got a newspaper, it

[105] Geneviève Bréton, *Journal 1867–1871* (1985), 64.

[106] Goncourts, *Journal*, 12:164.

[107] Gide, *Oeuvres complètes*, ed. L. Martin-Chauffier (1932–39), 10:250–52. Cf. Albert J. Guerard, *André Gide*, 2d ed. (Cambridge, 1969), 34–92; and Lejeune, *Le Pacte autobiographique*, 165–96.

[108] See "Femme née en 1900" and "Femme née en 1895," in Thiesse, *Le Roman quotidien*, 66, 72.

[109] Sand, *Oeuvres autobiographiques*, 1:637.

[110] Michel, *Mémoires*, 22.

[111] Beauvoir, *Mémoires d'une jeune fille rangée*, 47.

[112] Chateaubriand, *Mémoires d'outre-tombe*, 1:24.

was to read the whole thing! My mother and me, we read the serial."[113] In the presence of close family relations, women rarely read alone.

A similar literate network existed as well outside the household. Women tended to congregate whether or not they were related. The ardent feminist Jenny P. d'Héricourt recalled the serious intellectual interests of other activists who, like her, organized associations to promote women's rights.[114] Louise Michel also remembered two close friends: "How much I read then with Nanette and Joséphine, two young women of remarkable intelligence who never left the district! We talked about everything." In the same region, Michel noted a particular tradition of neighborhood female gatherings.

> Novels were used in the evenings devoted to the *écrègne*. . . . The *écrègne*, in our villages, is a house where during winter evenings women and girls gathered to spin, knit, and especially to tell or hear the old stories of the bogy-man [*feullot*] who danced in robes of flame out on the open land [*prèles*].[115]

Michel would continue reading with other women, as a schoolmistress in Paris and again as a political activist with Adèle Esquiros. At the turn of the century, working-class women would save money on newspapers and books by sharing their reading with others. "I cut out the serials, yes, I did, in order to read them all together," one older Parisienne stated. "In my neighborhood, the girls loaned out the serials they had bound themselves."[116] The exchange of books and readings was evidently an important feature of the female reading experience.

Since the eighteenth century at least, women preferred prose fiction to all other genres. Jean-Jacques Rousseau recalled how his late mother had left nothing but novels, her favorite reading, even though the boy and his father enjoyed a wide range of material.[117] In 1801, when Chateaubriand published *Atala*, his most enthusiastic audience was female. "Adolescent girls thirteen or fourteen years old were the most dangerous," he later wrote, "for knowing neither what they wanted nor what they wanted of you, they seductively blended your image into a world of fables, ribbons, and flowers."[118] The result was "a pile of scented letters" from his most avid readers, these adolescents. Stendhal, too, noted the same inordinate passion for Madame de Staël's *Delphine*, a novel he himself could not abide: "This book is a manual for young

---

[113] "Femme née en 1899," in Thiesse, *Le Roman quotidien*, 64.

[114] See La Femme, "Madame Jenny P. d'Hericourt," in *The Agitator*, in Karen Offen, "A Nineteenth-Century Feminist Reconsidered: Jenny P. d'Hericourt," *Signs* 13 (1987): 150–58.

[115] Michel, *Mémoires*, 29, 51.

[116] "Femme née en 1899" in Thiesse, *Le Roman quotidien*, 66.

[117] Jean-Jacques Rousseau, *Oeuvres complètes*, ed. Bernard Gagnebin and Marcel Raymond (1959), 1:8–9.

[118] Chateaubriand, *Mémoires d'outre-tombe*, 1:446.

women just entering society.''[119] But neither Chateaubriand nor Stendhal was
a disinterested observer of literate women. Suzanne Voilquin, the Saint-Si-
monian, recollects more incisively the place that fiction had in her development. She wrote that as a young girl,

> I loved reading passionately. I could give myself over to this penchant each eve-
> ning with my mother on the condition that I read to her, during her work, every-
> thing from a neighboring lending-library. Instead of the serious instruction that
> girls began receiving, I drew from these novels false notions of real life.[120]

This fascination with fiction continued into the twentieth century. In her adolescent rebellion, Beauvoir's childhood friend Zaza became absorbed by romantic novels, symbols of both her challenge and her concession to social
convention.[121]

In modern France, novels were often written especially for women, who
were not encouraged to develop interest in other genres. Most schools for girls
offered a particularly narrow curriculum that excluded ancient languages and
literature, philosophy and mathematics. Instead, girls studied domestic ac-
complishments and religion, subjects ill-suited to independent literary judgment.[122] For whatever reason, women limited their literate curiosity. Stern
recalls a forbidden cupboard filled with popular fiction that she read surreptitiously as a child: ''I read for a whole season innumerable novels: Madame
Cottin, Madame de Genlis, Madame Riccoboni, Anne Radcliffe, who put my
poor little brain in disarray.''[123] Little else got her attention. Similarly, working-class readers during the Belle Époque, for example, deliberately avoided
the political sections of the newspaper. Stated one woman born in 1883, ''My
husband took *L'Humanité*, but me, oh no! I didn't read it. I had no time to
read the newspaper. . . . I liked it better reading old books,'' that is, novels.[124]
About the same time, Marie Bashkirtseff, age 13, fought an unsuccessful battle with her conscience. ''I bought a novel in I know not what train station,
but it was so badly written that . . . I threw it out the window and I returned
to my Herodotus.'' Two years later she was still addicted to novels.[125] For the
most part, female intellectual culture was indeed narrowly circumscribed.

[119] Stendhal, *Oeuvres intimes*, 1:199.

[120] Suzanne Voilquin, *Souvenirs d'une fille du peuple, ou La Saint-Simonienne en Égypte*
(1978), 65.

[121] Beauvoir, *Mémoires d'une jeune fille rangée*, 250.

[122] Note the exceptional curriculum outlined for Beauvoir after her studies at the Cours Désir,
in ibid., 168. Cf. Linda Clark, *Schooling the Daughters of Marianne: Textbooks and the Socialization of Girls in Modern French Primary Schools* (Albany, 1984); and Marie-Christine Vinson,
L'Éducation des petites filles chez la comtesse de Ségur (Lyons, 1986).

[123] Stern, *Mes souvenirs*, 119.

[124] ''Femme née en 1883,'' in Thiesse, *Le Roman quotidien*, 70.

[125] Marie Bashkirtseff, *Journal* (1887), 1:68, 204.

In this gender-specific context, women's religious reading is particularly illuminating. George Sand, most notably, experienced a conversion, thanks largely to her reading of religious texts. After entering the convent school, she encountered *La Vie des saints*, which temporarily shaped her literate as well as her emotional life. "Miracles left me incredulous," she remembered, "but the faith, the courage, the stoicism of believers and martyrs seemed to me great things and responded to some secret cord that began to vibrate within me." With the added inspiration of a painting by Titian, Sand threw herself into other religious texts that ultimately brought her a profound sense of God's grace. "It was a stillness, a charm, a meditation, a mystery of which I never had an idea."[126] In time it was the contradictions in these books that led Sand to lose her pious enthusiasm; the paradox posed by the conflicting religious views of Jean Gerson, Chateaubriand, and Rousseau could only be resolved for Sand by a repudiation of strict Catholic doctrine. In the meantime, however, she lived her faith, like many other schoolgirls, through books. Chateaubriand's sister and Beauvoir's mother had similar experiences. Wrote Beauvoir about her mother's faith, "She took communion often, prayed assiduously, and read a number of pious books."[127] These works attracted the young Beauvoir, as well. For such women, reading fostered religious belief.

As one would expect, males and females responded differently to the same religious texts. Responses to one book in particular, Thomas à Kempis's *L'Imitation de Jésus Christ*, highlight significant features of gender-specific reading experiences. As a student, Sand knew this text by heart: "It charmed and persuaded me in every respect; but such logic is powerful in children's hearts. They do not know the sophisms and concessions of conscience. *L'Imitation* is a cloister book par excellence."[128] Sheltered from the outside world, girls like Sand were easily convinced of the book's truth. Young Beauvoir expressed a similar trust in this text: "I was very pious: I confessed to abbé Martin twice a month. I took communion three times a week, I read a chapter of *L'Imitation* every morning."[129] But in sharp contrast to Sand and Beauvoir's obliging faith, the young Michelet was profoundly skeptical from the start. "These religious stirrings," he noted in his student notebook, "did not last any longer than the distress that made me feel the necessity of getting away from the present moment."[130] The mature Baudelaire was far more scathing, likening it to the *orduriers*, or rubbish, of bourgeois love.[131] It is apparent from these differences that women not only preferred different texts, they also tended to read them less critically than men did.

---

[126] Sand, *Oeuvres autobiographiques*, 1:947, 953.
[127] Beauvoir, *Mémoires d'une jeune fille rangée*, 41.
[128] Sand, *Oeuvres autobiographiques*, 1:1040.
[129] Beauvoir, *Mémoires d'une jeune fille rangée*, 74.
[130] Michelet, *Écrits de jeunesse*, 187. Cf. Michelet reading *L'Imitation* in *Le Peuple*, 36.
[131] Baudelaire, *Oeuvres complètes*, 1191.

This clash in response may owe something to the rich imagination that women expressed in their journals and memoirs. Again, Sand recalls the vivid images that reading evoked for her as a child. For instance, she found the pictures in a book on mythology ample introduction to its content. "Without reading the text, I learned very quickly, thanks to the pictures, the chief features of ancient fable-telling, and that interested me prodigiously," she wrote later. The young Sand's imaginative predisposition affected her response to other books: "Certainly a love for the novel seized passionate hold of me even before I had finished learning to read."[132] In her childhood infatuation with fiction, Stern also remarked its lingering influence on her daydreams.

> Deprived of my books, I retained in my memory of them the names, the images, the novelistic adventures that I had accumulated for six months. I continued, myself apart, living in the company of beautiful princesses, in the enchanted groves where one sighed for love. I dreamed all the more of ravishers, sometimes white, always faithful shepherds. From then on I knew that perfect happiness was to see [before me] a handsome knight who swore to love his whole life.[133]

Here the child's passion for images has given way to the adolescent's fantasies that eventually became the adult's creative expression. Neither Sand's nor Stern's especially imaginative styles of reading changed very much over time. Nor would they differ markedly from those of other French women.

Many female readers responded creatively to texts. When a ridiculous suitor came to woo Louise Michel, the character of Agnès in Molière's *École des femmes* immediately came to her mind, because the man resembled so closely Michel's conception of Agnès's guardian, Arnolphe: "I gave him the same response, word for word—he didn't understand! Then in despair for good reason, I looked him in the face, and with the naiveté of Agnès, I impudently told him: 'Monsieur, is the other eye also made of glass?' (He had a glass eye.)"[134] And so Molière's text, and Michel's wit, saved the day. The young Beauvoir, too, read her life in a text by Louisa May Alcott. After devouring the entire "Bibliothèque de ma fille" only to encounter silly heroines and their insipid lovers, Beauvoir discovered *Little Women* "where I believed I recognized my face and destiny. . . . I passionately identified myself with Jo, the intellectual. . . . I shared her horror of sewing and housework, and her love of books."[135] Here was a role model Beauvoir could adopt, one that would endure her disappointment with Jo's subsequent marriage to a professor much older than she. By that time Beauvoir had found another fictional self—Maggie Tulliver in George Eliot's *Mill on the Floss*—still closer to her personal ideal. Like Michel, Beauvoir imagined her identity in a literary text.

---

[132] Sand, *Oeuvres autobiographiques*, 1:540, 541.

[133] Stern, *Mes souvenirs*, 119–20.

[134] Michel, *Mémoires*, 65.

[135] Beauvoir, *Mémoires d'une jeune fille rangée*, 89–90.

Most women's emotions played a profound role in their reading. To be sure, males and females alike shed tears over the fate of Julie de Wolmar and Saint-Preux in Rousseau's *La Nouvelle Héloïse* long after it was published in 1761.[136] But feelings and sentiments remained important to literate women when crying in public was no longer fashionable for men. At the end of her long life, Sand would write, "The world of emotions and ideas that these friends made me enter is an essential part of my true history, that of my moral and intellectual development."[137] Even more directly, Michel would find her love life exclusively in texts: "There are many songs of love that escape in the morning from the life and pages of old books. One can love within them as many men as one wishes."[138] Michel's lovers were the rebellious heroes of the past—the sons of Gaul, the great leaders of robber bands—whose ardent resistance to oppression she shared. In a poignant moment, the comtesse de Noailles's mother shared her passion for Zola's poetic prose, which she often read aloud to her daughter, handkerchief in hand, despite the apparent contradiction between reader and author.[139] A more typical response was Daniel Stern's disappointment in love that led her to take up Sir Walter Scott and other English romantics to forget her emotional misery: "After the comte de Lagarde's departure, reading was the only thing that for me made up in some manner for the loss of his support."[140] Love made many a novel richer and more important to women like Stern.

While socialization continued to inform the female experience, its historical impact on interpretive practice was certainly not exclusive. Some men also suffered both active and passive constraints on their reading; André Gide's family raised the young boy as a Protestant and instilled in him a strict moral code that guided and troubled Gide for the rest of his life.[141] Moreover, French men and women often shared the same social network of literate exchange: like Chateaubriand and Lucile, brothers and sisters read together; like M. de Beauvoir, fathers taught daughters about literature; and like the salons attended by Stendhal, literary gatherings included both sexes.[142] Women were not alone in their taste for the novel; professional literati, most of them male, not only wrote but also read prose fiction. Men also experienced religious conversions through texts; both Chateaubriand and Gide read for much of their lives as troubled Christians. Nor was imagination unique to literate females; like Beauvoir and Michel, Stendhal modeled himself after literary characters

---

[136] Stendhal, *Oeuvres intimes*, 2:716–17.

[137] Sand, *Oeuvres autobiographiques*, 2:272.

[138] Michel, *Mémoires*, 87.

[139] Pagnol, *La Gloire de mon père*, 44–45.

[140] Stern, *Mes souvenirs*, 242.

[141] See Gide, *Journal*, 587–606.

[142] See Chateaubriand, *Mémoires d'outre-tombe*, 1:89; Beauvoir, *Mémoires d'une jeune fille rangée*, 108–9; and Stendhal, *Oeuvres intimes*, 2:930.

in the novels that he read.[143] Nevertheless, gender-specific tendencies remained important. Men and women did not read and interpret the same texts in precisely the same way; they responded to their reading more often than not according to the sex roles defined for them in French society.

So strong in fact were these tendencies that it is not difficult to discover truly sexist readers. The Goncourt brothers rarely had good words to say about anyone in the arts, but they had even fewer compliments for women. The empress Eugénie and princesse Mathilde were their easiest targets, as was the literary autodidact Jeanne de Tourbey; "she has been persuaded that she knows how to read; she believes it and she speaks on literature."[144] Renard indulged in another stereotype, the mindless servant Augustine, "a real farmgirl . . . [with] just enough education to make an unlettered domestic in three or four years, since she will have forgotten everything she ever knew, that is to say, practically nothing."[145] Perhaps in spite of his Protestant upbringing, Gide was harshly critical of nearly all female literati. Few of them, according to his journal, ever seemed to have read the books they discussed. On the comtesse de Noailles's obituary for Anatole France in *Le Quotidien*, Gide wrote, "This is no longer even flattering criticism, it is swooning. Such excess, such intemperance, such inflation of words, emotions, and thoughts cheapens everything reasonable and sensible that one could go on to say."[146] Such absolute terms reveal much about Gide's misogyny. Whether or not it is appropriate to judge the past by present-day standards, male prejudices against literate females offer further evidence of sex roles in modern French literary life.

By now it should be clear that gender as well as region and class affected interpretive practice. In time, as nationalism, gender socialization, and class consciousness developed after 1800, their roles in intellectual life grew and influenced an increasing number of readers in France. These historical forces thus generated a plurality of approaches to the printed text, whatever the interpretive community, whatever the text. Towards the end of the nineteenth century, readers clearly responded according to their various locations within French society.

But region, class, and gender were not the only factors at work; as indicated by the artistic images and the prose fiction studied in Chapters 5 and 6, reading had a life of its own. From 1800 onward, people of all ages encountered print deliberately and alone; from childhood to maturity, readers acquired a new awareness of themselves in relation to the text. Interpretive practice thereby came to be marked by more self-conscious individuals as well as by the diver-

---

[143] See Stendhal, *Oeuvres intimes*, 2:896.

[144] Goncourts, *Journal*, 5:209.

[145] Renard, *Journal*, 1190.

[146] Gide, *Journal*, 784.

sity of modern social distinctions. In this way, the text was historically altered, enhanced, reduced, but always mediated by the world of the reader.

Such is the art of reading depicted in image, fiction, and memoir. Of course, the art and the act of reading are not identical. Few artists, novelists, and memoirists shared the historian's empirical passions; the artistic and literary works examined here remain imperfect historical documents. But the perceptions they express are in fact historical; and they offer rich insight into the changing nature of modern literate experience over time: from 1800 onward, more and more French men and women read alone, deliberately, and fully conscious of certain social realities. But above all, these works demonstrate that reading is a creative enterprise. Painters and writers portrayed reading in a world that was neither entirely true nor wholly false. From their perspective, comparable artistic and literary practices were at the heart of all literate culture, among both writers and their audiences. From the perspective of art and literature, as well, the individual's interaction with a text is central to an historical understanding of intellectual life, that is, of reading as creative interpretation. All literate activity requires considerable imagination and sensibility. Like creation, past and present, reception is indeed an art.

PART III

Historical Interpretive Practices: The Act of Reading

Chapter 8

FROM NOBLE SENTIMENT TO PERSONAL SENSIBILITY

ON AUGUST 8, 1921, soon after the news that he would be made a commander in the Legion of Honor, Georges Courteline received an effusive letter from Robert Rey. Apparently Courteline did not know Rey, but that fact did not deter the correspondent from congratulating the author. Courteline's work, Rey stated, had endured in the miserable circumstances of postwar France. With 1.5 million men dead and food prices beyond control, "our country so covered with wounds and burns" had given way to "a growing demoralization, a brutal cowardice without name, a degradation without precedent."[1] It seemed to Rey that French society had lost its bearings; self-interest and cynicism prevailed everywhere—except for Courteline: "You, you were to the side of all that, you, oh my master." Despite enormous contemporary problems, the author stood apart, his vision unaltered. "Towering over this period, hard and pure like a crystal, eternal and transparent, without bubble, without flaw, there was your work." Consequently, when Rey learned that the government would honor Courteline, he had new hopes for France: "This news brightens me up like an excellent augury . . . that one no longer awaits a precursory sign of a renaissance in taste, in justice, or in critical sense." Literary values, at least those represented by Courteline, seemed the unshakable bedrock of French culture.

If, as Robert Rey believed, the virtues of French literature remained unchanged, despite the vicissitudes of war and peace, the responses to those virtues most certainly did not.[2] From the eighteenth century onward, readers constituted many different interpretive communities whose reactions to various texts altered remarkably. This development in reader response owed much to an evolving historical context in publishing, literacy, politics, and culture. But these factors, important as they are, were neither the only nor the most decisive ones. Readers also experienced literature independently of context; they often received texts over time in another historical dynamic altogether.

At least one interpretive community, authors' personal correspondents, evolved in their response to literature from a presumed nobility of sentiment to a more profound personal sensibility. What this meant was a century-long transition in this group's initial proclivities to emphasize neoclassical literary

[1] Robert Rey to Georges Courteline, 8 Aug. 1921, in BA MS. 13892 fol. 96.

[2] Cf. correspondents as an interpretive community in Chapter 2, and literary critics in René Wellek, *A History of Modern Criticism 1750–1950*, 6 vols. (New Haven, 1955–86).

values and poetic truths; it also meant that these early nineteenth-century readers lived with contradictions of self-serving empathy, artistic analogies, and
personal reverie. Instead, by the outbreak of World War I, similar letter writers
expressed a more flexible classicism and prosaic reality; they showed a more
detached sympathy, a more pervasive interest in music as well as art, and a
better appreciation of the literary imagination. As contexts and texts changed
historically, so too did the interpretive practice of this well-defined network of
readers.

The correspondents' changing responses are well worth charting for a number of reasons. Above all, they shift the historian's attention from the art to
the act of reading. However important, creative perceptions cannot fully assess interpretation. Many aspects of interpretive practice eluded artists, novelists, and memoirists alike.[3] Changes in reader response over time, for example, are extremely difficult to document in art, fiction, and memoir; such
"documentation" can depict interpretation only indirectly, that is, from a distance defined by a particular artistic, literary, or narrative form. Readers must
be permitted to speak more spontaneously. Thanks to their personal correspondence, however, one can understand better the complex transaction between reader and text.[4] By choosing a specific group (the correspondents) responding to a limited range of texts (literature and criticism), one may define
more sharply the interaction between readers on the one hand and their texts
and contexts on the other. In effect, the transition from noble sentiment to
personal sensibility reflects one consequence of readers interpreting texts privately within a more diffuse milieu of social institutions and individual relationships. Correspondence thus constitutes a valuable source for examining
the evolution of French interpretive practice.

NOBILITY

In a perceptive letter to Madame de Staël about her novel *Corinne*, Prosper de
Barante expressed some aristocratic literary ideals, convictions in fact that
many other readers shared with him in 1807. He wrote,

> You have a character of style and of person that blends imagination and reality in
> a profoundly moving and heart-rending manner. . . . You knew to look for what
> good there was in me, and you encouraged it. . . . Rest assured that I will never
> make anything good of my life without dreaming of you—neither sacrifice, nor

---

[3] The independence of individual actors within a specific socioeconomic context remains de-
spite social scientists' unsuccessful attempts to define that independence. See Karl Mannheim,
Ideology and Utopia: An Introduction to the Sociology of Knowledge, trans. Louis Wirth and
Edward Shils (New York, 1936), 109–91.

[4] Cf. Louise M. Rosenblatt, *Literature as Exploration*, 4th ed. (New York, 1983), 27; Robert
Darnton, *The Great Cat Massacre and Other Episodes in French Cultural History* (New York,
1984), 215–56; and *Yale French Studies* 71 (1986), special issue.

devotion, nor all that will have any merit. Your memory is necessarily mixed with all the noble emotions that I will always feel.[5]

His infatuation with the author aside, Barante assumed here moral and social values that the French nobility claimed for itself in the early nineteenth century: sacrifice, devotion, merit, and true emotion. But by stating his assumptions explicitly, Barante's letter effectively defined a widely shared response to literary texts, namely, the tendency to perceive literature as a special preserve of the aristocracy.[6] In a long tradition of literary interests, as other readers besides Barante believed, the nobility was inclined to accept neoclassical rules in both art and poetry; and yet they also felt deeply the joys and sorrows of others in the same social class, indulging even in literary dreams that at first blush seem antithetical to enlightened rationality. Whatever the apparent contradictions, interpretation derived much from a social status enjoyed (or assumed) by the reader.

Madame de Staël's privileged audience was not unique; it expressed interpretive tendencies, especially neoclassical ideals, common to the readers of all prominent authors in the period.[7] When Félix Faure wrote to Stendhal about Buffon's *Discours sur l'homme*, he professed a marked preference for the True, the Beautiful, and the Good: "Truly, I had expected to find better, much better. I believed I would find the truth and instead I found an epic style, brilliant, harmonious, and little else much above all that."[8] In short, Faure found that overly delicate balance of form and content at the heart of Boileau's famous literary strictures. Louis Crozet also recognized the importance of Molière's work as a model worth careful study; as far as he was concerned, *Le Bourgeois gentilhomme*, "this masterpiece," could never be read too many times.[9] Despite the influence of romantic works, including some of his own, C.-A. Sainte-Beuve wrote approvingly of Stendhal's *Promenades dans Rome*: "I find there instruction and diversion," just as Horace found them in the works of ancient Greece and Rome.[10] Five months later in 1830, Astolphe de Custine would also call Stendhal's *Promenades* "a work so useful and yet so amusing."[11] This understanding was natural to readers who, like Barante and

[5] Prosper de Barante to Madame de Staël, 19 May 1807, in *Madame de Staël, ses amis, ses correspondants: Choix de lettres (1778–1817)*, ed. Georges Solovieff (1970), 310.

[6] Literature was never exclusive to the aristocracy in France. See John Lough, *Writer and Public in France from the Middle Ages to the Present Day* (Oxford, 1978), 68–163.

[7] See René Bray, *La Formation de la doctrine classique en France* (1951); and Henri Peyre, *Le Classicisme français* (New York, 1942).

[8] Félix Faure to Stendhal, [11 Dec. 1805], in Stendhal, *Corr.*, ed. Henri Martineau and Victor Del Litto (1967–68), 1:1153.

[9] Louis Crozet to Stendhal, 8 Jan. [1806], in ibid., 1:1170.

[10] C.-A. Sainte-Beuve to Stendhal, 8 Sept. 1829, in ibid., 2:839.

[11] Astolphe de Custine to Stendhal, [7 Jan. 1830], in *Cent soixante-quatorze lettres à Stendhal (1810–1842)*, ed. Henri Martineau (1947), 1:188.

Faure, espoused literary values appropriate to royal and aristocratic patronage. Neoclassicism would underlie many an early nineteenth-century reader's noble sentiments.

This conservative tendency lingered long after romanticism had passed as an issue in French literature. In 1869, for instance, E. Bosquet-Liancourt wrote approvingly of Ernest Renan's dedication of a text to Cornélie Scheffer: "This eloquent page is a masterpiece where the grace of the Gospels and the simple grandeur of ancient poetry breathe."[12] (The same could well have been said of a work written in the seventeenth century.) Certainly parnassian poets like José Maria de Heredia aspired to similar praise from their readers. And a number of their correspondents were happy to oblige. Noted Gustave Morcay of one Heredean sonnet collection in 1888, "All the pieces are pure marvels of a profound emotion and splendid form. . . . I reread and reread again with rapture these antique poems so modest and yet so lively."[13] A. Lécaille celebrated the same features of Heredia's poetry in a poem of his own: "When your pen depicts for us in sovereign verse, / The force and beauty of Hercules and Artemis, / It disperses the gloom and makes us whole again / And its grand vision makes all our souls serene."[14] The clear images, the classical allusions, the moderation of tone and mood noted here were all derived from literary principles appropriate to the age of Louis XIV. To be sure, poetry in particular lent itself to such elitist notions, but the force with which they lingered among readers in the nineteenth century is remarkable. Although the aristocracy was rapidly losing power and status to the wealthy bourgeoisie, its apparent influence remained in readers' neoclassical preferences.

This trend fostered a pervasive appreciation of poetic, as opposed to prosaic, truth. For the first half of the nineteenth century at least, most letter writers described realism in terms of traditional *vraisemblance*, whether or not the term was appropriate. In fact, readers used *vrai* and *vraisemblable* almost interchangeably. Thus in 1825, Auguste Mignet declared Stendhal's *Racine et Shakespeare* "very intelligent and very true," in much the same way Amédée de Pastoret in 1839 called the truth of *La Chartreuse de Parma* "profond."[15] For such readers, realism in the novel was never altogether free of moral value. This was equally so for Zulma Carraud when she told Balzac in 1834, "*Eugénie Grandet* has pleased me very much. If this is not the seductive woman incarnate, it is the true, devoted woman, as many others are, without brilliance. The illumination of her mind, with love's first sensation, is also true, very true."[16] Ten years later, C.-E. Guichard wrote Balzac, "Your nov-

---

[12] E. Bosquet-Liancourt to Ernest Renan, 16 June 1869, in BN NAFr 11494 fols. 85–86.

[13] Gustave Morcay to José Maria de Heredia, 10 Feb. 1888, in BA MS. 13566 fol. 1.

[14] A. Lécaille to Heredia, n.d., in ibid., fol. 49.

[15] Auguste Mignet to Stendhal, 25 Mar. 1825, in Stendhal, *Corr.*, 2:801; and Amédée de Pastoret to Stendhal, 3 April 1839, in *Cent soixante-quatorze lettres à Stendhal*, 2:170.

[16] Zulma Carraud to Honoré de Balzac, 8 Feb. 1834, in *Balzac: Corr.*, ed. Roger Pierrot (1960–66), 2:462.

els are without contradiction *the truest* analysis of man and woman.''[17] Dupont White praised the realism of *La Comédie humaine* for the same reasons. "Twenty years ago," he recalled, "when you still had only a few readers, I already admired in *Annette ou le criminel* the characters, the action, the passion, and this love for absolute truth.''[18] In each case, readers thought of the realistic novel as a contemporary poem, its truth more a literary than an empirical phenomenon.

Consequently, the novel's early readers also understood realism's moral and philosophic implications. In a letter to Balzac, Sanson de Pongerville, a member of the Académie française, expressed this common understanding of prose fiction's profundity.

> In your works, the analysis of man is complete: one finds there the well-informed examination of life's principles, and of emotion's power; the soul's resources are known to you as perfectly as the heart's secrets; your unfettered reason disdains the beaten track, and becomes all the more eloquent when it is bolder. . . . You have made a happy excursion into the ancients' domain, that is in effect the new and true manner. Antiquity and nature are [the] same thing.[19]

Few readers of the early realistic novel sought a simple depiction of life; literary truth required the author's reflections on the human condition. When Eugène Sue began to publish *Les Mystères de Paris* in 1842, for example, his correspondents praised not so much the accuracy of the novel's Parisian setting as the narrative's call for social reform. A retired military officer, Victor de Cabarrus, wrote, "Your philosophical sketches are of a very great authority, and the social renovation that one can no longer regard as a *hollow Utopia* after having read your humble production is, I believe at least, an Eldorado that Europe and France especially would be happy to possess.''[20] For another correspondent, notwithstanding its many realistic details, Sue's novel was nothing less than "a morality lesson.''[21] This sentiment was shared by a member of the Institut historique; he claimed to read *Les Mystères* with the interest "that a serious man carries to . . . a book where he finds great truths . . . , views of the most profound philosophy and a superior instruction.''[22] Such seemed the novel's noble truth.

Even though these interpretive tendencies were derived from well-defined literary norms, they were not without their contradictions. Neoclassical virtues and moral values were more appropriate to eighteenth-century poetry than they were to nineteenth-century prose fiction; but this impulse among the letter

---

[17] C.-E. Guichard to Balzac, 9 Oct. 1844, in ibid., 4:741 (emphasis in the original).

[18] Dupont White to Balzac, 1 July 1847, in ibid., 5:116.

[19] S. de Pongerville to Balzac, 12 July 1847, in ibid., 4:473.

[20] Victor de Cabarrus to Eugène Sue, 15 Dec. 1843, in BHVP Fonds Eugène Sue, cited in Nora Atkinson, *Eugène Sue et le roman-feuilleton* (1929), 70.

[21] X.Z. to Sue, 31 Mar. 1843, in BHVP Fonds Sue fol. 133.

[22] H.L.D. Rivail to Sue, 4 Sept. 1843, in ibid., fol. 382.

writers did not deter them from conceiving literary reality in pictorial, almost empirical terms. When letter writers early in the nineteenth century sought an analogy to describe a text, they most often chose painting. In so doing, they highlighted not the work's poetic features, but its representational qualities. "I have read *La Parole d'un croyant* [sic]," wrote Jules Gaulthier to Stendhal. "Love is painted there in divine colors."[23] And to Balzac:

> The descriptive portion of your novel is most remarkable; your pages have the effect of a landscape by Claude Lorrain or by Rémont [sic]; these are real beings who pass before you either covered with rags or handling the poacher's rifle; your paintings of home life are worth still more than the paintings sent to us by the Lyons school. In a word, you have little to acquire with respect to the art of painting physical nature; you have a treasure of images at your disposal that rival reality itself.[24]

Although painting had an older and more honorable place in aristocratic patronage than did the novel, the realism of art approximated best the poetic truth of prose fiction. Readers were undisturbed by the apparent confusion in their analogies.

Like art, prose fiction at least served a useful purpose: it made its subject matter immediately apparent to all who had eyes to see. If a painting can be easily understood, so can a novel. Ordinarily, poetry was the exclusive preserve of a social and intellectual elite, but fiction reached a much larger public. In this vein M. Menieux remarked to Sue, "You have been accused of threatening public morals thanks to the painting, however true, that you have done of a certain class of society . . . by placing this information in an interesting novel."[25] Up to now, however, Menieux asserted, only a small circle of people knew these matters. Hence the true moral danger of *Les Mystères de Paris* was its depiction of social problems so casually placed before the reader. The morality, or lack of it, in Sue's work lay in the eye of the beholder. Though apparent in the novel's imagery, not everyone saw the same picture. For Louis Jacquet, manufacturer and philanthropist, *Les Mystères* provided "the paintings imprinted by practical morality"; its straightforward rendering of crime and vice was an inducement for all its many readers to do good.[26] The same ambivalence appeared over the striking images developed in Charles Baudelaire's poetic art. The moral content of Baudelaire's *Les Fleurs du mal*, of course, subjected it to much legal trouble, perhaps because certain figures in the book were all too graphic for a middle-class public.[27]

---

[23] Jules Gaulthier to Stendhal, [25 June 1834], in *Cent soixante-quatorze lettres à Stendhal*, 2:72.

[24] Jean Thomassey to Balzac, [16 July 1834], in *Balzac: Corr.*, 2:528–29.

[25] M. Menieux to Sue, 22 Mar. 1843, in BHVP Fonds Sue fol. 115.

[26] Louis Jacquet to Sue, 15 Feb. 1843, in ibid., fol. 83.

[27] E.g., Hippolyte Valmore to Armand du Mesnil, in a letter from Mesnil to Charles Baude-

Another paradox among the correspondents was the passion of their responses. Seldom did reading leave readers indifferent. Noble sentiments in literature elicited the strongest feelings, most often of resounding approval. "I have hardly read more touching pages than those where you have painted Madame de Cerlèbe's father," wrote Chateaubriand to Madame de Staël in 1808 about her novel *Delphine*; "the blindman's scene is admirable."[28] In a moment of uncertainty, François Bigillion turned to *La Nouvelle Héloïse*, *Le Cid*, and *Andromaque* in the hope of reviving his flagging spirits. He told Stendhal in 1802, "I fear very much that all the world's tragedies seem to me but rags on which the most beautiful emotions have been traced for everyone but me at the moment."[29] It is not known whether or not these works provided the tonic Bigillion needed, but Sainte-Beuve's *Les Consolations* certainly moved Ludovic Vitet:

> Here it is less the poet than the man who has seized me. The convalescence of your soul has been for me a delightful story. . . . It has revealed or caused me a thousand emotions, a thousand sentiments; for beneath my calm and happy appearance I am the occasion of many torments, or at least of many impatient moments; I am powerless to speak of them, and so it is an ineffable pleasure when another reveals to me his soul, his agony, his recovery.[30]

The studied and careful reflection necessary to good reading is cast aside here for the intense emotions sought in Sainte-Beuve's poetic revelations. Despite the aristocratic pride in personal sacrifice and detachment from vulgar interest, the enlightened man of feeling endured, and indeed prevailed, well into the nineteenth century.

Accordingly, tears were a widely accepted form of literary appreciation. Until at least the Second Republic, weeping indicated the reader's profound empathy. "You have made me cry; and yet I am already old," Philippe Buchez told Sainte-Beuve in 1830. "In the name of these tears, I am speaking to you."[31] No doubt those tears were not solely for the poet; crying was more for the reader than for anyone else. For instance, Dr. Prosper Ménière, the physician to the duchesse de Berri, wrote Balzac that the novelist's *Louis Lambert* had moved the imprisoned Bourbon to tears: "She has cried, she has suffered. . . . Thank you, enchanter. You are the captive's Providence."[32] Apparently the duchesse felt as misunderstood as the young Louis. After read-

---

laire, 27 June [1859], in *Lettres à Charles Baudelaire*, ed. Claude Pichois (Neuchâtel, 1973), 257; and Joséphin Soulary to Baudelaire, 5 June 1860, in ibid., 362.

[28] F. R. de Chateaubriand to Madame de Staël, 8 Jan. 1803, in *Madame de Staël, ses amis, ses correspondants*, 214.

[29] François Bigillion to Stendhal, 24 Prairial an 12, in Stendhal, *Corr.*, 1:1078.

[30] Ludovic Vitet to Sainte-Beuve, [1830], in BSL D.595 fol. 54.

[31] Philippe Buchez to Sainte-Beuve, [1830], in ibid., fol. 6.

[32] Prosper Ménière to Balzac, 19 April 1833, in *Balzac: Corr.*, 2:291.

ing Edmond de Goncourt's account of his brother's death, a physician wrote in 1888, "I finished your journal with tears that did me some good; writers today no longer make me cry, yet the evils from which humanity has suffered must not be reflected in the doctor's eye."[33] Even as late as the Third Republic, a reader could still benefit from crying in a world given over to less tearful enthusiasms. Earlier in the century, such passionate responses were frequent and more typical of sensitive souls anxious to prove their refined sentiments, and by implication their higher social status. Intense feelings created their own special nobility.

Literature defined another world altogether for the correspondents. In the early nineteenth century, literate imagination tended towards reverie. Charles Viguier once explained to Sainte-Beuve, "The mysticism of an entirely subjective reverie does not allow the air outdoors, the sunshine, the life of the world to come into this sanctuary [i.e., Sainte-Beuve's *Les Consolations*]."[34] For this reader, poetry ought to isolate itself from the materiality of everyday life. Otherwise, why read it? Other readers felt the same about prose fiction. "Is there another world?" asked Henri Latouche of Balzac in 1829.[35] It was clear to Latouche that the imagination was powerful enough to obliterate everything outside the realm of literature. Not long afterwards, Zulma Carraud was completely possessed by one of Balzac's novels: "I am returning to *Le Médecin* [*de campagne*], for I cannot think of anything else. This book has taken me from all sides, has seeped into me. I cannot live without it."[36] Ordinarily, Carraud was not so easily removed from life on her estate, unlike the many anonymous women of more modest means who wrote Balzac about their reading. Typical of their response to *La Comédie humaine* was a letter from a woman who mistook a visitor for the character Vautrin. "Seized with terror in recognizing him, I let fall the spoon from my hands, and I asked myself if I were not living with Madame Vauquier [sic]."[37] (Mme. C.L. had just finished reading *Le Père Goriot*.) Whatever the correspondent's literary interests or social status, imagination was an ennobling sign.

What letter writers thought of the author also played a role in their responses. Correspondents repeatedly employed terms more appropriate to the writer than to the text. In 1802, DuPont de Nemours wrote to Madame de Staël about her *De la littérature*,

> I do not know anything more virile. One can count the passages that betray your sex. . . . We would not have done these passages as well as you, but none of us

[33] Dr. Becour to Edmond de Goncourt, 13 Aug. 1888, in BN NAFr 22451 fol. 139.

[34] Viguier to Sainte-Beuve, 25 Mar. 1830, in BSL D.595 fol. 52.

[35] Henri Latouche to Balzac, 22 [Jan. 1829], in *Balzac: Corr.*, 1:372.

[36] Carraud to Balzac, 17 Sept. [1833], in ibid., 2:368.

[37] C.L. to Balzac, [1835], in *Cahiers balzaciens, No. 2*, ed. Marcel Bouteron (1924), 20.

is better qualified for the rest, neither in the substance nor in the taste for erudition, nor in the poetry of style and the nobility.[38]

For DuPont, serious writing was men's work; *De la littérature* had to be the product of a masculine mind. Both its form and its content, however, could only come from a writer of Madame de Staël's position in society, which was well known for its taste, erudition, purity of style, and nobility of sentiment. The same logic was at work in the presumptions on the part of readers about an author's noble social status; letter writers frequently addressed Stendhal with the aristocratic particle before the novelist's name—his literary reputation ennobled both him and his works.[39] But even readers who knew the author personally were inclined to confuse his apparent social class and the qualities of his literary text. "Nothing resembles so much who you are," wrote Custine to Stendhal about *Les Mémoires d'un touriste*, "this independence of mind, this need for truth that rules everything, and at the same time this happiness of expression that would make one prefer interest even to lying."[40] For these readers, interpretive practice was a deliberate social act, literature a social ideal.

In the first phase of the realistic novel, then, at the height of the romantic movement, correspondents clearly sought from their reading the expression of a text's nobility of sentiment. Nothing seemed more important. The evidence, they thought, was easily found in a work's neoclassicism and poetic truth, whether or not these seventeenth-century principles applied to new genres like prose fiction. Truth, beauty, and virtue lay at the heart of poetry, the model for all great literature. Nor were these readers troubled by the contradictions in their frequent analogies to representational art, in their quest for profound emotions, or in their enjoyment of literary reverie. Painting provided the reader a clear image of an emotional and imaginative reality that both poetry and prose fiction not only made possible but also made more intense. All these qualities of literate response, however, appeared as expressions of elevated social status, be it the author's or the reader's, perhaps because literature itself remained a product of a restricted intellectual elite. The literary experience in the early nineteenth century remained a deeply moving one shaped by social as well as literary ideals—the noble soul, the aristocratic hero, the generous feeling—all vestiges of the Old Regime still alive long after the Revolution of 1789. Like the aristocracy, despite a rapidly changing context, much of French interpretive practice was an historical anachronism.

[38] DuPont de Nemours to Madame de Staël, 1 May 1802, in *Madame de Staël, ses amis, ses correspondants*, 203.

[39] E.g., M. *de* Stendhal, the author of *Le Rouge et le noir* in the reviews discussed in Chapter 4, p. 114.

[40] Custine to Stendhal, [11 Aug. 1838], in *Cent soixante-quatorze lettres à Stendhal*, 2:155.

MORALITY

Perhaps no topic more exercised literati in the nineteenth century than morality in literature. During the heyday of realism in the novel, from 1830 to 1880, moral issues also preoccupied the ordinary reader.[41] This preoccupation affected responses to poetry, as Astolphe de Custine reminded Baudelaire in 1857. "One pities," he wrote, "an epoch in which a mind and talent of so elevated a level are reduced to delight in the contemplation of things that it would be better to forget than to immortalize."[42] Why should Baudelaire have celebrated so vividly such disgusting images? As noted earlier, readers reserved literature for certain social ideals, not for the ugliness of everyday life. Nor was Custine alone in his opinions on this matter. Empirical realism and immoral writing were closely linked in the minds of readers at mid-century. The reasons for this are not hard to guess: the literary experience itself was undergoing a dramatic change. Neoclassical models of poetic truth were no longer appropriate; the inherent contradictions of reader responses to pictorial images, profound emotions, and personal dreams became more obvious; and collective ideals embodied by the aristocracy faded from view. Readers were clearly searching for new sources of literary inspiration. Realism thus became the victim of a transitional moment in modern French interpretive practice; readers in flux only saw its immorality.

For fifty years or more, letter writers and others like them were profoundly concerned with the moral implications of literature in general, and of literary realism in particular. Of course, most correspondents were sympathetic to the author's artistic interests, and so they usually defended his work from the accusations made by critics. Invariably readers tried hard to put morality aside. Charles de Montalembert wrote Balzac in 1831, "Whatever opinion I have of your works' tendencies, it is impossible not to be mastered by your style and originality." Otherwise, Balzac's "Thélémite morality is, frankly, execrable."[43] Female readers were especially torn by the portraits of women in *La Comédie humaine*. Wrote Madame C. in 1832, "Divining everything in us, you have the manner of Hoffmann; in consecrating us to God and the devil, in lavishing incense and mud on us, you have brought to light the strength and weakness of our nature."[44] Instead, she contended, Balzac should portray women as neither better nor worse than they actually are.[45] Male readers, however, were more generous. "I feel the need to tell you how much this book moved me and provoked my admiration," Samuel-Henry Berthoud stated

---

[41] Note discussion of the morality issue for French censors, another interpretive community, in Chapter 3, pp. 98–103.
[42] Custine to Baudelaire, 16 Aug. [1857], in *Lettres à Charles Baudelaire*, 109.
[43] Charles de Montalembert to Balzac, 17 Nov. [1831], in *Balzac: Corr.*, 1:610.
[44] Madame C. to Balzac, [before 26 April 1832], in *Cahiers balzaciens, No. 2*, 3.
[45] Cf. Madame Delannoy to Balzac, 27 July 1832, in *Balzac: Corr.*, 2:77.

about Balzac's *Le Médecin de campagne*. "It is the gospel of our time."[46] The positive influence of literature asserted by men and women alike emphasized a common moralistic approach.

A much more controversial writer, Eugène Sue, received similar letters during the serialization of *Les Mystères de Paris*. Charges of the work's immorality were so numerous that Sue's correspondents rushed to his defense, usually on the same interpretive ground as the accusers. In May 1843, Albert Privat d'Anglemont reported the advice given the Catholic faithful by Monseigneur Combalot at Saint Sulpice. No, Sue was not the "Voltaire of the new rabble," but the advocate of progress resisted by the church.[47] Privat followed up this flattery with another letter requesting assistance to prevent "the exploitation of educated foundlings," the struggling company of young unpublished writers like himself.[48] Another, less self-serving correspondent, J. Séry, refuted similar charges: "I have just finished, Monsieur, reading this product of your mind. I have found it full of interest, sound views, and morality in calling legislative attention to social ills that it would be possible to cure."[49] Most readers felt that the novel's careful descriptions of urban woes tended to obscure the author's munificent intentions. "I am pleased to recognize the profoundly moral thought in your work," wrote an anonymous *lecteur*. "Disguised as it is by the horrible and disgusting details in their sad truth, [that thought] can be misunderstood by many people."[50] Charges of Sue's immorality were countered by assertions to the contrary. The result was essentially the same preoccupation with the values implicit in the increasing number of realistic works on the market.

During the Second Empire, the debate continued with renewed intensity over Gustave Flaubert's *Madame Bovary*. The issue remained the morality of literary realism. Jules Sandeau listed the novel's most obvious shortcomings in a letter to Maxime Du Camp: "a harshness of tone, an absence of idealism, a denial of love."[51] For Sandeau, Flaubert's refined art in no way redeemed its disgusting subject matter. Although no one doubted Flaubert's stylistic gifts, his correspondents were unwilling to concede the immorality of the novel's plots or characters. For most sympathetic readers, *Madame Bovary* did have a lesson. "If you had not given a moral ending to your novel (virtue rewarded, *crime punished*)," argued one letter writer after Flaubert's trial, "you would have been condemned instead of being acquitted."[52] Similarly,

---

[46] S.-H. Berthoud to Balzac, [Sept. 1833], in ibid., 2:358.

[47] Albert Privat d'Anglemont to Sue, [30] May 1843, in BHVP Fonds Sue fol. 182.

[48] Albert Privat d'Anglemont to Sue, [31] May 1843, in ibid., fol. 184.

[49] J. Séry to Sue, 26 Mar. 1843, in ibid., fol. 120.

[50] "Un Lecteur des Mystères de Paris" to Sue, 28 Mar. 1843, in ibid., fol. 124.

[51] Jules Sandeau to Maxime Du Camp, [1857], in René Dumesnil, " 'Madame Bovary' et son temps (1857)," *MdF* (16 Nov. 1911): 300.

[52] Jacques ? to Gustave Flaubert, 28 Sept. 1857, in BSL H.1366 (B.VI) fol. 349 (emphasis in the original).

Virginie Du Hamel considered Flaubert's talent "grand and cruel": "In showing passionate souls the worst of the immense abyss where blooming youth's
celestial illusions are engulfed and all too often, alas! transformed into crimes,
you have taught them resignation, you have opened to them the path to
duty."[53] But only Léon Gozlan suggested that morality was irrelevant to art:
"Above all the confused though benevolent noise, I did not believe [*Madame
Bovary*] was so firmly sealed by a moral idea. It is, on the contrary, strikingly
true."[54]

Correspondents found Flaubert's acquittal far easier to understand than
Baudelaire's poetry. The poet's morality was less explicit and therefore
more difficult to discern, unless one simply considered the imagery in his
work. By lifting certain figures out of their poetic context, readers like Hippolyte Valmore could agree that *Les Fleurs du mal* was little more than "a
revel of corruption": "There are beauties in his *Fleurs du mal*," he wrote
Armand du Mesnil in 1857, "but [also] so many repulsive images, misdirected energies, unjustifiable visions. These are the paintings of carnage."[55]
Most letter writers were more sensitive to the special problems posed by realism in poetry. Perhaps better than anyone, Victor Hugo understood Baudelaire's achievement: "Like all poets, you are part philosopher," but most certainly not a moralist.[56] Other people were indignant that cant should be read
into his poetry. Émile Deschamps saw the actual problem not in Baudelaire
but in his accusers. "The real danger is a dirty orgy / Disguised as a handsome
gala," he versified; "The real danger is a hypocritical page . . . / Contagion
in verse is simply impossible."[57] Because Baudelaire's work brought him such
pleasure during a painful illness, Alfred de Vigny wrote the poet in 1862, "I
need to tell you how much these *flowers of evil* are for me the *flowers of
good*."[58] For whatever reason, however, correspondents resorted less often to
the moral benefits of reading Baudelaire's poetry than they did for Flaubert's
novel.

Concern with literature's morality peaked over Émile Zola's work. Little
had changed in the debate since Balzac, only the voices on both sides of the
issue had become more strident. When Zola published *L'Assommoir*, Lorédan
Larchey ran to his colleague's defense. "As for its morality," he wrote the
author, "it is incontestable. The lesson it emits is terrible. . . . I fear that it is

[53] Virginie Du Hamel to Flaubert, 11 May 1857, in BSL H.1362 (B.II) fols. 234–35.

[54] Léon Gozlan to Flaubert, [1857], in Dumesnil, " 'Madame Bovary' et son temps (1857),"
312.

[55] Valmore to Mesnil, in a letter from Mesnil to Baudelaire, 27 June [1859], in *Lettres à
Charles Baudelaire*, 257.

[56] Victor Hugo to Baudelaire, 30 April 1857, in ibid., 186.

[57] Émile Deschamps to Baudelaire, 13 Aug. 1857, in ibid., 127.

[58] Alfred de Vigny to Baudelaire, 27 Jan. 1862, in ibid., 382 (emphasis in the original).

understood only by those who do not need it.''[59] Zola's youthful disciple Paul Bourget also noted in 1877, ''There is morality in your success that no one sees. You are the only man at the moment who believes in the Will.''[60] Such blunt affirmations of Zola's virtue, however, were expressed much less often than a sincere interest in his scientific and artistic achievement. Hysteria over the moral implications of the naturalistic novel now coincided with a growing faith in its erudition and technique. In 1887, soon after the Manifesto of the Five against *La Terre* appeared, Émile Joindy wrote Zola,

> In truth, when I see in this ordinary volume so many things in a new light, so many characters so wisely described, a movement of the whole so gravely managed, where the useless is hard to find, where each thing in its place carries its own necessary contingency, I ask myself in truth, Gentlemen, if like Flaubert's accusers you are not finding Madame Bovary solely in the cab scene and the unlaced corset.[61]

M. de Roussen put the matter more succinctly in his letter to the author: ''This truth, this form, this study of a milieu has been judged both worse and better than it is, but in truth you alone have seen it.''[62] Eventually art and truth would triumph over both good and evil.

The question remains: Why were readers of literary realism so concerned with its morality? An adequate answer may be impossible. To be sure, as the correspondents noted, prose fiction presented new and unseemly details, and thereby elicited the outrage against it. The development of the realistic novel clearly altered the literary experience in nineteenth-century France. But texts alone cannot account for the correspondents' passionate intensity. Readers' moral indignation also shared in another historical development. At mid-century, the well-established sentiments of a small circle of literate elites were rapidly giving way to the aesthetic diversity of a larger, more varied public. People experienced an unsettling transition in their responses to new genres, and the result was a determined resistance to all literary change, at least until the variety of French intellectual life finally made it impossible to maintain old dogmas. The end of the century ultimately saw a new public responding with greater tolerance for, and in some cases indifference to, literary innovation. In the meantime, moral dogmatism was the logical concomitant of this dramatic shift in reader response—from expressions of noble principle during the First Empire to greater interest in aesthetic ideals by the outbreak of World War I. Preoccupation with morality may well have been a natural consequence of changing interpretive practice.

The adaptation of neoclassicism to prose fiction was the first and most ob-

---

[59] Lorédan Larchey to Émile Zola, [c. 25 Jan. 1877], EZRP Coll. Dr. F. Émile-Zola.
[60] Paul Bourget to Zola, [2 Feb. 1877], in BN NAFr 24511 fols. 284–85.
[61] Émile Joindy to Zola, 28 Nov. 1877, in EZRP Coll. Dr. F. Émile-Zola.
[62] M. de Roussen to Zola, 3 Jan. 1888, in EZRP Coll. Dr. F. Émile-Zola.

vious sign of this shift in literary reception. Despite the outcry against *Madame Bovary* when it appeared in 1857, correspondents were quick to note Flaubert's deliberate craftsmanship, an important neoclassical ideal. The novel "appears to me wisely conceived and eagerly executed," wrote M. Mulot of Rouen. "In short, in my opinion, Madame Bovary is not a novel, it is a history, a dramatically and conscientiously written history."[63] Similarly, Jules Duplan told Flaubert, "I find the whole book marvellously written. . . . Amusing in its numerous descriptions, the least details are extremely well done."[64] A friend since childhood, Caroline Le Poittevin d'Harnois particularly admired "these characters so well drawn . . . this style so correct and so perfectly mature that one believes it the work of an old author."[65] Since the realistic novel could not fulfill all neoclassical strictures, it still merited respect for its order, balance, unity, and stylistic tradition. But prose fiction was also praised for its truth and beauty. In 1893, M. H. Caro-Delvaille called Edmond de Goncourt's *Les Frères Zemganno* "a magnificent canticle to nature. It's lovely! It's grand and simple like the Bible."[66] Not long before, a journeyman printer had written of the Goncourts' "charming books in which you knew to maintain in a remarkable way the right note of the true, of the beautiful that makes you one of our epoch's premier stylists."[67] Such praise echoed literary values that were becoming more appropriate to the novel than to poetry.

In the same context, correspondents also made truth more prosaic. Alfred Cailteau thought *Madame Bovary* "a very grand study of our provincial mores . . . of portraits, of descriptions, of narratives, of charming speech, and of a striking truth."[68] Other readers seized upon Flaubert's character types as blends of poetic and novelistic reality. Noted Sainte-Beuve in a famous letter to the author, "M. Homais rises to height of a character-type. The stupidity, the silliness, the vulgarity, the routine, the monotony, the boredom, all that is rendered with an irony and a bitterness dissimulated under the various masks that have no inkling whatsoever of it all."[69] Almost always, readers saw precision as an expression of the novelist's mind and art. "The minute details into which you enter," wrote Charles Toirac, "announce a great mind for observation."[70] The same tendency to adapt neoclassicism to realism existed among the Goncourts' readers as well. In 1888, Georges Allewareldt wrote from Vienna, "Germinie [Lacerteux] has a very true, very genuine realism, a

[63] Mulot to Flaubert, 19 April 1857, in BSL H.1364 (B.IV) fols. 49–50.

[64] Jules Duplan to Flaubert, [1856], in BSL H.1363 (B.III) fols. 28–29.

[65] Caroline Le Poittevin d'Harnois to Flaubert, 10 June 1857, in BSL H.1363 (B.III) fols. 433–34.

[66] H. Caro-Delvaille to Edmond de Goncourt, 23 Dec. 1893, in BN NAFr 22456 fol. 146.

[67] V. Breton to Goncourt, 21 May 1887, in BN NAFr 22454 fol. 307.

[68] Alfred Cailteau to Flaubert, 2 June 1857, in BSL H.1361 (B.I) fols. 280–83.

[69] Sainte-Beuve to Flaubert, [1857], in Dumesnil, " 'Madame Bovary' et son temps (1857)," 314–15.

[70] Charles Toirac to Flaubert, 30 April 1857, in BSL H.1366 (B.VI) fols. 60–61.

warmth of frightening and very bitter passion, a very hard and very black disenchantment with things.''[71] Here literary profundity made room for empirical truth. In time, readers even began to reconsider the autobiographical features they perceived in literature.[72] For letter writers at mid-century, the realistic novel redefined poetic truth.

Similarly, readers became more self-conscious in their emotional responses to literary texts. The fervent empathy that had focused as much on the reader's own feelings as it had on those of others appeared less and less frequently in the fan mail that authors received at the height of the realistic novel's success. In fact, correspondents increasingly found their emotions inseparable from the novelist's art; the novel tended to ''objectify'' their responses in the text itself. For example, in 1857, after reading *Madame Bovary*, Paul de Saint-Victor wrote Flaubert, ''I am more and more touched and charmed. The death agony is poignant and the watch terrible. . . . Decidedly, it is a work. There is a mark of the master about it.''[73] Edmond About responded in a similarly detached fashion. ''The reading continues,'' he told Flaubert, ''the talent is appreciated because it is enlightened, and so is the passion because it is human.''[74] Unlike correspondents earlier in the century, both of these men were moved more by the work's technique than by its overt subject matter, a practice equally pervasive among readers of the Goncourt brothers. In 1860, Louis Bouilhet remarked of their *Les Hommes de lettres*, ''It is astonishing in its verve and wit; the observation there has a cruel truth; and the intimate drama that unfurls slowly, implacably, in the midst of all this biting envy, in the midst of all this killing weakness, has left me with an immense sadness.''[75] Even less sophisticated readers noted the special enchantment of the authors' work.[76]

Romantic reverie was also much less common. The responses to Flaubert's *Salammbô* illustrate particularly well a new literary imagination. Correspondents recognized the important element of fantasy in his novel, set in ancient Carthage. ''*Salammbô* was a literary fantasy that ought to be printed in a hundred copies, like a volume of poetry,'' quipped Champfleury in 1863, despite the author's patient attempt to reconstruct the novel's historical setting.[77] Eugène Fromentin likened the work to a vision: ''It is fine and robust, astounding

---

[71] Georges Allewareldt to Goncourt, 5 July 1888, in BN NAFr 22450 fols. 210–20.

[72] E.g., J. Barthélemier Le Hardy de Beaulieu to Goncourt, 19 Feb. 1887, in BN NAFr 22451 fols. 48–49.

[73] Paul de Saint-Victor to Flaubert, [1857], in Dumesnil, '' 'Madame Bovary' et son temps (1857),'' 300.

[74] Edmond About to Flaubert, [1857], in Flaubert, *Oeuvres complètes: Madame Bovary* (1930), 525.

[75] Louis Bouilhet to Goncourt, 9 Mar. 1860, in BN NAFr 22454 fol. 107.

[76] Serge Chapoton to Goncourt, 30 May 1892, in BN NAFr 22456 fol. 310.

[77] Champfleury [Jules Husson] to Flaubert, 14 Sept. 1863, in Flaubert, *Oeuvres complètes: Salammbô* (1934), 503.

in its spectacle and its extraordinary intensity of perspective. You are a great painter, my dear friend, better than that, a great *visionary*, for what are we to call this that creates realities so alive with its dreams and that makes us believe them?''[78] Like Fromentin, other readers regarded Flaubert's Carthage as a splendid illusion. ''It is the soul of Carthage,'' stated a close friend. ''It lives again in you . . . and you reproduce it in a splendid fashion with your chimerical genius that alone understands the profound meaning of the real world. . . . Nothing is more ideal than the real, and nothing is more real than the ideal.''[79] Thus readers' reveries became visions, their dreamworlds a novel's grand spectacle, appropriate to a new style of reading.

Underlying this transition in interpretive practice were new social ideals. The adaptation of neoclassicism to the novel, the prosaic qualities of poetic truth, the self-conscious literary emotion, and the reader's imaginative vision—all these developments coincided with a shift in the apparent social status of the author and the nature of his or her work. Correspondents tied literature less to the aristocracy than they did to the bourgeoisie. Increasingly, readers spoke of a work's energy, strength, and power in lieu of its refinement, taste, and subtlety.[80] Here is evidence of an intermediate stage in nineteenth-century reader response. In the letters, this transitional phase is represented by terms typical of readers earlier in the century—refined, delicate, subtle, and profound—but also appropriate to readers much later—vibrant, colorful, complex, and elaborate. Increasingly, correspondents responded to literature as if it were romantic, realist, *and* symbolist. Above all, the readers identified the author's stylistic and social individuality. By the end of the century, then, correspondents no longer felt threatened by innovation or diversity, either in literature or in their responses to it. It is precisely at this moment in the evolution of interpretive practice that the public concern over morality weakened, a victim of changes in the nature of French literary reception.

SENSIBILITY

In an 1891 letter to his good friend Anatole France, Paul Chéron defined a new sensibility among French readers. ''Your Thaïs is very pretty,'' he wrote.

> You tell your edifying stories with good humor, with a well-informed simplicity that recalls Zadig; here you are tender, moving, touching; there, biting to hurry along the scene—it is a connoisseur's delight, it is a gem of its kind—but the genre is dangerous, and I would have preferred that you had not taken it on. . . .

[78] Eugène Fromentin to Flaubert, 29 Nov. [1862], in Flaubert, *Oeuvres complètes: Salammbô*, 505 (emphasis in the original).

[79] Hélios to Flaubert, [1863], in BSL H.1363 (B.III) fol. 439. Cf. la duchesse de Castiglioni-Colonna to Flaubert, [1862], in BSL H.1361 (B.I) fols. 290–91.

[80] E.g., Antonin Bunand to Goncourt, 25 Feb. 1885, in BN NAFr 22454 fol. 349.

You are not an apostle; why is it necessary to cry aloud our most personal second-thoughts?[81]

In lieu of overt social or moral concerns, a deeply personal aesthetic matters most to Chéron. For him, *Thaïs* is the product of a good-natured intelligence capable of expressing a wide range of wit and emotion. If the author errs, it is because his book is too intimate. Otherwise, "the work is amusing and extremely well done. . . . What special erudition you possess. . . . But this is not all: besides an historical study, you have written an idyll and a satire." In his appraisal of France's work, Chéron expresses a clear preference for a modified classicism, a prosaic reality, a broad artistic knowledge, a rational sympathy, a controlled imagination, indeed an especial sensitivity to the novelist's persona in the text. Here the reader responds, not to the author's presumed nobility or morality, but to his apparent sensibility. This new emphasis in the correspondence is yet another step in the evolution of modern French interpretive practice.

Readers began to respond differently, even though realism and naturalism were still major forces in literature. As early as 1862, when Flaubert's *Salammbô* appeared, correspondents noticed the classical features of prose fiction—in Flaubert's case for obvious reasons.[82] *Salammbô*'s setting in the ancient city of Carthage echoed Latin texts studied in school. But even letters to Émile Zola expressed a remarkable interest in literary traditions. Writing from Luxembourg, L. van Deyssel noted in particular what he called the classical and modern aspects of Zola's *La Terre*, "his classical comedy and tragedy, and his modern melancholy." He needed to explain, he said, "the Epic of your work, which depicts the man-beast, like a great epic in centuries past, the man-beast with these essential and eternal qualities, beyond the passing skin that philosophic and social movements had him wear."[83] Like van Deyssel, readers were surprisingly concerned to resurrect the old debate between romantics and classicists. Some correspondents placed Zola among the former, as Jules Troubat did in his letters to the author. "You are finishing the decapitation of aristocratic and academic art," he wrote, making Zola something of a latter-day Victor Hugo.[84] But most readers described the naturalist's achievements in more classical terms. The workers in Zola's *L'Assommoir* were for Théodore Bainville "marvellous tragic characters."[85] Guy de Maupassant later lamented the effects of serialization, because the artificial breaks

---

[81] Paul Chéron to France, 18 April [1891], in BN NAFr 15432 fol. 172.

[82] E.g., to Flaubert from Heredia, 11 Nov. 1879, in Flaubert, *Oeuvres complètes: Salammbô*, 506; from Édouard Le Barbier, 1 Dec. 1862, in BSL H.1364 (B.IV) fols. 172–73; and from V. Cibiel, 15 Dec. 1862, in BSL H.1361 (B.I) fols. 366–67.

[83] K.J.L. Alberdingk Thijn (L. van Deyssel) to Zola, [1887], in EZRP Coll. Dr. F. Émile-Zola.

[84] Jules Troubat to Zola, 9 Dec. 1887, in BN NAFr 24524 fols. 307–8. Cf. Albert Delpit to Zola, 29 Nov. 1887, in BN NAFr 24517 fols. 345–46.

[85] Théodore Bainville to Zola, 27 Nov. 1876, in BN NAFr 24511 fol. 1.

in the narrative, he said, destroyed its grandeur and composition; instead, details ruled and Zola's art suffered.[86]

Anatole France's readers were still more impressed by the classicist features of his work. His deliberate allusions to the Greek and Roman world, of course, contributed significantly to this response. But France's correspondents were more likely to mention less apparent traditions in his work. A former seminary student, G. Cistier, wrote in 1917 of his discoveries in *Le Puits de Sainte Claire*. Even though the novel was far from what Cistier had been schooled to appreciate in Fénelon and Bossuet, it did have "style, thought, harmony, . . . precise and luminous expression." And so, Cistier realized, Corneille and Racine were not necessarily "what literature had produced of the most elevated, the most perfect, indeed the most sublime."[87] After his own fashion Anatole France had achieved as much. Other readers noted France's carefully crafted style, "the most judicious and most beautiful language," as a French politician put it in 1924.[88] A book collector wrote in 1922, "I profoundly admire the sublime elegance of your mind, the amiable profundity of your genius, and your smiling philosophy." As a consequence, Anatole France was "one of these centuries' great humanists."[89] Letter writers singled out the *esprit* of the author's work more than any other quality, perhaps because it captured modern French literature's debt not to neoclassical rules, but to the more enduring creative impulses behind them. In this way, readers shaped old virtues to new literary experiences.

The correspondents also redefined the novel's veracity, one distinct from both poetry and life. A natural tendency for readers had been to take the naturalists at their word: the novel was a human document, a slice of life, an account of reality. In 1887, both Eugène Cros and Émile Collet called Zola's *La Terre* a "study."[90] A less sophisticated reader assured Zola that his view of peasants was exact and not at all exaggerated; he then recounted two anecdotes about peasants who resembled closely Zola's characters.[91] This confusion of the literary and the everyday, however, was far from universal. Most letter writers understood that prose fiction's mirror refracted rather than reflected the world. One anonymous correspondent compared *Les Mystères de Paris* to *L'Assommoir*, much to Zola's credit:

When one compares these improbabilities of form and action to the pathetic but striking paintings of real life, to these scenes so true and so rigorously written of

[86] Guy de Maupassant to Zola, [Jan. 1888], in BN NAFr 24522 fols. 79–80.
[87] G. Cistier to France, 27 Sept. 1917, in BN NAFr 15439 fols. 194 bis–194 ter.
[88] Bracke [Deputy] to France, 15 April 1924, in BN NAFr 15431 fol. 3.
[89] E. Bruell to France, 28 Feb. 1922, in ibid., fols. 137–40. Cf. Annie Joachim-Daniel to France, 15 Dec. 1921, in BN NAFr 15434 fols. 660–62.
[90] Eugène Cros to Zola, 1 Dec. 1887; and Émile Collet to Zola, 12 Dec. 1887, both in EZRP Coll. Dr. F. Émile-Zola.
[91] Brachmann to Zola, 30 July 1887, in EZRP Coll. Dr. F. Émile-Zola.

miseries that you investigated in *L'Assommoir*, one cannot keep one self from casting aside Sue's volume with a shrug of the shoulders and returning to what is truly a work.[92]

André Theuriet protested that Zola had chosen to portray only exceptional aspects of rural life in his novel, "but you have shown in this collection the admirable talent of an artist and a poet."[93] Few readers failed to note the novel's mediation of reality.

Anatole France's correspondents were also engaged by his novels' special combination of poetry and erudition. In 1887, the vicomte Melchior de Vogüe praised *Le Livre de mon ami* for "its profound truth and its superior poetry."[94] M. Harmigny of Tours expressed a similar enthusiasm in verse.[95] Repeatedly, France's readers recognized the special artful knowledge of his prose fiction. For Hortense Sellon in 1922, the life of "le petit Pierre" "is in many respects more marvellous, more difficult to relate, to render so true that one does not know where art begins or where the truth (of facts) ends."[96] But in time, yet another notion of literary truth intruded into the correspondence, namely, literature as a phenomenon to study. Readers corrected the author's grammar, pointed out misquotations, and wrote articles on France's place in literary history. Maxime-Lévy discussed the increasing use of France's work in lycées and collèges, while a French professor at St. Lawrence College in Canton, New York, questioned the author's use of the word "torve" (scowling).[97] A schoolboy in Tours even wrote France for help on a composition assignment; the lad was to explain what the author meant by the phrase, "To live is to act."[98] Consequently, by the turn of the century, prose fiction had come to define not only a reality of its own, but also an object of new scholarship. Literature was increasingly a world unto itself.

Personal sensibilities required different analogies from what readers had used to characterize the literary experience. Correspondents turned more often, for example, to music. To be sure, early in the nineteenth century, discussion of poetry had used figures of speech derived from another classical art. Marcelline Desbordes-Valmore could naturally celebrate Sainte-Beuve's *Les Consolations* with some music of her own: "Oh poetic ferver! Oh holy illness! / Oh eternal youth! Oh vast melody! / Invisible tool, limpid and con-

---

[92] C.G. to Zola, [1887], in EZRP Coll. Dr. Émile-Zola.

[93] André Theuriet to Zola, 6 Dec. 1887, in BN NAFr 24524 fols. 77–78. Cf. Antoine Guillemet to Zola, 3 Feb. 1877, in EZRP Coll. LeBlond E.24.

[94] E. Melchior de Vogüe to France, 24 Mar. [1887], in BN NAFr 15439 fol. 275.

[95] L. Harmigny to France, 3 Nov. 1917, in BN NAFr 15434 fols. 407–8.

[96] Hortense Sellon to France, 15 May 1922, in BN NAFr 15438 fols. 453–55.

[97] Maxime-Lévy to France, 2 July [?], in BN NAFr 15436 fols. 207–8; and L.E.M. Vernier Du Pontet to France, n.d., in BN NAFr 15439 fols. 233–34.

[98] Jean Le Bodo to France, 6 June 1921, in BN NAFr 15435 fols. 415–16.

tained, / Like a profound voice in a beloved book.''[99] Similarly, Charles Gounod likened Hugo's poetry to an ''immense organ of thought, all of whose
keys reverberate under your fingers, all of which thrust onto the soul a sonority
so powerful that one no longer dares to include there a feeble note.''[100] No
fewer than six of Baudelaire's correspondents used comparable similes.[101] But
readers like Zulma Carraud occasionally described the novel, as well, in such
musical terms. In 1833, she wrote Balzac, ''With thoughts from the condemned man for his mother, *L'Auberge rouge* [is] like a melody to everyone,
or like chromatics to musicians.''[102] After reading *Madame Bovary* in 1857,
Henry Morel also wrote Flaubert of ''your style's music.''[103] But these were
exceptions to the general rule throughout the nineteenth century. For most
letter writers, poetry was to music what prose fiction was to painting.

From the appearance of realism onward, however, these analogies were often reversed. In a letter to Heredia in 1871, Théodore de Banville emphasized
the pictorial quality of the poet's ''La Détresse d'Atahualpa'': ''All your
paintings are cast in pure light with all the dazzling crudeness of color that it
permits, and yet you have come to this harmony without sacrificing anything.''[104] Readers of Anatole France's early poetry also noted its visual aspects. Eugène Manuel remarked how ''full of light'' were France's *Les
Poèmes dorés* when they appeared in 1873, just as Soulary wrote the poet of
''the true color'' in *Les Noces corynthiennes* three years later.[105] The concrete
images used by Heredia and France played a role in this trend, but no more so
than those used by the romantics earlier in the century. Reader responses had
shifted in the interim. Now correspondents also compared the language of
prose fiction to music. In 1897, Lucie-Félix Faure wrote Anatole France,
''With joy I have found . . . all the poetry of the sea that your prose sings in
an exquisite music.''[106] The novelist's style was especially sonorous to Milly
G., who thanked France profusely for the music of his language.[107] And for
A. Buisseret, writing in 1924, ''The style is a light and a music.''[108] While
most correspondents continued to think of literary realism pictorially, a significant number were sensitive to its other artistic resonances, suggesting a
neoromantic synergism of the arts.

In the same period, the ways in which literature moved readers also changed

[99] Marcelline Desbordes-Valmore to Sainte-Beuve, [1830], in BSL D.595 fol. 12.

[100] Charles Gounod to Hugo, n.d., in BN NAFr 24803 fol. 203.

[101] See *Lettres à Charles Baudelaire*, 76, 128, 250, 285, 370, 389.

[102] Carraud to Balzac, 1 [Mar. 1833], in *Balzac: Corr.*, 2:261.

[103] Morel to Flaubert, [1857], in BSL H.1365 (B.V) fol. 38.

[104] Théodore de Banville to Heredia, 27 July 1871, in BA MS. 13566 fol. 2.

[105] Eugène Manuel to France, 10 Feb. 1873, in BN NAFr 15436 fol. 51; and Soulary to France,
25 April 1876, in BN NAFr 15438 fol. 562.

[106] Lucie-Félix Faure to France, 7 Jan. 1897, in BN NAFr 15433 fol. 481.

[107] Milly G. to France, 22 July 1922, in BN NAFr 15434 fols. 358–64.

[108] A. Buisseret to France, 22 April 1924, in BN NAFr 15431 fol. 156.

noticeably. The tearful solipsism that letter writers expressed in response to Stendhal and Balzac continued among Émile Zola's audience, but to a much more limited extent. To Zola, J. K. Huysmans wrote about *L'Assommoir*, "It's beautiful. . . . Gervaise working the sidewalks in the mud, and watching the indecent movements of her shadow is admirable, and the refrain: 'Monsieur, listen to me,' that returns incessantly is poignant to the point of tears."[109] Georges Lys de Bonnerive could not resist crying either, over both Gervaise and the abbé de Mouret.[110] Others, however, enjoyed Zola's Rabelaisian good humour in *La Terre*, what Henry Févre called its "huge gaiety."[111] But these appreciations tended more to an emotional detachment. Readers cried and laughed self-consciously; the correspondents experienced emotion in literature as if they were concerned about what others would think. For instance, Bourget told Zola in 1877, "You have invented a manner. It is troubling like all discoveries overthrowing so many received ideas"—his particular response informed by the naturalist cause.[112] In 1887, Octave Mirbeau fell victim to a similar purposiveness: "In naturalism's fact, haven't the latter-day romantics been tormented, haven't they surrendered all they can? This same peasant I can see, I have encountered his like in Perche, in Mayenne, in a portion of Normandy. And I am always moved."[113] Literary passions were, in short, dampened by more deliberate readers.

By the turn of the century, correspondents expressed a less literal imagination. Still free from the fantasy favored by people earlier in the century, these readers apparently felt more secure in their literary experience, its contradictions notwithstanding. Lys de Bonnerive could still speak of himself as "a dreamer," but he was exceptional.[114] Rather, France's readers declared a fascination with the author's own world in the text. Although English, G. I. Petty expressed a common sentiment in his letter of 1921: "At first the truths you showed me caused me exquisite anguish, but I was a fascinated victim of the potent spell you exercised over my rude imagination by means of your art."[115] Later readers would make distinctions between the literary visions of different genres. The correspondence sent to Albin Valabrègue fell neatly into two parts, one addressed to the professional dramatist and the other addressed to the amateur philosopher. Only Valabrègue's sister, Louise, had encountered both visions; in 1895, she wrote him of her fear that *La Philosophie du XXe siècle* would expose him to unnecessary ridicule when his plays were doing so

[109] J. K. Huysmans to Zola, 7 Jan. 1877, in BN NAFr 24520 fol. 410.

[110] Georges Lys de Bonnerive to Zola, 1887, in EZRP Coll. Dr. F. Émile-Zola.

[111] Henry Févre to Zola, 28 Nov. 1887, in BN NAFr 24519 fols. 163–64. Cf. Huysmans to Zola, [19 Nov. 1887], in BN NAFr 24520 fols. 334–35.

[112] Bourget to Zola, [2 Feb. 1877], in BN NAFr 24511 fols. 284–85.

[113] Octave Mirbeau to Zola, 29 July 1887, in BN NAFr 24522 fol. 192.

[114] Lys de Bonnerive to Zola, 1887, in EZRP Coll. Dr. F. Émile-Zola.

[115] G. I. Petty to France, 23 Nov. 1921, in BN NAFr 15437 fols. 112–14.

well.[116] While Louise thus warned her brother, however, an administrator of the Théâtre de l'Odéon critiqued one of his plays, *Père et fils*: "This is elementary theater, I want to say, containing only the *elements* of a good play . . . from which an author knowing his job would have drawn a good resolution."[117] By then, literature did not send the reader dreaming but thinking.

Readers also identified new literary ideals. Neither the aristocracy nor the bourgeoisie provided appropriate terms of praise for Anatole France's correspondents. His work developed personal rather than social attributes. For readers at the turn of the century, his fiction was not noble or elevated, powerful or energetic, but delicious and witty. "There is much passion in this volume," wrote Georges Brandes from Copenhagen about *Le Lys rouge*. As for *L'Anneau d'améthyste*, it had "a depth of delightful irony."[118] Raymond Poincaré called France's character of Pierre Nozierre "a philosopher who is more tender, more moving and of a less distinctive irony" than M. Bergerat in the same work.[119] "I say thank you," Milly G. stated in 1922, "for the charm of your incomparable thoughts, for the beauty that you sow in your books, for the serenity and the peace that come from so much beauty."[120] Such seemed the novelist's persona. Less self-assured letter writers remarked the work's profundity, whether or not they fully comprehended it. "Can you imagine sometimes the reverberation that a lofty and serene thought like yours can have on the minds of ordinary people who, like me, read and reread you?" asked M. A. Isoard of France in 1922.[121] For all these readers, the author's achievement transcended class entirely; in their correspondence, the social dimensions to literature had given way to more purely individualistic features.

This sharpened interest in the author's aesthetic persona marked the end to a century-long development. One important community of interpretation, the correspondents with French authors, evinced a major shift in their responses to literature and criticism, a shift from noble sentiments to personal sensibility. Strict neoclassicism yielded to a more flexible classicism; poetic truth passed in favor of prosaic realism; analogies to art broadened to all the arts; self-contained empathy became a more reflective sympathy; reverie evolved into imagination; and elite social ideals gave way to authorial integrity. In the interim, at the height of the realistic and naturalistic novel, these unsettling changes fostered a profound concern with morality in literature; unshakable moral principles provided a bulwark against the uncertainties and insecurities of new interpretive practices for a new reading public. For a brief period, in

---

[116] Louise Valabrègue to Albin Valabrègue, 5 Jan. 1895, in BA MS. 13598 fol. 10; and Louise Valabrègue to Albin Valabrègue, 11 Mar. 1895, in ibid., fol. 11.

[117] L'Odéon Administration to Valabrègue, [189?], in BA MS. 13598 fol. 50.

[118] Georges Brandes to France, 12 April 1899, in BN NAFr 15431 fols. 9–10.

[119] Raymond Poincaré to France, 15 July [1899], in BN NAFr 15437 fol. 329.

[120] Milly G. to France, 22 July 1922, in BN NAFr 15434 fols. 358–64.

[121] A. Isoard to France, 24 Jan. 1922, in BN NAFr 15434 fols. 623–24.

the middle of the nineteenth century, modified neoclassicism, poetic realism, aesthetic emotion, and above all bourgeois social ideals pervaded the responses of French readers. Moral intensity was thus a logical concomitant, if not consequence, of an underlying historical development. While reception after 1900 had not ceased to evolve, it certainly appeared more stable, more secure—indeed, more enduring.

It is interesting to note here the correspondents' variations on literary and intellectual movements in the nineteenth and twentieth centuries. For the letter writers, the Enlightenment's preoccupation with empirical knowledge, among other concerns, lingered long after 1800, while romanticism took a long time to penetrate the consciousness of this interpretive community. The nobility of sentiment was preeminently a feature of neoclassicism throughout the romantic first half of the nineteenth century. And bourgeois morality, with its inflexible principles, largely defined the response to realism, even though the middle classes also cried over all kinds of literature in the nineteenth century. Other literary sensitivities did not appear quite so pervasively. It was not until the rise of the symbolists in the Third Republic, however, that readers developed romantic tendencies of their own. Towards the end of the century, correspondents became introspective and interested in self-discovery to the same extent that authors had been several decades earlier.

Literary developments among readers were thus very curiously off-phase from their appearance among writers and in their texts. In the history of modern French interpretive practice, romantic reception lagged considerably behind romantic creation; features of the eighteenth century—in many different manifestations, of course—indelibly marked French responses to literature throughout the modern period. It would appear, then, that reception belies the basic elements of French literary history, a world focused more on authors than on readers, at least as scholars continue to conceive of it. Clearly, the historical act of reading involved far more than either the text or its context. At least one literate public, the correspondents with published French authors, re-created literary works in a distinct and remarkable tradition all its own.

Chapter 9

RESPONSES TO GENRE

IN THE INTEREST of national defense during World War I, military censorship of the mail followed very precise procedures.[1] The French army established dozens of commissions, each composed of more than 200 soldiers and civilians, to sort, classify, and read the correspondence to and from the front. But because so much was at stake in the war, the commissions were given specific guidelines, formulas in fact, to facilitate the detection of information potentially valuable to the enemy. The Army General Staff issued the same instructions to each commission specifying the way letters should be read.[2] After an initial screening to reduce the number of items for close examination, the readers were required to stop all letters pertaining to "the military, diplomatic, political, or moral situation of France and the allied countries."[3] Absolutely nothing suspicious in the slightest was to pass. Moreover, censors were tasked with surveying the letters to collect information useful to the allied war effort. In time, the General Staff drew up a checklist that formed the basis of weekly reports to Army Intelligence from each postal section. Even before the mutinies in the wake of the Nivelle offensive, military censors had information, sector by sector, on how the troops perceived their hygiene, the war, politics, and the home front.[4] The result was an enormous archive devoted to a particular interpretive practice, one defined during the war in effect by bureaucratic fiat.

Although the historian can never know how well, or how poorly, the military effected its own procedures, the instructions and the reports do offer intriguing insight into the conventions of reading in modern France. Each genre of writing, and not just letters during World War I, made certain demands on all reading publics.[5] As discussed in Chapters 3, 4, and 8, responses to litera-

---

[1] See instructions in AMG 16N 2704 d. Surveillance du commission, janvier–août 1915.

[2] E.g., see reports in AMG 7N 952 d. Lyon.

[3] Instructions in AMG 16N 2704.

[4] See questionnaires in AMG 16N 2705 d. 3. Cf. reports in ibid. and in AMG 16N 1470 d. Sondages. Cf. also Gérard Baconnier et al., *La Plume au fusil. Les Poilus du Midi à travers leur correspondance* (1985).

[5] On genre, see titles listed in L. E. Shiner, *The Secret Mirror: Literary Form and History in Tocqueville's "Recollections"* (Ithaca, 1988), 13 n. 1; Adena Rosmarin, *The Power of Genre* (Minneapolis, 1985), 3–51; Paul Hernadi, *Beyond Genre* (Ithaca, 1972); Heather Dubrow, *Genre* (London, 1982); and Alastair Fowler, *Kinds of Literature: An Introduction to the Theory of Genre* (Cambridge, Mass., 1982).

ture, for example, differed markedly over time from one community to another. But responses also changed from one genre to another. Readers brought different expectations to poetry, drama, and other, less well-defined literary forms like criticism, newspaper articles, and personal letters. Readers also perceived different features in those forms—for instance, poetry's images, drama's action, prose fiction's descriptions, and the like. Despite the remarkable variety of communities and their different interpretive practices from romanticism to symbolism, each genre elicited a curiously narrow range of reactions. Within the diversity of readers there was some unity appropriate to the kind of text they considered. Most readers, of course, did not have the careful instructions that military censors used for personal letters during the war. But they did assume that each form of writing made specific demands of them.

These implicit limits to reception deserve closer study. Interpretive traditions no more determined reader response than did their historical context. Correspondents with authors, the reading community examined in the last chapter, received books in ways specific to the histories of their practices, but also specific to the histories of publishing, education, censorship, and culture that were considered in Part I. This much is evident even in the art, fiction, and memoirs of other readers examined in Chapters 5, 6, and 7. What matters here, however, are aspects of the texts themselves, or more specifically, the generic expectations that readers had and the apparent fulfillment of those expectations by the texts. Each reader, no matter what the interpretive community, entered into a dialogic relationship with each work within the bounds set, among other things, by that work's genre. As intellectual historians and literary specialists well know, the type of writing placed before a reader can shape his or her response.[6] This additional feature to the history of reading complements the limits established by the reader's historical context of response, either as a member of a particular interpretive community or as a figure in the larger cultural landscape. Precisely how the conventions of genres affected response, however, requires consideration of the textual clues that people actually used in the act of reading.

CORRESPONDENCE

For centuries, before the widespread use of the telephone, the most commonly read, sustained text was the personal letter. The collected correspondence of prominent political and intellectual figures numbers many volumes, even though much of their handwritten communication has been lost. After the Sec-

[6] E.g., I. A. Richards, *Practical Criticism: A Study of Literary Judgment* (New York, 1929), 1–18, 173–287; Wayne C. Booth, *The Rhetoric of Fiction* (Chicago, 1961), 3–165; and Peter J. Rabinowitz, *Before Reading: Narrative Conventions and the Politics of Interpretation* (Ithaca, 1987), 15–169.

ond Republic issued the first prepaid stamp, ordinary French men and women increasingly sent and received correspondence and thereby learned firsthand the conventions of both letter writing and letter reading.[7] Recipients naturally came to expect dates, addresses, greetings, closings, and signatures, as well as messages directed to them in particular by individuals of their acquaintance. Indeed, it was these generic formalities that suggested to the reader the specific context for the letter's content and defined the conventions of an appropriate response. Whatever the actual message, knowledge of the author as friend, relative, lover, or enemy, for example, made a dramatic difference to the reader. Modes of address, even time of day, played similar roles in determining a letter's meaning, or apparent lack of it. Readers inattentive to such matters can easily misconstrue what the writer intended for the recipient. Although the letter was not a formal literary genre, its form and format provided readers, past and present, with clues to its personal import.[8]

Perhaps nowhere were the conventional features of correspondence so important to reader response than in the case of an open letter by Anatole France.[9] Soon after the German shelling of Reims cathedral in September 1914, France sent a personal protest to Gustave Hervé, editor of *La Guerre sociale*, a newspaper well known for its socialist sympathies before the war. The desecration of so celebrated a monument was only the latest in a series of German atrocities reported from Liège and Nancy. And so the author felt moved to speak out. He apparently sent his letter to *La Guerre sociale* to reaffirm Hervé's vigorous denunciation of the German action that appeared in the September 21 issue.[10] Whereas both the editor and the novelist expressed elsewhere their socialist opposition to the war, here they unambiguously stated their patriotic sensibilities for all to read. The outraged response of France's readers, however, left him in some doubt as to the wisdom of his published remarks. Within a week, several journalists and nearly four dozen correspondents criticized him sharply for the views expressed in his protest. However appalled France had been by the German decision to shell the cathedral, the readers of his open letter in *La Guerre sociale* were of another mind. Their anger moved the author to publish another letter offering to give up writing

---

[7] See Eugène Vaillé, *Histoire générale des postes françaises*, 6 vols. (1947–55), abridged in idem, *Histoire des postes françaises jusqu'à la Révolution* (1947); and idem, *Histoire des postes françaises depuis la Révolution* (1947).

[8] See Charles Porter, "Foreword," *Yale French Studies* 71 (1986): 1–16.

[9] See Pierre de Quirielle, "Notes et aperçus. Anatole France et la guerre," *Correspondant* (10 Aug. 1915): 547–51; Carter Jefferson, *Anatole France: The Politics of Skepticism* (New Brunswick, N.J., 1965), 190–91; Marie-Claire Bancquart, *Anatole France. Un Sceptique passionné* (1984), 345–47; and APP BA 1586.

[10] See Gustave Hervé, "Répresailles," *Guerre sociale* (21 Sept. 1914): 1. Cf. protests in other French newspapers, esp. *La Presse, Le Siècle, Le Temps, La Libre Parole*, and *Le Figaro*.

and to join the fighting at the front.[11] How could he have been so widely misunderstood? How did the implicit rules of letter reading contribute to this interpretive incident?

The letter itself is not very long and deserves quotation in full.[12] It reads:

My dear Hervé,

I am bringing to *La Guerre sociale* my indignant protest against the destruction of the cathedral at Reims. Invoking the god of Christians, the barbarians have shelled one of Christianity's most magnificent monuments.

They have thus covered themselves with an immortal infamy; and the name German has become execrable to the entire thinking world. Who on earth, then, can doubt now that they are the barbarians and that we are fighting for humanity?

The war will be without mercy. Soldiers in the right, we will remain worthy of our cause; we will show ourselves formidable and magnanimous to the end.

As you said in your noble article of yesterday, my dear Hervé, we will take a pitiless revenge on these criminals.

We will not sully our victory by any crime; and on their soil, when we will have vanquished their last army and reduced their last fortress, we will proclaim that the French people befriend the defeated enemy.

I extend to you a patriotic hand. Anatole France.

From a vantage point many years later, Anatole France's message seems entirely appropriate to the period. His letter sounds angry, stern, and proud. The very first paragraph forthrightly protests the shelling and labels the Germans as both barbarians and hypocrites. Such actions, the author declares, render the enemy infamous and execrable. Germany is thus the aggressor and France the defender in this conflict over the fate of humanity. From these stereotypical propositions, the writer then draws three conclusions: the French are in the right to vanquish the Germans, and in so doing show themselves both formidable and magnanimous; the French shall take a pitiless, unrelenting revenge against these criminals; and the French themselves shall commit no crimes, but in fact will proclaim their friendship once the enemy has been thoroughly defeated. The author then closes with a patriotic gesture. Under the circumstances of the war soon after the battle of the Marne, the letter appears unexceptionable. At least to the American editors of *The New York Times* who published an otherwise accurate English translation, the letter could be summarized, albeit very crudely, in the accompanying headline, "Invokes Pitiless Vengeance. But Anatole France Warns Against Destroying Ger-

---

[11] Anatole France, "Une Nouvelle Lettre d'Anatole France," *Guerre sociale* (28 Sept. 1914). Cf. his letter to the minister of war in *Le Matin* (1 Oct. 1914).

[12] France, "La Protestation d'Anatole France," *Guerre sociale* (22 Sept. 1914).

man Monuments.''[13] Other prominent public figures in France, like Hervé, had said as much in their own protests at the time. But none of them provoked such an angry outburst.

The first angry responses to France's letter appeared in the newspapers. The very next day, *L'Écho de Paris* published the reaction of Albert de Mun, who considered France's protest part of a defeatist plot, one that must be stamped out immediately.[14] The source of his disgruntlement, and that of many other readers, was the penultimate sentence calling on the French people to befriend the defeated enemy. De Mun seized upon this suggestion; and without mentioning anything else in France's letter, he declared the author a traitor. On September 27, de Mun reiterated his concern in an article published in *La Guerre sociale* where he rendered France's offending sentence in a peculiar fashion: "To the German people, when it has been vanquished and when it has thrown up its Hohenzollerns, that is to say, when it has made the sole *mea culpa* that will disengage it from the butchers of Louvain, Senlis, and Reims, to this German people our master Anatole France promises the French people's friendship.''[15] Put in even harsher language than the original, this idea remained abhorrent to de Mun and to the other journalists who were deeply disturbed by the very thought of friendship with the enemy—all Germans were complicit in the atrocities committed by their troops on Belgian and French soil. What Anatole France must have thought a noble gesture inspired dismay on the part of readers who were still traumatized by the nearly successful German attack in the early stages of the conflict. Like other journalists, de Mun ignored the rest of the famous author's stout protest.

This selective reading was not unique. As one would expect in the monarchist *L'Action française*, Charles Maurras termed Anatole France's postwar magnanimity "an atrocious folly . . . a cruel philanthropy.''[16] The Germans must be subdued and contained for a century or more before they would deserve so much as a smile from the French. But Republican newspapers were equally condemnatory. In *L'Homme libre*, Georges Clemenceau thought that if Anatole France's words of friendship were written seriously, they were indeed treasonous.[17] Similar responses appeared in other provincial papers. Pierre Jay, a journalist for the *Salut public de Lyon*, wrote, "Tomorrow the French people will be composed in large part of widows and of mothers whose

[13] Anon., "Invokes Pitiless Vengeance. But Anatole France Warns Against Destroying German Monuments," *The New York Times* (23 Sept. 1914).

[14] Albert de Mun in *L'Écho de Paris* (23 Sept. 1914). Cf. Benjamin F. Martin, *Count Albert de Mun: Paladin of the Third Republic* (Chapel Hill, 1978).

[15] De Mun in *La Guerre sociale* (27 Sept. 1914), as quoted by Michel Ney to France, 28 Sept. 1914, in BN NAFr 25436 fols. 465–66.

[16] Charles Maurras in *L'Action française* (23 Sept. 1914). Cf. Eugen Weber, *Action Française: Royalism and Reaction in Twentieth-Century France* (Stanford, 1962), 12.

[17] Georges Clemenceau in *L'Homme libre* (Bordeaux, 27 Sept. 1914).

sorrow and grief, in the expression of one of our finest poets, remain unnamed. I am chilled to the depths of my soul at the thought of the friendship for which they would rekindle Germany.''[18] While so many families are still mourning their dead, Jay stated, Anatole France's sentiments were nothing short of indecent, the author himself disgusting. As for the official newspaper of the Social Democrats, *L'Humanité*, Anatole France had been no less patriotic than Alfred de Mun; but under the circumstances, this was obvious and very lame special pleading for a longtime political friend. Here France's letter was clearly of less concern than de Mun's.[19] At best the novelist was ignored when he was not vilified in the French press soon after his protest appeared in *La Guerre sociale*.

Concerned individuals also admonished the author in dozens of hostile letters. However different their interpretive community, the correspondents were as angered by the issue of friendship as the journalists had been. About 80 percent of the correspondence France received during the controversy attacked his apparent generosity to the Germans. Typical of these letters was one by M. Surlané of Paris, who on September 24 referred angrily, and illogically, to another issue not even mentioned in France's protest.

> To dare proclaim, at the very moment when millions of French families mourning their dear ones are devoured by agony and uncertainty, have had their homes savaged by the bloodthirsty brutes whom the entire world reproves—to dare proclaim that germany [sic] is not big enough and that it must take territory from austria [sic] to enable it in some years to completely annihilate us, that surpasses all imagination—that is criminal or that is insane![20]

Outrage at least as trembling as Surlané's appeared in more than thirty-five other letters addressed to France, most of them anonymous. One satirical spirit posing as the kaiser sent him a postcard of appreciation: "Bravo for your fine article in *La Guerre sociale* and for your friendship after the war. So much the worse if the French are not pleased. Very cordially yours, Wilhelm.''[21] One-third of the letters noted bitterly the irony of the author's last name, and made it a point to address him as "Anatolich Deutschland" or "Anatole the Prussian.''[22] Evidently the sharp contrast between the war's intensity on the one hand and France's detachment on the other was simply too much for his readers to bear in silence.

After venting their spleen, most correspondents attempted to account for

---

[18] Pierre Jay, "Bulletin du jour," *Salut public de Lyon* (24 Sept. 1914), in BN NAFr 15439 fol. 557.

[19] Pierre Renaudel, "Assez," *Humanité* (26 Sept. 1914).

[20] M. Surlané to France, 24 Sept. 1914, in BN NAFr 15438 fols. 628–29.

[21] Guillaume to France, 24 Sept. 1914, in BN NAFr 15439 fol. 553.

[22] E.g., letters to France in BN NAFr 15436 fols. 468–69; BN NAFr 15438 fols. 223–24; and BN NAFr 15439 fols. 555, 560.

the author's apparent lack of patriotic fervor. And their explanations were less
than flattering to the man they were addressing. Like Surlané, nine others
thought France insane or senile.[23] M. Duroyers noted, for example, "In order
to be an Academician, one must be sometimes a perfect idiot." The author's
official status confirmed his enfeebled intellect even before the pronouncement
in *La Guerre sociale*.[24] Like Clemenceau in *L'Homme libre*, seven correspondents accused France of treason, which made him a criminal pure and
simple. "You are ripe for the padded cell or passable for the guillotine," wrote
Henri Erpeldinger. "In any case it is certain that the enemy will not thank you
for your *good* intentions."[25] Two correspondents called the author a coward,
while two others condemned his greed and vanity. Of all the blatantly *ad hominem* responses to France's letter, the most generous recalled a quip from
Talleyrand; his gesture of friendship was worse than a crime, it was a blunder.
France's broad-mindedness merely stirred up rabid war feelings rather than
allayed them, if that was what he indeed intended by his public protest. Asked
a reader of *La Bataille syndicale* and fellow leftist sympathizer, "Master, why
use your certain influence in order to encourage spirits further in this stupid,
misguided, and unhealthy hatred?" The answer, no doubt, lay in France's
illogic. Otherwise there seemed no rational explanation for this self-defeating
protest.[26]

More than half the letter writers, however, turned their attention from the
author to themselves. If Anatole France's motives seemed inscrutable, then
the correspondents suggested more personal reasons for their deep sense of
betrayal. The most frequent, and most obvious, source was the actual or likely
loss of a loved one in the fighting. With all the passion of a mother, Mme.
L. Diodonat of Paris wrote,

> I have two sons under fire and a widowed son-in-law with two children who have
> left him, as well. My heart also rises in disgust to think that a Frenchman can ask
> pity for those who strangled a poor lost hunter in the very country where my sons
> found themselves August 15. . . . I have the heart of a mother; I would not want
> my sons to finish as a casualty, but on the battlefield at no price [will there be]
> pity for them. Will you give me back my sons with your pity for the enemy?[27]

More painful still was the letter that France received from M. G. Henry.
"How could you wish," he asked, "that a family father like me (and we are
legion), having raised a son to age 24 (and who was killed on August 24), to
be of your opinion?"[28] Nearly all readers who had close relatives at the front

---

[23] E.g., Un Français de France to France, [22 Sept. 1914], in BN NAFr 15439 fols. 567–68.

[24] M. Duroyers to France, 25 Sept. 1914, in BN NAFr 15433 fol. 359.

[25] Henri Erpeldinger to France, 22 Sept. 1914, in ibid., fols. 403–4 (emphasis in the original).

[26] Anon. to France, 23 Sept. 1914, in BN NAFr 15439 fols. 581–82.

[27] Mme. L. Diodonat to France, [Sept. 1914], in BN NAFr 15433 fol. 242.

[28] M. G. Henry to France, 26 Sept. 1914, in BN NAFr 15434 fols. 481–82.

posed similar questions, though with less simplicity and poignancy. Because of their own fear or suffering, France's correspondents often sought in themselves an explanation for his seemingly callous statements. And so as they read, these people sought some understanding of very real personal problems arising from the war.

Twenty percent of Anatole France's correspondents were far less critical of his letter, even though his sentiments there still evoked intense feelings. At least three letter writers were deeply ambivalent: M. G. Cantel thought that France was right, but had addressed the wrong audience; Pierre Renard also agreed with the letter, but wished its message had been published before the war; René Gillouin tried hard to see reason in both France and his critics.[29] In their attempts to find common ground with the author, three other people redefined what he meant by friendship. The term was too vague, according to Hervé: "If you could have explained your word 'friendship,' you were wrong to retract it."[30] Apparently, the editor himself thought that France's second, more overtly patriotic letter to *La Guerre sociale* on September 27 had been unnecessary. " 'Friendship' is much less than fraternity," wrote René Helleu, a suggestion echoed by Gabriel Marty.[31] Nevertheless, three other correspondents fully endorsed France's original language. A schoolteacher, M. Ris, wrote from Bourges, "Are you not in the proper tradition of the French Revolution that did not wage war on people but on tyrants, and that meant in all countries independence with liberty?"[32] Another individual unknown to the author actually attacked militarism in an unapologetically pacifist spirit; for him, friendship was absolutely correct. If anything, France had not emphasized it enough.[33] But like the other correspondents, whether or not they agreed with the author, this man responded selectively and personally.

Closer analysis of this correspondence, however, reveals the crucial role played by implicit conventions of letter reading. For example, both the date and the address of Anatole France's protest contributed much to the readers' response. September 22, 1914, marked less than two months of military conflict between France and Germany, most of it on French soil. Only two weeks earlier, General von Moltke had ordered a general withdrawal from Nancy to the Vesle, bringing an end to the first major German offensive of the war. The Schlieffen Plan had come very close to defeating the French who, as it was, still ceded several northeastern departments to German military occupation. In light of the tremendous loss of life and property, the French took little sat-

[29] Letters to France from M. G. Cantel in BN NAFr 15431 fols. 536–37; from Pierre Renard in BN NAFr 15438 fol. 119; and from René Gillouin in BN NAFr 15434 fols. 210–11.

[30] Hervé to France, 8 Oct. 1914, in BN NAFr 15434 fol. 511.

[31] René Helleu to France, 4 Oct. 1914, in BN NAFr 15434 fols. 461–62; and Gabriel Marty to France, 14 Oct. 1914, in BN NAFr 15436 fols. 123–26.

[32] M. Ris to France, 21 Oct. 1914, in BN NAFr 15438 fol. 170.

[33] Anon. to France, 25 Sept. 1914, in BN NAFr 15439 fol. 583.

isfaction in the victory, while heavy fighting continued to secure the army's left flank on the English Channel in the famous race to the sea. Nationalistic feelings ran extremely high in the wake of the greatest threat to the country since the Franco-Prussian War. With published reports and many more unconfirmed rumors of German atrocities compounding the enormous casualty figures, the country was truly in shock.[34] Anatole France could not have chosen a worse moment to write his public letter in the relative safety of his estate in Touraine, far from the front, far from Paris, which had been threatened by German troops before the French counteroffensive. Under the circumstances of the war, the time and place of the author's letter, prominent features of all correspondence, were in themselves potent messages to France's audience.

The letter writers were acutely aware of date and location; they also noted origin and destination. As the correspondents lamented the impact of the war on their lives, they could not ignore the author as sender and themselves as receivers of his protest. Anatole France had addressed that letter to them. And they responded accordingly to these features specific to the genre. The author, they knew, had opposed war in general, if not this war in particular, upon the same socialist principles as the editor of *La Guerre sociale*. Even before he had written his letter, France was well known for his pacifist leanings; and his readers were well accustomed to seeing them in his work.[35] The correspondents referred to him variously as a utopian, a humanitarian sophist, an ultra-socialist, an atheist, as well as a pacifist, in their attempt to make sense of his conciliatory proposal once the war was over.[36] Besides providing a partial explanation for the author's sentiments, this name-calling, or more precisely, this scapegoating assuaged the letter writers' profound personal anguish. More than one-fourth of the correspondents had husbands, brothers, or sons at the front; still others feared for the safety of their friends or neighbors in uniform. The *ad hominem* response to France's protest thus followed logically from the conventions of letter reading: the date, the address, and knowledge of the sender as well as of the receiver ensured the highly emotional temper of the published and unpublished archive on France's open letter.

No matter what the reading community, then, personal letters required special attention to a particular form. Both reviewers and correspondents responded in the same way to Anatole France's protest letter published in *La Guerre sociale*. Attention to the letter as a genre was also at the heart of military censorship of mail during the war, just as the same concern appears, albeit implicitly, in the principal correspondences published since the eighteenth

[34] See Marc Ferro, *The Great War, 1914–1918*, trans. Nicole Stone (London, 1973), 49–55; B. H. Liddell Hart, *The Real War, 1914–1918* (Boston, 1930), 54–81; and *Les Armées françaises dans la grande guerre* (1930), vol. 1.

[35] On France's politics, see Jefferson, *Anatole France*.

[36] See letters to France in BN NAFr 15433 fols. 321–22; BN NAFr 15436 fols. 463–64; and BN NAFr 15439 fols. 576–80.

century.[37] Naturally, other factors, such as the recipients' assumption of a private message addressed directly to them, shaped responses to this kind of text. But to the extent that these elements were specific to the letter as a form, they obviously contributed to the meaning that readers construed from each instance. The same is true about other genres, some of them well defined, such as poetry, drama, and fiction, some of them less well articulated, such as advertisements and encyclopedias. Each of them made subtle, and not so subtle, demands of the reader; and they informed the dialogic relationship between text and context underlying interpretive practices throughout the modern period.

OPINION

French readers encountered another literary form that posed still more interpretive problems than the letter: the essay. Although Michel Montaigne had created the genre in the sixteenth century, explicit rules were never developed for either its composition or its reception.[38] The essay form lacked some of the letter's most obvious features that were important to its reception, such as a specific location in time and space. Published more often than not, its message was intended for a general audience; its narrative could be written in the third as well as the first and second persons; and it usually made much broader use of literary devices. Length, structure, point of view, tone, mood, and figures of speech all varied considerably from one instance to another. Because the genre itself was so difficult to define, its audience found it challenging to read, to define its meaning as well as its form. This was especially true during the Second Empire, when Jules Michelet published two extended essays on love and women, *L'Amour* (1858) and *La Femme* (1859).[39] Here again, two different interpretive communities, reviewers and correspondents, responded with the same hostile embarrassment to a particular text, this time to book-length literary works on another controversial contemporary issue: the place of women in French society. Like the readers of Anatole France's letter in 1914, Michelet's audiences were guided by a genre's implicit conventions—or, in this case, a form's apparent lack of substantive clues to what the author actually meant.

First, the texts. Despite the author's intention to discuss the moral and natural history of love—belabored in the lengthy notes at the end of each volume—Michelet's two books are in fact more literary than historical. Both

---

[37] See correspondence listed in *Yale French Studies* 71 (1986): 12.

[38] See Gustave Lanson, *Les Essais de Montaigne. Étude et analyse* ([1930]); Pierre Moreau, *Montaigne. L'Homme et l'oeuvre* (1933); and Erich Auerbach, *Mimesis: The Representation of Reality in Western Literature*, trans. Willard R. Trask (Princeton, 1953), 285–311.

[39] See Jules Michelet, *L'Amour-La Femme*, in *Oeuvres complètes*, Tome 18, ed. Paul Viallaneix et al. (1985).

works are structured by a common stylistic device, the human life cycle. In *L'Amour*, after a substantial introduction, the exposition charts the natural progress of an imaginary couple from courtship, betrothal, consummation, child-rearing, and maturity to widowhood. *La Femme* follows a similar course, except that it focuses on the life cycle of the woman from childhood to late adulthood, or from "education" to "family" to "society." Within this cyclical organization, the essays also create a frame by opening and closing on related ideas. *L'Amour* begins with a chapter on puberty and ends with a chapter on the rejuvenation of love during widowhood. As for *La Femme*, the bright sunlight and healthy air of a spring morning in the country are richly described in the first and last chapters.

It is precisely in their literariness, however, that Michelet's texts make their most important demands of readers.[40] Just as the formal structure of the works seems to belie their thematic content, so their stylistic features contradict their explicitly prosaic nature. Michelet's language frustrates a literal reading. The texts constantly use interesting tropes, like the infant's brain in the fourth chapter of *La Femme*, but they then undermine these figures within a decidedly prosaic context.[41] The themes literally overwhelm the author's metaphorical impulses in these essays' natural imagery. Apparently, in writing each book in less than four months while busily engaged in other work, Michelet was not given to develop his figures fully.[42]

The problems created for readers by these tropes adapted to the essay form arise often in *L'Amour* and *La Femme*, but those posed by the less self-conscious play of oppositions in language intrude even more often. A major stylistic feature here is paradox, the most important example of which is the theme itself, the conflict between mind and body. The books are deliberate attempts to redress this opposition in the natural and social worlds. On the level of language, however, contradiction multiplies and may be found on nearly every page. The most evident concern differences between the sexes, what the texts term "a sweet harmonious combat" at one point and "a secret hostility" at another.[43] Similarly, the nature of women—"She has nothing but furnishes everything"—is as ambivalent as the relations between men and women: "She is his daughter . . . his sister. . . his mother," while he is "her father . . . her mother."[44] Less obvious but no less important contradictions concern the love and happiness found in pain and sorrow. For the narrative, "love is the *brother of death . . . the brother of suffering*," especially for the

---

[40] See Edward K. Kaplan, *Michelet's Poetic Vision: A Romantic Philosophy of Nature, Man, and Woman* (Amherst, 1977); and Linda Orr, *Jules Michelet: Nature, History, and Language* (Ithaca, 1976).

[41] Michelet, *La Femme*, 440–41.

[42] See Michelet, *Journal: Tome II (1849–1860)*, ed. Paul Viallaneix (1962), 458–94.

[43] Michelet, *L'Amour*, 61; *La Femme*, 517.

[44] Michelet, *L'Amour*, 68, 73; *La Femme*, 518.

woman in her first sexual relations and again later in childbirth. She loves her husband "for the blood that she sheds and for her torn flesh."[45] Accordingly, "one must suffer, love, think. That is the true life of humankind," but of women in particular, since they are ill in ways that men can never be.[46] Women are not simply invalids because of their monthly indisposition, however inescapable; but because in the social world without men they are incomplete, their moral as well as biological functions unfulfilled. In short, "*woman does not live without man.*"[47] In this paradoxical language—is Michelet to be taken literally or not?—the texts exaggerate the already ambiguous nature of the essay genre.

An even more troublesome generic element in the texts is the rapid and unexpected shifts in voice from the third to the first and second persons, from the most impersonal of scientific prose to the most subjective of personal statements. At one point the author reminisces, "I remember, like yesterday, how on the day after my grandfather's funeral, as it rained that night, my grandmother said in a tone that still makes me cry forty years later, 'My God. It's raining on him!' "[48] Elsewhere the author adopts a more objective pose: "One can say that even the best foundling hospitals are cemeteries. The one in Moscow saved 1,000 out of 37,000 in twenty years. The one in Dublin saved 200 out of 12,000, that is to say, one-sixtieth of the infants."[49] Moreover, the texts seem directed at a heterogeneous audience. In *La Femme* it is composed of young girls, older women, and unmarried men, all of whom are addressed as "ma fille," "madame," or "monsieur," as appropriate. The author also adopts a variety of personas, especially of the precise audiences that are expected to contest some controversial points. More often, the voices are paraphrased from sources both genuine and imaginary; nature itself is given a moment to speak its mind.[50] This medley of voices breaks up the surface of the expository prose, but it appears so frequently, sometimes indiscriminately, that it blunts the impact of its highly figurative language. The result is a normative tone rather than an illuminating vision.

Like the few readers of these texts today, those in 1859 and 1860 were often bored, but invariably puzzled by *L'Amour* and *La Femme*. Reviewers contemporary with the author found Michelet's language and subject matter contradictory, as if the texts had been written by more than one person. A number of reviewers discerned as many as three figures in the texts—a materialistic scientist, a moralistic poet, and a secular priest. For instance, in *La Revue des deux mondes*, Émile Montégut castigated this quality of *L'Amour*: "It is truly

[45] Michelet, *L'Amour*, 119, 130 (emphasis in the original).
[46] Ibid., 56, 62ff.
[47] Michelet, *La Femme*, 415 (emphasis in the original).
[48] Michelet, *L'Amour*, 205.
[49] Michelet, *La Femme*, 439.
[50] Ibid., 518.

the *Song of Songs* mixed up with treatises on physiology'' written by a man posing as doctor, poet, and moralist. But Michelet's book was ''too lyrical to be scientific and too scientific for poetry,'' while its conservative view of marriage made it ''for better or for worse essentially a catholic book.'' The result for Montégut was at best a platitude appropriate to neither science nor poetry nor religion: ''In the last analysis I do not know if the author wanted to recommend to the men of his time anything other than to be respectful and tender towards their wives.''[51] Montégut was not alone in this quandary over Michelet's genre. Most Second Empire readers could not clearly identify the author or the literary form he had adopted. As often as not, despite or even because of the literary features, readers chose to treat the works as marital guides with the disturbing characteristics of a medical treatise, a prose poem, and a new religious scripture.

All reviewers were concerned with labelling Michelet; most simply seized upon the most singular characteristic about the author in the normative qualities of the text and its genre. In this way, the largest proportion of published reviewers singled out in the books Michelet's apparent evangelism. For Léon Aubineau in *L'Univers*, *L'Amour* was the confusing expression of ''the Gospel of marriage. . . . To cite or to analyze here seems equally difficult. Refined filth, etherization of materialism, deification of sensuality, it is a little of all that.''[52] Nearly every critic shared this perspective. But if Michelet was for most reviewers an intrusive doctor of the soul, he was for others an equally imposing doctor of the body. ''The priest of love is doubled as a physiologist who in deference to his patients spares you not a syllable of his terrible science,'' stated Elme-Marie Caro.[53] Ironically, Michelet's prophetic work also represented a materialism whose nature required an uncomfortably close attention to female anatomy. For Second Empire reviewers, in part because of form, morality and science strangely coexisted in these texts.

There were, however, many fewer critics of Michelet the stylist in *L'Amour* and *La Femme*, a more difficult but less controversial subject. What appeared most often were oblique remarks about the poetic qualities of the prose. A physician, better informed than most reviewers about the fragile scientific basis of Michelet's work, commented, ''I beg the pardon of writers, but art in general and literature in particular exist only in physiological error. . . . Frankly, my future colleague, you write of childbirth just as I would write of history.''[54] But whatever the response, the works were not placed within the discursive context of Michelet's other belletristic writings on natural history.

[51] Émile Montégut, ''De l'amour et du mariage selon M. Michelet,'' *RdDM* n.s. 18 (1858): 934–35, 943, 949. Cf. collected reviews in Michelet, *Oeuvres complètes*, 18:285–360, 655–746.

[52] Léon Aubineau, ''L'Amour,'' *Univers* (16 Dec. 1858).

[53] Elme-Marie Caro, ''L'Amour,'' *Constitutionnel* (14 Dec. 1858).

[54] Charles Pajot, ''L'Amour,'' *Moniteur des hôpitaux. Revue médico-chirurgicale de Paris* 7 (1859): 169–70.

Only six of twenty-five selected reviews mentioned his other work, including the histories, even though *L'Amour* and *La Femme* have much in common with Michelet's earlier quasiliterary works on the bird (1856) and the insect (1857).[55] Rather, for Michelet's contemporaries his texts were a *sui generis* blend of mysticism and science in poetic trappings.

The most interesting published response to Michelet's essays was by a self-styled free-thinker, C.-P. Marie Haas, who wrote an entire book responding to *L'Amour* in 1859 (and another on *La Femme* in 1860).[56] A mid-level bureaucrat in the prefecture of the Haute-Marne and author of statistical studies of rural France, Haas attacked the first book at length for its patently secular perspective on love and women, one of the more common conservative criticisms of Michelet. What makes this extended analysis significant, however, is not its *ad hominem* criticisms or its emphasis on religion—these were prominent in nearly all reviews of controversial books in the period. Rather, it is how Haas responded to Michelet's text by *non sequitur* instead of by careful gloss. Illustrating this mode of reading a complex and undefinable genre, two passages in particular merit quotation in full, one by Michelet, the other by Haas in response to him:

Very often seated and pensive before the deep sea, I spied the earliest agitation, at first perceptible then sensible, growing and formidable, that recalled the tide flooding to the shore. I was preoccupied, absorbed by the immense electricity that floated over the army of waves whose crests glittered. But with still how much more emotion, with what religion, what tender respect, I noted the first signs— sweet, delicate, continuous, then painful and violent—of the nervous impressions that periodically announced the flux and reflux of that other Ocean, woman![57]

M. Michelet has had leisure in his life, a happiness we have not yet known. He has been able to sit on the cliffs that rise above the Ocean, to contemplate the movement of the agitated tide, the immense electricity floating over the numerous waves with glittering crests. He can still, before this fine spectacle, admire the grandeur of God's works and compose above all a hymn of thanksgiving. But this does not prove that the sea—calm, sensible, growing, formidable, and terrible— can resemble Woman. No, woman is not *an invalid, a suffering Ocean.* Woman is a creature of God, subject to the laws of her being, powerful mysterious laws that the *well-informed* man does not deny and does not reveal to the profane who misunderstand because they cannot comprehend—even with the help of modern chemistry.[58]

[55] Cf. Paul Viallaneix, *La Voie royale. Essai sur l'idée du peuple dans l'oeuvre de Michelet* (1971), 432–33.

[56] C.-P. Marie Haas, *L'Amour. Renversement des propositions de M. Michelet par un libre penseur* (1859); and idem, *La Femme. Réfutation des propositions de M. J. Michelet* (1860).

[57] Michelet, *L'Amour*, 62.

[58] Haas, *L'Amour*, 80–81 (emphasis in the original).

Evidently of no concern in contemporary readings of *L'Amour* and *La Femme*, however crucial to their achievement, was the language of Michelet's chosen genre, at once prosaic and metaphorical, scientific and lyrical. In the text's play of tropes, paradoxes, and voices, Haas sought only its most apparent persona. Here, for instance, he has reduced the work's complex surface to a literal statement of personal belief, presumably to demonstrate Michelet's materialistic denial of religious dogma despite the book's heavy-handed moralizing. The confusion that Haas and others like him felt in reading a difficult genre literally overwhelmed their sensitivity to the obvious but ambiguous literary features of the texts themselves.

This generic conundrum was equally evident in the letters sent to Michelet in the same years as the reviews. If anything, it was even more pronounced, perhaps because the correspondents had clearer ulterior motives in writing than did the reviewers. Most letters were from relatives, friends, or acquaintances inclined to like Michelet's work in the first place. More than ten percent of the letters expressed little more than glowing compliments. A fragment of one letter reported the enthusiasm of Alexandre Dumas *fils*; for him *L'Amour* was "one of the finest . . . and one of the most useful books in our time."[59] In another letter, Madame de Herrage wrote from Brussels, "You are a distinguished, noble, and great man! . . . Your book entitled *L'Amour* . . . is imposing in its veracity."[60] Similarly detached from Michelet's literary achievements were letters from irate readers (less than five percent of the total), whose criticisms closely resembled those in the reviews. "What good is this book that is nothing but an error from one end to the other?" asked one correspondent not quite brash enough to sign her name. "If I were the prefect of police, I would condemn Monsieur Michelet to go to Notre Dame, barefoot, the [penitent's] rope around his neck and a flame in his hand, to make honorable amends to the sex that he flagellates all the while it is prostrate at his feet."[61] Such emotive reactions required little or no understanding of genre or its language. Instead, they expressed a singular interest in the author's identifiable personality in the essays.

While even approving correspondents also reflected the same extraliterary concerns as the reviewers, especially the search for the author's true voice in the texts, they appreciated *L'Amour* and *La Femme* in a far more intimate sense. The works, however evangelistic or scientific, evoked in nearly every letter sent to the author a personal testimony of the book's importance to the correspondent's life. As if confessing in particular to Michelet the moralist, more than thirteen individuals included brief autobiographical sketches in their

[59] Anon. to Michelet, n.d., in BHVP Fonds Michelet, Tome 11, Liasse A4748 fol. 5. Cf. Michelet, *Oeuvres complètes*, 18:625–53.

[60] Madame la baronne de Herrage to Michelet, 15 Jan. 1859, in BHVP Fonds Michelet, Tome 11, Liasse A4748 fol. 13.

[61] Anon. to Michelet, 10 Mar. 1859, in ibid., fol. 24.

letters. Marie-Sophie Leroyer de Chantepie of Angers, for instance, wrote in imperfect French, ''Already your previous works have inspired in me an admiration for your fine character, an esteem mixed with confidence, that gives me the courage to ask of you the moral support that I lack.''[62] Leroyer de Chantepie then detailed how her education at the hands of religious fanatics had ruined her life and induced moral hallucinations. As a consequence, the only person in the world she could ever love was her ailing mother. Still hungry for the affection that fate had denied her, however, this ''old girl of 58'' had recently adopted a poor family as a surrogate for her own. Now Michelet's charming book, *La Femme*, had given her the courage to write for advice and consolation from a man whose work revealed him to be of high intelligence and good heart. ''Our appreciations are the same. Never has a novel [sic] so sharply impressed me!'' This personal, indeed intimate perspective appeared in more than half of the correspondents, all of whom felt compelled at least to explain why they were moved to take the liberty of writing the author. Despite the variety of other impressions they made, Michelet's works struck a responsive chord among more sensitive readers. While the reviewers were repelled by the author's apparent intentions, the correspondents were drawn more by the books' emotional suggestiveness. In either case, the unclear generic conventions left them without any sure guide through the texts.

The confusing literary character of *L'Amour* and *La Femme* thus seemed to have stirred their audiences in two ways: by drawing on the most personal experiences of some readers (like the correspondents), and by antagonizing the deeply felt prejudices of others (like the reviewers). For both groups, however, the texts' surface became almost a pretext for concerns that were not shared by the author or even expressed in his work. The reviews of his books and the letters sent to the author expressed a discernible disjuncture between the prosaically minded reader and the apparent literary text, one evident in the response of several feminist writers sensitive to the more obvious contradictions in Michelet's attitudes towards women. Five letters and two books addressed the moralist in the text and his conservative perspective on women's issues without very careful attention to the metaphorical features of what the author had actually written.[63] In this way they were, of course, not very different from other readers in the Second Empire, and certainly no more shrill than the males who attacked Michelet for other reasons. In a long letter on *La*

---

[62] Mlle. Marie-Sophie Leroyer de Chantepie to Michelet, 12 Aug. 1859, in ibid., fol. 14. Cf. Daniel Brizenue, ''Une Correspondance de Flaubert: Mademoiselle Leroyer de Chantepie,'' *Amis de Flaubert* 16 (1960): 3–12; 17 (1960): 3–10.

[63] See Adèle Esquiros, *L'Amour* (1860); Jenny P. d'Héricourt, *La Femme affranchie. Réponse à MM. Michelet, Proudhon, É. de Girardin, A. Comte et aux autres*, 2 vols. (Brussels, 1860); and letters in BHVP Fonds Michelet, Tome 11, Liasse A4748 by Angélique Arnaud (fol. 8); Aymé Cecyl (fol. 9); N. L. Trélat (fol. 11); Louise Mesnier (fol. 33); and Émilie Venturi (fol. 37).

Femme, for example, Angélique Arnaud complimented Michelet on his responses to her earlier review of *L'Amour* in *La Gazette de Nice*, including his now more sensible consideration of women's education before marriage, of their various strengths apart from men, and of their ability to think and act constructively. ''I have devoted my life to this question concerning woman's emancipation, regarding it as the capital question of the century, the pivotal center of human morality.'' And yet she reproaches Michelet, and men generally, for their ''systematic spirit: that is to pursue an axiom to its last consequences instead of elucidating well this point of departure,'' a proclivity that she herself and other readers shared. ''Your ideal of woman . . . is an arbitrary conception that can trouble her development and thereby falsify her nature.''[64]

Although it would be valuable for many reasons to pursue further the feminist critique of *L'Amour* and *La Femme*, its interest here is the type of generic response the feminists had in common with other readers contemporary with them, whatever the merit of their respective viewpoints.[65] For nearly all of them, the text was more a sounding board than an icon, its figurative language of apparently little or no import whatsoever in the readers' need to identify one or more of the author's personas—and by implication, the genre of the books he wrote. This extraliterary interpretive practice was expressed unconsciously but well by one anonymous correspondent who wrote in 1858:

> If the book *L'Amour* appeared Saturday, you must have received today Monday more than a hundred letters, for love calls and creates love. These letters, even those coming from the most unknown and obscure, you cannot ignore them, for they are a distant echo that responds to your powerful voice. . . . Considering your work like a book of moral medicine, I need to tell you how much I have been touched by the magnetic picture that you have drawn of *woman*, the queen of the home—I have known that woman.[66]

For this correspondent, the material on love naturally evoked an emotive response that was only ''a distant echo'' of the author's text, its power derived largely from the reader's relationship to his own mother. While the mysterious individual with the initials J.T.D.S.G. may not have realized the implications of his remarks, he suggested a style of reception typical of Michelet's documented audience. Reading essays in the past owed as much to personal predispositions for or against a particular expository voice as it did to the complexities of literature itself, especially in the absence of clear interpretive cues in the genre.[67]

---

[64] Arnaud to Michelet, in Michelet, *Oeuvres complètes*, 18:644–50.

[65] E.g., see Thérèse Moreau, *Le Sang de l'histoire. Michelet, l'histoire et l'idée de la femme au XIXe siècle* (1982), 105–44; and Jeanne Calo, *La Création de la femme chez Michelet* (1975).

[66] J.T.D.S.G. to Michelet, 22 Nov. 1858, in BHVP Fonds Michelet, Tome 11, Liasse A4750 fol. 29 (emphasis in the original).

[67] See Jonathan Culler, *On Deconstruction: Theory and Criticism after Structuralism* (Ithaca,

LITERATURE

Perhaps the oldest and most fully established literary form is drama. Since the fourth century B.C., when Aristotle's *Poetics* described ancient Greek comedy and tragedy, the theater has been a well-prescribed art.[68] Dramatists, actors, and spectators all know that a play almost invariably requires characters, action, dialogue, and a stage. From the seventeenth century onward, as the theater evolved as a public institution in France, drama became even more of a ritual, one with certain rules regulating its participants and the various roles they play on and off the stage. Elaborate costumes and props contribute as well to the theater's special interaction of illusion and reality in a variety of settings and situations. In time, however, these specific features of theatrical events have affected the way they are read as well as viewed. Drama reading has developed similar interpretive conventions, despite a variety of different audiences. Besides spectators, there have been censors, critics, actors, and other authors who responded to dramatic texts long before they were ever staged. Émile Augier's controversial play, *Le Fils de Giboyer* (1862), provides an excellent opportunity to study the formalities of drama reading among these particular communities. Their ample records show how important were their respective expectations of the play as a genre that obviously shaped their responses.

Augier's *Le Fils de Giboyer* itself is a five-act comedy of manners with two closely related plots.[69] The first concerns an elaborate political attack on France's secular University by a circle of monarchical sympathizers; the second concerns the attempt of the marquis d'Auberive to marry his natural-born daughter, Fernande, to his cousin, the comte d'Outreville. Both intrigues demand the cooperation of M. Maréchal, a wealthy middle-class deputy anxious to create an enduring alliance between the old aristocracy of blood and the new aristocracy of merit. The marquis d'Auberive and his political "committee," including the shadowy baronne Pfeffers, have arranged for Maréchal's recent election to the Legislative Corps, where he is to give an important speech setting out a new conservative political agenda. Because the deputy is politically inexperienced, the marquis has a talented but unscrupulous journalist, Giboyer, write the speech, and makes Giboyer's natural son, Maximilien Gérard, Maréchal's secretary. But the marquis has another reason to take a special interest in this provincial bourgeois: Maréchal's late wife was the

---

1982), 82–225; Harold Bloom et al., *Deconstruction and Criticism* (New York, 1979); and Josué V. Harari, ed., *Textual Strategies: Perspectives in Post-Structuralist Criticism* (Ithaca, 1979), 17–72.

[68] See Eric Bentley, *The Life of the Drama* (New York, 1967); Gaston Baty and René Chavance, *La Vie de l'art théâtral des origines à nos jours* (1932); and Paul Blanchart, *Histoire de la mise en scène* (1953).

[69] See Émile Augier, *Le Fils de Giboyer*, in idem, *Théâtre complet* (1895), 5:1–194.

marquis's mistress and had borne him a daughter, Fernande, whom Maréchal takes for his own. To continue his family fortunes, the marquis patronizes the new deputy and finds a socially acceptable suitor for Fernande. The two plots thus come together in the Maréchal household, where political and social ambitions during the Second Empire collide.

All the elements necessary to comedy appear in the play. The scheming marquis matches wits with the shrewd journalist and his equally quick-witted son. At stake is Maréchal's political allegiance and Fernande's hand in marriage. In the end, all of the aristocrat's plans miscarry, to the delight of everyone he tries to manipulate: Maréchal finds his true political interests with the liberals, and Fernande marries Giboyer's son with the marquis's and Maréchal's grudging approval. In the meantime, the play's dialogue and action cast an ambivalent light on each of the characters, including the obvious heroes and villains. In several scenes, especially with his grasping servant and the irredeemable baronne Pfeffers, the evil marquis actually shows considerable good humor, one clearly manifested in the last scene of the play when he settles his entire estate on Fernande and Maximilien's future children. Nor does the heroic Giboyer escape completely unscathed; at one point he confesses to the marquis his numerous moral compromises, all for the sake of his son: "It has pleased me to be a dung heap and to sustain a lily."[70] Similarly, Fernande is initially cold and haughty to Maximilien, who first appears on stage reading Lamartine's *Jocelyn* to please Fernande's swooning stepmother. It is hard to decide who is the more ridiculous, the reader or his audience. Even the dupe Maréchal develops a kind of dignity in his rebellion against the marquis and his political circle. His awakening moral conscience rescues his spineless though amusing performance earlier in the play.

Like all comedies, *Le Fils de Giboyer* resolves its conflicts in a community of love and sincerity.[71] Its other features are ultimately subordinated to this end. And so the monarchical political plot is central to the development of nearly every major character in the play: the marquis repents, the deputy defects, and the journalist finally triumphs over adversity. From the viciously insincere baronne to Fernande's sentimentally lascivious stepmother, each figure is a type essential to comic situations in nearly every scene. The baronne, for instance, shows Fernande a rug that she pretends to have hooked herself, but in fact Fernande had made the rug; she had given it to the poor woman who sold it to the baronne. Fernande then attempts to spare the hypocritical baronne the embarrassment that, of course, arises when Mme. Maréchal stupidly insists upon examining the rug herself. The false woman is reproved, and Fernande's genuine regard for others is generously highlighted. Moreover, the play uses witty language and clever scenic devices to ensure the

---

[70] Ibid., 47.

[71] See Wylie Sypher, ed., *Comedy* (Garden City, N.Y., 1956), 193–255.

comic effect intended by Augier, who, as a privileged sociétaire of the Théâtre français, knew precisely which actors would assume the roles he created. In an effort to save the marquis's marriage plans for Fernande, for example, Madame Maréchal tries to insult Maximilien, but misses her mark and insults the marquis's cousin instead. In short, *Le Fils de Giboyer* is a typical comedy of social manners following nearly all the conventions of a genre well known to readers, theatergoers, and actors alike.

Accordingly, interpretive communities all recognized Augier's text as a comedy, even though they emphasized aspects of particular interest to individual readers. Government censors, for instance, considered *Le Fils de Giboyer* a political satire. In a long, detailed report to the minister of state, four members of the official examining commission carefully analyzed the play's implications for Second Empire authorities, leaving the minister himself to decide whether or not the work should be staged.[72] What disturbed the censors most was the satirical treatment of monarchical and religious politics during the Second Empire. They felt that Maréchal's conservative speech, expressing perfectly honorable and widely held sentiments, was a source of ridicule. "In effect, in these doctrines presented as troublesome and retrograde, there is nothing more ordinary that the believer, the least fanatic and least fervent man, the most indifferent spirit in political and religious matters would concede." But the play presented these ideas as instruments of the counterrevolution, "a thesis as false as it is dangerous in the theater." Furthermore, the playwright satirized prominent people who were easily recognizable through their very thin disguises. Without mentioning the individuals by name, the censors singled out a Catholic polemicist, a former minister, and several members of the Legislative Corps. The comedy had turned the genre's most effective weapons against the government. As a literary form, the readers suggested, the play was perhaps too good a satire.

The censors paid particular attention to the work's comic language. They identified several offending passages to stress the serious implications of the playwright's humor. Indicated not once but twice for special concern was the marquis's description of Déodat, the staunch monarchical journalist, "this angelic pamphleteer, *conviciator angelicus*, this hussar of orthodoxy."[73] The censors also underlined the marquis's words about the comte d'Outreville the "sacristan" and Maréchal "the former Voltarian, liberal, and subscriber to *Le Constitutionnel*."[74] Although morality was not an issue, the report did highlight the play's explanation for Madame Maréchal's lewd behavior: "This is a novelistic but platonic person," the censors quoted the marquis. "Her hero is not obliged to participate in her novel. She persuades herself that she

---

[72] See report on *Le Fils de Giboyer*, 3 Oct., in AN F21,966 d. 1862.

[73] Cf. Augier, *Le Fils de Giboyer*, 5:15 (based on Louis Veuillot).

[74] Cf. ibid., 5:28, 19.

is loved, she delivers herself from terrible struggles, and in the end, she triumphs over her danger by sending the seducer to a better job."[75] This inflammatory tone throughout the play, the report noted, was insulting to the respectable political and religious sentiments expressed by this woman and her husband, "such as the hope for a better World, manifestly sensible ideas such as Faith and God assimilated by all the reasonings to which there can be no reply." In this way censors took one part of the play for the whole, but the satire remained an important feature of the genre all the same. And they may have been right: two months later, the prefect of the Haute-Garonne reported a series of disturbances at the play's performances in Toulouse; monarchical sympathizers had protested the work's insult to their political ideals.[76] The comedy apparently struck some funny bones too hard.

Drama critics, most of them hostile, were equally sensitive to genre in their reviews of *Le Fils de Giboyer*. A representative account of the play by Théodore de Banville criticized Augier's bourgeois, utilitarian conception of art's contribution to social progress. This was not the nature of true comedy, he felt. The actual originality of comic drama lies less in its use of contemporary issues, people, and situations—Augier's source of misplaced pride—than in a significant variation on established literary conventions—the real strength of great comedy. Although he dealt with current events, Banville noted, Augier had in fact borrowed even more heavily from the stock of comic themes, characters, and plots. None of Augier's figures was unusual; most had been taken from Murger's *La Vie de Bohème*, just as the situations came from Commerson's *La Famille improvisée*. Maréchal, for instance, was merely M. Prudhomme in different clothes. Consequently, according to Banville, Augier's comic characters were nothing new to the genre. "These are Parisians for provincials, what one calls, in tailor's jargon, ready-made. Paradoxical material, chimerical cuts, illusionary doublets, the whole tailored for patrons by the dozen."[77] In short, *Le Fils de Giboyer*, with all the features of a vaudeville, was nothing but vulgar hackwork. Despite staging his work at the Théâtre français, Augier was a slave to the lowest variety of dramatic expression.

Politically more conservative, Léon Lavedan echoed the same concerns expressed by Banville and the censors. "The reproach that everyone makes to Giboyer's father," wrote Lavedan, "is to have outraged defenseless men and

---

[75] Cf. ibid., 5:90.

[76] Prefect of the Haute-Garonne to the Minister of State, 11 Jan. and 1 Feb., in AN F21,996 d. 1863.

[77] Théodore de Banville, "Théâtres. *Le Fils de Giboyer*," *Boulevard* (7 Dec. 1862): 2. Cf. the dossier of criticism in [Evariste Thévenin], *Le Tour de France du Fils de Giboyer, ou Recueil complet des jugements exprimés par les principaux journaux politiques et littéraires de Paris, de la province et de l'étranger* (1864), and the controversy centered on Louis Veuillot, *Le Fond de Giboyer. Dialogue avec prologue et pièces justificatives* (1863).

disarmed parties.'' But in fact, the critic argued, Augier had committed a far worse sin: he had misunderstood the nature of satire. After devoting more than a third of his review to an anecdotal history of this comic form, Lavedan admonished the playwright for having divided the entire world into two groups, cads and dupes, and passed off this simplistic division as a comedy of manners. For the reviewer, satire was not merely ''the banal rehabilitation of the bastard and the bankrupt at the expense of the rich and the honest.'' All Augier's characters were ''a series of bad caricatures and a collection of false grotesques.'' Perhaps because he shared their political perspective, Lavedan bridled at the play's mockery of Catholics and monarchists. But he accused Augier of besmirching the principles of 1789, as well: ''He evidently hopes to have everyone believe that the immense majority of the nation is composed of intriguers, idiots, hypocrites, and rascals!''[78] As a result, Lavedan, like Banville and other reviewers, considered *Le Fils de Giboyer* a comic distortion; Augier had misunderstood the essential element of comedy, namely, its generosity in the interest of community—hence the antagonism of censors and critics alike toward the play.[79]

One interpretive community far from hostile to Augier's work included the directors and actors of the Théâtre français, where it was first staged. The theater's often fractious jury had accepted the play unanimously in September 1862.[80] Obviously the sociétaires had fewer qualms about either the genre or the playwright's particular contribution to it. But no record exists of their response to *Le Fils de Giboyer*.

Other plays by Augier had already been staged by the Théâtre français, and so this dramatist's work was formally exempt from preliminary readings. On the other hand, the theater's copious archives on many other plays like it provide insight into how actors read drama and the importance of literary form to their reading. The most important of these records are the preliminary reports of the theater's readers recommending whether the committee should even consider a manuscript submitted to the Comédie française.[81] Hundreds of these reports remain, as do some of the directors' individual written explanations for voting to accept or reject plays at the Opéra-comique, especially during the Restoration.[82] These precious records document the concerns that theater professionals expressed in their consideration of new plays. Here is ample

[78] Léon Lavedan, ''Théâtre français. *Le Fils de Giboyer*,'' *Correspondant* 21 (Dec. 1862): 831, 836, 837.

[79] See Henri Gaillard de Champris, *Émile Augier et la comédie sociale* (1910), 423–83.

[80] See the record of this vote in ''Théâtre français. Comité de lecture. 1859–1878,'' in BTF Archives de la Comédie française, Register fol. 109.

[81] See dossiers in BTF Archives de la Comédie française ''Rapports de lecture.'' Cf. anon., ''Le Comité de lecture,'' *Gazette anecdotique* 21 (15 Nov. 1894): 276–81; and H. Duveyrier to Eugène Scribe, 9 Dec. 1855, in BN NAFr 22549 fols. 275–76.

[82] See AN AJ13,1057, Liasse 1.

documentation of one marked interpretive style concerning a specific literary genre, a style very similar to that of the censors and the reviewers in its special attention to the dramatic features of the text.

The key question posed in each preliminary report was nearly always the same: Given a reasonably interesting idea, does the play develop it dramatically? Unfortunately for the author of one typical manuscript submitted in 1857 and again in 1872, the reader's answer was "no." The earlier report concluded,

> When the idea is original, the form that it takes in the work too often lacks force, luster, power. . . . It needs a larger brush, one less slow with more character, a less verbose style, a more animated sequence of scenes, and sometimes a more certain taste—in a word, a more constant preoccupation to disguise the straight line of its plot.[83]

Despite a different reader fifteen years later, the manuscript was accorded the same reception on the basis of considerably different criticisms: "One can reproach the play for its slight originality, the extreme slowness of its action that stops at useless scenes, on repetitions, with overdeveloped accessory characters, and that instead of advancing [it] always turns in the same circle."[84] In each case, the readers at the Théâtre français were especially attuned to a play's technical features. A work's subject matter received relatively brief consideration; its theme had to be sufficiently elevated and grand, its morality impeccable, and its interest topical and appropriate to a Parisian bourgeois clientele. But a play's structure, plot, pacing, language, dialogue, and other aspects specific to drama earned considerably more attention. When a reader waxed enthusiastic about *Croquenouille et Percinet*, a fantastic comedy considered in 1915, he praised its rich and gracious details, its skillful handling of delicious scenes, its irresistible good humor.[85] By comparison, its subject seemed unimportant.

A similar response appeared among those jury members who bothered to justify their votes for or against accepting new plays. The sociétaires of the Opéra-comique answered seven questions about each submission for several years during the Restoration.[86] Each question focused attention on aspects unique to productions at the Opéra: Was the work appropriate to the theater? Was it interesting? Was the action clear and well directed? Was the poetry suited to music? Was the suggested composer appropriate to the work required? What corrections should be made? And finally, was the play acceptable? Although most answers were simply yes or no, some of them provided

---

[83] "Rapport," *L'Article 762* (1857), in BTF Archives de la Comédie française "Rapports de lecture" d. Ar.

[84] "Rapport," *L'Article 762* (1872), in ibid.

[85] "Rapport," *Croquenouille et Percinet* (1915), in ibid., d. Cqry.

[86] AN AJ13,1057. Liasse 1.

more extensive consideration of the technical problems posed by the work. In the same period, the Opéra-comique's juries summarized their readings of new plays in a similar fashion. Explaining the acceptance of Capelle's *Le Mariage de poste* on January 17, 1823, a secretary noted, "The play is well written; it is managed with art; the poetry is smooth and gracious; but the subject is so thankless that it requires all the author's wit to handle it." Consequently, the jury asked the playwright to cut it by one act.[87] But like the preliminary readers of manuscripts at the Théâtre français, the directors of the Opéra-comique studied each play primarily as an instance of a particular genre, the drama. It is no accident that literary form shaped their response, just as it did for government censors and dramatic critics. Once again, genre defined response.

Aside from these institutional archives, there are few records of how other interpretive communities responded to Augier's play. Little of his personal correspondence remains.[88] But other playwrights, like Eugène Scribe, Arnold Mortier, and Georges Courteline, kept better track of the letters they received.[89] And their papers reveal a similar interest among readers in the special nature of drama. Albin Valabrègue's literary correspondents, for example, dwelt almost exclusively on the comic forms he had mastered. In response to a critical review of Sacha Guitry's *Je t'aime*, M. J. Vincent disagreed with the playwright. "Without intrigue and without plot," the play was neither "a theatrical revolution" nor "an absolutely new genre," as Valabrègue had contended. Rather, it was merely bad work; dramatic conventions, Vincent stated, were not so easily ignored in successful plays.[90] Similarly, Pierre Wolff protested that one of Valabrègue's works had a major problem: the fourth act was too short, only eight pages or five minutes of action, for an entirely new stage set. Why not simply make it a scene somewhere else in the play?[91] At various times, Maurice Ordonneau, Valabrègue's sometime collaborator, congratulated the dramatist on his latest work, such as one play that Ordonneau thought was "made according to the true formula."[92] All the dramatist's conscious craft went into Valabrègue's comedy, and nearly all his correspondents recognized its "ingeniousness," "logic," and "dexterity." The letters sent to Augier in December 1862 probably said as much about *Le Fils de Giboyer*.[93]

[87] "Rapport," *Le Mariage de poste*, 17 Jan. 1823, in ibid.

[88] Note the small archive of letters by Augier in the BTF.

[89] See letters to Scribe in BN NAFr 22544–52, to Mortier in BA MS. 13435, and to Courteline in BA MS. 13892.

[90] M. J. Vincent to Albin Valabrègue, 31 Dec. [?], in BA MS. 13597/97.

[91] Pierre Wolff to Valabrègue, n.d., in ibid., 153.

[92] Maurice Ordonneau to Valabrègue, 30 Nov. 1899 and 15 Dec. 1888, in BA MS. 13596/33 and 17.

[93] Cf. considerations of other literary genres. In poetry: Maurice Grammont, *Le Vers français*, 4th ed. (1937); Thierry Maulnier, *Introduction à la poésie française* (1939); and Henry A. Grubbs and J. W. Kneller, *Introduction à la poésie française* (Waltham, Mass., 1962). In prose fiction:

Genre was thus important to reading, to making sense of texts within specific contexts. As readers encountered a variety of written forms from street signs to sacred scripture, they often felt it necessary to classify them as a first step towards assessing their particular meanings. The import of personal letters depended upon a precise location in time and space; Anatole France's public protest thus elicited replies that were entirely appropriate to wartime Paris. Similarly, essays like Michelet's *L'Amour* and *La Femme* employed a much richer language to often confusing effect, at least for readers during the Second Empire; Michelet's play of tropes, paradoxes, and voices in these complex narratives challenged and ultimately embarrassed his contemporaries. And plays, especially comedies, followed rules essential to audience interest; Augier's *Le Fils de Giboyer* and comic productions like it made ample use of theatrical conventions—character types, amorous intrigue, and social satire—to insure the happy ending that readers had come to expect. Occasionally the interpretive cues provided by the text were missed, resulting in some curious responses, such as the reader challenging the author to a duel.[94] But these were aberrations. Most literate experiences resulted in a less violent interpretive practice, one that required the reader to recognize certain conventions specific to the text's genre.

These generic clues were never explicit rules, like those laid down for the censorship of correspondence during World War I. Nor were they necessarily the most important ones that scholars have studied. Rather, readers responded to the conventions that were most obvious to them as members of different interpretive communities—as literary critics, as public censors, as actual or presumed acquaintances of the author. Each group had its own expectation of what the text should do. But in most cases, whatever the readership, the letter was a personal message, the essay an authorial persona, and the play a conflict resolved. These generic expectations seemed to have been stable throughout the nineteenth and early twentieth centuries, even though reader response altered as genres and interpretive communities changed. In this way, then, readers negotiated the intricate relationship between text and context at the heart of historical interpretive practice. Specific generic rules, used by the text but identified by the reader, clearly defined the act of reading for a century or more in France after 1800.

Robert Scholes, ed., *Approaches to the Novel: Materials for a Poetics* (San Francisco, 1966); Philips Stevick, ed., *The Theory of the Novel* (New York, 1967); and Michel Raimond, *Le Roman depuis la Révolution* (1967).

[94] E.g., Mermeix, "Paris au jour le jour. Lundi, 29 mars. Robert Caze," *France* (30 Mar. 1886) on the duel between author Robert Caze and critic Charles Viguier; and a document, dated 20 Aug. 1876, settling Josué Milhaud's dispute with Albin Valabrègue, over the latter's article in *Égalité* (Marseille), in BA MS. 13598/2. Cf. V. G. Kiernan, *The Duel in European History: Honour and the Reign of the Aristocracy* (Oxford, 1986), 258–70.

Chapter 10

READING THE NOVEL

IN RESPONSE TO a proliferation of popular literature during the July Monarchy, Alfred Nettement wrote a series of critical essays on the serial novel.[1] A publicist with strong Catholic and legitimist sympathies, Nettement was especially outraged by the phenomenal success of Eugène Sue's *Les Mystères de Paris* (1842–43); he devoted all four of his "lettres à une femme du monde," first published in *La Gazette de France*, to deploring the threat that this work posed to the social order.[2] But in doing so, Nettement also felt the responsibility that all serious literary critics have to outline their analysis clearly, logically, and succinctly. "My observations bear on the conception, on the plan, on the outline of the book," he wrote. This analytical framework required Nettement to include commentary "on the types [that the novel] contains, on the author's literary procedures, on his style, on the morality of his work, [and] on the motives to which one must attribute its success."[3] Although some of these concerns, morality especially, no longer matter to most readers today, Nettement expressed a specific interpretive style, one as appropriate to prose fiction in general as it was to Sue's novel in particular. His other interests aside, this conservative writer responded self-consciously to the distinct nature of literary narrative. In effect, what Nettement did in his essays was to define the rules for reading the modern novel.

Nettement's attention to narrative conventions was far from complete; the work of recent reader-response critics is more extensive. Peter Rabinowitz, for example, has devoted the major portion of a book to the implicit rules that people follow in reading prose fiction.[4] What Nettement termed his "observations," Rabinowitz called the "rules of notice," the way in which a reader sorts out the relevant details from the plethora of stimuli in any narrative. The title, opening and closing scenes, and the like are important interpretive clues in every literary text, but especially in the novel because of all its extraneous material. Moreover, what Nettement called "conception," Rabinowitz termed the "rules of signification," that is, the work's larger meaning expressed in both form and content. Here narrative voice takes a leading role in defining

[1] See Edmond Biré, *Alfred Nettement* (1901).

[2] Alfred Nettement, *Études critiques sur le feuilleton roman* (1847), 1:231–330.

[3] Ibid., 1:236.

[4] See Peter Rabinowitz, *Before Reading: Narrative Conventions and the Politics of Interpretation* (Ithaca, 1987), 15–169. Cf. Wayne Booth, *The Rhetoric of Fiction* (Chicago, 1961), 23–148.

the reader's understanding of the work. Another set of Rabinowitz's rules appeared in Nettement's "plan" or map of the work's unfolding. As Rabinowitz argues, the narrative's "configuring conventions" guide reader response as it develops over time from the first to the last chapters. And finally, Nettement's "outline" prefigures Rabinowitz's "rules of coherence," or how a narrative suggests to readers its unity as a literary work. On this issue, the reviewer is clearly distinguished from the ordinary reader, since until recently the critic's main task has been to characterize the narrative as an artistic whole; few other people are so concerned with a novel's coherence.[5] Nevertheless, all readers, critics or not, are subject to the same rules in their encounters with prose fiction.

In this fashion, a nineteenth-century writer anticipated the ideas of a twentieth-century literary specialist. Like Rabinowitz, though with far less deliberation, Nettement outlined the conventions of reading a genre for every interpretive community. Both book reviewers and fan-mail writers responded appropriately not only to Sue's *Les Mystères de Paris*, but also to Gustave Flaubert's *Madame Bovary* (1857), Émile Zola's *L'Assommoir* (1877), and Anatole France's *Le Lys rouge* (1894). Over a fifty-year period, from late romanticism to early symbolism, actual readers followed the narrative's rules of notice, signification, configuration, and coherence, all fundamental features of the French novel as it developed in the nineteenth century. Each work made certain demands of its readers, who responded appropriately, depending upon their skills and the narrative's clues. Different audiences thus interacted with specific works in yet one more element important to the history of interpretive practice: the text itself.[6] The contexts of publishing, education, ideology, and culture all shaped the literate experience, as did the tradition of response within reading publics and the nature of various genres. This much is clear. But the text also played a major role; it guided the act of reading in ways that can be well documented historically.

NOTICE

As any literature teacher knows, long fictional narratives pose special problems to young readers: What are the most significant details? How are they distinguished from the irrelevant? Of course, significance depends much upon the reader's ultimate interpretation, but the text does provide some obvious

---

[5] See Frank Lentricchia, *After the New Criticism* (Chicago, 1980), 102–55; and Geoffrey H. Hartman, *Criticism in the Wilderness: The Study of Literature Today* (New Haven, 1980), 284–301.

[6] See Jane Tompkins, ed., *Reader-Response Criticism from Formalism to Post-Structuralism* (Baltimore, 1980); Susan Suleiman and Inge Crosman, eds., *The Reader in the Text: Essays on Audience and Interpretation* (Princeton, 1980); and Elizabeth Flynn and Patrocinio Schweickart, eds., *Gender and Reading: Essays on Readers, Texts, and Contexts* (Baltimore, 1986).

clues.[7] A reasonable narrative will help its audience to establish a hierarchy of detail, to privilege some information, in short, to suggest a framework of understanding. As literature, the novel naturally directs the reader's attention, even though the actual focus may shift somewhat from reader to reader. In most cases, people will attend to the title, to opening and closing scenes, and to dramatic changes in the course of the narrative. These are all common features of the modern novel. It is no accident, then, that French readers noticed and made good use of them in their responses. This is certainly true of Sue's audience for *Les Mystères de Paris*; this novel provoked considerable commentary from both the author's correspondents and his critics, who followed the rules of notice in the long narrative itself (especially its title, its first and last installments, and its shifts in theme, characterization, and setting). Each of these features guided the reader of Sue's text as it was published serially in the *Journal des débats* from June 1842 to October 1843.[8] Despite ambiguities, *Les Mystères de Paris* provided its readership the help it needed to make sense of an otherwise enormous and poorly conceived work.

In irregular biweekly installments, Sue spun out the diverse fates of a long list of characters. The novel had little unity of plot, structure, characterization, tone, or mood in its nearly 900 pages of narrative.[9] Rather, the work was organized episodically; its most consistent focus rested on the activities of Prince Rodolphe of Gerolstein in his quest for social justice in nineteenth-century Paris. A high-minded reformer, often disguised as a fan-painter in order to seek out honest but impoverished workers deserving of his charity, Rodolphe discovers his natural-born daughter, Fleur-de-Marie, whom he rescues from prostitution (despite the machinations of her hard-hearted mother, Lady MacGrégor). Before the resolution of this conflict, however, Rodolphe encounters the cutthroat Chourineur, the lapidary Morel, and the seamstress Rigolette—each of them possessing a heart of gold that an evil urban environment has endangered. Rodolphe rescues them, as well. But other characters are not so deserving: the brutal thief le Maître d'école and his ruthless accomplices, la Chouette and Tortillard; the grasping notary Jacques Ferrand; the homicidal Squelette; Calabash; and the widow Martial, among others. Like Lady MacGrégor, all of these evil figures seek to frustrate Rodolphe's generous designs, unsuccessfully, of course, in this deliberately melodramatic narrative. In the end, each villain dies. Otherwise, only the reiterated theme of

---

[7] See Rabinowitz, *Before Reading*, 47–75.

[8] See Eugène Sue, *Les Mystères de Paris*, ed. Jean-Louis Bory (1963), based on the text in the *Journal des débats*.

[9] See Jean-Louis Bory, *Eugène Sue. Le Roi du roman populaire* (1962), 243–97; Pierre Chaunu, *Eugène Sue et la Seconde République* (1948); Peter Brooks, "The Mask of the Beast: Prostitution, Melodrama, and Narrative," *New York Literary Forum* 7 (1980): 125–40; Georges Jarbinet, *Les Mystères de Paris d'Eugène Sue* (1932); and *Europe: Revue littéraire mensuelle*. *Eugène Sue* 60 (1982): nos. 643–44.

bleeding-heart social reform—by individual charity and not by political action—provides a modicum of aesthetic unity to the innumerable details competing for the reader's attention.[10]

But one important convention did help Sue's audience: the work's title. By its very nature, *Les Mystères de Paris* suggested a world unfamiliar to the literate bourgeoisie, whether or not they lived in the French capital. The novel's particular mysteries—the poverty, crime, vice, and violence so common among the laboring classes—were its most obvious subject matter, as many readers testified.[11] Wrote Désiré Laverdant in the Fourierist newspaper *La Phalange*, "M. Eugène Sue wanted to investigate the mysteries of a civilized capital."[12] And he was echoed by more than two-thirds of the novel's reviewers. Socialist, liberal, and conservative commentators alike noted the work's call to reform "the mysteries of injustice, . . . these mysteries in society and Parisian civilization," as Nettement put it.[13] Occasionally, hostile critics like the reviewer in the Catholic *L'Univers* mocked the author's depiction of immorality, "a secret that he ought to explain."[14] C.-A. Sainte-Beuve appropriately quoted the abbé Combalot of Saint Sulpice: "The mysteries of Paris ooze with crime."[15] Such confusion of title and subject was deliberate. But Sue's correspondents were more generous in their responses. An overwhelming majority of them singled out the work's truths. Charity workers like Caroline Angebert and an anonymous letter writer sent serious proposals for social reform thanks to the narrative's heavy-handed commentary.[16] Clearly, the title alerted these readers to this particular feature in Sue's bewildering text.

Another textual clue guiding readers was the novel's dramatic first installment set in Paris's criminal underworld, the dark streets and wineshops of la Cité. Within a week of its appearance, Laverdant noted this bold scene: "Monsieur Eugène Sue, in effect, has opened to the public those obscure and frightful cesspools that accumulate criminal scum, the precise types in jailbird hangouts where men from the prison hulks are given refuge, where crime is

[10] See Edward Tannenbaum, "The Beginnings of Bleeding-Heart Liberalism: Eugène Sue, *Les Mystères de Paris*," *Comparative Studies in History and Society* 16 (1981): 491–507; John Moody, *Les Idées sociales d'Eugène Sue* (1938); Marc Angenot, *Le Roman populaire. Recherches en paralittérature* (Quebec, 1975), 71–87; and Umberto Eco, *The Role of the Reader: Explorations in the Semiotic of Texts* (Bloomington, 1984), 125–43.

[11] See Louis Chevalier, *Labouring Classes and Dangerous Classes in Paris during the First Half of the Nineteenth Century*, trans. Frank Jellinek (London, 1973), 359–417.

[12] D.L. [Désiré Laverdant], "Feuilleton de la Phalange. Revue critique," *Phalange* (13 Nov. 1842), col. 961.

[13] Nettement, *Études critiques*, 1:239.

[14] Cited in D.L., "Feuilleton de la Phalange. Revue critique," *Phalange* (19 Feb. 1843), col. 1639.

[15] C.-A. Sainte-Beuve, *Chroniques littéraires (1843–1845)* (1876), 132. Cf. Alexandre Privat d'Anglemont to Sue, 30 May 1843, in BHVP Fonds Sue fol. 180.

[16] Caroline Angebert to Sue, 28 Feb. 1843, and Lecteur des Mystères de Paris to Sue, 28 Mar. 1843, in BHVP Fonds Sue fols. 96, 124.

contemplated, where trips to the gallows are prepared.''[17] This graphic setting earned the attention of other readers, as well. One woman unwilling to sign her name admonished the author for having frightened her by his work's opening action. It was much too threatening for sensitive people like her.[18] Similarly, two years later Jules Michelet complained, without mentioning the author or his text by name, that Sue's first pages had defamed the working people: "A great and terribly phantasmagorical talent [has] given, in lieu of our urban communities, the life of a place where the police keep an eye on former offenders and released convicts.''[19] Consequently, one of the novel's more notable features, the beginning, not only provoked its readers, but informed their views of the entire work as it unfolded for the next seventeen months. In actual interpretive practice, first impressions lingered.

Because of its privileged position in the text, the last word impresses at least as much as the first. And so as *Les Mystères* continued, installment after installment, book reviewers and correspondents often wondered when and sometimes how the novel would end. A hostile critic and a disgruntled letter writer both thought Sue's work "interminable.''[20] In *La Revue des deux mondes*, Paulin Limayrac wrote angrily, "M. Sue accumulates volume upon volume, and his pen once launched never stops.''[21] There seemed no obvious way for the work to conclude after hundreds of loosely linked episodes that, according to Nettement, made it "a nomad and vagabond narrative.''[22] Less hostile readers sometimes spoke of the sense of closure they experienced with each installment, despite the deliberate suspense invariably created by the last line, "To be continued in the next issue." Noted Laverdant, "M. Eugène Sue's fecundity is marvellous. Each chapter of his book contains the elements of an entire play or novel.''[23] But for the most part, the text provided few clues about its end until September 1843, when correspondents wrote of their impending disappointment. "Rumor has it that there will be several volumes. Is this true?'' asked Ernestine Dumont, who hoped that the news she heard would delay the return of Prince Rodolphe and Fleur-de-Marie to the principality of Gerolstein, the logical end to their adventures in Paris.[24] In a serial novel like Sue's, however, the reader's need for conclusion was continuously frustrated.

---

[17] D.L., "Feuilleton de la Phalange. Revue critique," *Phalange* (26 June 1842), col. 1235.

[18] Une Inconnue to Sue, 20 June 1842, in BHVP Fonds Sue fol. 19.

[19] Jules Michelet, *Le Peuple* (Lausanne, 1945), 28.

[20] See review in *Le Constitutionnel*, quoted in D.L., "Feuilleton de la Phalange. Revue critique," *Phalange* (19 Feb. 1843), col. 1639; and H.D. to Sue, 25 April 1843, in BHVP Fonds Sue fol. 151.

[21] Paulin Limayrac, "Simples essais d'histoire littéraire. IV. Le Roman philanthrope et moraliste. Les Mystères de Paris," *RdDM*, n.s. 2 (1844): 94.

[22] Nettement, *Études critiques*, 1:249.

[23] D.L., "Feuilleton de la Phalange. Revue critique," *Phalange* (29 Mar. 1843), col. 1903.

[24] Ernestine Dumont to Sue, 24 Sept. 1843, in BHVP Fonds Sue fol. 416.

Another novelistic feature that focuses the reader's attention is a shift in the narrative. Whenever a text adds new material or changes direction in the development of character or plot, the audience is sure to notice. As *Les Mystères* progressed, the narrative took up new themes, and Sue's readers responded. Most of them, like one anonymous correspondent, remarked the richness of the author's interests that invited suggestions of other worthy themes for him to develop. In this case, the reader proposed that Sue consider writing about a virtuous wife driven to prostitution by the incarceration of her husband for unpaid debts.[25] But most of the time, readers were surprised by the narrative's sudden shifts from one subject to another. Nettement complained of "continuous surprises." George Sand was hardly more indulgent: "This is a jumble of scenes that criss-cross, follow one another and seem to progress haphazardly, so vague and poorly indicated is its point."[26] Coming to the author's defense, Laverdant saw some merit in the text's many twists and turns: "M. Sue approaches the most incisive criticism of Society with a profundity, a wisdom, and an energy worthy of every glory; and if it is proclaimed only in the contrasts, it is solely because there are certain people who must be taught somehow by surprise."[27] However they reacted to shifts in Sue's work, readers noted them as the text grew longer and harder to understand as a unified narrative.

Besides material intrusions in the narrative—and occasionally long interruptions from installment to installment—readers noticed the work's change in setting.[28] As a German prince, Rodolphe also appears in elegant social circles, the *beau monde* of the French aristocracy, whose vices the narrative contrasts with those specific to the urban poor. "M. Eugène Sue has a manner," Laverdant wrote, "of comparing the fate of civilized people with the fate of beasts whose effect is striking and terrible."[29] The narrative's deliberate juxtaposition of these two worlds captured the attention of other readers, though rarely with Laverdant's evident enthusiasm. Louis Reybaud remarked, "The regions where the convict's language is spoken hold no more secrets for [Sue]; he has taken on the task of diminishing the distance that separates the criminal from the elegant world."[30] For another critic in *La Gazette de France*, the

---

[25] Anon. to Sue, 26 April 1843, in ibid., fol. 153.

[26] Nettement, *Études critiques*, 1:327; Eugène Faure [George Sand], "Les Mystères de Paris, par M. Eugène Sue," *Revue indépendante* 8 (1843), in Helga Grubitzsche, ed., *Material zur Kritik des Feuilletons-Romans, "Die Geheimnisse von Paris" von Eugène Sue* (Weisbaden, 1977), 43.

[27] D.L., "Feuilleton de la Phalange. Revue critique," *Phalange* (26 June 1842), cols. 1235–36.

[28] See Sophie Dorloclot to Sue, 30 April 1843, and Dr. Frédéric Maîtrejean to Sue, 7 July 1843, in BHVP Fonds Sue fols. 157, 261.

[29] D.L., "Feuilleton de la Phalange. Revue critique," *Phalange* (9 Dec. 1842), col. 1138.

[30] Louis Reybaud, "La Société et le socialisme. La Statistique, la philosophie, le roman," *RdDM*, n.s. 1 (1843): 806.

novel was nothing less than "a systematic attack" on the entire social order.[31] But the correspondents actually welcomed Sue's decision to bring Parisian high life and its problems into the work. When Clémence d'Harville first made her appearance in a March 1843 installment, two women wrote Sue to praise her fortitude in a tragically unhappy marriage. For Ernestine Dumont, this aristocrat was as much an example to the middle classes as Rigolette was to the laboring poor.[32] Meanwhile, Virginie Prignot could not praise Clémence's character enough, the same figure whom Nettement had called "la Goualeuse with 100,000 francs in dividends."[33] The narrative's sudden shift in focus, from the misery of the poor to the vices of the rich, was noted by contemporary readers.

Another major change remarked in the narrative was in the character of Fleur-de-Marie, whose motives intrigued Sue's audience. On the one hand, she was a prostitute, a fact that irremediably condemned her in the eyes of hostile respondents. Limayrac could not believe that the author had created this moral abomination: "Such is how the author imagines a prostitute in la Cité, innocent and completely candid, who in the novel's first chapter exercises her abominable trade and who at the end of the book becomes the princess of a royal court in Germany!"[34] Sand was similarly bemused: "What then does Fleur-de-Marie lack to be the most charming creature in modern poetry? The truth."[35] On the other hand, this character was a victim of circumstances beyond her control. More sympathetic readers seized on her relationship to Prince Rodolphe, surprisingly revealed in the twelfth installment of the novel, as evidence of her purity. "The prostitute breathes this frail and delicate grace that only privileged races breathe," stated Reybaud.[36] Given her parentage, she could do nothing truly wrong. The correspondents were particularly adamant in this conviction. Noted Castellane de Contades, "Marie . . . is a pretty person of whom you must be very proud."[37] Towards the end of the novel, readers worried about her fate. At least two people pleaded, in vain of course, that she not die.[38] Even though Fleur-de-Marie was not the central character in the novel, the narrative's unexpected revelations made her a much more prominent figure.

Fleur-de-Marie was only emblematic, however, of a much more pervasive feature that readers noticed in Sue's work: its thematic contradictions. The

---

[31] Anon., no title, *Gazette de France* (15 Feb. 1843).

[32] Ernestine Dumont to Sue, 13 July 1843, in BHVP Fonds Sue fol. 268.

[33] Nettement, *Études critiques*, 1:279; Virginie Prignot to Sue, 17 May 1843, in ibid., fol. 186.

[34] Limayrac, "Simples essais d'histoire littéraire," 87.

[35] Faure [Sand], "Les Mystères de Paris," 46.

[36] Reybaud, "La Société et le socialisme," 806.

[37] Castellane de Contades to Sue, 6 Sept. 1843, in BHVP Fonds Sue fol. 386.

[38] E.g., Dumont to Sue, 24 Sept. 1843, and Louis Jacquet to Sue, 15 Feb 1843, ibid., fols. 416, 83.

novel's title and dramatic changes in character, plot, and setting all indicated matters of import, but so did flagrant violations of narrative logic, the most obvious of which was the moral condition of the Parisian poor. While the text exonerated some characters like Fleur-de-Marie of personal responsibility for their acts, it condemned others like Lady MacGrégor and le Maître d'école, both of whom suffer painful deaths. There seemed no consistent rationale for the narrative's tone towards its characters. As Nettement put it, "M. Sue . . . has an astoundingly fecund imagination in finding excuses for the most blameworthy acts; and he pleads extenuating circumstances with a superiority that has assured him a fine place before the bar in a criminal court." Why should the reader, Nettement asked, respect le Chourineur, for example, who kills but never steals? He is an odious type, all the same.[39] Other readers could not accept the narrative's apparent "social fatality," or what Karl Marx called "false consciousness," at work in the narrative.[40] For those people better disposed to the author's theme, however, this illogic was more easily reiterated than explained. Wrote one anonymous correspondent, "*Les Mystères de Paris* . . . exposes the particular turpitudes and virtues that demonstrate the irresistible influence of legal and social institutions on the deterioration or amelioration of individuals."[41] This reader also noted the text's obvious contradictions, but chose to ignore their implications.

Obviously, then, Eugène Sue's documented audience did follow some important rules of notice. Both book reviewers and correspondents established a hierarchy of detail within an analytical framework of their own making, one most certainly guided by the text. These interpretive communities noted the work's title, *Les Mystères de Paris*, and explained what it seemed to mean; they remarked the first and last installments; and they responded to all disruptions in the narrative created by the introduction of new material, by unexpected changes in plot, character, and setting, and by various contradictions and inconsistencies in the work. Each of these features of Sue's text was noted by his audience, even though the significance of these features varied from one person to the next. Ideology undoubtedly intruded at this point, as many social and cultural commentators have observed recently, but Sue's readers first had to respond to the text.[42] What they saw there was in large part determined by the narrative itself, whose conventions directed attention to specific elements. Not surprisingly, the debate over *Les Mystères de Paris* concerned the details less than what those details meant. The details themselves were never in question; they were all too evident to readers in 1843.

[39] Nettement, *Études critiques*, 1:267, 295.

[40] See Karl Marx and Friedrich Engels, *The Holy Family; or The Critique of Critical Criticism*, trans. Richard Dixon and Clemens Dutton (Moscow, 1975), 218–21.

[41] Anon. to Sue, 18 Aug. 1843, in BHVP Fonds Sue fol. 338.

[42] Cf. titles in note 10 above.

SIGNIFICATION

Another set of rules implicit in the novelistic text facilitates the reader's sense of its significance.[43] Beneath the literal surface, the narrative requires the attentive reader to answer a series of questions that suggest a limited range of interpretations: Who is speaking—the author, a character, a narrator, or someone else? What is one to make of that voice's judgment of character and action? Who is that voice addressing? What does the text expect the reader to assume, and why?[44] In making sense of fictional narratives, every reader needs to consider these conventions. This is especially true of Flaubert's *Madame Bovary*, whose interest arises directly from the different answers readers give to the questions it poses. Flaubert's free, indirect style removes the author almost completely from the narrative and frustrates all pat conclusions drawn from the most apparent voice in the text. Similarly, the narrative seems not to judge so much as to ridicule the characters, good and bad alike, leaving its audience unsure whom it is addressing. In short, the text's assumptions are ambiguous. Readers are therefore left without the assurances that one expects from works like Sue's *Les Mystères de Paris*. An examination of the actual responses to *Madame Bovary* highlights the narrative conventions of signification, largely because of their ambiguity throughout Flaubert's creative work.

The story itself is not difficult to summarize: Emma Bovary's adulterous infatuations with a local squire and a law clerk in a small provincial town lead in the end to her suicide and her disillusioned husband's premature death. But the narrative is much more complex. The critical problems it poses have been the object of considerable attention since the work's publication in *La Revue de Paris* in 1856.[45] Despite Flaubert's apparent intention to portray an incurable romantic—a victim of her extravagant novel-reading at odds with her more prosaic world—*Madame Bovary* undermines the very ground on which this simple moral lesson stands. The reader is distanced from every character, including the heroine, by long detailed descriptions of surface detail provided by an utterly impersonal narrative voice. The result is confusion over what moves the characters. For the most part, their motives are inscrutable. Readers learn more explicitly about Charles Bovary's hat, for instance, than they do about the man's relationship with his wife; the audience is left alone to relate externals without guidance from the narrator. For this reason, the rules of sig-

---

[43] See Rabinowitz, *Before Reading*, 76–109.

[44] See Booth, *The Rhetoric of Fiction*, 169–398.

[45] See Bernard Weinberg, *French Realism: The Critical Reaction 1830–1870* (New York, 1937), 159–76; Raymond Giraud, ed., *Flaubert: A Collection of Essays* (Englewood Cliffs, N.J., 1964), 88–140; Benjamin Bart, ed., *"Madame Bovary" and the Critics: A Collection of Essays* (New York, 1966); and R. Debray-Genette, ed., *Flaubert: Miroir de la critique* (1970).

nification in Flaubert's text are never very clear, and his contemporary reading public responded accordingly.[46]

From the very first page, *Madame Bovary* challenged its readers to identify the narrator.[47] The style was so impersonal that few of Flaubert's contemporaries could easily characterize its voice. Like most critics, Edmond Duranty disliked the narrative that was "always material description and never personal impression."[48] There was a sterile, antiseptic quality to what Léon Aubineau called "a medicinal style," because the narrative seemed so tightly controlled, crafted, or more precisely, tooled like a jewel.[49] Its language, Granier de Cassagnac remarked, was "full of ease, clarity, and force. It is supple without softness, correct without pedantry, concise without harshness. It is a firm and noble instrument."[50] That tool, however, was not a pen but a scalpel—both Paulin Limayrac and Marie-Sophie Leroyer de Chantepie borrowed Sainte-Beuve's famous surgical analogy—probing the hearts of the novel's characters "without tenderness, without idealism, without poetry, and . . . without soul."[51] Although Flaubert's correspondents were more comfortable with this cold narrative voice, they recognized its impersonality as well as the critics had. As a result, Edmond About wrote Flaubert, "From the first pages of your novel, one recognized the true life of the provinces studied up close," its stylistic objectivity a matter otherwise unexceptionable to the author's friends and family.[52]

Who, then, was speaking in the narrative? Few people claimed to know for sure. While readers answered the question variously, most of them turned to science for their terms. "M. Flaubert is not only a painter who has mistaken his vocation," wrote Gustave Merlet, "but a surgeon who applies to character analysis the cruel cold-bloodedness of an anatomist."[53] Only physicians

[46] Cf. Dominick LaCapra, *"Madame Bovary" on Trial* (Ithaca, 1982), 126–49.

[47] Cf. Francis Steegmuller, *Flaubert and Madame Bovary: A Double Portrait* (New York, 1950); Jonathan Culler, *Flaubert: The Uses of Uncertainty* (Ithaca, 1974); and Michael Riffaterre, "Flaubert's Presuppositions," *Diacritics* 11 (1981): 2–11.

[48] Edmond Duranty, "Nouvelles diverses," *Réalisme* (15 Mar. 1857): 79.

[49] Léon Aubineau, "Variétés. G. Flaubert et Paul Destuf," *Univers* (26 June 1857), in René Dumesnil, *"Madame Bovary* et son temps," *MdF* (1 Dec. 1911): 473.

[50] Adolphe Granier de Cassagnac, "La Bohème dans le roman. *Madame Bovary,*" *Réveil* (16 Jan. 1858), in Dumesnil, *"Madame Bovary* et son temps," 479.

[51] Paulin Limayrac, "Des causes et des effets dans notre situation littéraire," *Constitutionnel* (10 May 1857), in Dumesnil, *"Madame Bovary* et son temps," 468; Marie-Sophie Leroyer de Chantepie to Flaubert, 18 Dec. 1857, BSL H.1364 (B.IV) fols. 229–30; C.-A. Sainte-Beuve, *"Madame Bovary,"* *Moniteur universel* (4 May 1857), in *Causeries du lundi* (1869), 13:349, 350; and Jules Barbey d'Aurevilly, "M. Gustave Flaubert," *Pays* (6 Oct. 1857), in René Dumesnil, *La Publication de "Madame Bovary"* (1927), 116–17.

[52] Edmond About to Flaubert, [1857], in Flaubert, *Oeuvres complètes: Madame Bovary* (1930), 525.

[53] Gustave Merlet, "Le Roman physiologique. *Madame Bovary* par M. Gustave Flaubert,"

would write such prose that contained "neither emotion, nor sentiment, nor life."[54] Sainte-Beuve used the same medical terminology in his assessment of the novel: "Son and brother of distinguished physicians, M. Gustave Flaubert holds the pen as others hold the scalpel. Anatomists and physiologists I still find you everywhere!"[55] Others agreed; they called the narrator a sawbones [carabin], an entomologist, and a mathematician.[56] Almost all critics, both friendly and hostile, recognized the detached scholarly features of Flaubert's apparent narrative persona. The more poetic voice at work in the text was hardly ever mentioned, except among the author's correspondents, who, like René de Marcourt, made the narrative into a sacred script: "I read and reread you as a true believer reads the *Imitation [of Christ]*," he wrote.[57] Otherwise, the voice speaking in the text could be none other than Flaubert himself, a logical resolution of the puzzle posed by the narrative's implacable, impassive surface that few readers liked, much less understood, whatever the terms they used to describe it.

In fact, the most common response to the narrative voice in *Madame Bovary* was to call it Flaubert's. Confusing narrator and author was, of course, habitual in the nineteenth century; readers often claimed to hear novelists in their texts throughout the period. But Flaubert's audience persisted despite the impersonality of the author's prose. Jean Rousseau, a critic for *Le Figaro*, spoke for many readers when he wrote, "There is in M. Gustave Flaubert's novel a forgotten character and that it does not name: it is the author."[58] As a rule, Flaubert's correspondents addressed both author and narrator; Charles Toirac, Ulric Guttinguer, and Champfleury, for instance, all considered Flaubert the narrator in this "fine study of the period, mores, [and] feelings."[59] "An author ordinarily puts his heart and soul into his work," Leroyer de Chantepie stated emphatically, "for this work is himself."[60] Consequently, even critics who decried the narrative's free, indirect style still tended to see the author in the text. Wrote M. Dumesnil in *La Chronique artistique et littéraire*, "Ma-

---

Revue européenne (15 June 1860), in idem, *Le Réalisme et la fantaisie dans la littérature* (1861), 114.

[54] Duranty, "Nouvelles diverses," 79.

[55] Sainte-Beuve, "*Madame Bovary*," 13:363.

[56] Edmond Texier, "Chronique littéraire," *Illustration* (9 May 1857), in Flaubert, *Oeuvres complètes: Madame Bovary*, 536; Barbey d'Aurevilly, "M. Gustave Flaubert," 119; and Duranty, "Nouvelles diverses," 79, respectively.

[57] René de Marcourt to Flaubert, 30 Dec. 1866, BSL H.1364 (B.IV) fols. 286–91.

[58] Jean Rousseau, "Les Hommes de demain. II. M. Gustave Flaubert," *Figaro* (27 June 1858).

[59] Ulric Guttinguer to Flaubert, [1857], in Dumesnil, "*Madame Bovary* et son temps," *MdF* (16 Nov. 1911), 312. Cf. Charles Toirac to Flaubert, 30 April 1857, BSL H.1364 (B.IV) fols. 60–61; and Champfleury to Flaubert, [30 Jan. 1857], BSL H.1361 (B.I) fol. 302.

[60] Leroyer de Chantepie to Flaubert, 15 Mar. 1857, in Flaubert, *Corr.*, ed. Jean Bruneau (1980), 2:680.

dame Bovary remains no less than one of the most curious and most personal works of our time."[61] Neither the prosecuting nor the defense attorney during Flaubert's obscenity trial ever made the critical distinction between the author and his narrative, for an obvious reason: the law held writers responsible for their language. "The principal accused," declaimed Ernest Pinard, "is the author, M. Flaubert."[62]

Some readers did make a distinction between the author and the narrative voice, and thereby understood better the significance of Flaubert's accomplishment. As Sainte-Beuve put it, *"Madame Bovary* is above all a book, a well-considered and composed book, where everything is in its place, where the pen leaves nothing to chance, and in which the author, the artist rather, has done precisely what he wanted from one end to the other."[63] By distinguishing the artist from the author, Sainte-Beuve implicitly distinguished the narrative from Flaubert. Similarly, Rousseau noted "the style of artist and poet where the picturesque word and image abound." These words and images, Rousseau thought, were prominent features of the text, not the author.[64] In this way the work took on a different meaning, one that A. A. Cuvillier-Fleury remarked in his careful review of the book:

> The scenes of a singular boldness and revolting crudeness abound in M. Flaubert's work. Has the author put them there complacently? In fairness, no, and I believe as well that once given the heroine's character, the situations force her author willy-nilly into these perilous analyses.[65]

The result was a new truth, a new realism in the novel that had never existed before. Readers were left to draw their own conclusions from the narrative, written in what Jules Habans called "the language of the daguerreotype."[66] The author was simply the photographer, his novel the reproduction of the world in which everyone existed.[67]

Because there was indeed a voice distinct from the author's addressing a different audience in the text, readers sought its judgment of the characters and their behavior. Some critics, like Charles de Mazade had difficulty assessing it: "This novel evidently contains an idea, a social thought, in such a way that it is not easy to disentangle."[68] But most people had no trouble discerning

[61] Dumesnil, note, *Chronique artistique et littéraire*, in Flaubert, *Oeuvres complètes: Madame Bovary*, 534.

[62] Ernest Pinard, "Réquisitoire," in Flaubert, *Madame Bovary*, ed. Édouard Maynial (Garnier frères edition, n.d.), 344.

[63] Sainte-Beuve, "*Madame Bovary*," 13:347.

[64] Rousseau, "Les Hommes de demain."

[65] A. A. Cuvillier-Fleury, "*Madame Bovary*," *Journal des débats* (26 May 1857).

[66] Jules Habans, "*Madame Bovary*. Roman par M. Gustave Flaubert," *Figaro* (28 June 1857) in Dumesnil, "*Madame Bovary* et son temps," *MdF* (1 Dec. 1911): 475.

[67] Jacques ? to Flaubert, 28 April 1857, BSL H.1364 (B.IV) fol. 349.

[68] Charles de Mazade, "Chronique de la quinzaine," *RdDM* (1 May 1857): 218.

the implicit narrator's often bitter mockery. Despite the impersonality of the text written by "a stone pen," reviewers like Nestor Roqueplan found "an excellent store of irony, taste, and feeling."[69] "Irony is always just beneath the surface," wrote Sainte-Beuve, so much so that it tended to outright ridicule. "The raillery of a systematic hostility" was aimed at nearly every figure in the text.[70] "At heart M. Gustave Flaubert is a satirist," noted Cuvillier-Fleury.[71] Flaubert's correspondents remarked this feature of the narrative as well, one perhaps too harsh toward life in the provinces and the people who live there.[72] One correspondent simply stated, "I have also known this large and fine egoist of a farmer; this ridiculous bourgeois who discusses, judges, and settles without knowing anything . . . ; this avid and clever merchant who dupes you while he obliges you; and these young men ready to profit by a woman's weaknesses."[73] Consequently, Leroyer de Chantepie told Flaubert that the book's moral lesson was clear to all who had eyes to read: come what may, wives must be faithful to their husbands.[74]

But matters were hardly so clear to people less kindly disposed to the narrative's ironic stance. Those readers who confused author and narrator were particularly harsh in their response to the book's apparent (im)moral tone. Jules Barbey d'Aurevilly, a recent Catholic convert, wrote, "M. Flaubert is too intelligent not to have in himself firm notions of right and wrong, but he invokes them so rarely that one is tempted to believe that he does not have them."[75] Other reviewers threw up their hands in frustration and declared the book obscene. "Art ceases the very moment it is invaded by filth," opined Aubineau.[76] Both Pontmartin and Granier de Cassagnac considered the novel nothing less than a poison, like democratic politics, sure to destroy French society.[77] Other critics condemned the work's cruel, often lascivious irony. Nettement called the novel "a long calumny against human nature"; Émile Chevalet deplored its cynicism, "the crudeness with which M. Flaubert presents us licentious scenes."[78] To the extent that the narrative voice seemed to

[69] "Une Plume de pierre," according to Barbey d'Aurevilly, "M. Gustave Flaubert," 118. Cf. Nestor Roqueplan, "Courrier de Paris," *Presse* (16 May 1857), in Flaubert, *Oeuvres complètes: Madame Bovary*, 534.

[70] Sainte-Beuve, "*Madame Bovary*," 13:358; Merlet, "Le Roman physiologique," 118.

[71] Cuvillier-Fleury, "*Madame Bovary*," in Flaubert, *Oeuvres complètes: Madame Bovary*, 531.

[72] Anon. to Flaubert, n.d., BSL H.1366 (B.VI) fols. 347–48.

[73] Jacques ? to Flaubert, 28 April 1857, BSL H.1364 (B.IV) fol. 349.

[74] Leroyer de Chantepie to Flaubert, 18 Dec. 1857, BSL H.1364 (B.IV) fols. 229–30.

[75] Barbey d'Aurevilly, "M. Gustave Flaubert," 117–18.

[76] Aubineau, "Variétés. G. Flaubert et Paul Destuf," 473.

[77] Armand de Pontmartin, "Le Roman bourgeois et le roman démocratique. MM. Edmond About et Gustave Flaubert," *Correspondant* (25 June 1857), in Flaubert, *Oeuvres complètes: Madame Bovary*, 533; and Granier de Cassagnac, "La Bohème dans le roman," 479.

[78] Alfred Nettement, "Gustave Flaubert," in *Le Roman contemporain* (1864), 123; and Émile

judge, its treatment of Emma seemed too severe, too superfluous in fact for prose realism; she was too trivial an individual to die in the end.[79] Only a handful of friendly critics and correspondents, like Frédéric Baudry, accepted the narrative voice's moral judgment.[80] Otherwise, whether or not readers recognized the integrity of the narrative, *Madame Bovary*'s apparent significance was sharply criticized. Its voice, its audience, and thus its meaning were not so easily discerned.

Given the text's ambiguous rules of signification concerning its narrative voice, readers sought what understanding they could. In his shrewd review of *Madame Bovary*, Charles Baudelaire identified the most common interpretive difficulty that Flaubert's audience encountered: "It is for the reader to draw conclusions by inference."[81] The text provided insufficient interpretive clues and thus forced readers to assess the novel's meaning all by themselves. Rousseau touched on this problem when he wrote, "A suspicion has come to me several times in running through this book: it is that I have not read a novel but a memorandum. . . . That would explain the faceless characters and banal situations—and at the same time it would also explain the minute care with which the author details these trivialities."[82] For Rousseau there were no causal links between the items on this aimless list of details. Rational explanation of the story also defeated Gustave Vapereau: "The entire unity of the book is in the heroine's character," he wrote, "and there is nothing sadder than such a unity; it is fatality, always fatality in its many different guises."[83] But this inevitability did not shed much light on either Emma's behavior or the lesson the reader was to draw from it. "From the heroine's first false step, you know that she was born and that she will die a *courtisane*. That is the sole formula that explains it."[84] The audience found no other source of meaning in a literary world without explicit suggestions from the narrative.

Second Empire readers, then, were troubled because the rules of signification in *Madame Bovary* were unclear. Few members of Flaubert's documented audience could make sense of the narrative voice; after the first chapter, in which the author seemed to be simply another figure in the novel, the narrator disappeared altogether. What voice there was, however, created an uncomfortable distance from the characters and their activities; the implicit narrator was detached, ironic, often satiric. This distant voice refused to assess or to

---

Chevalet, "*Madame Bovary*," *Les 365. Annuaire de la littérature et des auteurs contemporains, par le dernier d'entre eux* (1858), 193.

[79] Rousseau, "Les Hommes de demain."

[80] Frédéric Baudry to Flaubert, 30 Dec. 1856, in BSL H.1361 (B.I) fols. 122–23.

[81] Charles Baudelaire, "*Madame Bovary* par Gustave Flaubert," in Baudelaire, *Oeuvres*, ed. Y.-G. LeDantec (1954), 1008.

[82] Rousseau, "Les Hommes de demain."

[83] Gustave Vapereau, *L'Année littéraire et dramatique*. Première année 1858 (1859), 53.

[84] Merlet, "Le Roman physiologique," 131 (emphasis in the original).

judge any aspect of the story, except perhaps to ridicule good intentions and provincial life. Consequently, there was no causal or moral explanation that Flaubert's readers could identify with confidence in the plethora of textual detail. In an underdetermined text such as *Madame Bovary*, the normal conventions assisting, directing, guiding readers to some understanding of the author's achievement were obscure; and the response was confusion, frustration, bemusement, and for many readers, anger. Indeed, much of the moral outrage over the novel when it first appeared stems, in part at least, from these ambiguous features of the text. The ordinary narrative rules clearly defining its meaning simply did not apply in this case. Flaubert's audience made what it could from a text that permitted the Second Empire's moralism to determine its meaning.

CONFIGURATION

A third set of rules important to reading prose fiction made possible answers to a single question: How will this narrative, in all probability, work out?[85] As a novel unfolds, it typically creates expectations about its course and outcome. All characters generate speculation about the rewards the story holds in store for them; in most narratives, crime is punished and virtue rewarded. An audience naturally assumes a moralistic universe unless the text drops hints along the way that its world is structured differently. When a story fools the reader and belies these preliminary predictions, the response is either surprise or discomfiture, usually both. A reader's tolerance for reversals, for betrayals of expectations derived from the text, is often very limited. This is true for the novel's most prominent features—its characters, plot, and setting—on which a literate audience focuses its greatest attention from the very beginning. Most expectations concern who does what and where in the novel. One can see these rules at work in the responses to Zola's *L'Assommoir* when it was published both serially and in book form in 1876–77.[86] Here readers recognized the author's programmatic preface at work; they reacted sharply to how it seemed to achieve his stated intentions; and finally, they drew their conclusions from what they learned of Gervaise, Lantier, Coupeau, and their life in Paris. In this way Zola's audience responded to the conventions appropriate to the author's evolving narrative.

    L'Assommoir provided its audience ample indication of the characters' im-

---

[85] See Rabinowitz, *Before Reading*, 110–40.

[86] See Léon Deffoux, *La Publication de "L'Assommoir"* (1931); Jacques Dubois, *"L'Assommoir" de Zola. Société, discours, idéologie* (1973); Jacques Allard, *Le Chiffre du texte. Lecture de "L'Assommoir"* (Montreal, 1978); and Henri Mitterand, *Le Renard et le signe. Poétique du roman réaliste et naturaliste* (1987), 209–29.

placable fate.[87] Once reaching Paris, Gervaise and her lover Lantier are destined to a difficult working-class existence. An incurable idler, Lantier leaves Gervaise to support their two children by herself. The struggling woman then marries Coupeau, a zinc worker, and together they manage a brief prosperity after Gervaise opens her own laundry business on borrowed money. But their life is troubled by heredity and circumstances beyond their control. Coupeau is badly injured in a roofing accident and turns to drink, squandering all of Gervaise's savings from the shop. Soon she, too, takes up drinking and loses customers. At Coupeau's suggestion, Lantier returns; he moves in with the unfortunate couple until they can no longer support him. Gervaise's laundry fails, Coupeau dies of delirium tremens, and Gervaise's rotting body is found soon afterward in a staircase closet. From the start, these characters have all too little chance to defy either the alcoholism they inherit or the environment they inhabit. The narrative presents an unrelieved portrait of Parisian brutality and degradation from which there is no escape. As the story develops, it draws the reader inexorably into the lives of its characters and their point of view; the narrative thereby creates a pessimism as unavoidable as the sympathy the reader feels for these apparent victims.

As one would expect, Zola's readers responded to the plot's inevitable course. Those people who felt that everyone is a responsible moral agent naturally condemned this feature of the narrative. "Beginning with this book *L'Assommoir*," wrote Barbey d'Aurevilly, "M. Émile Zola—and for me this is hardly praise—must be taken for the most accentuated, the most resolute, the most systematically exaggerated realist in a literature that has a heart for nothing and a heart sick from nothing."[88] By 1877 realism had become a more neutral term for Zola's deliberately provocative naturalism, a literary project first outlined in his "Le Roman expérimental." Because of naturalism's focus on the working class, however, Armand de Pontmartin objected as a matter of political principle: "M. Zola's work is the Republic."[89] And *L'Assommoir* was no exception; from the first page onward, it fit the mold perfectly. Consequently, when Anatole France reviewed the novel, he began with an overview of the author's previous work; for him *L'Assommoir* appeared in what was by then a predictable pattern.[90] Zola's naturalistic colleagues took up the same theme in their response to the novel. Observed Louis Jacquet, "*L'Assommoir* is thus not a novel for little girls, nor for prudes . . . but it pleases

---

[87] Cf. David Baguley, "Event and Structure: The Plot of *L'Assommoir*," *PMLA* 90 (1975): 823–33; and Auguste Dezalay, *Lectures de Zola* (1973).

[88] Jules Barbey d'Aurevilly, "Zola. *L'Assommoir*," *Le XIXe siècle. Des oeuvres et des hommes*, ed. Jacques Petit (1966), 2:278.

[89] Armand de Pontmartin, "M. Émile Zola," *Nouveaux samedis* (1877): 326.

[90] Anatole France, "Variétés. Les Romanciers contemporains. M. Émile Zola," *Temps* (27 June 1877).

us, this novel where we find a living reality."[91] For readers like Jacquet and Zola's correspondents, literary expectations extraneous to the text itself complemented well the certain progress of the story and its characters.

So predictable did *L'Assommoir* seem to its original audience, critical reviews of it appeared long before the last serial installment in *La République des lettres*. Only one critic, Albert Wolff, admonished his colleagues for judging a work still in progress.[92] But this tendency to anticipate Zola's work continued unabated. Henry Houssaye expressed his disappointment in terms as unoriginal as he felt the author's work: "And it took M. Zola," he wrote sarcastically, "six hundred pages of close text to recount such an epic and to come to this new conclusion, that evil conduct engenders misery!"[93] Zola's severest critics expected and were not disappointed by his new work's ignoble material, which rendered all literary art impossible, according to Barbey d'Aurevilly.[94] The vast majority of reviews, however, noted the narrative's clear and unimpeded course. "From the perspective of the work's unity, of continuous plot development," remarked Jacquet, "this book is one of the best made that we have ever read."[95] Jacquet was particularly put out by the interruption of the novel's serialization in midstream when *Le Bien public* turned it over to *Le République des lettres*. Even more than the critics, Zola's correspondents, especially those thanking him for copies he had sent, spoke of the narrative in the future tense. Ferdinand Fabres intended to pass several "good hours" reading *L'Assommoir*, while Gabriel Guillemot looked forward to "ineffable enjoyments."[96] Writing from Warsaw, Jules Guillemain told Zola that he was not surprised by the critical debate over such "conscientious and unstinting work of exploration into reality."[97]

Consequently, Zola's audience expressed little satisfaction with those aspects of the novel which betrayed their expectations of it. A narrative on working-class life, one radical republican wrote, ought to be more sympathetic to the poor: "On first reading *L'Assommoir*, I asked myself if this work, with its ever brutal, often disgusting realism from which arises no philosophy, moral, or conclusion, was not a bad deed and more, a reactionary work?"[98] What Zola should have written and what Secondigné promised to write himself was a novel depicting the true source of working-class degradation: the Second Empire's politics of debauchery. Other readers expressed their surprise at Zo-

[91] Louis Jacquet, "Chronique. *L'Assommoir*," *Bien public* (7 Feb. 1877).

[92] Albert Wolff, "Gazette de Paris," *Figaro* (5 Feb. 1877).

[93] Henry Houssaye, "Variétés. Le Vin bleu littéraire. *L'Assommoir*, par M. Émile Zola," *Journal des débats* (14 Mar. 1877).

[94] Barbey d'Aurevilly, "Zola. *L'Assommoir*," 278.

[95] Jacquet, "Chronique. *L'Assommoir*."

[96] Gabriel Guillemot to Émile Zola, 17 May [1877], in BN NAFr 24519 fol. 428.

[97] Jules Guillemain to Zola, 1 Feb. 1877, in EZRP Coll. Dr. F. Émile-Zola.

[98] A. Secondigné, *Les Kerney-Séverol. Histoire d'une famille française au XIXe siècle. L'Assommé* (1877), iii.

la's achievement. While most critics, like Wolff, resented the work's unrelenting attention to social ills, the correspondents had their own reservations about the narrative's unexpected turns. Paul Bourget thought that for so unified a work, *L'Assommoir* lacked a center; in light of the narrative's obvious sympathy for Gervaise, its tragic end was insufficiently intimate.[99] Anatole France was similarly bemused by the novel's artless quality.

> [Zola] believes that disorder is natural. He does not understand that all our conceptions of order come from nature alone and that ideas of the world and of order are identical. . . . I do not wish to impose on contemporaries the forms of the past; but art has its laws that will endure as long as humankind, because they conform to the nature of humankind.[100]

In short, France implied, Zola was not naturalistic enough.

Ordinarily, readers focused on the novel's most apparent message. But the nature of that theme varied from one person to another. These different assessments of *L'Assommoir*'s central idea resulted, of course, in a variety of expectations and predictions about the text as it unfolded. It is therefore no accident that the novel's most critical audience identified themes drawn from the text's most objectionable subject matter. Pontmartin in particular was struck by how "the municipal pawn shop, the hospital, the criminal court, the prison all preach the same antithetical homily."[101] These features of working-class life had no place in art. Readers more favorably inclined to Zola's text also varied remarkably in their assessments of *L'Assommoir*'s theme, but none of these differences was enough to disturb the author's fans; accordingly, none of their expectations was disappointed. Jacquet identified Zola's interest in the destructive aspects of poverty; Wolff remarked the determining roles of heredity and environment; Élizé de Montagnac understood the ambivalent consequences of work that leads as much to misery as it does to wealth; and Jan ten Brink analyzed the naturalistic principles in literary art.[102] As Frédéric Erbs put it, "Zola gives us a good idea of the mores appropriate to a certain class of people from eccentric localities—especially of those people who desert the home for the tavern, tools and books for gambling and drinking."[103] And his judgment of Zola's work followed logically: *L'Assommoir* was a perfect example of naturalism in prose.

What was true for perceptions of theme also held for views of character-

---

[99] Paul Bourget to Zola, [2 Feb. 1877], in BN NAFr 24511 fols. 184–85.

[100] France, "Variétés. Les Romanciers contemporains."

[101] Pontmartin, "M. Émile Zola," 331.

[102] Jacquet, "Chronique. *L'Assommoir*"; Wolff, "Gazette de Paris"; Élizé de Montagnac, *À propos de "l'Assommoir." Monseigneur Mermillod et Monsieur Zola. Étude contemporaine publiée en avril 1877 dans Le Courrier des Ardennes et le journal La Défense* (Chareville, 1877), 26; and Jan ten Brink to Zola, 31 Dec. 1876, in BN NAFr 24512 fol. 5.

[103] Frédéric Erbs, *M. E. Zola et son Assommoir. Étude critique* (1879), 75.

ization. Zola's readers responded to Gervaise, Coupeau, and Lantier in ways that affected their expectations of these figures in the narrative itself. Houssaye called them hideous exceptions.[104] Given such assumptions, the narrative's sympathetic tone could only provoke this critic's anger. On the other hand, those readers, like Jules Lermina, who considered Zola's characters superb types were less unpleasantly surprised by the text.[105] "The author wanted," wrote Philippe Gille, "by introducing everyone to the mores of Paris's lowest class of workers, to preach against the drunkenness that decimates them every day and to show us the real types who resemble none of Eugène Sue's conventional workers. From this point of view, he has completely succeeded."[106] For Gille, the narrative's characterizations both promised and delivered. Théodore Bainville also thought the characters consistent; he told Zola, "Like you I think that pure heroes must resemble peasants and savages more, and that is why I like them so much. Moreover, one has always known these perfect primitives, how they drink as well as eat, where they sleep as well as why they act as they do."[107] The author understood all his characters so well, J.-K. Huysmans felt, that he was past master at portraying minor figures, even faceless crowds.[108] Consequently, so captured was he by the narrative's account of Gervaise, Ferdinand Fabres cried when he learned of her death in the last installment, even though he knew it was coming.[109]

Commentary on *L'Assommoir*'s plot varied much less, but the responses were still keyed to the continuities or ruptures that readers perceived in the text. Some correspondents were particularly struck by scenes that interrupted the flow of action. In his letter to Zola, Huysmans pointed out Gervaise in the street soliciting passersby in her desperation, and again Gervaise and Coupeau in the snow passing each other without saying a word.[110] These poignant moments, Huysmans believed, were the best of the novel, and more, the best of all Zola's work. But the dramatist William Busnach found that these scenes, strung together, did not make for a unified whole. As drama *L'Assommoir* promised "sketches and not a play."[111] The inevitable progress of Gervaise's demise, however, created other expectations of the text. Houssaye disliked the intrusion of chance events; they did not belong in a tightly structured plot; the characters did not need any help to die: "The progress of their fall is not well

[104] Houssaye, "Variétés. Le Vin bleu littéraire"; and Montagnac, *À propos de "l'Assommoir,"* 15.

[105] Jules Lermina to Zola, 27 Jan. 1877, in BN NAFr 24521 fol. 259.

[106] Philippe Gille, "Revue bibliographique," *Figaro* (12 Oct. 1876), supplement.

[107] Théodore Bainville to Zola, 27 Nov. 1876, in BN NAFr 24511 fol. 1.

[108] J.-K. Huysmans, "Émile Zola et l'*Assommoir*," in Huysmans, *Oeuvres complètes* (n.d.), 2:187–88.

[109] Ferdinand Fabres to Zola, 31 Dec. 1876, in BN NAFr 24518 fol. 425.

[110] Huysmans to Zola, 7 Jan. 1877, in BN NAFr 24520 fol. 410.

[111] William Busnach to Zola, 21 Aug. 1877, in BN NAFr 24513 fols. 16–19.

rendered. Their slow decline is entirely fortuitous.''[112] Jacquet, on the other hand, saw the entire plot as of a piece: *"L'Assommoir*'s subject does not, in effect, take much conceptual effort. . . . It is the story of a worker's household that declines bit by bit to the lowest degrees of shame and misery.''[113] Whatever happened to the characters came as no surprise, their fate was perfectly predictable.

Perhaps *L'Assommoir*'s most controversial feature was its setting, one that encouraged a wide variety of predispositions towards the rest of the novel. Few readers could restrain from judging the working-class world in which Gervaise struggled so unsuccessfully. In the minds of conservatives, Zola's deliberate choice of setting condemned his entire narrative *a priori*. Critics more favorably disposed to the author's naturalistic project were also uncomfortable with the novel's depiction of Paris. Deeply ambivalent himself about the narrative, Édouard Rod asked, ''How can you wish to see with a tranquil eye the vice that approaches everywhere? And how can you wish it painted and branded without showing it in all its ugliness? That it be on display and make us shudder, such is what M. Zola wants.''[114] But the author's apparent moral intention did not stand up to scrutiny. As Secondigné pointed out, Zola pretended to know more about this world than he actually did; his use of working-class argot, for instance, was merely a cover for this ignorance.[115] In fact, the novel's crude language represented an extremely risky artistic strategy, noted Huysmans: ''[It is] to have the people speak just as they speak, to recount in their language their miseries and their joys, and at the same time to create a work of art.''[116] While Huysmans was convinced that the author had succeeded, most other critics and some of Zola's correspondents were sure that he had not. *L'Assommoir*'s setting seems to have spoiled the literary experience for much of its readership.

Thus Zola's audience responded to the implicit rules of configuration in the novel. The unfolding narrative created specific expectations of the course that it would take. Undoubtedly, readers brought extratextual concerns to the text, especially their interest in or loathing of naturalism. But these matters actually complemented rather than conflicted with predilections arising directly from the work itself. On the basis of a few installments in *Le Bien public*, readers anticipated the rest of the novel. Some predictions of the narrative's course were readily made within the first few pages. Consequently, Zola's audience developed a limited tolerance for sudden changes in ideological content or literary form; his reading public often felt betrayed whenever their predispositions ultimately proved wrong or inappropriate. Moreover, readers ex-

---

[112] Houssaye, ''Variétés. Le Vin bleu littéraire.''

[113] Jacquet, ''Chronique. *L'Assommoir*.''

[114] Édouard Rod, *À propos de "l'Assommoir"* (1879), 33.

[115] Secondigné, *Les Kerney-Séverol*, ix.

[116] Huysmans, ''Émile Zola et l'*Assommoir*,'' 2:182.

pressed a variety of perspectives on the work's theme, characters, plot, and setting that led to a variety of anticipations of where the narrative was headed. And not all people, not even Zola's friends, were necessarily pleased by the narrative's outcome. In this way the text played a part in shaping reader response, as much by what it promised as by what it ultimately did. The narrative's configuring conventions pervaded interpretive practice; actual readers' projections in fact depended upon them.

COHERENCE

Readers also respond to a novel's unity.[117] The rules of coherence inherent in the prose narrative enable people to answer the question, "How does one make sense of all this?" Most works provide ample evidence of their totality, and few readers have trouble comprehending them. But many novels are problematic because in one way or another they are incomplete, contradictory, or open-ended—sometimes all three.[118] Usually the reader is left to fill in gaps, to sort out irrelevancies, and to piece together the text's various elements, even though the narrative guides the process more or less adequately. A murder mystery, for example, rewards in particular the active reader who can make sense of the text's many clues. Achieving closure, that is, coming to a logical conclusion, is ultimately the reader's responsibility. To that extent, at least, a text cannot read itself. A good historical example of a literate audience's completing, resolving, and concluding a complex narrative arose in response to Anatole France's *Le Lys rouge*. The peculiar qualities of this *fin-de-siècle* novel required readers to seek its totality in the author's carefully crafted style. How the textual conventions suggesting the work's coherence actually worked appears in the responses that this text elicited from its original audience when symbolism was just becoming a force in French literature.[119] Again, the text explicitly shared in literate experience.

Le Lys rouge openly invites the reader to complete its narrative.[120] Thérèse Martin-Bellême, the central figure, grows disenchanted first with her husband, a prominent politician, and then with her lover, Robert Le Ménil, before she falls rapturously in love with the artist Jacques Dechartre. For the first time in

---

[117] See Rabinowitz, *Before Reading*, 141–69.

[118] Cf. Wolfgang Iser, *The Implied Reader: Patterns of Communication in Prose Fiction from Bunyan to Beckett* (Baltimore, 1974), 274–94.

[119] See Jean Pierrot, *The Decadent Imagination 1880–1900*, trans. Derek Coltman (Chicago, 1981), 147–237; Michel Raimond, *La Crise du roman. Des landemains du naturalisme aux années vingt* (1985), 194–212; and Pierre-Olivier Walzer, *Littérature française. Le XXe siècle. I: 1896–1920* (1975), 209–32.

[120] See Jean Levaillant, *Les Aventures du scepticisme. Essai sur l'évolution intellectuelle d'Anatole France* (1965); Drehan Bresky, *The Art of Anatole France* (The Hague, 1969); Julien Cain, "Le Drame amoureux du *Lys rouge*," *Figaro littéraire* (20 Sept. 1955); and Edwin Preston Dargan, *Anatole France, 1844–1896* (New York, 1937).

her life Thérèse experiences passion to its fullest measure. And Jacques, too, seems enthralled by his new lover's awakening sensuality. But this passion is not meant to last. Jacques is fiercely jealous; he must possess Thérèse entirely. So when he inadvertently catches her in a lie about Robert and suspects that she still loves the man despite her protestations, Jacques leaves Thérèse. The narrative ends ambiguously, for it is unclear what will become of her. Readers must decide this matter for themselves as they attempt answers to other questions implied in the work: Is sensual love ever fulfilled? Does the Parisian *beau monde* preclude personal passion? How conducive to love is life in another culture, such as Italy, where most of the novel's action occurs? The author's ironic language throughout the novel drops few hints to help its audience. There are frequent omissions, digressions, and ambiguities that readers must address on their own. The lovers' passion is suggested indirectly; curious secondary characters divert attention from the principal couple; and the end is deliberately held in suspense. How readers actually resolved France's text underscores the rules of coherence at work in his narrative—and in their response.

With few exceptions, readers of *Le Lys rouge* sought its unity in the author's stylistic persona.[121] Reviewers in particular noted Anatole France's special voice that, for them, gave the novel its clearest form, in language itself. In his account of the play derived from the narrative, drama critic Robert de Flers noted "the 'gentle nihilism,' 'the inalterable skepticism,' and the serene indifference" of the original text whose author was to be found in every word.[122] Gaston Deschamps was also impressed by France's apparent "wide-ranging erudition, his active philosophy, his irony moistened by tears."[123] It is hard to determine whether these qualities pertained to the novelist or to the novel he wrote. But few critics made much of a distinction; as if to make sense of the text, they identified the man with the work and its particular style. Asked Paul d'Armon in *Le Voltaire*,

> Perhaps he wanted only to modulate ironic couplets on love and the political milieu of our time? Perhaps he sought only to express a literary refinement for his pleasure and even more for ours as well? Let us accept this latter suggestion in order to enjoy fully the exquisite grace of *Lys rouge*, however a bit deliquescent its style.[124]

Such impressionist attributions of the author in a text were most clearly expressed in Jules Lemaître's assessment of the novel's language as "the latest

---

[121] See Paul Giselle, "Sur la popularité d'Anatole France," *Revue mondiale* (1 Nov. 1924); and Chapter 4, note 33.

[122] Robert de Flers, "*Le Lys rouge*, de M. Anatole France," *Le Théâtre et la ville. Essais de critique—Notes et impressions* ([1895]), 18.

[123] Gaston Deschamps, "M. Anatole France," *La Vie et les livres* (1899): 231.

[124] Paul d'Armon, "*Le Lys rouge*," *Voltaire* (11 Aug. 1894).

flowering of the Latin genius.''[125] From this perspective, coherence lay in the author's voice as evidenced most profoundly in the language of his work.

This personal stylistic approach to *Le Lys rouge* was even more obvious in the correspondence the author received. It is interesting to note that in a sample of 270 letters sent to Anatole France over his long lifetime, only one letter—from the Danish critic Georges Brandes—made direct reference to this novel.[126] In fact, relatively few letters concerned any one text in particular; most people spoke of his work in general, citing oftentimes the charm of his characters and the wisdom of his prose in a number of different novels. But for France's correspondents, the heart of the literary experience was the author's voice. Like the critics, the letter writers praised the novelist profusely for his style, his language, and the persona they suggested. Jules Lecornu, for example, remarked ''this skepticism . . . this secularity . . . this free thought'' in *Le Puits de Sainte Claire*.[127] These stylistic features were France himself. Similarly, Raymond Poincaré wrote the author of the charm of his prose, what Madame Jean Peyret in her letter called his grace and finesse.[128] His language was enchanting in itself, but it also represented the novelist's most significant achievement. As Jules Puch put it in 1916, ''It is your wisdom and your taste that keep me in the present enchantment.''[129] For France's audience, the narrative voice, the author's own, seemed to provide the underlying coherence to all his work, and not just to *Le Lys rouge*.

Critics stressed the extent to which style actually unified an otherwise uncomposed novel. ''We are much less interested in the course of the narrative so often interrupted,'' wrote Georges Pellissier, ''than in the diversions from which it wanders on its way. However remarkable the novelistic part of *Le Lys rouge*, it is only truly superior in its episodes,'' each one of which was exquisitely written.[130] Charles Arnaud agreed: ''Anatole France's *Le Lys rouge* is a news item garlanded by treatises''—the better the individual discourses, the better the work.[131] Teodor de Wyzewa corrected the common sentiment that the novelist structured his works poorly; ''on the contrary, I believe that he composes his work marvellously, but it has nothing to do with the novel form.''[132] France's splendid language created a genre all its own.

[125] Jules Lemaître, ''Anatole France. *Le Lys rouge*,'' *Les Contemporains. Études et portraits littéraires*, 6th ser. (n.d.), 395.

[126] Georges Brandes to France, 12 April 1899, in BN NAFr 15431 fols. 9–10.

[127] J. Lecornu to France, 5 Feb. 1913, in BN NAFr 15435 fols. 427–28.

[128] Raymond Poincaré to France, 11 Mar. [1901]; and Mme. Jean Peyret to France, 26 Nov. 1921, in BN NAFr 15437 fols. 320, 122.

[129] Jules Puch to France, 10 Nov. 1916, in ibid., fol. 518.

[130] Georges Pellissier, ''*Le Lys rouge*; par A. France,'' *Revue encyclopédique* (15 Oct. 1894): 451.

[131] Charles Arnaud, ''*Le Lys rouge*, de M. Anatole France,'' *Polybiblion* (Feb. 1895): 112.

[132] Teodor de Wyzewa, ''Les Livres nouveaux. *Le Lys rouge*, de M. Anatole France,'' *Revue politique et littéraire. Revue bleue* (1 Sept. 1894): 284.

"There are in our literature no more polished models of free, abundant, ornate conversation that is enlivened by fantasy and fertile in its wingèd grace."[133] While René Doumic identified the form France had chosen, few other reviewers were so courageous. Asked Deschamps, "What is this? Is it a photographic album? A collection of rough sketches? A pack of epigrams? A fagot of thorns disguised beneath the flowers of incomparable rhetoric? . . . What does it matter? It is so well written!"[134] For most critics, the central feature of *Le Lys rouge*, like much else France wrote, was its beautiful style. What form it took or what it expressed seems not to have mattered. Language was all, the whole, the source of the work's unity.

This stylistic preference reinforced another important tendency: the coherence of the reader's response. Reviewers not only praised the author's language, they also reveled in how it affected them. From their deliberately subjectivist perspective, critics found a certain order in the extreme pleasure they took in France's text. Noted the Belgian poet and critic Émile Verhaeren, "It is very pleasant reading; as artistic flavoring, it is delicate; one sucks on it like a candy at once fragrant and pungent. But these last features dissolve in the mind's saliva; there is no other sensation (not without cost) than that of some charmingly spent hours."[135] Most such readers were willing to locate the unity of the work in their response. Philippe Gille, for example, was especially charmed by the details, the ingenious observations, the particular and personal way of seeing things in France's novel.[136] So was Wyzewa: "The reverie and conversation remain there strong enough to divert our minds and to charm our senses for the entire narrative."[137] Neither the plot, nor the characters, nor the setting sustained as much interest as the author's suggestive tone and mood. The reader's delight was justification and coherence enough for the critics. Consequently, the ambiguous ending did not disturb Albert Le Roy: "For a novelist, here is such supreme competence that it leaves the last chapter to mislead the female reader's imagination!"[138]

Even more than the critics, France's correspondents made their response the novel's focus. Jacques Bereilh-Liegaux's warm appreciation was typical. "Thank you," he wrote, "for having contributed to instilling in me so healthy a taste for beautiful, pure, clear, and concise French prose."[139] Younger readers expressed a similar enthusiasm for the author's influence on them. Wrote Renée Chevalier, "It seemed that after the student's arid, suffocating work, a

---

[133] René Doumic, "Revue littéraire. M. Anatole France," *RdDM* (15 Dec. 1896): 933.

[134] Deschamps, "M. Anatole France," 243, 244.

[135] Émile Verhaeren, "Anatole France. *Le Lys rouge*," *Art moderne* (30 Sept. 1894): 307.

[136] Philippe Gille, "Anatole France. *Le Lys rouge*," *Les Mercredis d'un critique* (1895): 172–73.

[137] Wyzewa, "Les Livres nouveaux," 284.

[138] Albert Le Roy, "Profiles littéraires. *Le Lys rouge*," *Événement* (30 Aug. 1894).

[139] Jacques Bereilh-Liegaux to France, 23 Aug. 1916, in BN NAFr 15430 fols. 284–85.

fresh hand was placed on my forehead; my thoughts became harmonious and sweet.''[140] For this student, notwithstanding France's impressionistic language, the text imposed a refreshing order on her own intellectual and emotional world. The author's classical style in particular seemed to have made this coherence possible, not only for Chevalier, but also for Lecornu. ''What draws me to you especially,'' this reader wrote, ''is the admirable and pure style. . . . It is this Attic form that characterizes you.''[141] And so when Georges Brandes spoke of the remarkable passion in *Le Lys rouge*, he meant more than Thérèse's newfound sensuality; he experienced it as well in his own response.[142] France's correspondents frequently confused the text with its effects on them, as M. Harmigny noted in the verses that he sent the author about his work: ''How he makes us smile or provokes a tear. / Whatever the subject he takes, he charms, / And his work forms a harmonious whole,'' as much in the reader as in the text.[143]

Although *Le Lys rouge* left readers room to create their own conceptions of its achievement, they still did so within the usual conventions of coherence. France's audience filled in gaps in the text, the uncertain conclusion for instance, to complete the narrative. His readership also sorted out extraneous details such as the long digressions on various topics of interest to the characters. And the author's reading public gave order to the chaotic narrative, whose elements did not in themselves constitute a unified whole. For critics and correspondents alike, these challenging tasks were facilitated by France's commanding persona in the text. His voice made closure, for example, much easier, because it offered a focus of attention, a foundation on which the work could be reconceived. Similarly, the very language identified this persona; its style constituted another source of unity in an otherwise disparate text. But ultimately France's readers found the surest resolution of his problematic work in their responses to it. *Le Lys rouge* was a delight, an enchantment, a sustained pleasure. Even if the novel had no structure whatsoever, its audience found order in an enjoyment derived from few other texts. Perhaps the reason why Anatole France is no longer read much now is that his narrative voice no longer speaks so immediately; his readers today are no longer willing to impose the same kind of order in their response to his works. In short, the rules of coherence in the text are perceived differently, and the result is another subjective, but less favorable, perspective on France's fiction.

The particular conventions at work in France's *Le Lys rouge* shaped its audience's sense of the whole. And they did so in much the same way that the rules of notice in Sue's *Les Mystères de Paris* had affected its readership fifty years earlier. In fact, what was true for the specific roles played by these texts

---

[140] Renée Chevalier to France, 21 Dec. 1919, in BN NAFr 15432 fols. 180–81.

[141] Lecornu to France, 5 Feb. 1913, in BN NAFr 15435 fols. 427–28.

[142] Brandes to France, 12 April 1899, in BN NAFr 15431 fols. 9–10.

[143] L. Harmigny to France, 3 Nov. 1917, in BN NAFr 15434 fol. 407.

in their readers' responses also held for those played by Flaubert's *Madame Bovary* and Zola's *L'Assommoir*; the rules of signification and of configuration helped audiences make sense of the latter novels, either as an authorial voice or as an unfolding narrative, even though the texts themselves were often deliberately ambiguous. In each case, the work and its clues gave rise to certain interpretive practices appropriate to the text as well as to the audience. The act of reading therefore appears historically as a dialogue between the work and the reader, between the text and the context, both functioning in the literate experience. Despite the vagaries of individual readers, the narratives did provide some boundaries within which people responded.

It should be noted that the conventions were not exclusive to the works themselves: the rules of notice guided readers in other texts besides *Les Mystères de Paris*, just as the rules of signification, configuration, and coherence promoted the interpretation of other novels besides *Madame Bovary*, *L'Assommoir*, and *Le Lys rouge*, respectively. People responded to titles, voices, expectations, and gaps in all the novels they read. Only rarely, as in serial novels, did some conventions seem to preclude the others. As a matter of course, readers require and use as many interpretive clues as they can find in every narrative they encounter.

But from 1800 onward, there was a discernible development in the textual conventions most appropriate to historical changes in literature and interpretive practice. For instance, at the height of romanticism in France before 1850, new kinds of texts privileged the rules of notice, at least among reviewers and fan-mail writers. The romantic reaction to the emotional and aesthetic sterility of neoclassicism meant that critics were reluctant to embrace any new literary enthusiasms; they focused on a work's subject matter, refusing to appreciate so much as to judge a text, like Stendhal's *Le Rouge et le noir* or Balzac's *La Peau de chagrin*, that seemed alarmingly new or potentially dangerous to its audience. Similarly, the rise of romantic literature contributed to serious contradictions in the correspondents' apparent nobility of sentiment. Despite the pervasive challenge to older literary forms, letter writers continued to express their allegiance to aristocratic ideals of neoclassicism and poetic truth; at the same time, they also projected their feelings onto texts, drew analogies to the plastic arts, and indulged in a deeply personal reverie, one frequently detached as much from empirical reality as from the literary work. In each interpretive community, romanticism and its explosive creativity fostered responses for which titles, openings, closings, and narrative shifts were especially important. These particular conventions focused attention on the dramatically new features of romantic literature, and above all on the contradictory elements of the texts themselves. In short, the rules of notice shared in the complexities already inherent in romantic works and their reception.

In time, with the appearance of realist works from 1850 to 1880, another set of rules guided interpretive practices. Realism's mirror held up to the everyday world, succeeded by naturalism's quasiscientific endeavor to explain that reality, encouraged critics and correspondents alike in concerns appropriate to signification and configuration. Reviewers now focused on the author and the impact this creative individual had on an impressionable audience. Like Sainte-Beuve, these critics considered novels by Flaubert and the Goncourts as enormously influential monuments to literature's special place in an increasingly literate society. Moreover, the letter writers reinforced this development with their heightened interest in morality. Critics also discussed this issue, but correspondents expressed perhaps more clearly the new social basis for this response, namely, the bourgeois ideals of proper subject matter and language in literature. The moral outrage provoked by realist and naturalist publications like Zola's *La Terre*, for example, stemmed from these new interpretive practices—and more, from the new importance of clues to meaning and chronology in the texts themselves. Flaubert's use of free, indirect style confused authorial and narrative voices, made the identification and judgment of those voices more difficult, and undermined the readers' understanding of causation. Likewise, Zola's inexorable plots created expectations about the unfolding narrative and limited the readers' tolerance for surprises in theme, characterization, setting, and action. Thus the textual conventions concerning narrative voice and continuity were called into play by the texts and audiences of both realism and naturalism.

Symbolism from the *fin-de-siècle* to the interwar period meant still more new works, new rules, and new responses. In a neoromantic reaction to realism, creating a new literary context for a limited audience of aesthetes, the symbolists' medley of metaphors challenged the more ordinary reader to make sense of some very difficult texts. Critics at the time naturally had relatively little trouble, since they shared with symbolism an abiding interest in self-discovery, especially their own. Consequently, book reviewers were far from hostile to the particular innovations they saw, for example, in Proust's *À la recherche du temps perdu*. Even Sartre's existentialist project in *La Nausée* seemed a bit dated. Anatole France's correspondents, on the other hand, adapted symbolism's creative concerns to a new personal sensibility. Their ideals were neither overtly aristocratic nor crudely bourgeois, but apparently were more literary; their quest for the self disavowed morality per se and embraced instead a more flexible aestheticism. Besides their tolerance for classicism and acceptance of prosaic truths in literature, these readers expressed a more detached sympathy for the characters, more eclectic analogies to all the arts, and a broader literary imagination. It is certainly no accident, then, that the conventions of coherence became increasingly central to both symbolist texts and audience responses. In works like France's *Le Lys rouge*, but also in even more ambiguous works, readers had to fill in gaps, to sort out details, to resolve contradictions—in effect, to unify their conception of the author's often opaque achievement. Symbolism actually required its audience to participate more actively in making sense of literary texts; from this new demand, neither critics nor correspondents were exempt.

So there was indeed a complex relationship between developments in literary expression and reader response throughout the modern period. At least two different communities of readers responded to different genres like the letter, the essay, the theater, and the novel, in ways that obviously required a text. To be sure, their interaction with literature changed over time not only as the reading public changed, but also as the works and their rules developed. From period to period, however, the immediate situation of that interaction changed as well. Notwithstanding the complexities that remain for further study, such as how reception delayed and distorted literary trends from romanticism onward, it is now clear that from a historical perspective, texts do not read themselves, readers do, and that audiences do so at a specific intellectual moment. Every reader functions within at least one interpretive community's tradition of response, as well as within the context of new literary movements, new genres, and their specific conventions. Clearly, a work has no meaning until readers make of it what they can, given certain changing historical circumstances and interpretive practices appropriate to them, even though all literate experience begins first and foremost with the printed text and the particular rules essential to its reception.

AT THE BEGINNING of this book, Henri Fantin-Latour's 1859 portrait of his two sisters suggested that reading had a past worth exploring. This intriguing depiction of two women, together with other historical evidence, raised at least three serious questions: In what circumstances did people read from the eighteenth century onward? How did they read? What did their reading mean to them and why? Although there may be no entirely satisfactory answers, those ventured in the ensuing chapters identified issues for a full-scale history of reading in modern France. Literate milieus required texts, people to read them, laws and leaders to guide if not regulate their activity, and a culture to inform their responses. This easily described historical context, of course, did not explain entirely the way in which reading participated in art, literature, and memoir—some of the richest but most difficult historical sources on the subject. Artists, novelists, and memoirists drew deliberately upon literate experience in their creative endeavors; and in so doing they artfully characterized the subjective nature of interpretive practice in the past. But two communities of readers in particular—literary critics and authors' correspondents—also demonstrated some widely accepted conventions appropriate to different genres of writing. By negotiating a complex dialogue between text and context, their reading resulted in a remarkably narrow range of changing responses. Why precisely people read as they did, then, is no less amenable to study than their historical circumstances are.

As closer examination shows, reading's context in modern France seemed to change in surprising ways. What people read changed dramatically in form but relatively little in content. There have indeed been important developments in French intellectual life since 1800, but the most widely read text in the eighteenth century, the almanac, ultimately gave way to the newspaper, a more updated compendium of information. Yet only a small percentage of people read these increasingly diverse forms of print regularly and well, less than 40 percent of the population. From 1870 to 1940, a structural limit existed not only on the production of books and newspapers, but also on the absolute and relative number of serious readers in France's major urban centers. Ironically, this period was preceded by rapid growth in both publishing and literacy, despite an enduring ideology of legal control over what people could read. But once censorship lapsed, the growth in literate activities that had worried political authorities in the nineteenth century actually seemed to have waned. Nevertheless, French readers expressed a pervasive cultural mentality that privileged classical norms, empirical reality, and rational values. Book reviewers rarely welcomed experimentation; correspondents shared their books in social networks of like-minded readers; and schools instilled a Cartesian mode of thinking in nearly all the children who attended them. These constitutive rules remained much the same from 1800 to 1940, and they underscored the curious continuities in the historical context of modern French literate culture.

Within this particular milieu, the art of reading sheds light on how people encountered texts. Artists like Honoré Daumier saw creative possibilities in depicting groups, pairs, and individuals with printed matter. At the height of representational art, painters often portrayed literate activities in various social settings; by the end of the nineteenth century, these settings were less and less communal. In an increasingly educated world, oral readings seemed particularly inappropriate, unless they pertained to public institutions such as schools or legislative assemblies. The individual reader was more alienated from other people, even within the intimacy of the family. In time, besides the sitter, literate culture itself was painted, since nearly everyone could read and books were no longer the special preserve of a select few in French society. Similarly, the *roman de formation* depicted the important place that reading had in the development of its principal characters. At each stage of the life cycle from childhood to maturity, the modern French novel used literate life to emphasize the peculiarly "intertextual" features of growing up—in and with prose fiction. Like figures in the novel, the writers of journals and memoirs also created a reading self that was subject to social forces. Readers changed as they matured, but they also differed from region to region, from one social class to another, and from one sex role to another. Accounts of the reading experience indicated the remarkable influence of social location—as Parisian, Frenchman, peasant, aristocrat, bourgeois, male, or female. Each identity distinctly shaped interpretive as well as creative practice.

The actual responses to print provided by book reviewers and correspondents underwent a curious historical development as well. Critics adapted their principles in daily practice from 1800 onward. They learned to apply neoclassicism to a wide range of new works as French literature evolved in the nineteenth and twentieth centuries. Similarly, during the heyday of romanticism, the writers of letters to authors expressed their perceptions of aristocratic ideals in the text, particularly a nobility of sentiment, that in time gave way to a bourgeois concern with morality, especially with prose realism after 1850. Later, in response to symbolist texts, correspondents expressed more strictly literary values, a personal sensibility in fact, far more in keeping with authorial intentions. These traditions of response, whether the correspondents' or the reviewers', did not necessarily prevail over the conventions of reading. Each genre had its own "rules" that shaped its reception. Whatever the community of interpretation, the clues in letters, essays, plays, but especially novels guided readers to some textual meaning. In a few cases, such as wartime mail censorship, these conventions took on a formulaic quality. But ultimately, the literary text made more complex demands that shaped historical response every bit as much as the historical context in which it was received.

However disparate these developments, the history of reading does appear to follow a discernible pattern, a course of modernization in effect, from the Old Regime to the present. On the one hand, the circumstances in which people read moved from overtly collective to increasingly individual settings. In the eighteenth century, when literacy was rare and texts expensive, when political and cultural institutions attempted to control the printed word more or less directly, readers tended to share literate activity with others. In these circumstances, reading in groups seemed both natural and logical. This tendency, however, became unnecessary as literacy spread and printed material grew more accessible. By the twentieth century, individuals no longer experienced the same contextual constraints on their reading habits. On the other hand, interpretation also became less and less public. More often than not, because of older traditional social structures, Old Regime interpretive practices were regulated by recognized authorities like the church, the monarchy, and the aristocracy. But with the rapid decline of these authorities under the twin pressures of politicization and industrialization, people were left to their own resources within a much looser, overlapping network of communities and associations. Individuals today turn far more often to authorities of their own choosing, and in some cases define their own responses to texts, to the extent that they are free to do so. Thus, like many other features of French society, reading as both context and practice has taken on all the recognizable characteristics of modern life.[1]

From this perspective, it would seem, historians have yet another revolution to record. The early modern transition from "intensive" to "extensive" reading had its natural complement in another shift from religious to secular interpretive passions. Both Rolf Engelsing and Robert Darnton consider these major changes in interpretive activities during the eighteenth century.[2] Rousseau's readers certainly experienced *La Nouvelle Héloïse* very differently from the way in which the faithful had memorized devotionals and liturgies since the Reformation. People like Jean Ranson immersed themselves in a new world of secular texts with a remarkable alacrity that once had been reserved for sacred works alone. Although this celebration of Rousseau's novel marked a radical departure from the past, literate practices did not cease to develop in the nineteenth century. The immersion of readers in new texts continued and

---

[1] Cf. Peter N. Stearns, *European Society in Upheaval: Social History since 1750*, rev. ed. (New York, 1975); Georges Dupeux, *La Société française 1789–1970* (1972); Theodore Zeldin, *France 1848–1945* (Oxford, 1973–77), 1:11–282; and Roger Price, *A Social History of Nineteenth-Century France* (New York, 1988).

[2] See Rolf Engelsing, *Der Bürger als Leser. Lesergeschichte in Deutschland 1500–1800* (Stuttgart, 1974), 182–215; and Robert Darnton, *The Great Cat Massacre and Other Episodes in French Cultural History* (New York, 1984), 215–56.

changed; the noble sentiments and enthusiasms in response to the romantics in time evolved into the outrage over immoral monuments of prose realism. This in turn gave way to the personal sensibilities and identities of readers encountering the symbolists in the twentieth century. Moreover, readers responded according to new textual conventions in the novel. From rules of notice and signification to rules of configuration and coherence, people learned to follow the guides provided by literary narratives as they too developed in the nineteenth century. Consequently, the radically new mode of reading Rousseau was followed by still other modes of reading the romantics, realists, and symbolists. In fact, the modern revolution in reading continued unabated for at least 140 years.

Significance

Clearly reading has a history; it is also an active historical force. Literate culture, for example, played a prominent role in the context that so obviously affected it. Rapid growth in the production of print was owed directly to comparable growth in the number of readers; as the rise in literacy leveled off after 1870, reducing the new demand for print, the publication of books leveled off as well, reflecting among other things the importance of reading to one sector of the French economy. Other factors surely had an effect, but changes in production cannot be insulated completely from consumption patterns. Moreover, reading helped to define social classes as French society moved from a traditional hierarchy of Old Regime landed elites to a more open structure based on modern sources of wealth, power, and status. Once free, compulsory, secular elementary education was established, nearly everyone shared in higher levels of reading competence; but only a select few attended the secondary schools and universities that in time created new social distinctions. Consequently, well-educated, urban, white-collar professionals rose to new prominence as readers and as social elites after 1870. In politics, literate activity posed a long-standing threat to centralized power. So long as the legitimacy of France's various constitutions was challenged, as it was for most of the nineteenth century, censorship in one form or another remained intact. And serious threats to national security in the twentieth century, such as World War I, meant a reimposition of state-sponsored controls on both expression and reception. Similarly, widespread literacy resulted in the demise of a predominantly face-to-face oral culture, one that lingered on in some rural areas of France until 1914.[3] So literate life was indeed an historical agent.

Reading was a force in creative life, as well. More than 500 artistic images of readers appeared between 1800 and 1940—after the classical idealism of the eighteenth century and before the abstract expressionism of the twentieth

---

[3] See Eugen Weber, *Peasants into Frenchmen: The Modernization of Rural France 1870–1914* (Stanford, 1976), 3–191.

virtually precluded such representations of everyday events. Literate life provided opportunities for satirical artists, like Daumier, to poke fun at the foibles of a rapidly growing reading public. But realist portraits also made good use of books to reveal the sitter's inner nature in a medium otherwise incapable of penetrating deeply into its subject matter. As for modern novelists, reading was a major incentive to write. Although few writers knew their audience precisely, they often assumed one in their work and thus created the textual counterpart to the implied narrator.[4] Moreover, authors used reading to develop characters, especially in modern fiction, as literate activity became increasingly self-conscious after 1900 among novelists like Marcel Proust and André Gide. Reading in fact earned a new respect from symbolists, whose deliberate obscurity required serious effort from their audience to make sense of their work. Writers of journals and memoirs emphasized another side of the close relationship between reading and meaning. As they defined themselves in their literary creations, self-reflective authors drew on vast stores of experience possible only in a literate context. Reading as Parisians, as bohemians, as men or women all entered into personal accounts of what it meant to be or to become a self-conscious individual in modern France. Reading, in short, was a creative activity.

Interpretive practice itself influenced French intellectual life. To the extent that readers formed groups or established networks, they treated the text as a medium of social exchange. The book was not solely a cultural code or a commodity in the marketplace; it was also a vehicle for ties between individuals sharing a common endeavor. Correspondents expressed how their interest in print was due to friends, relatives, colleagues, and neighbors. These readers helped predispose others for or against certain works, often providing the texts as well. If such linkages overlapped or intensified, they constituted communities of interpretation that in time created traditions of response to various texts. Book reviewers, for instance, wrote for periodicals with well-established editorial, that is political, interests. It is therefore no accident that conservative critics decried prose realism's apparent moral challenge to the Second Empire when few publications stayed long in print without official sanction; the reviews of works by Flaubert, the Goncourts, and Baudelaire in effect foreshadowed the legal proceedings against them.[5] Furthermore, schools and universities privileged certain styles of reading, the *explication de texte* in particular, to institutionalize one community's interpretive influence. No doubt attentive readers throughout the modern period gave their books meanings that few authors intended. An audience sometimes even offered suggestions to novelists like Eugène Sue on the course that a particular narrative

[4] See Jane Tompkins, ed., *Reader-Response Criticism from Formalism to Post-Structuralism* (Baltimore, 1980), 7–25.

[5] See Roger Bellet, *Presse et journalisme sous le Second Empire* (1967), 119–36.

should take. By no means was literate culture an entirely passive feature of French life.

By now it should be clear that despite considerable overlap, the significance of reading in history is not the same as that of literacy.[6] Interpretive culture entails far more than the widespread circulation and use of print. Active reading and literate skills are simply not the same. Of course, all readers are technically literate, even if they cannot write. On the other hand, not all literate people are serious readers; the possession of a particular skill does not mean that it will be used. Functional literacy often denotes some measure of competence in dealing with texts, though the specific measure is extremely difficult to define. Other factors, such as cultural background, can affect an individual's ability to decipher a written message.[7] Some of Sue's audience, for example, missed entirely the classical references in *Les Mystères de Paris* and thus could not make sense of the book's distinctions between certain instances of good and evil. But the particular issues raised by the history of reading also require attention to what may be called "interpretive literacy," that is, the ability to participate in a community of readers. No one can easily appropriate a complex text alone; a reader usually takes meaningful cues from other people whose views are more decided. In this way, the making of textual meaning is a collective effort, much like the treatment of sacred scripture during the Reformation or like the Conseil d'état's rulings on the constitutionality of administrative decrees.[8] Here the role of reading as interpretation, beyond the notion of mere literacy, takes on much greater historical significance.

This field is also distinct from recent work on the history of the book.[9] Early modern historians in particular have explored the implications of printed texts from the Renaissance to the Enlightenment, and their findings occasionally suggest what people did with the books produced for them. The most provocative research has actually attempted to describe the mentality, the state of mind, even the mental equipment of readers, largely by analyzing a period's most widely circulated texts.[10] This procedure, however, often says more about historians than it does about historical readers. Careful study of interpretive practice, such as the history of literary criticism, shows how much

[6] See Harvey J. Graff, Jr., *The Legacies of Literacy: Continuities and Contradictions in Western Society and Culture* (Bloomington, 1987), 245–85.

[7] Cf. E. D. Hirsch, Jr., *Cultural Literacy: What Every American Needs to Know* (New York, 1988), 1–32.

[8] See Natalie Zemon Davis, *Society and Culture in Early Modern France* (Stanford, 1975), 189–226; and David Thomson, *Democracy in France since 1870* (London, 1969), 99–101.

[9] See Roger Chartier, "Frenchness in the History of the Book: From the History of Publishing to the History of Reading," *Proceedings of the American Antiquarian Society* 97 (Oct. 1987): 299–329. Cf. Lynn Hunt, ed., *The New Cultural History* (Berkeley, 1989), 154–75.

[10] E.g., Robert Mandrou, *De la culture populaire aux 17e et 18e siècles. La Bibliothèque bleue de Troyes* (1975). Cf. Dominick LaCapra and Steven L. Kaplan, eds., *Modern European Intellectual History: Reappraisals and New Perspectives* (Ithaca, 1982), 13–46.

misunderstanding can arise from texts. And there is certainly no guarantee that a twentieth-century reading, no matter how popular the work, will re-create the actual understanding that contemporaries had of a text. In his own time, Balzac's novels were a scandal; even his closest friends and colleagues had reservations about them. Today Balzac's works mark the origin of prose realism; *La Comédie humaine* has now taken on a completely new meaning that few in its original audience ever dreamed possible. Without careful consideration of critical practice, it is risky speculation indeed for historians to infer climates of opinion from the study of popular literature. The danger of anachronistic reading is a real one in the history of the book, and even more in the history of popular culture and its many different artifacts.[11]

But this problem also arises in the history of ideas, at least in the version practiced since Arthur O. Lovejoy.[12] Historians of *mentalité* accused older intellectual historians of privileging elite texts and thus of distorting their accounts of the past. But this so-called Lovejoy fallacy is joined by another that historians of interpretive practice identify. Readers perceived literary movements, for instance, very differently from the way authors did. Textbook accounts of the Enlightenment's exploration and celebration of human reason, natural law, and cultural progress rarely discuss the deep personal emotion that Rousseau's readers experienced with *La Nouvelle Héloïse*. Similarly, the romantics' reaction to the neoclassicists' creative sterility seems not to have affected readers for a generation or more. It was not until the end of the nineteenth century that interpretive practice can be said to have caught up with authorial inspiration during the symbolist movement, when readers were required to make sense of erudite, often very private works. Moreover, the reading public tended to distort the nature of literary movements. Romanticism became a cause of noble enthusiasms, realism a matter of moral influence, and symbolism a source of self-discovery—whatever the actual nature of the works themselves that represented these developments in French literary history. Readers' predispositions and preoccupations prevailed over the precise features of texts that writers wanted to emphasize. In the historical record, creation and interpretation simply did not match up as neatly as some scholars have assumed.[13]

There is, of course, nothing new in this perspective; literary specialists have taken very similar positions. For more than thirty years, structuralists have argued that the meaning of a text is not found in its referents so much as in the

---

[11] E.g., cf. James Smith Allen, *Popular French Romanticism: Authors, Readers, and Books in the Nineteenth Century* (Syracuse, 1981), 65–73, 213–22; and Martyn Lyons, *Le Triomphe du livre. Une Histoire sociologique de la lecture dans la France du XIXe siècle* (1987), 105–28.

[12] E.g., Arthur O. Lovejoy, *The Great Chain of Being: A Study of the History of an Idea* (Cambridge, Mass., 1936), 3–23, 315–33.

[13] See W. K. Wimsatt, *The Verbal Icon: Studies in the Meaning of Poetry* (Lexington, 1967), 3–39.

language it uses, or more correctly, in the language that uses it.[14] Authors do not necessarily speak in their own right, because they depend upon a preexisting discourse to make sense of the world. Thus all reality is mediated through linguistic structures, especially in the knowledge possible in literary texts. Deconstructionists have taken this argument several steps further by contending that logocentricism, or the apparent sense of language, is in fact only an illusion.[15] Textual meaning is undetermined and leaves infinite interpretive possibilities, so much so that a complex literary work always defies the critic's resolution of its ambiguities, its vagaries, its evasions. In any case, literary theorists are reluctant to define meaning in language. But a history of reading suggests that reception has its own discourse, one quite distinct from that of either author or text. As this book has shown, texts are only one ingredient of interpretive practice. The linguistic structures that theorists have elaborated, perhaps reified, do not include the actual language of reading and readers in the past. It appears from historical study that meaning lies more in a dialogue between the world of the text and that of its audience, each contributing some portion of the literate experience (and one's understanding of it), to the extent that it can be known empirically. Neither discourse is sufficient in itself; neither can preempt or co-opt the important role played by the negotiation between two different linguistic structures, the reader's as well as the text's.

Literary specialists in reader response have also explored the theoretical problems posed by reception, especially in the function of interpretive communities. More than anyone, Stanley Fish has championed the critical predispositions inherent in professional criticism and scholarship, most often centered in the university, the most important source of critical influence in literature today. It is these "interpretive communities, rather than the text or the reader, that produce meanings and are responsible for the emergence of formal features."[16] The particular strategies that these groups formulate ultimately "determine the shape of what is read." This position has provoked considerable controversy, especially over the exclusive focus of Fish's attention upon a handful of readers. From an historical perspective, schools of criticism are only one of many different and competing sources of influence on reception. Opinion leaders, social scientists know, exist in a host of fields; and the groups gathered around them, either formally or informally, tend to for-

[14] See Richard Macksey and Eugenio Donato, eds., *The Structuralist Controversy: The Language of Criticism and the Sciences of Man* (Baltimore, 1972); Robert Scholes, *Structuralism in Literature: An Introduction* (New Haven, 1974); and Frank Lentricchia, *After the New Criticism* (Chicago, 1980), 102–55.

[15] See Harold Bloom et al., *Deconstruction and Criticism* (New York, 1979); Jonathan Culler, *On Deconstruction: Theory and Criticism after Structuralism* (Ithaca, 1982), 85–225; *The Yale Critics: Deconstruction in America*, Theory and History of Literature, vol. 6, ed. Jonathan Arac et al. (Minneapolis, 1983); and Lentricchia, *After the New Criticism*, 156–210.

[16] Stanley Fish, *Is There a Text in This Class? The Authority of Interpretive Communities* (Cambridge, Mass., 1980), 14.

mulate interpretive strategies very much like Fish's communities of critics and scholars.[17] Although schools and universities establish and promote more comprehensive and more critical reading styles, other institutions, like literary reviews, salons, professional associations, book clubs, and the like, serve similar functions. Tighter definition and analysis of those groups and their influence require more effort, but for now interpretive communities are an extremely useful tool of historical investigation into the nature of readers and reading.

Until recently, Jonathan Culler and his students have argued for "literary competence" as a central feature of critical practice. Because certain interpretive skills are required of good readers, contends Culler, their "understanding depends upon mastery of a system" of rules and conventions appropriate to the text under consideration.[18] The more competent the reader, the richer his or her response will be, especially to literary masterworks. Although he does not posit, like Michael Riffaterre, a hypothetical "superreader" capable of all different interpretations to a text, Culler does value some readings over others, the arbiter of which must ultimately be the reader's command of language itself.[19] But neither Culler nor Riffaterre allows for much diversity in the use of language. Historically, systems change, and so too do the strategies that readers adopt to make sense within them. As authors developed different narrative conventions in the nineteenth century, readers followed as well as they could, some with more alacrity than others. Much depended upon the reader's age, education, social class, and psychological state. Other factors affecting historical reader response included gender, nationality, and culture. This much is clear from a history of interpretive practice. People simply make out what they can from the discourse around them and reach what seems in retrospect some curious conclusions about their reading. Whether they are competent or not, they respond in ways that are appropriate to the historical moment as well as to the skills particular to all readers, past and present. But the result is often critically idiosyncratic.

Texts do provide cues, and miscues, to their interpretation. Literary theorists and critics are quite right to study them. Every experienced reader recognizes, indeed expects, certain conventions in literature. As I. A. Richards noted in 1929, university students presuppose that poetry is distinguished by the technical features that pertain to it, such as prosody, density, and meta-

[17] E.g., Elihu Katz and Paul F. Lazarsfeld, *Personal Influence: The Part Played by People in the Flow of Mass Communications* (New York, 1955), 15–133; and Morris Rosenberg and Ralph H. Turner, eds., *Social Psychology: Sociological Perspectives* (New York, 1981), 320–43, 653–82.

[18] Jonathan Culler, *Structuralist Poetics: Structuralism, Linguistics, and the Study of Literature* (Ithaca, 1975), 114.

[19] See esp. Michael Riffaterre, *Text Production*, trans. Terese Lyons (New York, 1983).

phor.[20] The arrangement of words on the page immediately alerts the reader to the nature of a text. Similarly, nearly all prose fiction narratives develop character and plot within a recognizable setting to maintain reader interest from beginning to end. Nor will anyone deny the essential role of conflict at the heart of drama. Each feature thus suggests an interpretive function, as well, to guide the reader through the text. But textual clues are not the only factors at work in reading, a complex act dependent upon extratextual considerations. The special concerns of different communities will highlight or actually efface many otherwise obvious features of a text. Flaubert's carefully controlled prose, for example, was overlooked by his original audience, who decried the apparent immorality of his subject matter. Moreover, some individuals will respond in a fashion that appears unrelated to either the text or its apparent context. However predictable the kind of response, specific interpretations can be erratic, some of them evidently derived from another aspect of the reader's life and mind, whatever the work and whatever the community. As Wolfgang Iser put it, "The convergence of text and reader brings the literary work into existence."[21] The same is equally true of literary response.

Historical analysis, in fact, promises a contribution to the debate over subjective criticism. Even more radically than Fish—in some cases to legitimate literary affect—literary theorists like David Bleich and Norman Holland suggest that readers alone make meaning; indeed, texts are but pretexts, little different from other life experiences, in an individual's quest to define an evolving identity.[22] Consequently, literature can become whatever readers care to make of it, notwithstanding the linguistic systems, literary competencies, interpretive communities, and textual cues that other theorists have used to explain, and occasionally to justify, various critical practices. In an historical approach to reading, however, this is only one dimension to a more complete study of interpretation; text and context quite obviously also matter, at least in the responses that actual communities left of their reading in the nineteenth and early twentieth centuries. People, then, no more read out of context than they read without texts. Of course, print in itself does not mean anything, nor does its milieu determine interpretation, but it is also clear (*pace* some literary theorists) that readers must have something to respond to and a setting in which to do so. This empirical situation leads logically to the identification

[20] I. A. Richards, *Practical Criticism: A Study of Literary Judgment* (New York, 1929), 275–87.

[21] Wolfgang Iser, *The Implied Reader: Patterns of Communication in Prose Fiction from Bunyan to Beckett* (Baltimore, 1974), 275. Cf. idem, *The Act of Reading: A Theory of Aesthetic Response* (Baltimore, 1979); and idem, *Prospecting: From Reader Response to Literary Anthropology* (Baltimore, 1989).

[22] See David Bleich, *Subjective Criticism* (Baltimore, 1978), 10–37; Norman N. Holland, *Five Readers Reading* (New Haven, 1975), 1–12, 113–29, 201–91; and Michael Steig, *Stories of Reading: Subjectivity and Literary Understanding* (Baltimore, 1989), 3–38.

of the principal historical forces at work in the act of reading: the text, the context, and the reader engaged with both. As a result, the subjective element in reading must be contained within the overlap of these three essential elements. It would make little sense otherwise to omit serious analysis of any one of them.

An historical understanding of reading thus offers significant insight into the dialogic constraints on interpretive subjectivity, especially in the negotiation actually undertaken by readers in the past with literature and the world around it. The specific conditions affecting this relationship over time resulted in interpretive practices defined by contemporary communities of readers, by the development of literate culture, and by the evolution of literature itself. These factors cannot be studied in isolation from one another. The simple tracing of taste, as long practiced by literary historians, has never entirely succeeded in explaining interpretation.[23] Nor, for that matter, has an exclusive focus on the text, intertextuality, or discourse, as emphasized by other literary specialists. The most important work on literary and theoretical audiences, especially those defined within the text, would benefit greatly by a more empirical, more broadly historical perspective.[24] There remains as much to know about actual readers and their perceptions, past and present, as there is to discover about apparent readers and their roles in literature. Until now, few scholars have bothered to pose even the most obvious questions about reading: who read what, where, when, how, and why? The present history proposes some tentative answers for modern France. Its approach suggests what this new knowledge of documented audiences and their reading has to offer the disciplines of literature and history alike.

ANTICIPATIONS

Reading in the past deserves further exploration, especially in the early modern period during the long historical transition to print culture. Already Roger Chartier and others have discovered the remarkable interdependence between oral and written cultural practices long after the invention of printing.[25] For example, popular images nearly always accompanied the elite texts prepared for distribution in the *bibliothèque bleue*; without some kind of visual emblem, it seems, the poorly edited tales and religious admonitions themselves would have been virtually unintelligible even to a relatively well-lettered audience.

---

[23] E.g., René Wellek, *A History of Modern Criticism 1750–1950*, 6 vols. (New Haven, 1955–86).

[24] Cf. Tompkins, *Reader-Response Criticism*; and Susan Suleiman and Inge Crosman, eds., *The Reader in the Text: Essays in Audience and Interpretation* (Princeton, 1980); Wayne Booth, *The Company We Keep: An Ethics of Fiction* (Berkeley, 1988); and I. Crosman Wimmers, *Poetics of Reading: Approaches to the Novel* (Princeton, 1989).

[25] See Roger Chartier, ed., *Pratiques de la lecture* (Marseille, 1985); idem, *Lecteurs et lectures dans la France d'Ancien Régime* (1987); and idem, ed., *L'Usages de l'imprimé* (1987).

Moreover, these crude publications aimed at civilizing the lower orders did not always hit their marks; their readership was varied and their reception often distorted by local resistance to obvious and overt attempts at social control during the Counter-Reformation. Ambiguities in the sixteenth-century "Return of Martin Guerre"—did Bertrande de Rols truly collude with Arnaud du Tilh?—left ample room for readers to adapt the story to popular customs, even though it was written down by Jean de Coras and others for didactic purposes of their own.[26] On the other hand, servants often imitated the literate lives of their masters, learning to read and buying books, ostensibly to distinguish themselves from other social groups in eighteenth-century Paris.[27] As Elizabeth Eisenstein has shown, the printing press was a complex agent of historical change whose cultural implications are not easily summarized in textbook remarks about the dissemination of information. Reading mediated the impact of this new technology, but precisely how it did so requires more study.[28]

Similarly, the changing nature of reading in contemporary life also poses serious challenges. French schoolchildren today continue to sort out the nonsense, as well as some of the good sense, in what they read for class, depending upon the text's appropriateness to their immediate lives.[29] Social control through the printed word is no more effective today than it was 500 years ago. One can still see in the electronic media the same interdependence between oral and literate cultures that existed in early modern Europe. Even though news reporters seem to be talking to the television viewer, they are in fact reading a teleprompter; and few advertisements fail to include print with their striking images and assuring voices. The apparent reversion to preliterate face-to-face exchange in the computer age is fraught with similar contradictions and delusions. Despite the telephone, people are sending and receiving more mail; and the demands for higher-order reading and writing skills insure the continued utility of word processors as well as photocopying machines. Furthermore, the alarming statistics concerning the functional illiteracy of 20 percent or more of the adult population actually underscore the increased literacy requirements of a postindusrial society.[30] High technology and higher education for more people are, of course, tightly linked. Even billboards continue to rely upon the insatiable literate eye roving the highway for some visual

[26] Natalie Zemon Davis, *The Return of Martin Guerre* (Cambridge, Mass., 1983). Cf. Robert Finlay, "The Refashioning of Martin Guerre," *American Historical Review* 93 (1981): 553–71; and Davis, " 'On the Lame,' " *American Historical Review* 93 (1981): 572–603.

[27] Daniel Roche, *Le Peuple de Paris. Essai sur la culture populaire au XVIIIe siècle* (1981), 204–41.

[28] Elizabeth L. Eisenstein, *The Printing Press as an Agent of Change: Communications and Cultural Transformations in Early Modern Europe* (Cambridge, 1979), 129–36.

[29] E.g., Laurence Wylie, *Village in the Vaucluse* (Cambridge, Mass., 1973), 55–97.

[30] See Daniel Resnick and Lauren Resnick, "The Nature of Literacy: An Historical Exploration," *Harvard Educational Review* 47 (1977): 370–85.

stimulation not provided by the passing scenery. Marshall McLuhan may have overstated his case, but his insights into the implicit messages of media to different audiences deserve closer investigation.[31]

It would seem, then, that the historical development of literate culture is far from complete anywhere in the West, much less in France.[32] The extent to which reading matters culturally, of course, varies over time and generally grows with modernization. With few local exceptions, an industrial economy and a constitutional government correlate with higher rates of literacy from the eighteenth century onward.[33] But even widespread elementary education did not guarantee the cultural importance of reading. Other conducive factors, such as urban growth, humanistic institutions, and inexpensive print, all took time to develop. And so, according to François Furet and Jacques Ozouf—two social historians with anthropological interests—the popular adaptation to fully literate culture in France took at least four centuries.[34] Early in the nineteenth century, this acculturation to print was still incomplete; readers of the romantics were often more interested in their own emotional responses than they were in the literature that evoked them. Similarly, friends, family members, and neighbors persisted in borrowing and lending books long after printed matter became cheaply and widely available. By the twentieth century, however, the work itself had become more the focus of attention, as suggested by the replacement of rhetoric by the *explication de texte* in the Third Republic's literary pedagogy. Obviously the modern period stands at the end of this long process, but personal and external modes of interpretation indicate the continued reluctance of people to enter completely into the abstract world of texts. Historians clearly need to know more about the curious history of print culture.[35]

Another problem worth further research is the context of reading in countries other than France. Thanks to considerable work already undertaken in Britain, Germany, and the U.S., cross-cultural histories of the book are not only possible but necessary.[36] The rise of the serial novel was international,

[31] Marshall McLuhan, *The Gutenberg Galaxy: The Making of Typographic Man* (Toronto, 1962).

[32] See the annotated bibliography in David R. Olson et al., eds., *Literacy, Language, and Learning: The Nature and Consequences of Reading and Writing* (Cambridge, 1986), 412–26. Cf. Suzanne de Castell et al., eds., *Literacy, Society, and Schooling: A Reader* (Cambridge, 1986); and Eric A. Havelock, *The Muse Learns to Write: Reflections on Orality and Literacy from Antiquity to the Present* (New Haven, 1988).

[33] Cf. Harvey J. Graff, Jr., *The Literacy Myth: Literacy and Social Structure of a Nineteenth-Century City* (New York, 1979).

[34] François Furet and Jacques Ozouf, *Lire et écrire. L'Alphabétisation des Français de Calvin à Jules Ferry* (1977), 1:349–69.

[35] Cf. Robert Darnton and Daniel Roche, eds., *Revolution in Print: The Press in France 1775–1800* (Berkeley, 1989), 141–289.

[36] See Robert Darnton, "First Steps toward a History of Reading," *Australian Journal of*

as various translations of Eugène Sue's *Les Mystères de Paris* amply testify, but the mechanisms of its publication from one country to another remain unknown. Literacy, too, progressed at different rates in England, France, Germany, Italy, and Russia, complicating all generalizations about acculturation to print in the West. In fact, as Jeffrey Brooks has argued recently for prerevolutionary Russia, the later development of elementary education did not necessarily delay the impact of cheap popular literature; the rural networks of distribution, both commercial and social, were extensive even when literacy rates were extremely low.[37] Moreover, comparative studies of censorship promise greater illumination of variations in the ideology of control from one political system to another. Not all regimes were uniformly repressive or efficient in their enforcement of laws restricting printed expression and its reception. Further, there have been few comparative studies of mentality. With the exception of some structuralist studies of fairy tales, *mentalité* remains a French specialty.[38] But this need not prevent other historians from examining similarities and differences in the mental equipment of men and women across national cultures that defined the conceptions of value, reality, and knowledge in modern literate activity.

Besides comparative study of reading's historical context, historians should examine interpretive practices cross-culturally. This research can go beyond comparing the structures of literary texts, for example, by considering how a single work was received in different countries. Especially after the 1886 Berne convention, which secured international property rights, authors like Émile Zola and Anatole France authorized translations of their work. In this way, more scrupulous editions of their novels reached new audiences, who then published reviews in newspapers and journals. Many more readers also wrote letters to the novelists. Such reviews and letters permit careful compar-

---

French Studies 23 (1986): 5–30 (also published in idem, *The Kiss of Lamourette* [New York, 1989], 154–87). Cf. Philippe Ariès and Georges Duby, eds., *Histoire de la vie privée* (1986), 3:113–61; Susan Zimmerman and Ronald Weissman, eds., *Urban Life in the Renaissance* (Newark, 1989), 103–20; Gilles Quinsat et al., eds., *Le Grand Atlas des littératures* (1991), 260–333; Richard Altick, *The English Common Reader: A Social History of the Mass Reading Public 1800–1900* (Chicago, 1957); Richard Hoggart, *The Uses of Literacy* (Harmondsworth, 1958); Jon P. Klancher, *The Making of English Reading Audiences, 1790–1852* (Madison, 1987); Rudolf Schenda, *Volk ohne Buch. Studien zur Sozialgeschichte der populären Leserstoffe 1770–1910* (Frankfurt, 1970); Peter Uwe Hohendahl, ed., *A History of German Literary Criticism* (Lincoln, 1988); Nina Baym, *Novels, Readers, and Reviewers: Responses to Fiction in Antebellum America* (Ithaca, 1984); and William J. Gillmore, *Reading Becomes a Necessity of Life: Material and Cultural Life in Rural New England, 1780–1835* (Knoxville, 1989).

[37] Jeffrey Brooks, *When Russia Learned to Read: Literacy and Popular Literature, 1861–1917* (Princeton, 1985).

[38] E.g., Darnton, *The Great Cat Massacre*, 9–74. Cf. Carlo Ginzberg, *The Cheese and the Worms: The Cosmos of a Sixteenth-Century Miller*, trans. John and Anne Tedeschi (Baltimore, 1980); and Henry Nash Smith, *Virgin Land: The American West as Symbol and Myth* (Cambridge, Mass., 1950).

ison of their interpretations of a translated text in several different European countries. Variations of response to both form and content promise insight into the role of culture in the history of reading. Did Anatole France's German audience note his style as often and as favorably as did his French readership? Did readers in Russia also call Zola's work obscene? Was there the same quest for personal identity among literate Italians at the turn of the century? Answers to these questions would indeed shed new light on cultural practices and their illustration of national differences, and similarities, over time. Perhaps other communities of readers, like government censors and secondary-school students, left similar records of their responses to French literature in translation. In any event, so long as appropriate sources exist, comparative study of reception outside of France would clearly complement work on historical context.

Moreover, the history of reading will remain incomplete until scholars attend to the influence of prior interpretations on subsequent responses to the same text. Almost everyone depends upon predecessors for help in a first encounter with a complex literary work, and some distortion of response almost inevitably results. This problem Hans-Georg Gadamer addressed in his important work on hermeneutics, *Truth and Method*.[39] It makes sense to consider the way in which not only philosophers but also more ordinary mortals sorted out the various readings of a text to arrive at one of their own. In its quest to know God's word, the Catholic Church certainly privileges readings of the Bible, just as Supreme Court justices must attend to precedent in their decisions on what the U.S. Constitution actually means.[40] Less institutional situations, however, also reflect the important role played by earlier readings. For instance, successive translations of a classic text like Dante's *The Divine Comedy* show how much, or little, generations of literary specialists have borrowed from their predecessors. Another history of reading in modern France should treat the layers of interpretive practice evident in successive readings of an influential literary figure like Voltaire from the eighteenth century onward.[41] Of course, it would be wise to restrict the focus of this approach to a single community of readers, such as poets or dramatists, for comparative study of their responses. The results could well measure the precise degree of continuity and change at work in reader responses in France over a long historical period.

At least one other feature of reading worth more historical study is the precise nature and function of interpretive communities. Although book review-

---

[39] Hans-Georg Gadamer, *Truth and Method*, trans. Garrett Barden and John Cumming (New York, 1975), 245–73.

[40] E.g., Frederic Farrar, *History of Interpretation* (Grand Rapids, Mich., 1961); and Hans W. Frei, *The Eclipse of Narrative: A Study of Eighteenth- and Nineteenth-Century Hermeneutics* (New Haven, 1974). Cf. Jörn Stuckrath, *Historische Rezeptionsforschung* (Stuttgart, 1979), 1–12, 107–27; and Gunter Grimm, *Rezeptionsgeschichte* (Munich, 1977), 10–161.

[41] E.g., Jean Sareil, *Anatole France et Voltaire* (Geneva, 1961).

ers and correspondents formed such groups, they were neither the only ones nor the most significant. Schools, for example, certainly taught specific interpretive styles for much of the Third Republic, but their success in creating self-conscious readers is less easily discerned than their transmission of other cultural capital.[42] In its attempt to control commentary on scripture and doctrine, the Catholic Church was also influential, guiding the faithful and provoking the anticlerical. To what extent did less formal groups like friends and family affect reader response? How did other institutions, such as public agencies and professional associations, inform literate activities? Christophe Charle has studied a closely related problem: the sides taken by French authors in the Dreyfus Affair in 1894–1906.[43] Because the polemic initially concerned different assessments of a single document—the famous *bordereau* found in the German embassy—writers often read Dreyfus's guilt or innocence as members of various Parisian intellectual circles. The young, socially marginal avant-garde generally supported Dreyfus, while the older, better-established academicians usually became staunch anti-Dreyfusards. Thus the remarkable predispositions for or against the Jewish captain, prejudices reinforced in effect by social networks, literary salons, government bureaucracies, and political parties, decided Dreyfus's fate by the way in which these communities read as well as wrote about his case. It remains to be seen how such groups interpreted texts at less dramatic moments in history.

Historians of modern France might also consider what the history of reading has to say about the evolution of cultural mentalities. Early modern historians have already explored popular value systems, especially on the eve of the 1789 revolution. But scholars have been reticent in pursuing the implications of these systems in the nineteenth and twentieth centuries, perhaps because most approaches to recent history tend to preclude an independent role for culture.[44] Modern revolutions in politics and the economy tore the seamless web of history, directing attention away from slow, long-term development in thought and feeling. Nevertheless, subtle changes in literate culture did occur and affected the everyday lives of ordinary people nearly everywhere in France by World War I. The economy produced more printed matter; a literate society provided greater demand for different kinds of reading material; political re-

[42] Pierre Bourdieu and J. C. Passeron, *Les Héritiers* (1964); and Pierre Bourdieu, *La Reproduction* (1971).

[43] Christophe Charle, "Champ littéraire et champ du pouvoir. Les Écrivains et l'Affaire Dreyfus," *Annales: E.S.C.* 32 (1977): 240–64 Cf. Jean-Denis Bredin, *The Affair: The Case of Alfred Dreyfus*, trans. Jeffrey Mehlman (New York, 1986), 275–84.

[44] See Lucien Febvre, *Le Problème de l'incroyance au 16e siècle. La Religion de Rabelais* (1942); Robert Mandrou, *Introduction to Modern France, 1500–1640: An Essay in Historical Sociology*, trans. R. E. Hallmark (New York, 1975); and Michel Vovelle, *Piété baroque et déchristianisation en Provence au XVIIIe siècle* (1978). Cf. Peter Burke, *Popular Culture in Early Modern Europe* (New York, 1979); and David Warren Sabean, *Power in the Blood: Popular Culture and Village Discourse in Early Modern Germany* (Cambridge, 1984).

gimes enacted laws restricting the world of print; and popular conceptions of value, reality, and knowledge informed reading activities. As literate skills and habits spread, texts became increasingly important in French life. Indeed, they pervaded art, literature, and memoirs to make modern culture very much a textual experience. Artistic creation, the life cycle, and social identity all acquired a literate dimension. Similarly, the interpretive practice of various communities of readers developed traditions of response to certain kinds of texts whose conventions facilitated the process by which people made meaning. Consequently, the modern French mentality is linked to the context, the art, and the act of reading from the Old Regime onward.

The implications are even more numerous for reading in France after World War II. The postmodern sensibility is self-consciously interpretive, perhaps its single most distinguishing feature.[45] As literary theory considers linguistic and discursive systems as well as the way deliberately ambiguous texts defy determination, recent literature makes new and more sophisticated demands of the reader. In the New Novel, for example, the audience is expected to play a more active, more creative role in completing the text. Michel Butor's *La Modification* (1957) is, in fact, a narrative jumble that the reader must reorder to make sense of it. Similarly, the plot of Alain Robbe-Grillet's *Les Gommes* (1953) is never resolved, nor is the blank space in his *Le Voyeur* (1955) ever filled; despite their excessive detail, both texts are incomplete. But the same invitation, or provocation, to co-creation appears elsewhere in Europe.[46] The narrative in Italo Calvino's *If on a Winter's Night a Traveller* (1979) is picked up by a succession of readers, as characters in the novel, suggesting what its audience should also be doing for itself. The metaphor of the mad bibliophile destroying himself and his books in Elias Canetti's *Auto-da-Fé* (1935) nicely illustrates, among other things, a tendency in postmodern literature to force the impassioned reader, in a world apart, to take responsibility for the author's work—or for its destruction. There can be no more fitting tribute to the critical politics that has consumed literary specialists in their acrimonious battles over readings that concern texts less than they do the act of their interpretation.[47]

Besides reading's growing importance to postmodern literature and criticism, literate activities continue to invite further social-science research. Psychologists, sociologists, anthropologists, and education specialists, along with historians, critics, and creative writers, are exploring the nature of interpretive practice. Despite the different approaches they take, social scientists are no less committed to a fuller understanding of what people do with texts. Exper-

[45] Germaine Brée, *Twentieth-Century French Literature*, trans. Louise Guiney (Chicago, 1983), 167–236.

[46] Roland N. Stromberg, *After Everything: Western Intellectual History since 1945* (New York, 1975), 87–118.

[47] See Josué V. Harari, ed., *Textual Strategies: Perspectives in Post-Structuralist Criticism* (Ithaca, 1979), 17–72.

imental psychology specializes in the study of reading as a physical act whose characteristics can be measured and analyzed statistically.[48] If clinical psychology is less inclined to enumerate, it has uncovered the complex relationship between literate culture and the unconscious.[49] Social psychology and sociology, on the other hand, focus on contextual issues; more specifically, their work examines the influences on and implications of reading in modern industrial societies, even though anthropology does much the same in other cultural settings.[50] But the field of education leads all others in related research. The educational literature on reading is enormous, though of uneven quality, for at least one very good reason: literacy is an essential educational skill at all levels of schooling.[51] As the demands for a better-educated work force increase, education specialists will not only develop more effective teaching methods, but they will do so on the basis of better knowledge of how meaning is made from print. In this endeavor, however different their assumptions, social scientists share a common goal with their humanist colleagues.

In the meantime, as research proceeds in other disciplines, historians have a new field to pursue. Reading indeed has a long and rich past whose development over time can be traced within changing historical circumstances. But interpretive practices did more than respond to formative forces in the economy, society, politics, and culture; they exerted a considerable influence of their own—in promoting economic growth, defining social status, transforming ideologies, and shaping cultural mentalities. An active agent of continuity and change, reading became a prominent feature of modern French art, literature, and memory. How people interpreted texts over 140 years marked reception, of course, but much more; it was at the heart of intellectual life itself. Ideas did not belong to writers alone; readers had some of their own. Interpretive communities responded to different genres of writing in traditions that complemented the author's creative task. In short, reading in France and elsewhere has a significant history that deserves further exploration.

[48] See Eleanor J. Gibson and Harry Levin, *The Psychology of Reading* (Cambridge, Mass., 1975).

[49] E.g., Victor Nell, *Lost in a Book: The Psychology of Reading for Pleasure* (New Haven, 1988).

[50] E.g., R. J. Spiro et al., eds., *Theoretical Issues in Reading Comprehension: Perspectives from Cognitive Psychology, Linguistics, Artificial Intelligence, and Education* (Hillsdale, Ill., 1980); and Sylvia Scribner and Michael Cole, *The Psychology of Literacy* (Cambridge, Mass., 1981).

[51] Cf. Ben F. Nelms, *Literature in the Classroom: Readers, Texts, and Contexts* (Urbana, Ill., 1988); and P. David Pearson et al., eds., *Handbook of Reading Research* (New York, 1984).

APPENDIX
TABLES

TABLE A.1
Printers' Declarations in Paris, 1815–81

Year	Mean no. sampled	Mean edition size/year	Median	Range	No. of sets in sample
1815	281	882	500	30–8,000	20
1816–20	368	1,366	1,000	30–20,000	28
1821–25	450	1,378	1,000	25–30,000	39
1826–30	563	1,574	1,000	7–36,000	35
1831–34	416	1,529	1,000	25–25,000	31
1838–40	472	1,817	1,000	15–100,000	37
1841–45	448	1,680	1,000	15–100,000	1
1846–50	389	2,295	1,000	12–100,000	13
1851–55	537	2,114	1,000	10–100,000	10
1856–60	640	2,476	1,000	10–300,000	12
1861–65	660	2,070	1,000	20–200,000	19
1866–70	650	2,014	1,500	15–400,000	3
1871–75	619	2,213	1,000	14–180,000	8
1876–80	564	2,666	1,500	12–1,800,000	8
1881	604	3,153	1,500	25–300,000	14

Source: AN F18,II*1–183.

Note: Declarations for titles projected to include two or more printed sheets only. Samples included at least five percent of registered titles annually; variation in sample percentages from year to year, as well as variation in the number and size of multivolume sets, accounts for deviation in mean sample numbers. Data for 1835–37 are unavailable, as are some data about multivolumed sets.

TABLE A.2

Formats of Titles Declared by Printers in Paris, 1815–81

Year	Mean yearly percentages						
	Folio	In-4	In-8	In-12	In-16	In-18	In-32
1815	1.4	5.7	69.4	12.8	0.7	8.9	1.1
1816–20	0.8	7.1	60.7	18.4	0.6	10.3	1.8
1821–25	0.7	8.3	53.0	23.5	0.9	10.7	2.3
1826–30	1.2	9.0	48.1	16.9	0.4	19.3	5.0
1831–34[a]	1.2	10.1	63.2	14.1	0.5	8.8	1.8
1838–40	1.4	12.1	56.7	10.6	1.0	15.3	2.0
1841–45	1.2	15.4	50.3	9.6	0.7	18.0	4.2
1846–50	2.2	13.9	51.7	9.4	1.4	18.0	3.2
1851–55	2.1	18.6	43.3	9.7	4.1	19.3	2.7
1856–60	1.4	19.0	45.3	8.9	1.8	20.2	3.9
1861–65	1.0	16.2	44.4	8.3	3.2	24.8	1.9
1866–70	1.1	21.7	43.3	5.4	5.4	20.6	2.3
1871–75	1.2	21.5	42.5	4.4	9.4	18.1	2.6
1876–80	1.0	22.0	44.5	4.2	6.2	17.9	3.8
1881	0.5	24.5	36.4	3.8	12.3	19.9	2.0
Mean edition size	1,455	1,622	1,475	2,406	3,851	2,882	3,996

Source: An F18,II*1–183.

Note: Percentages in each five-year period do not total 100, because other declared formats, especially in-24 and in-64, are not listed.

[a] Registers for 1835–37 are missing from the Archives nationales.

TABLE A.3

Circulation of Parisian Newspapers, 1832–1938/39

	Date founded	Circulation					
		1832	1840	1870	1880	1910	1938/39
Action	1903					19,000	
Action française	1908					19,000	45,000
Aurore	1897					10,000	
Auteuil Longchamp	1886					35,000[a]	
Auto	1900					100,000[a]	100,000
Autorité	1886					22,000	
Capitole	—		1,534				
Charivari	1832		2,794	(1,661)			
Citoyen de Paris	1880				3,000		
Civilisation	1879				10,351		
Cocarde	1888				3,735	25[a]	
Commune	1880				21,304	26,000	
Comoedia	1907						
Constitution de 1830	1830	424					
Constitutionnel	1814	10,776	5,944	7,831	2,135	50[a]	
Corsaire	1822	236	557				
Courrier de l'Europe	—	1,102					
Courrier du soir	1878				1,919	1,050	
Courrier français	—	4,084	4,069				
Croix	1880				4,288	140,000	140,000
Défense sociale et religieuse	1876						
Démocratie	1910					30,000	
XIXe siècle	1871				14,881	1,500	

TABLE A.3 (cont.)

	Date founded		Circulation				
		1832	1840	1870	1880	1910	1938/39
Droit	1835				3,111		
Écho de Paris	1884					118,000	183,844
Écho des courses	—					15,000[b]	
Écho français	—	1,164	1,977				
Éclair	1888					102,000	
En avant	1879						
Époque	1852				4,948	50[a]	80,000
Estafette	1875		(5,046)		8,846	30[a]	
Étendard	1882					40[a]	
Événement	1872				14,085	4,000	
Excelsior	1910					140,000[c]	132,792
Figaro	1854	(540)		63,890	104,924	35,000	80,602
Français	1868			4,962	4,718		
France	1861			7,788	43,752	500	
France nouvelle	1871	(280)	(1,193)		14,554		
Gaulois	1866			45,894	14,854	30,000	
Gazette de France	1631	7,496	5,165	6,108	5,864	2,600	
Gazette des tribunaux	1825		2,936		2,918		
Gil Blas	1879				28,257	5,000	
Globe	1879	1,896			4,625		
Grand Journal	1880				10,236		
Grand National	1902					2,500	
Humanité	1903					65,000	349,587
Intransigeant	1880				71,601	70,000	134,462
Jockey	—					35,000	
Jour	1890					100	183,844
Journal	1892			(1,665)		815,000	411,021
Journal à un sou	1879				5,643		

Journal des débats	1789	6,011	10,583	8,475	6,935	26,000	10,000
Journal du commerce	—	814	4,642			1,000	
Journal du soir	1904				12,847	4,000	2,000
Justice	1880				150,531	33,000	
Lanterne	1877					500	
Liberal	1886						
Liberté (2 editions)	1866			24,298	17,921	59,000	15,000
Libre parole	1892				28,818	49,000	
Marseillaise	1880			(49,542)		670,000	312,597
Matin	1874				24,000[a]	2,800	
Messager de Paris	1896						
Messager des chambres	—	1,273					
Messidor	1907		1,301			25[a]	
Monde	1860		3,363	2,990	6,130		
Moniteur parisien	—		2,767		13,872		
Moniteur universel	1789	751		21,041	16,316		
Mot d'ordre	1879				25,631		
Napoléon	1880						(60,000)
Nation	1885					100	
National	1830	1,910	4,502	26,306	14,543	1,200	
Nouveau Journal	1877				27,384		
Nouvelle Presse	1888					500	
Nouvelles	1876					6,000	250,000
Oeuvre	1915						
Ordre	1871				3,153	50[a]	12,000
Paix	1879				52,949	50[a]	
Paris	1878			(9,067)	18,100[e]	500[a]	
Paris-Courses	—					4,500[a]	
Paris-Journal	1868			13,617	6,051	42,000	
Paris-Soir	1931						1,739,584
Paris-Sport	1886			(6,840)	3,250	35,000[b]	
Parlement	1879						
Patrie	1841			11,751	6,434	40,000	

	Date founded	Circulation					
		1832	1840	1870	1880	1910	1938/39
Pays	1849			3,964	6,715	25[a]	
Petit Caporal	1875				25,051	300	
Petite Presse	1867			160,000	22,629	50[a]	
Petite République française	1876					52,000	
Petit Journal	1863			320,000	196,372	780,000	178,327
Petit Journal du soir	1880				583,820		
Petit Moniteur	1864			130,000	16,200	100[a]	
Petit National	1866				100,476	40[a]	
Petit Parisien	1876				46,837	1,375,000	1,022,401
Petit Républicain	1880				39,419		
Petit Sou	1899				9,890	50[a]	
Peuple français	1893			(32,225)	9,463	7,500	
Politique coloniale	1891					700	(16,600)
Presse	1836		10,186	7,920	2,048	60,000	
Prolétaire	1878				3,500[d]	5,606	
Public	1883			5,674		50[a]	
Quotidienne	—	3,433	3,143				
Radical	1881					29,000	
Rappel	1869			34,293	33,535	30,000	
République française	1871				10,431	4,000	
République radicale	1883					100	10,000
Réveil social	1880			(7,474)	13,316		
Révolution de 1830	1830	1,679					
Siècle	1836		33,366	37,290	15,082	5,000	
Signal	1893					300[a]	
Soir	1869			7,105	4,556		
Soleil	1873				43,190	22,000	
Souveraineté nationale	—					50	

Title	Founded	1832	1840	1870	1880	1910	1938/39
Sports	—					50,000	
Télégraphe	1877				8,464	36,000	68,556
Temps	1861			4,348	13,618	22,764	
Tribune	—	869	2,049				
Union	1847			6,376	4,592		
Univers	1833		1,584	1,110	10,367	12,000	
Veine	1901					28,000[b]	
Vérité	1880				12,263	20,000[f]	
Voltaire	1878				11,506	400	5,000
Total daily circulation		49,086	108,701	1,068,009	2,094,170	5,336,941	6,056,864
Number of dailies		19	21	38	67	81	91
Mean daily circulation		2,583	5,176	28,106	31,256	65,888	66,559
Circulation of four largest dailies		28,631	60,079	550,000	1,035,647	3,640,000	3,522,593
Percentage of total daily circulation		58	55	51	49	71	58

Sources: Circulation data for 1832: Gilles Feyel, "La Diffusion nationale des quotidiens parisiens en 1832," *Revue d'histoire moderne et contemporaine* 34 (1987): 37.

Circulation data for 1840: Jean-Pierre Aguet, "Le Tirage des quotidiens de Paris sous la Monarchie de Juillet," *Revue suisse d'histoire* 2 (1960): 216–86; and Charles Ledré, *La Presse à l'assaut de la monarchie, 1815–1848* (1960), 244.

Circulation data for 1870: AN F18,294 d. 1870.

Circulation data for 1880 and 1910: Michael B. Palmer, *Des petits journaux aux grandes agences. Naissance du journalisme moderne* (1983), 320–28.

Circulation for 1938/39: APP BA1712 d. Correspondance échangée à la suite de la saisie du journal "La Guerre sociale"; and Claude Bellanger et al., *Histoire générale de la presse française* (1969), 3:511.

() Circulation of a different newspaper under the same title.

[a] Circulation approximated.

[b] Circulation for 1909.

[c] Circulation for 1912.

[d] Circulation for 1881.

[e] Circulation for 1882.

[f] Circulation for 1915.

Lending Activity of French School Libraries, 1865–90, and of Coulommiers Municipal Public Library, 1891–1935

	Mean no. of libraries per yr.	Mean no. of vols. per yr.	Mean no. of vols. lent per yr.	Mean % of vols. lent per yr.
France				
1865	4,833	180,854	179,267	99
1866–70	11,927	916,199	737,484	81
1871–75[a]	17,891	1,627,127	894,340	55
1876–80	21,269	2,124,553	1,640,920	77
1881–85	31,773	3,363,825	3,881,867	115
1886–90	36,838	4,534,627	5,816,041	129
Coulommiers				
1891–95		10,209	4,034	40
1896–1900		14,270	4,986	35
1901–5		17,364	6,786	39
1906–10		18,275	5,977	33
1911–15		19,755	9,482	48
1916–20		21,411	9,846	46
1921–25		22,940	7,753	34
1926–30		24,208	5,834	24
1931–35		24,715	4,591	19

Sources: For France: AN F17,10735–55. For Coulommiers: AN F17,17402. d. Coulommiers, Seine-et-Marne.

[a] Does not include the Department of the Seine. Reports after 1870 also do not include the departments ceded to Germany as a consequence of the Franco-Prussian War under the terms of the 1871 Treaty of Frankfurt.

Primary Schools and Students in France, 1817–1938

Year	Mean no. of schools per year	Mean no. of students per year
1817–20	24,520[a]	987,667[a]
1821–30	30,996[b]	1,358,000[b]
1831–40	39,522[c]	2,314,500[c]
1841–50	59,697[c]	3,228,250[c]
1851–60	—	—
1861–65	69,230	4,352,667
1866–70	70,671	4,515,000
1871–75	70,853	4,765,500
1876–80	72,656	4,583,000
1881–85	76,996	5,364,400
1886–90	80,972	5,577,000
1891–95	82,734	5,558,400
1896–1900	84,004	5,533,800
1901–5	83,496	5,550,400
1906–10	81,858	5,624,400
1911–15	82,790	5,668,667
1916–20	68,021[d]	3,933,667[d]
1921–25	78,128	4,172,400
1926–30	80,223	3,996,200
1931–35	80,304	5,018,400
1936–40	81,226	5,363,000

Source: Ministère de l'Économie et des Finances, Statistique Générale de la France, Annuaire statistique. Résumé retrospective (1941), 23*, 24*, except as noted below.

[a] Data taken from Chanoine Adrien Garnier, Frayssinous. Son rôle dans l'Université sous la Restauration (1822–1828) (1925), 481.

[b] Data taken from Maurice Gontard, L'Enseignement primaire en France de la Révolution à la loi Guizot (1959), 424.

[c] Data taken from Antoine Prost, Histoire de l'enseignement en France, 1800–1967 (1968), 108, 294.

[d] Data from territory occupied by German troops not included.

TABLE A.6
Students Enrolled in French Lycées and Collèges, 1810–1938

	Annual mean no. of lycées and collèges	Annual mean no. of students	Annual mean % of pop. aged 12–17
Boys only			
1810		31,481	1.1
1820		33,762	1.2
1830		42,228	1.4
1840		41,865	1.3
1850		47,941	1.4
1851–55		46,076	1.4
1856–60		53,371	1.6
1861–65		62,637	1.9
1866–70		69,431	2.1
1871–75		70,428	2.2
1876–80		81,720	2.5
Boys and girls			
1881–85	373	94,355	2.9
1886–90	394	91,029	2.8
1891–95	397	89,842	2.8
1896–1900	405	89,223	2.7
1901–5	416	99,568	3.1
1906–10	455	103,317	3.2
1911–15[a]	465	95,407	2.9
1916–20[a]	474	99,161	—
1921–25	527	121,851	3.6
1926–30	528	124,031	3.8
1931–35	521	162,710	6.0
1936–38	522	185,763	6.4

Sources: Number of students and schools in Ministère de l'Économie Nationale et des Finances, Statistique Générale de la France, Annuaire statistique. Résumé retrospective (1941), 26*, 27*. Percentage of students enrolled calculated from age-structure reconstruction data in J. Bourgeois-Pichat, "The General Development of the Population of France since the Eighteenth Century," in Population and History: Essays in Historical Demography, ed. D. V. Glass and D.E.C. Eversley (London, 1965), App. 2, Table 1, 498–99.

[a] Data do not include schools or students in territory occupied by German troops.

TABLE A.7
Estimate of Active Readers in France, 1801–1936

Year	Men				Women			Literate population[c]	Percentage of population urban	Total urban readers[d]	Percentage of total population[e]	Percentage literacy increase[f]
	Total population	Older than 14	Literacy rate (%)	Literate men[a]	Older than 14	Literacy rate (%)	Literate women[b]					
1801	28,288,000	9,172,000	50	4,586,000	9,793,000	28	2,742,040	7,328,040	20.5	1,502,248	5.3	—
1811	29,561,000	5,586,000	52	4,984,000	10,415,000	32	3,332,800	8,317,520	21.5	1,788,267	6.0	13
1821	31,065,000	10,054,000	54	5,429,160	11,083,000	35	3,879,050	9,308,210	22.5	2,094,347	6.7	12
1831	32,991,000	11,025,000	53	5,843,000	11,680,000	40	4,672,000	10,515,250	23.5	2,471,084	7.5	12
1841	34,414,000	11,753,000	61	7,169,330	12,185,000	46	5,605,100	12,774,430	24.5	3,129,735	9.1	21
1851	35,902,000	12,515,000	68	8,511,200	12,708,000	52	6,608,160	15,118,360	25.5	3,855,182	10.7	18
1861	37,427,000	13,351,000	70	9,345,700	13,418,000	55	7,379,900	16,725,600	28.9	4,833,698	12.9	21
1871	37,124,000	13,406,000	73	9,786,380	13,260,000	60	7,956,000	17,742,380	31.0	5,500,138	14.8	15
1881	37,738,000	13,656,000	85	11,607,600	13,644,000	77	10,505,880	22,113,480	34.8	7,695,491	20.4	38
1891	38,471,000	13,979,000	92	12,860,680	14,130,000	87	12,293,100	25,153,780	37.4	9,407,514	24.5	20
1901	38,784,000	14,243,000	96	13,673,280	14,540,000	94	13,667,600	27,340,880	42.0	11,483,169	30.0	22
1911	39,193,000	14,177,000	98.2	13,921,814	14,922,000	97	14,447,840	28,369,154	46.0	13,049,810	33.3	11
1921	38,797,000	13,740,000	99.1	13,616,340	16,238,000	98.4	15,978,192	29,594,532	48.0	14,205,375	36.6	10
1931	41,228,000	15,118,000	99.5	15,042,410	16,651,000	99.3	16,534,443	31,576,853	50.0	15,788,426	38.3	5
1936	41,180,000	14,670,000	99.5	14,596,650	16,332,000	99.5	16,250,340	30,846,990	51.0	15,731,964	38.2	-0.3

Sources: J. Bourgeois-Pichat, "The General Development of the Population of France since the Eighteenth Century," in Population and History: Essays in Historical Demography, ed. D. V. Glass and D.E.C. Eversley (London, 1965), App. 2, Tables 1a and 1b, 498–99; Adna Ferrin Weber, The Growth of Cities in the Nineteenth Century: A Study in Statistics (Ithaca, 1963), 68, 71; and Table 2.1.

[a] Literacy rate (men) times men older than 14.
[b] Literacy rate (women) times women older than 14.
[c] Literate men plus literate women.
[d] Percentage of population urban times literate population times percentage of urban population in tertiary sector (= 45 percent, from Georges Dupeux, La Société française 1789–1970 [1972], 30–31).
[e] Total urban readers divided by total population.
[f] One minus (total urban readers each decade divided by total urban readers the following decade).

TABLE A.8

Correspondents Previously Acquainted with Selected French Authors, 1800–1924

Author and year	Not aquainted %	N	Acquainted %	N	Closely acquainted %	N	Number known	Number unknown
Staël (1800)	40.9	27	48.5	32	10.6	7	66	63
Stendhal (1830)	19.1	13	44.1	30	36.8	25	68	87
Balzac (1835)	16.5	15	59.3	54	24.2	22	91	63
Sue (1843)	95.7	111	4.8	5	0	0	116	23
Baudelaire (1857)	33.0	34	51.5	53	15.5	16	103	0
Michelet (1860)	81.8	54	15.2	10	3.0	2	66	8
Flaubert (1862)	10.1	9	65.2	58	24.7	22	89	8
Goncourt brothers (1853–96)	49.3	34	50.7	35	0	0	69	1
Zola (1887)	56.1	110	33.3	65	10.7	21	196	71
France (1868–1924)	82.6	219	16.6	44	0.8	2	265	5

Sources: Mme. de Staël: Random sample of 129 names from the list of all correspondents with Mme. de Staël in *Madame de Staël, ses amis, ses correspondants: Choix de lettres (1778–1817)*, ed. Georges Solovieff (1970), 539–48.

Stendhal: All 155 correspondents listed in *Corr.*, ed. Henri Martineau and Victor Del Litto (1967–68), 2:1137–49.

Balzac: All 154 correspondents listed in *Balzac: Corr.*, ed. Roger Pierrot (1960–66), 2:801–27.

Sue: All 139 correspondents in letters addressed to Sue concerning *Les Mystères de Paris* (1842–44) in BHVP Fonds Eugène Sue.

Baudelaire: All 103 correspondents listed in *Lettres à Charles Baudelaire*, ed. Claude Pichois (Neuchâtel, 1973), 411–14.

Michelet: All 74 correspondents in letters addressed to Michelet about *L'Amour* and *La Femme* (1858–60) in BHVP Fonds Jules Michelet, Liasse A4748, fols. 1–44 and Liasse A4750, fols. 1–57.

Flaubert: All 97 correspondents in letters addressed to Flaubert concerning *Madame Bovary* (1857) and *Salammbô* (1862) in BSL H.1361–66: B.I–VI.

Goncourts: Random sample of 70 correspondents in letters addressed to the Goncourt brothers (1853–96) in BN NAFr 22450–79.

Zola: All 267 correspondents having sent letters to Zola in 1887 listed in the *fichiers* of the Émile Zola Research Program, John P. Robarts Library, University of Toronto.

France: Random sample of 270 correspondents in letters addressed to France (1868–1924) in BN NAFr 15430–39, 24197.

Published Authors among Correspondents with Selected French Authors, 1800–1924

Author	Males		Females		Total	
and year	%	N	%	N	%	N
Staël (1800)	36.8	35	21.9	7	32.6	42
Stendhal (1830)	29.9	40	10.0	2	27.1	42
Balzac (1835)	31.0	35	23.7	9	28.6	44
Sue (1843)	16.7	17	11.1	4	15.1	21
Baudelaire (1857)	48.5	47	16.7	1	46.6	48
Michelet (1860)	37.1	13	15.6	5	24.3	18
Flaubert (1862)	44.2	38	27.3	4	43.3	42
Goncourt brothers (1853–96)	49.2	30	44.4	4	48.6	34
Zola (1887)	35.3	83	14.3	2	31.8	85
France (1868–1924)	14.1	27	1.3	1	10.4	28

Sources: See Table A.8. For data on publications, see BN, *Catalogue général des livres imprimés de la Bibliothèque nationale: Auteurs*, 238 vols. (1897–); Otto Lorenz et al., *Catalogue général de la librairie française*, 34 vols. (1867–1945); Joseph-Marie Quérard et al., *La France littéraire, ou Dictionnaire bibliographique des savants, historiens et gens de lettres de la France*, 10 vols. (1827–39); and idem, *La Littérature française contemporaine, 1827–1849*, 6 vols. (1840–57).

TABLE A.10

Males and Females among Correspondents with Selected French Authors, 1800–1924

Author	Male		Female			
and year	%	N	%	N	Known	Unknown
Staël (1778–1817)	74.8	95	25.2	32	127	2
Stendhal (1830–42)	87.0	134	13.0	20	154	1
Balzac (1829–38)	74.8	113	25.2	38	151	3
Sue (1843–44)	73.9	102	26.1	36	138	1
Baudelaire (1843–67)	94.2	97	5.8	6	103	0
Michelet (1858–60)	52.2	35	47.8	32	67	7
Flaubert (1857–62)	88.7	86	11.3	11	97	0
Goncourt brothers (1853–96)	87.1	61	12.9	9	70	0
Zola (1887)	94.4	235	5.6	14	249	18
France (1868–1924)	71.8	191	28.2	75	266	4

Sources: See Table A.8.

Mean Ages of Correspondents with Selected French Authors, 1800–1924

Author, year, and age	Male		Female		Total		
	Mean	N	Mean	N	Mean	N	Unknown
Staël (1800), age 34	34.2	71	35.8	20	34.6	91	38
Stendhal (1830), age 47	43.9	89	39.1	16	42.8	106	49
Balzac (1835), age 36	38.9	71	43.3	20	39.8	91	63
Sue (1843), age 39	41.3	13	37.8	8	40.0	21	118
Baudelaire (1857), age 36	38.4	84	45.0	4	38.6	88	15
Michelet (1860), age 62	46.7	14	35.4	5	43.7	19	55
Flaubert (1862), age 41	46.4	39	46.8	4	46.5	43	54
Goncourt brothers (1853–96), ages 31–74	40.3	34	42.4	5	40.6	39	31
Zola (1887), age 47	38.2	98	46.3	3	38.4	101	166
France (1868–1924), ages 24–80	33.5	87	30.5	51	32.4	138	132

Sources: See Tables A.8 and A.9.

TABLE A.12
Age Structure of Correspondents with Selected French Authors, 1800–1924

Author and year	Less than 21		Between 21 and 59		More than 59		Known or approximate	Unknown
	%	N	%	N	%	N		
Staël (1800)	6.5	7	85.2	92	8.3	9	108	21
Stendhal (1830)	0.7	1	90.7	127	8.6	12	140	15
Balzac (1835)	4.8	6	92.7	115	2.4	3	124	30
Sue (1843)	3.1	3	91.7	88	5.2	5	96	43
Baudelaire (1857)	4.9	5	90.3	93	4.9	5	103	0
Michelet (1860)	12.2	5	75.6	31	12.2	5	41	33
Flaubert (1862)	2.1	2	88.7	86	9.3	9	97	0
Goncourt brothers (1853–96)	1.4	1	95.7	67	2.9	2	70	0
Zola (1887)	4.3	8	91.8	169	3.8	7	184	83
France (1868–1924)	20.9	41	69.9	137	9.2	18	196	74

Sources: See Tables A.8 and A.9.

TABLE A.13

Residence of Correspondents with Selected French Authors, 1800–1924

Author, year, and residence	Correspondents residing in Paris		Correspondents residing elsewhere in France		Correspondents residing elsewhere in Europe		Non-European correspondents		Known	Unknown
	%	N	%	N	%	N	%	N		
Staël (1800), Coppet	26.1	30	7.0	8	61.7	71	5.2	6	115	14
Stendhal (1830), Paris	59.5	148	9.5	14	31.1	46	0	0	148	7
Balzac (1835), Paris	75.6	99	13.7	18	9.2	12	1.5	2	131	23
Sue (1843), Paris	61.3	76	22.3	28	16.1	20	0	0	124	15
Baudelaire (1857), Paris	62.1	64	16.5	17	18.4	19	0	0	100	3
Michelet (1860), Paris	37.2	19	41.2	21	21.6	11	0	0	51	23
Flaubert (1862), Croisset	33.0	32	41.2	40	8.2	8	0	0	80	17
Goncourt brothers (1853–96), Paris	50.7	35	31.9	22	14.5	10	2.9	2	69	1
Zola (1887), Médan	45.9	112	25.0	61	25.0	61	4.1	10	244	23
France (1868–1924), Saint-Cyr-sur-Loire	27.3	66	44.6	108	15.3	37	12.8	31	242	28

Sources: See Tables A.8 and A.9.

TABLE A.14

Socioeconomic Background of Correspondents with Selected French Authors, 1800–1924

Author and Year	Landed wealth		High administration		Clergy		Military		Professionals		Employees	
	%	N	%	N	%	N	%	N	%	N	%	N
Staël (1800)	28.0	33	33.1	39	2.5	3	7.6	9	6.8	8	1.7	2
Stendhal (1830)	12.4	19	20.3	31	2.0	3	7.2	11	13.1	20	7.8	12
Balzac (1835)	19.7	26	6.1	8	0.0	0	1.5	2	12.1	16	11.4	15
Sue (1843)	13.8	13	7.4	7	1.1	1	4.3	4	17.0	16	16.0	15
Baudelaire (1857)	7.1	7	3.1	3	0.0	0	2.0	2	13.3	13	18.4	18
Michelet (1860)	19.4	7	5.6	2	2.8	1	5.6	2	13.9	5	11.1	4
Flaubert (1862)	18.2	12	4.5	3	0.0	0	0.0	0	15.2	10	9.1	6
Goncourt brothers (1853–96)	12.3	8	9.2	6	0.0	0	0.0	0	18.5	12	12.3	8
Zola (1887)	3.0	6	5.0	10	0.0	0	2.0	4	18.3	37	15.8	32
France (1868–1924)	3.5	6	4.7	8	1.7	3	18.0	31	13.4	23	14.0	24

Author and Year	Writers %	N	Students %	N	Businessmen %	N	Workers %	N	Peasants %	N	Background known	Background unknown
Staël (1800)	8.5	10	4.2	5	6.8	8	0.8	1	0.0	0	118	11
Stendhal (1830)	13.3	20	0.7	1	21.6	33	2.0	3	0.0	0	153	2
Balzac (1835)	15.9	21	3.8	5	28.0	37	1.5	2	0.0	0	132	22
Sue (1843)	7.4	7	3.2	3	8.5	8	21.3	20	0.0	0	94	45
Baudelaire (1857)	32.7	32	5.1	5	18.4	18	0.0	0	0.0	0	98	5
Michelet (1860)	25.0	9	8.3	3	8.3	3	0.0	0	0.0	0	36	38
Flaubert (1862)	40.9	27	3.0	2	9.1	6	0.0	0	0.0	0	66	31
Goncourt brothers (1853–96)	27.7	18	1.5	1	16.9	11	0.0	0	1.5	1	65	5
Zola (1887)	37.6	76	4.0	8	13.9	28	0.5	1	0.0	0	202	65
France (1868–1924)	16.3	28	20.9	36	4.7	8	2.9	5	0.0	0	172	98

Sources: See Tables A.8 and A.9.

SELECTED BIBLIOGRAPHY OF ARCHIVAL SOURCES

ARCHIVES DE LA PRÉFECTURE DE POLICE, PARIS (APP)

BA472. Inscriptions et placards séditieux ou injurieux enlevés par la police de 1880–83.

BA475–79. Placards injurieux ou obscènes enlevés par la police municipale (1871–83).

BA697–736. Guerre de 1914. Censure. Visa des chansons et des programmes.

BA744–48. Guerre de 1914. Censure. Résumés de la presse (parisienne et départementale), 1913–17.

BA755–64. Censure des télégrammes ayant un intérêt politique et échappage des journaux (1915–18).

BA770–73. Censure des pièces et revues. Enregistrement et analyse des pièces et revues.

BA1586. Dossier Anatole France.

BA1712–13. Presse. Affaires diverses.

ARCHIVES DU DÉPARTEMENT DE LA SEINE ET DE LA VILLE DE PARIS (ADSVP)

DM4,16. Déclarations des imprimeurs—St. Denis et Sceaux—1828–32, 1835–44.

ARCHIVES DU MINISTÈRE DE LA GUERRE, VINCENNES (AMG)

7N952. Création et transformation des commissions de contrôle postal . . . 1915–20.

7N979–1001. Commissions de contrôle postal, 1916–18 (by region).

16N1380–81. Organisation et fonctionnement des commissions de contrôle postal . . . 1914–19.

16N1470. Rapports du contrôle postal de la correspondance venant de l'intérieur . . . février-septembre 1918.

16N2703–4. Bulletins des armées: . . . instructions aux commissions de contrôle postal relatives à la surveillance des correspondances. . . .

16N2705–6. Commissions de contrôle postal: comptes rendus hebdomadaires, 15 septembre 1915–27 décembre 1916; résumés des comptes rendus des commissions de contrôle postal, février 1916–août 1917.

ARCHIVES NATIONALES, PARIS (AN)

AJ13,1050. Opéra—Divers . . . Censure des théâtres de Paris, 1799–1840.

AJ13,1057. Opéra—Administration . . . Comité de lecture, 1818–23.

BB18,1010/1112/1166/1742/1800–1. Cour Royale de Paris—Dossiers particuliers.

BB21,633. Cour Impériale de Paris—Dossiers particuliers.

BB24,494–99. Justice—Recours en grâce—Rapports.

F17,1547–55. Procès-verbaux des séances de la Commission d'examen des livres élémentaires, 1829–48.

F17,9146. Réponses aux circulaires du Ministère de l'Instruction Publique, 1866–67.

F17,10735–55. Rapports relatifs aux bibliothèques scolaires, 1863–96.

F17,17314,1–2. Bibliothèques populaires du Département de la Seine, 1880–1940.

F17,17317–430. Dossiers des bibliothèques par département, XIXe siècle–début XXe siècle.

F18,39. Conseiller d'État—Préfet de Police—Correspondance.

F18,40. Direction générale de l'imprimerie et de la librairie—Surveillance.

F18,43–119. Déclarations des imprimeurs de Paris, 1817–34.

F18,120–56. Déclarations des imprimeurs des départements, 1817–35.

F18,157–67. Déclarations et dépots des imprimeurs de Paris, 1835–53.

F18,168. Déclarations d'imprimeurs, Seine: Sceaux et Saint-Denis, 1835–53.

F18,294. Division de la presse—Notes et statistiques générales, 1858–89.

F18,312–425. Presse—Paris—Dossiers des journaux, 1820–94.

F18,431–514. Presse—Départements—Affaires générales—Dossiers des journaux, 1811–81.

F18,551–55. La Commission du colportage, 1852–60.

F18,567. Imprimerie—Paris—Affaires diverses, 1815–54.

F18,2295–309. Statistiques des imprimeurs et des libraires par département, 1851–79.

F18,I*58. Registre des pièces de théâtre soumises à la censure, le 17 mars 1896–le 31 décembre 1900.

F18,II*1–183. Déclarations des imprimeurs—Paris—Années 1815–81.

F21,966–995. Théâtre—Paris—Procès-verbaux de censure, 1804–67.

F21,1079. Théâtre Français—Administration.

BIBLIOTHÈQUE DE L'ARSENAL, PARIS (BA)

MS.13435–37. Lettres adressées à Arnold Mortier.

MS.13566. Lettres et pièces de vers adressées à José Maria de Heredia.

MS.13591–98. Lettres reçues par Albin Valabrègue.

MS.13744–52. Lettres adressées à Gustave d'Eichthal.

MS.13814.–15. Lettres adressées à L.-F. Rouquette à suite de la publication de 'L'Épopée blanche.'

MS.13892. Lettres et billets adressées à Georges Courteline.

Coll. Renduel Rf37,378–99. *Le Fils de Giboyer.*

BIBLIOTHÈQUE HISTORIQUE DE LA VILLE DE PARIS (BHVP)

Fonds Eugène Sue

Lettres adressées à Sue sur *Les Mystères de Paris* (1842–43).

Fonds Jules Michelet

Tome X, Liasse A4745, fols. 1–136. Lettres adressées à Michelet sur *Le Prêtre, la femme et la famille* (1845).

Tome XI, Liasse A4747, fols. 1–33. Lettres adressées à Michelet sur *Le Peuple* (1846).

Tome XI, Liasse, A4748, fols. 1–44. Lettres adressées à Michelet sur *L'Amour* (1858).

Tome XI, Liasse A4750, fols. 1–57. Lettres adressées à Michelet sur *L'Amour* (1858) et *La Femme* (1859).

Tome XII, Liasse A4751, fols. 1–133. Lettres adressées à Michelet sur *Le Prêtre, la femme et la famille* (1845).

Fonds Louise Bouglé: Papiers de Céline Renooz

Boites 1–9. Lettres à Céline Renooz, 1855–1927.

Boites 16–18. "La Femme cachée" (Mémoires).

Fonds George Sand

G.5707–92. Lettres d'admiration pour l'oeuvre de George Sand.

Bibliothèque de l'Institut Pédagogique National, Paris (BIPN)

Cahiers d'élèves, XIXe–XXe siècles.

Bibliothèque Nationale de France, Paris (BN)

Département des Estampes

Kb matières 1. Scènes de lecture.

Oa 22. 340–359. Soirées en famille.

Département des Manuscrits

NAFr 5001–02. Procès-verbaux de censure, 1811–13.

NAFr 10739. Rapports de censure par L.C.J. de Manne, 1811–14.

NAFr 11494–95 (1–2). Papiers Renan: Correspondance diverse.

NAFr 15430–39, 24197. Lettres adressées à Anatole France.

NAFr 15507–10, 20781–98. Lettres adressées à Edgar Quinet.

NAFr 16533–35. Lettres adressées à Henri Barbusse.

NAFr 21035–54. Papiers et rapports relatifs aux bibliothèques publiques, an VII–1830.

NAFr 21129. Papiers et lettres relatifs aux imprimeurs et aux libraires du XIXe siècle.

NAFr 22450–79. Lettres adressées aux frères Goncourt.

NAFr 22544–52. Lettres adressées à Eugène Scribe.

NAFr 24225–33. Lettres adressées à Louis Veuillot.

NAFr 24510–25. Lettres adressées à Émile Zola.

NAFr 24636–39, 14663–69. Lettres adressées à Alexandre Dumas fils.

Uncatalogued. Lettres adressées à Maurice Barrès.

Uncatalogued. Journal de Geneviève Bréton.

Bibliothèque Spoelberch de Lovenjoul, Chantilly (BSL)

A.312–18. Lettres adressées à Honoré de Balzac.

C.491–501. Lettres adressées à Théophile Gautier.

D.597–616. Lettres adressées à C.-A. Sainte-Beuve.

D.595. fols. 1–169. Lettres reçues par Sainte-Beuve au sujet des *Consolations*.

E.934–35. Lettres adressées à George Sand.
H.1361–66: B.I–VI. Lettres adressées à Gustave Flaubert.

BIBLIOTHÈQUE DU THÉÂTRE FRANÇAIS, PARIS (BTF)

Papiers et pièces relatifs à Émile Augier.
Registres des pièces, 1800–1910.
Rapports de lecture, 1830–1920.

ÉMILE ZOLA RESEARCH PROGRAM, JOHN P. ROBARTS LIBRARY, UNIVERSITY OF TORONTO (EZRP)

Letters to Émile Zola, 1858–1903.
Miscellaneous archival files.

MUSÉE NATIONAL DE L'ÉDUCATION, MONT-SAINT-AIGNAN (MNE)

Cahiers littéraires d'élèves primaires et secondaires, XIXe–XXe siècles.
Correspondance privée des écoliers, XIXe–XXe siècles.

INDEX